DECENTRALIZED MULTILEVEL PLANNING : PRINCIPLES AND PRACTICE

(Asian and African Experiences)

About the Author

K.V. Sundaram was a Senior technocrat of the Indian Planning Commission during 1973-1987 and was intimately associated with the formulation and implementation of three five year plans in the country. He also served as Chief Technical Advisor/Consultant to FAO/UN and other International Agencies. He pioneered the evolution of multilevel planning in India and many other Asian and African countries. With more than thirty years of professional experience in Multilevel/Regional/Local level planning and development issues, the book represents the quintessence of his vast experience and knowledge in this field.

DECENTRALIZED MULTILEVEL PLANNING
Principles and Practice
(Asian and African Experiences)

K.V. SUNDARAM

CONCEPT PUBLISHING COMPANY, NEW DELHI-110059

ISBN 81-7022-580-9

First Published 1997

Published and Printed by
Ashok Kumar Mittal
Concept Publishing Company
A/15-16, Commercial Block, Mohan Garden
NEW DELHI-110059 (India)
Phones : 5504042, 5554042

To

Providence for the myriad gifts in my life and

My Spouse Girija and all my children and grandchildren

for shedding sweetness, light and joy

in my journey through life

“The time has come, the Walrus said—
To talk of many things;
Of ships and sails and sealing wax,
Of cabbages and kings”

—*Anonymous*

“Societies grow in historical time,
Characterized by irreversibilities and
History does not perform controlled
experiments for our benefit”

—*Sukhumoy Chakravarty*

PREFACE

My interest in Decentralized Multilevel Planning has been kindled since the 1970s through many events and circumstances in my life. Among them, I must specially mention the late Prof. Sukhumoy Chakravarty's seminal paper on the subject in 1970* and my subsequent appointment in the Indian Planning Commission in 1973, with the major responsibility for Multilevel Planning. The seventies and eighties were critical times for the Planning Commission, when several ideas on multilevel/area development/microlevel (district and block) planning were circulating. In this I played a crucial role, by conducting policy analysis and studies and writing extensively on the subject. In this manner, I sought, in my own modest way, to further policy decision-making on several vital issues. This was also the period, when certain important national committees were appointed by the Planning Commission to deliberate on the relevant issues of the time and advise the Centre and the States on taking several forward steps. Today, their reports have become milestones. These included the Working Group on Block Level Planning (known as Dantwala Committee, 1977), the Working Group on District Planning (known as Hanumantha Rao Committee, 1982) and the Committee to review the existing arrangements for Rural Development and Poverty Alleviation Programmes (CAARD, otherwise known as G.V.K. Rao Committee, 1985). In all these committees, I played a very important role as an actor, facilitator and scribe in various capacities as Division Chief/Member-convenor/Permanent Invitee, etc., in preparing discussion papers, drafting reports, making case studies and preparing guidelines for state governments. During this period, I also authored a book (with Prof. R.P. Misra) on *Multilevel Planning and Integrated Rural Development in India*, 1980, which was the first ever published document on this subject at that time. Simultaneously, my participation in various National and International Seminars and interaction with numerous scholars clarified many issues on multilevel planning. I was articulating

---

* S. Chakravarty, "The Planning Process in India : An Appraisal and a Framework." (Planning Commission, Mimeographed, 1970).

these ideas in several papers, many of which were published. Gradually, a district planning process also evolved in some States in the country. It must be emphasized that those were the formative years and several actions pursued at the Planning Commission level acted as a catalyst and pushed the process of multilevel planning in a meaningful direction.

In 1987, I was invited by the Food and Agriculture Organization of the United Nations and this provided me further opportunities to pursue my specialization in an international context, particularly in the countries of Asia and Africa. I also held a field posting in Nepal as Project Co-Manager and Chief Technical Adviser during 1988-1990 and subsequently went on various missions to the African countries of Uganda and Ghana. Besides, I had the opportunity to travel around and document the decentralization experiences of Asian countries and of Sub-Saharan Africa and prepared two major reports for FAO under the following titles :

(i) Toward Improved Multilevel Planning for Agricultural and Rural Development in Asia and the Pacific (FAO Economic and Social Development Paper 52, Rome 1990); and
(ii) Decentralized Agricultural Sector Planning in Sub-Saharan Africa.

During my tenure in Nepal, I was instrumental in preparing a Training Manual on Decentralized Planning (district level) for Nepal in eight volumes with case studies and exercises.

Having spent years trying to understand and grapple with the perplexities and incongruities of the decentralization policy and multilevel planning in the various developing countries, I thought I should set down some rare-bits of my learning through experience. Although the literature on decentralization is fairly extensive, the treatment of this theme in the context of multilevel planning, incorporating both theory and practice, is rare to come by. Hence this book.

In the present work, I have drawn upon all my previous works and have attempted to present a coherent account of the concepts, principles and practices in Decentralized Multilevel Planning. In preparing this for publication, I had to wade through a mass of material accumulated by me during my professional career, consisting mostly of my notes, lectures in training programmes, discussion papers, keynote papers prepared for International and National Seminars as well as my publications scattered in various journals and books. This material has been collated, up-dated and edited for the current publication. While doing so, some overlaps have been maintained because each chapter of the book is designed to be an independent presentation and certain thoughts must necessarily recur because they bear on the argument. This enhances the usability of the book for both academicians and practitioners.

I must acknowledge my deep debt of gratitude to Mrs. Girija Sundaram, and Mrs. Seetha Ravi, who helped in retrieving most of the material referred to, and in organizing them in some order for speedy reference. This greatly facilitated my task. But for their dedicated assistance, much of the material would have found its way to the dustbin and lost. I shall be failing in my duty if I do not express my gratitude to Dr. Anu Kapur, Lecturer, Miranda College (University of Delhi), for going through the entire manuscript of this book and helping me with several valuable suggestions.

This book reflects the quintessence of my life-time work and experience in this field. Several academicians, bureaucrats (both from the Centre and the States) and professionals from various countries with whom I have had the privilege of interacting and discussing during my professional career, extending over three decades, have helped, directly and indirectly, in moulding my thinking and crystallizing the ideas that are reflected in this work. They are far too many to be individually named. I leave my thankful acknowledgement to them open-ened.

The book has been divided into four parts : Part I deals with "Concepts and Principles"; Part II with "Issues and Problems"; Part III with "Country Experiences"; and Part IV with "Human Resource Development. Each Part carries an "Introduction", which seeks to highlight the content and scope of the contribution. In the "Country Experiences', I have limited the scope to two Asian (India and Nepal) and two African (Ghana and Uganda)", countries, whose developmental experiences I have had the privilege to study in depth during my professional career. These countries differ in their range and depth of experience in decentralized planning and implementation of decentralized policies. Undoubtedly, much more in-depth studies of decentralization experiences of individual countries are needed to sharpen our understanding of multilevel planning in the Third World countries. This is a task for future researchers.

Decentralized multilevel planning, which may be a narrow specialization, is yet a vast field. I have not covered all its aspects in this book. With every attempt at factual precision and clarity of presentation, still some errors of commission and omission are bound to be there for which I take the sole responsibility. I hope the book will be useful to students, professionals and practitioners.

Finally, I am grateful to Shri Ashok Kumar Mittal of Concept for doing an excellent job in converting my manuscript into its present form.

New Delhi
November, 1996

K.V. SUNDARAM

CONTENTS

PART III
COUNTRY EXPERIENCES

PART IV
HUMAN RESOURCE DEVELOPMENT

LIST OF TABLES

LIST OF FIGURES

Figures

PART I

CONCEPTS AND PRINCIPLES

I keep six honest serving men
(They taught me all I know);
Their names are What and Why and When
And How and Where and Who

—*Kipling*

PART 1

INTRODUCTION

The six chapters of this part discuss various concepts like decentralization, multilevel planning and the two-way planning process, development from below and development from within. Chapter 1 on "Decentralization : Context and Concept" draws attention to the four major shifts in the emphasis on decentralization that have occurred over time, all of which are related to the contexts in which decentralization figured as a public policy. The meanings of the terms Decentralization and its variants (Deconcentration, Devolution, Delegation and Privatization) are explained and the four major dimensions of decentralization, viz. Functional, Financial, Administrative and Political, are elaborated. The problem of integrating "administrative" and "political" decentralization through appropriate institutions/structures has been emphasized.

Chapter 2 on "Multilevel Planning and the Two-Way Planning Process" discusses the merits of multilevel planning and its six major principles, viz. function-sharing, financial decentralization, administrative decentralization, public participation, iteration and the nesting and integration of plans. The two-way planning process is elaborated in terms of flows and interactions across different levels in an iterative top-down and bottom-up process of planning/organizations and linkages, which are critical to the operation in a multilevel system are specifically discussed and the various actions needed to operationalize a multilevel planning process have been elaborated.

In Chapter 3 on "Sectoral Decentralization," the principles of administrative decentralization are broadly set out and the nuances involved in organizing the agriculture and forestry sectors on multilevel planning principles are indicated in detail. The problems and challenges met with in this context have been pointed out.

Chapters 4 and 5 deal with two local level planning concepts, viz. "Development from Below" and "Development from Within." The distinction between the two is subtle in that it reflects the nature and intensity of the people's participation and relation to the role of government. "Development from Within" is in the nature of "capillary effect" or "trickle-up effect", while "Development from Below" is government controlled, albeit with an element of public participation. A view has been expressed in these chapters that in the context of current macro-economic policies, the role of the State in local and regional development is being reduced and the domain of responsibility of the people and the local institutions increased. The regional and local communities, therefore, must find their own development centres of gravity to respond to the new policy changes.

In Chapter 4 on "Development from Below," the changes in the development paradigm have been reviewed, and it has been emphasized that if development planning is to be scientifically practiced, it has to be done at three territorial levels, viz. National, Regional and Local. The differences in planning at these levels in regard to their aim, approach, command, methodology, resources and nature of public participation are indicated. The five major concepts on which development from below is based, viz. Decentralization, Area Development, Public Participation, Sustainable Development and Integration are fully discussed. This is followed by a clear elucidation of the sequence of operational phases and analytical steps involved in a decentralized planning methodology. This chapter is heavily loaded in terms of concepts and principles. To balance this theoretical slant, applied aspects have been discussed in the latter portion of the chapter. The Midnapore experiment (West Bengal) of village-based district planning and the Kerala experiment of Panchayat level resource mapping have been cited as illustrations.

Chapter 5 on "Development from Within" stresses the self-reliant approach, i.e. the idea that "development at the local community level has to be self-generated, self-organized and self-sustained". The key components of such an approach would be : (a) public participation, (b) decentralization and empowerment, (c) self-reliance, (d) self-management through collective action, and (e) poly-centric in structural arrangement. The salient features of these components are dealt with in the chapter. How Development from Within could be a planning tool for sustainable development from the grassroots level is illustrated.

In Chapter 6 on "Chemistry of Micro-Level Development," the idea that success in development efforts follows from a "mix" or combination of certain factors has been emphasised. These have been identified as "Technocratic, Academic and Democratic Mix" (TAD MIX). The case of "Kundrakudi development" in Tamil Nadu is discussed to illustrate a success story in micro-level development.

1

DECENTRALIZATION : Context and Concept

Decentralization has been a subject of intensive debate since the 1970's, when the orientation and structure of development planning changed from growth to redistribution with growth, with the accompanying objectives of increasing the productivity and incomes of all segments of society, providing the basic minimum needs to the population, raising the living standards of the poor and ensuring sustainable development of earth's natural resources. According to Prof. Lakdawala, "The logic of decentralization is so powerful that it has been almost universally accepted. It is now a well-recognized doctrine that since local resources are to be harnessed, local needs to be consulted, and local knowledge is needed, a large degree of decentralization is essential for the success of developmental efforts. This is especially so for those developmental efforts which aim at transforming the lives of the people or where the masses are involved."[1]

Many governments in the Third World countries have increasingly adopted decentralization policies and programmes in recent times particularly during the last decade. These have been informed by varying degrees and methods of public participation. These experiments have been diverse. One of the objectives of this book is to examine the principles and practice of decentralization in the developing countries.

Shifts in the Context of Decentralization

Decentralization, like development, has been shifting its emphases in the Third World countries during the last four decades.[2] These shifts in emphases are, by and large, linked with the contexts in which they figured as a public policy. At least four major shifts are discernible.

First, the period from the mid-1950s to the early 1960s was a time which was characterised by the establishment or strengthening of local governments in a number of countries. Many leading ideas on local governments emerged during this period. The seminal writings of Hicks[3] and Maddick[4] exemplify this trend. They dwell at length on the advantages and disadvantages of decentralized systems of government, the various forms which they may take and their organization and management. The second marks the period from the early 1970s to early 1980s, when many nation-states in Asia and Africa attained independence and were consolidating their power and authority. At this stage, the emphasis shifted to the role of decentralization as a means of national development and for achieving a variety of development objectives, ranging from popular participation to better management of rural development and maintenance of national unity. This period also marks the Third Development Decade of the UN, when the meaning of development came to be questioned and ideas of growth with equity or redistribution emerged, along with rural development programmes emphasizing poverty alleviation, basic needs, employment and quality of life. These trends increased the complexities of planning and administration of the multitude of central government departments and specialized agencies that had to take on considerably added functions to bolster and manage the new programmes with their thrust on specific areas and target groups. Now planning and development administration had to be organized through various layers of territorial space, extending from the centre through the state/region, district, sub-district, field units of central ministries, local government and para-statal bodies. Also, such planning and development had to be rendered increasingly relevant and specific to the requirements of the respective areas / administrative units and the people for whom the development benefits were intended. This led to the idea of the two-way process in planning—top-down and bottom-up or multi-level planning,[5] which came to be recognized as crucial for orderly planning and development for any country. In this context, decentralization acquired its in-depth meanings as a tool to bring about functional, financial and administrative deconcentration to the various area levels, with people's participation providing a critical and meaningful input. This marks the third stage. By any standards of evaluation, this third stage in the decentralization concept is the most significant and has placed development administration and management in its true context of function-sharing and capacity-building for territorial management and development administration. During this stage of evolution of the concept, the imperative for decentralization has been interpreted as stemming from three converging forces :

(i) Disillusionment with the results of central planning and control of development activities;
(ii) The implicit need for participatory management of development programmes to conform to the "growth with equity" strategy of the 1970s; and
(iii) The realization that, with expansion of government activities and resulting complexity, it is difficult to plan and administer all development activities from the centre.[6]

A concomitant realization during all these shifts in emphasis involving changes is the central idea that these changes are not "just technical and administrative; they are political. They involve a transfer of power from the groups who dominate the Centre to those who have control at the local level". (Griffin, 1981).[7]

Present Context and Imperatives

The evolution of thc decentralization concept brings us to the present context. This is the 1990's and in this fourth stage the imperative for decentralization has emerged in a different context—to afford the best chance for survival in a crisis-ridden situation. The crisis referred to here is "the debt crisis" being faced by a number of Third World countries today, particularly most of the African countries during the 1970s and 1980s. To cope with the crisis, several of these countries are involved in structural adjustment programmes, which are based on a resurgence of neo-classical macro-economic theories, under the guidance of the World Bank. Structural adjustment often involves a severe cutback in services to rural people. The spiral of economic decline which has led to the crisis situation has, in itself, created the preconditions for increased local initiatives. The governments, either by choice or necessity, are unable to provide adequate development services and the local people now cannot wholly depend on the State to provide them with sufficient means to improve their quality of life. What is needed is, therefore, a "self-reliant approach", in which local initiatives must lead development efforts. It depends on decentralization and devolution of the structure of government, education and sensitization of local communities to decide their own development priorities and to mobilize the resources necessary towards the solution of their own development problems.

Besides the debt crisis, there are three other imperatives which have rendered the concept of decentralization very relevant to the developing countries today. Since the mid-80's, the "environmental crisis" has surfaced as an important concern, and "sustainable development" has emerged as the strategy appropriate to all countries to arrest the rapid depletion of global natural resources. This needs to be approached in a decentralized manner. At the macro-level, this calls for a substantive and extensive analysis of (a) the implications of various macro-economic, trade and sectoral policies for management of the natural resource base, and (b) alternative policy options that explicitly take into account the resource constraints of the most vulnerable economic groups in society. At the meso-level, it calls for the operationalization of regional, economic development-cum-environmental planning. At the micro-level, it calls for eco-development planning with participatory action.[8]

Currently many countries in Africa and Asia are engaged in re-structuring and re-inventing their governments. The challenge is to find the proper balance between centralized and decentralized arrangements and to link them in ways that promote development most effectively. The optimal mix is not easily determined. In India, the government has recently passed a bold legislation, conferring constitutional status on the local bodies and following this, the Panchayati Raj bodies are being revived. The subjects of decentralization and district and local planning are once again under intensive discussion in all states in the country.

Yet another historical event, which has contributed to a favourable climate for decentralization is the collapse of the centrally planned regimes of Eastern Europe. The UN Human Development Report (1993) observes that "with free enterprise winning out over central planning and the courageous voices of democracy quieting the terrors of authoritarianism, people everywhere are asserting their right to determine their own destiny". It seems to have proved that highly centralized methods are manifestly ineffective, especially in implementing local development programmes.

The above four imperatives have undoubtedly increased the awareness and the need for operationalizing decentralized multilevel planning in many parts of the world.

Decentralization and its Variants

The dictionary meaning of decentralization as "The process of transferring the functions from the Central Government to the local units"[9] masks the many nuances associated with this term. Even the definition contained in the *Encyclopaedia of Social Sciences*[10] that decentralization denotes "the transference of authority, legislative, judicial or administrative from a higher level of government to a lower level" does not capture all the essential features of decentralization. The basic idea of decentralization is sharing the power of decision-making with lower levels in the organization. But this power can be shared within the system at a lower level or by creating new mechanisms in the system. Power can also be shared with outside organizations or agencies.[11] Depending on the extent and the means by which power can be shared with the lower levels, Rondinelli *et al.*[12] have recognized the following types :

(i) Deconcentration,
(ii) Delegation,
(iii) Devolution, and
(iv) Privatization.

Deconcentration

Literally it means "breaking the bulk" into smaller parts. In the sense in which it is used in the development context, it involves the redistribution of administrative responsibilities within the central government by shifting the work load from a central government ministry or agency headquarters to its own field offices, *without* transferring to them the power to make decisions or exercise discretion. Deconcentration is also sometimes called "Administrative Decentralization". It is really the transfer of some administrative responsibilities from the central government to the regional, zonal and district level government offices (geographic decentralization), retaining all powers of control and authority with the centre.

Deconcentration implies limited transfer of central government powers, functions and resources to its field units.

Deconcentration in local administration may be of two types : Integrated and Unintegrated.

Integrated Local Administration is a form of deconcentration, in which the field staff of central ministries work within a local jurisdiction under the supervision or direction of a chief executive of that jurisdiction, who is appointed by and is responsible to the central government. In one form of integrated provincial administration in East Africa, for instance, the Province Commissioner has the power to supervise and coordinate the work of various ministry staff working within the province. Although the field staff may be hired, paid, trained, promoted, and transferred by central ministry officials, the field officers act as technical staff to the Province Commissioner and are accountable to him for the efficient performance of their duties within the province.

Unintegrated Local Administration is an arrangement, wherein the field staff of central ministries and administrative staff of local jurisdictions operate independently of each other. Both sets of officials are responsible to central authorities but they have little or no formal power over each other. Each technical officer is responsible to his own ministry headquarters in the national capital and the administrative staffs of the local jurisdictions are supervised by the jurisdiction's chief executive, who has little or no control over the central ministry personnel. Coordination takes place informally, if at all, and each technical officer operates in accordance with the guidelines prepared by supervisors in the national capital.

Delegation

It is assigning some tasks to the lower level for administrative convenience. It implies that the central government creates or transfers to an agency or administrative level certain specified functions and duties, which the latter has broad discretion to carry out. The agencies to which powers and functions are delegated may or may not be under the direct control of the central government, but the ultimate responsibility for these functions rests with the central government and, as such, *indirect control* is implied in "delegation".

> ***To illustrate what delegation of authority really means, one may quote the advice given by a district collector in British India to his sub-divisional officers. "This is your job. These are the lines on which I want it to be run. Now go and run it. If you make a really serious mistake, I shall have to over-rule you. Otherwise I shall not interfere. If you want advice, I am here to give it. If you want a definite order, you are free to ask for it. But if you make a habit of wanting either, you will be of very little use to us."***

Devolution

This involves creating or strengthening independent levels or units of government through transfer of functions and authority from the central government. In this case, the local units of government to which functions and authority are devolved would be mostly autonomous, with the central authority only exercising indirect, supervisory control over them. For instance, in the context of Nepal, the transfer of authority effected from the central government (HMG/N) to the District and Village Development Committees (VDC) is a case of devolution. Devolution, in fact, implies political decentralization, i.e. decentralization of power to a political body such as sub-national legislature. In India, the state governments, which have their own legislatures and have defined powers and responsibilities under the Constitution, are an example of this kind.

Local units, which are conferred, through devolution, wide functions, powers and responsibilities are said to enjoy "Local Autonomy". By "local autonomy" is meant the ability of local communities to govern and serve themselves, to determine their own future, and — in practice as well as in law — to initiate, integrate and take decisions and actions, with a minimum of outside direction, approval, help or other forms of intervention (particularly by central authorities).

Devolution implies a situation in which lower ranking units acquire greater autonomy in respect of certain defined functions, including decision-making authority.

Devolution of functions, powers and responsibilities is normally effected through legislation. For example, in the context of Nepal, the District and Village Development Committees enjoy devolution of certain functions, powers and responsibilities through a legislation— Dcentralization Act, 1982.

It should also be noted that devolution is a form of decentralization in which the people's participation is maximized and their say in the decision-making powers is quite important.

The authority handed over to the Local Development Committee through devolution can be taken back only after making amendments in the law.

Privatization

This is another form of decentralization, in which the government transfers some responsibility or public functions to voluntary, private or non-governmental organizations. Voluntary organizations may include trade and industrial associations, professional groups, cooperatives, etc. Sometimes, the act of the government in allowing certain functions to be performed by private enterprises may also come under the scope of privatization.

> ***Privatization is a form of decentralization in which the government may transfer functions to voluntary organizations or allow certain functions to be performed by private enterprises.***

Delegation of Authority to Public Corporations and Regional Development Authorities

Between the two extremes of "Deconcentration" and "Devolution" of power, there are various degrees of delegation of functions and various mixes of shared responsibility between the state and organizations set up to perform specified functions. These may be in the form of parastatals, public corporations or regional/area development authorities. This is a way to short-circuit the normal government machinery and endow certain organizations with specified functions, so as to enable them to function with drive, coherence and authority to plan and pursue economic development. It is felt that this arrangement has distinct advantages over entrusting such functions to regular government agencies. Their executives could make decisions more expeditiously would be free from bureaucratic red tape and political manoeuvring characteristic of administrative agencies and could operate outside of the sometimes tight constraints imposed by legal regulations and civil service requirements. Moreover, a separate and usually higher-level salary scale, the prestige of a corporate image and the ability to use business procedures within these special authorities would attract the most highly qualified personnel and motivate them toward better performance. The MUDA Irrigation Authority in Malaysia, the Command Area Development Authorities and Small Farmers Development Agencies set up in India are examples of such organizations.

Decentralization : Its Real Meaning

Distinct from the above four expressions, the term Decentralization is an arching concept or an "umbrella term," which defies any single attempt at definition or interpretation.

Decentralization literally means the action or fact of reducing or undoing "centralization" or "concentration". In the political sense, complete or total decentralization would mean "the withering away of the state".

However, in the context in which the term is used in the development literature, it refers to the transfer of authority to plan, make decisions and manage public functions from the national level to any organization or agency at the sub-national level. Thus the sub-national area level, to which decentralization is effected, will have a particular "role" in the development process. This would mean assigning both "powers and responsibilities" for its activities. The power assigned may also include the power to raise local resources. When powers and responsibilities are fully decentralized to the sub-national level, the latter will have also control over the determination of their development goals and targets.

> ***Decentralization refers to a situation in which lower-ranking decision-units acquire all powers and responsibilities and have also control over the determination of their goals and targets.***

True decentralization implies three things :

1. Assigning of responsibilities (i.e. functions) with matching powers and requisite finances.
2. Rendering the decentralized level fully accountable for its activities.
3. Ensuring participation of the local population in planning and implementation.

Thus a clear role with adequate powers and finances, accountability (to the higher levels of administration as well as to the public) and public participation constitute the hallmarks of decentralization. The concept of autonomy is an important component of decentralization and that for autonomy to be meaningful, it should take place along three dimensions—administration, finance and delivery system.

To increase our clarity of understanding, the alternative forms of decentralization are depicted in Fig. 1.1. It should be noted that each form of decentralization has different implications for institutional arrangements, the degree of transfer of authority and power, local citizen participation, preconditions for successful implementation and advantages or benefits for the political system. In reality, although there are differences among the various forms of decentralization, they are not mutually exclusive. All governments consist of some combination of these forms, with the amount of authority transferred to decentralized units differing from country to country.

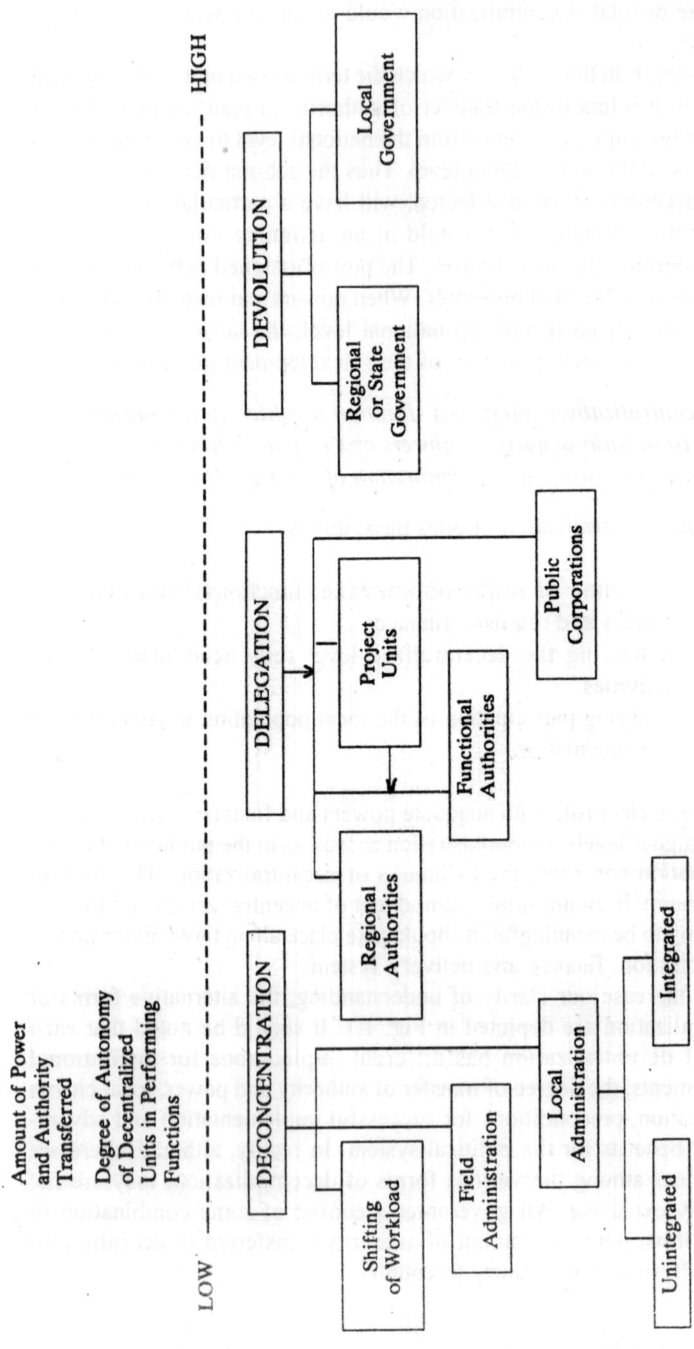

FIG. 1.1 : Alternative Forms of Decentralization

Dimensions of Decentralization

There are four major dimensions of decentralization, *viz.* (i) Functional, (ii) Financial, (iii) Administrative and (iv) Political. We may now devote some attention to these dimensions.

Functional Decentralization

The question of what types of functions are to be decentralized to the different sub-national levels is an important issue in decentralized planning. This cannot be done in a mechanistic omnibus manner by "listing" subjects in a schedule in the concerned enactment. This is because the "functions" have to be matched with the "capabilities" available and the "powers" proposed to be delegated by the government departments. The line ministries/departments do not give up the powers easily. The experience of many developing countries reveals that the lack of adequate capability at the lower levels to take on all new functions and responsibilities "in one go" is a serious constraint. The requisite capabilities to govern take a long time to develop. It is, therefore, apparent that the devolution of functions will have to proceed in steps, matching the building up of capabilities.

Government institutions at the sub-national levels of the central legislature (in case of unitary states) or the state legislature (in a federal set-up) can exercise only those powers and functions that are specifically assigned or delegated to them. Depending upon their nature and instrumentality, the powers and functions may be said to fall under three categories.[13]

(i) Governmental and departmental functions which arise out of *executive orders* of government and are not covered by statutes. A good part of plan schemes, welfare pensions and scholarships and allowances will come under this category;

(ii) Powers and functions *entrusted by the statute and its subordinate legislation,* creating the local government institutions; and

(iii) Powers and functions *assigned and delegated* to local government institutions (different powers being delegated to different local government institutions) in the subject matter enactments and their subordinate legislation.

While effecting functional decentralization, two issues must be considered: (i) The type of functional activities to be decentralized; and (ii) The nature of powers over each activity being decentralized.

While listing the functional divisions of government activity in any enactment or subordinate legislation or delegation through executive orders of the government, it is necessary to be very clear and specific. This is because, it is usual for any one functional (sectoral) activity to be divided between national and sub-national levels of government. Thus to take the example of education, one needs to consider different types of education, i.e. primary, secondary, tertiary, vocational, adult, etc., and different types of functions with regard to each kind of service such as day-to-day administration, location of new schools, curriculum design, teacher training and so on.[14]

What powers over each activity are decentralized is a relevant question, because those powers will determine the effective control or authority which sub-national levels of government or administration have over those functional activities. The powers that may be decentralized fall into three main categories : policy-making powers, financial powers and powers over personnel matters. Each of these powers can, in turn, be sub-divided. Thus policy-making powers are sub-divided into law-making and executive powers, financial powers into those concerning revenue and expenditure (each of which is further sub-divided) and personnel powers into those relating to conditions of service, establishments, appointments and promotions, transfers and direction and discipline (many of which could also be further sub-divided). Diana Conyers has summarized in a tabular form (Fig. 1.2) the main types of power which may be decentralized with regard to any particular activity (referred to in the diagram as activity one).[15]

The demarcation/division of planning and plan related functions between the national and sub-national levels is always a tricky problem. While it is ultimately a political/bureaucratic decision, there could be several criteria on which a rational decision could be arrived at. Some of these criteria are :

(i) *Selective closure* : Territory and Function have close affinities. Each particular function has a certain "territorial reach". Sudhir Wanmali's field surveys in Andhra Pradesh[16] have shown that under Indian conditions, economic distance is an important factor. Thus a primary school commands a service area of about 25 sq.kms, a secondary high school about 120 sq.kms., a branch

Type of powers			Level to which decentralized			To whom decentralized			How decentralized		
			Level in hierarchy	Population (ave)	Area (ave)	Politician/ bureaucrat/ 'mixed'	Indiv. or group	Specialist or general	Const. legis.	Ord. Legis.	Admin. Deleg.
Policy making	Law making										
	Executive										
Finance	Revenue	Tax									
		Grants									
		Loans									
	Expend	Budget									
		Alloc.									
		Control									
		Acc/ audit									
Personnel		Services conds.									
		Estabs.									
		Appoint/ promotion									
		Transfer									
		Direct/ discip.									

FIG. 1 2 : Analysing Decentralization

post office about 50 sq.kms. and so on in the rural areas. Thus based on "access norms", various functions could be allocated along spatial levels;

(ii) *Location of schemes/investments and the geographical spread of beneficiaries* : This is particularly relevant in assigning territorial control over specific poverty alleviation programmes, where the geographical spread of beneficiaries is an important consideration;

(iii) *Divisibility/indivisibility of a scheme or activity* : Some schemes require a unified control by an authority at a particular spatial level, e.g. Command Area Development activities. Splitting such functions across different spatial levels would cause complex administrative problems;

(iv) *Interdependence and complementarity between functions/ activities* : The linkage effects of development demand that interdependence and complementarity between functions be taken into account in deciding the allocation of functions to particular area levels. For example, the improvement in agriculture in an area depends on complementary developments in irrigation, rural electrification, roads, transport, banking, service provision and agro-industries. Integrated development would be greatly facilitated, if complementary functions could be controlled at the same spatial level; and

(v) Economies of scale must also be recognized as one of the criteria. For instance, economies of scale may direct certain functions to the sphere of a higher spatial level, e.g. Large-scale and strategic industries the responsibility of the centre; small-scale industries, the responsibility of the regions and so on.

In many Indian states, the criteria, by and large, for determining whether a particular plan scheme belongs to the state sector or the district sector are : (a) the location of the scheme, and (b) the area intended to be benefited by the scheme. Generally speaking, the schemes which are intended to promote the interests of the people of the state as a whole are classified as state-sector schemes. The schemes which are mainly for the benefit of the people of a particular district are identified as the district-sector schemes. In actual practice, however, the application of such criteria may present some problems, as benefits of certain schemes may cut across district boundaries. In such cases, the proportion of the benefit to the district in relation to the state is taken into account for deciding its classification.

Financial Decentralization

Financial devolution and the powers to mobilize local resources are very critical aspects of decentralization. As an FAO document puts it, "Planning at any level without necessary financial resources and authority is an exercise in futility. In all countries, including the federal ones, most financial resources are mobilized by the central government, which then distributes them to the lower levels. In a federal structure, the states have a right to certain shares in these resources and the Constitution provides for the periodic revision of Centre-State financial relations. In unitary systems, the financial resources of the provinces and the lower levels are received through the process of devolution. Multilevel planning processes are facilitated to the extent that the magnitude and rules for such devolution are clearly laid down and periodically revised".[17]

Local governments derive revenues from two main sources :

(i) External sources, which are not within the authoritative jurisdiction of the local government. Examples of this kind are the central government grants and loans and credits provided by domestic lending institutions;

(ii) Local sources, which include :

  (a) Taxation, i.e. those taxes imposed by the local bodies pursuant to the provisions contained in the appropriate legislation;

  (b) Rentals, charges and fees; and

  (c) Earnings from public utilities or public enterprises.

Based on various studies conducted in different developing countries, one may generalize that not more than 35 to 40 per cent of local body financial resources come from local sources and much of the resources of local bodies are derived from national government assistance through devolution.[18] It is also apparent from many studies that in spite of wide taxation powers available to local bodies, in a number of countries, the same have not been utilized fully, with the result that the inadequacy of local finances is a nagging problem with all local bodies. For this reason, most local authorities have failed to render effectively the services they are supposed to provide.

Therefore, the mobilization of larger internal resources to augment the financial capability of the local bodies is a crucial issue. Such mobilization does not merely mean the raising of more taxes or their rates.

Plugging of tax evasion and arrears, and curbing waste and inefficiency would also increase the flow of resources. Besides the internal mobilization of resources, we should also consider the transfer of resources from the centre.

This, in turn, raises many complicated issues of revenue sharing as well as the question of rationality in the transfer of development resources from the national to the sub-national levels.

For deciding the sharing of revenue between the centre and the sub-national levels, different countries have adopted their own procedures. In India, this is decided by a statutorily appointed Finance Commission for the transfer of finances from the Centre to the States. Recently, a similar device (i.e. a Local Finance Commission) has been stipulated for the transfer of financial resources from the states to the districts. For the disaggregation of development plan funds from the state to the districts and below. The major objectives are : (a) to nourish the grassroots planning and decision-making, and (b) to achieve a fair degree of regional equity in the allocation of development finance and the provision of services. Governments adopt various criteria for the allocation of development funds from the centre to the sub-national levels. Theoretically, the following socio-economic considerations hold good :

(i) Area;
(ii) Population size;
(iii) The degree of relative backwardness;
(iv) The measure of tax effort;
(v) Special locational (physical or environmental) and social characteristics; and
(vi) Commitment to major national schemes.

Each of the above factors may be given a special weight and a formula may be devised to calculate the contribution to each sub-national entity (e.g. district). In this method, the degree of relative backwardness is a crucial factor. It is used to rank the sub-national units, say, in terms of income per capita, services per capita and government expenditure per capita. Many other factors could be incorporated in this measure, such as infrastructural facilities, the rate of unemployment and nutritional status. The underlying argument is that an area, which is relatively more backward, should receive relatively higher grants, both from equity and efficiency considerations. The argument about efficiency is that when a backward area (particularly if it is potentially rich) is enabled to grow and develop and on its own feet, its future contribution to the national economy may more than outweigh the subsidy originally paid for its rescue.

In India, some state governments have adopted a rigorous formula approach. Broadly, the method consists of dividing the total plan outlay into "divisible" and "indivisible" pools, which indicate the resources available for the district-sector schemes and the state-sector schemes respectively. The "divisible pool" of resources is then distributed among the districts on the basis of a formula (incorporating various criteria) adopted by the State government. As an illustration, the criteria and the weightages given in the disaggregation formula for four Indian states is shown in Table 1.1.

At one time, Sri Lanka influenced by political considerations adopted the "equal-weighting approach" for making districtwise allocations, which means that the spatial disparities in development were ignored. In many African countries, no systematic or sophisticated criteria are being adopted for the allocation of central grants. The approach is ad hoc. Among those countries which follow some procedures, that of Ghana may be cited. In the criteria for the allocation of central grants, called "ceded revenue" in Ghana, three variables, viz. equality, population and development status of the districts, have been given some weight. A certain proportion of the funds (which is not a constant, but varies from year to year) is divided among the districts on an equal-sharing basis. The remaining funds are shared by taking population and development status into account in the proportion of 3:2. The criterion of development status is related to deprivation or backwardness. For example, the presence of settlements qualifying as towns is regarded as the indicator of "developedness". Using such rule-of-the-thumb methods, the level of backwardness of the districts is measured.[19]

In India, the states generally earmark funds meant for district schemes. But mere earmarking of funds for district schemes does not automatically confer autonomy on the district planning bodies for utilizing these funds. This is because most of the funds allocated to the districts may be pre-empted for various departmental schemes, the decision-making for which rests with the departmental heads at the state level. Therefore, unless some "un-tied funds" are kept at the disposal of the district planning bodies to be utilized according to their discretion, the district planning will be only in name. This constraint has been sought to be tackled to some extent in one of the states, Gujarat, by dividing the district outlays into three categories, viz.:

TABLE 1.1 : **India—Formula for Disaggregation of Plan Funds to the District level**

(Weightages %)

Criteria	States			
	Maha-rashtra	Gujarat	Karna-taka	Uttar Pradesh
1. Population				
(a) Total Population	60.0	40.0@	50.0	50.0
(b) Urban Population	5.0	—	—	—
2. Backwardness of Weaker Sections				
(a) Population of Scheduled Castes and Scheduled Tribes	5.0	15.0	2.5	5.0
(b) Small and Marginal Farmers and Population of Agricultural Labourers	—	2.5	2.5	10.0
3. Backwardness in respect of				
(a) Agriculture Production/value of output	5.0	10.0	5.0	5.0
(b) Irrigation	4.0	10.0	5.0	—
(c) Industrial Output	5.0	5.0	5.0	5.0
(d) Communications	5.0	10.0	2.5	5.0
(e) Drinking Water	—	—	—	5.0
(f) Financial infrastructure as measured by the size of population served by each Commercial and Cooperative Bank	—	—	2.5	—
(g) Medical and health facilities (No. of hospital beds)	—	—	5.0	5.0
(h) Power Supply	—	—	5.0	5.0
4. Backwardness in respect of the targets of other selected Minimum needs	—	5.0	—	—
5. Special Problems				
(a) Drought Prone Area	3.0	—	2.5	—
(b) Coastal Areas	1.5	—	—	—
(c) Forest Areas	1.5	—	2.5	—
6. Local Tax Effort	—	—	5.0	—
7. Incidence of unemployment as measured by the proportion of registrants at the Employment Exchange	—	5.0	—	—
8. Unallocated amount for meeting Special Problems	5.0	—	—	—
9. Incentive Provision	—	5.0	—	—
Total	100.0	100.0	100.0	100.0

@ For computing the population for the purpose of the formula in Gujarat, only rural population and population of towns with less than 50,000 people were taken into account.

Source : Govt. of India, Planning Commission, "Report of the Working Group on District Planning", May 1984.

(1) Eighty per cent of the provision is retained for normal schemes to be proposed by the sectorial departments;
(2) Fifteen per cent of the outlay is provided for schemes suggested by the district planning bodies in response to local needs and priorities and to exploit local potential; and
(3) The remaining 5 per cent is earmarked as incentive grants against which additional funds are to be raised at the district level.

What this means is that 20 per cent of the funds is provided as "discretionary outlay" to the local bodies and the remaining 80 per cent of the outlay is meant to be spent by the departments, over which the local bodies have little or no say.

Thus the above formula approach seeks to compromise the interests of departmental bureaucrats and the local planning authority. Ideally if the district planning has to manifest itself in its full meaning, all funds flowing into the district should be pooled together and placed at the disposal of the district planning authority. This does not happen, because the departments are not prepared to give up their hold on financial resources. The excuse usually advanced for this is that the districts do not have an adequate planning capability for formulating a systematic district plan and utilizing the funds rationally and in an accountable manner.

In the pattern of district plan outlays as evolved by Gujarat state in India, it may be noted that the provision of a 20 per cent discretionary outlay (including 5 per cent incentive outlay), which the district planning bodies have the freedom to use, has generated a lot of enthusiasm and is said to have resulted in the formulation of schemes of real local need and interest. But for this freedom, works like the provision of some missing links in development works would not have been taken up. The experiment of incentive outlay has also been very well received and has resulted in the mobilization of sizable local resources, in the shape of a matching contribution by the local population. The incentive outlay requires 50 per cent or 25 per cent matching contribution from the districts depending upon the pattern prescribed, which is based on the relative backwardness of the area. While the relatively advanced areas have to provide a matching contribution of 50 per cent, certain categories of relatively backward areas are required to contribute only 25 per cent. Thus differential incentives have been provided for according to the degree of backwardness.

From the above country experiments, we get many useful clues about financial decentralization methods. We also understand that in any scheme of financial decentralization, adequate incentives must be provided for, to encourage the local mobilization of resources. This would lead to a sense of participation among the people and increase their motivation to help themselves as far as possible and to achieve a certain measure of self-reliance. An FAO document says that "the local mobilization processes in a community are not generated spontaneously. Catalytic intervention of some sort is often a crucial initial step. One of the ways of motivating a community is to incorporate an incentive element in the resource transfer formula itself, such as a performance and efficiency criterion. Alternatively, a small part of the transfer could be earmarked for a matching contribution by the sub-national community, (i.e. an incentive grant)".[20]

It should be noted that devoid of a substantial element of local resource mobilization and with reliance only on the central financial flows, local development becomes wholly dependent on a whimsical exercise by the state in the deconcentration of the national development budget to the local level. Consequently, the local bodies are throttled by barely or totally insufficient funds, with which to meet their local felt needs and tackle all their local problems. Unfortunately, this is the prevailing state of affairs in the local bodies of many Third World countries

Administrative Decentralization or Deconcentration

Administrative decentralization or "Deconcentration" as it is known, is considered to be a watered-down surrogate of true decentralization. It encompasses a wide range of structural, planning, personnel, procedural and managerial issues, which are all administrative in nature. Administrative decentralization is certainly a necessary component of decentralization for any country, but not sufficient.

Administrative decentralization essentially means deconcentration of functions and some powers from the headquarters of the national government departments and agencies to their respective field offices. It may also mean divesting of some responsibilities to corporate institutions and para-statals. Through such means, the centre "unloads" a part of its administrative burden at the top. The "command", however, is retained at the top. The deconcentrated administrative institutions, which owe their allegiance to their vertical hierarchies, work within top-down lines of command.

First and foremost, administrative decentralization means taking a range of administrative actions to partly off-load governmental activities. These include :

(a) Setting up offices at the regional and various local levels, so as to improve the "reach" and "access" of the governmental administration and move closer to the people;
(b) Designating the decentralized subjects or functions for each of the spatial levels in the hierarchy;
(c) Making necessary delegation of powers;
(d) Assigning adequate finances;
(e) Determining appropriate financial powers for ensuring accountability, laying down budgetary procedures for framing the budget, for financial release, accounting and reappropriation of funds;
(f) Posting of adequately qualified personnel through deputation or fresh recruitment;
(g) Establishing work procedures and framing departmental rules and regulations for coordinated functioning;
(h) Providing technical guidelines to field officers and establishing a time-bound programme of activities to nest into the national planning process;
(i) Taking suitable steps for capability building among the personnel through the institution of training, re-training and refresher programmes;
(j) Instituting a planning process with top-down and bottom-up procedures meshing into one another; and
(k) Establishing institutional mechanisms for an effective policy analysis, planning, coordination, monitoring, review and evaluation.

All the above tasks amount to the building-up of an efficient "administrative framework", which would have the necessary capabilities to take over the responsibilities of effectively implementing a decentralized policy and manage the decentralized development activities. This means not merely the acquisition of skills by the bureaucracy and the technocracy, but also gradually developing in them an attitudinal change and a frame of mind in favour of working with the people and their representatives. In other words, it means "laying the ground work" for the more desirable "democratic decentralization", about which we shall discuss more in the next Part. In this conception, administrative decentralization is seen more in its positive role as a pace-setter and facilitator of democratic decentralization. However, it should not be forgotten that sectoral administrative decentralization really means, enabling the building up of an insulated, free-wheeling and isolationistic vertical empire in each sector of activity, characterized by an excessive "departmentalism" and "ivory tower attitude", which thwarts all attempts at coordinated and integrated development. According to Benninger,[21] the more "fine grain" the pattern of deconcentration, the more ugly and corrupt will be the face of the administration. He views administrative decentralization as a process of extending central control in a more fine-grain pattern through "supervisory" officials down to "contact" officials in the field. In its extreme form, it may lead to an excessive bureaucratic control and may even encourage corruption.

Whatever be the negative aspects of "administrative decentralization" in the strict sense of this term, it is a necessary component of decentralization because it enables the various governmental sectors of activity to descend to the critical spatial levels in the sub-national hierarchy and provide greater access to the government's services and delivery systems to a large part of the population. In many countries in sub-Saharan Africa characterized by political centralism, the real problem is how to extend the "reach" of the government to the periphery. In this context, the question of administrative reforms preceding democratic decentralization does not arise. By at least decentralizing development administration in ministries, line agencies and departments, it would be possible to extend the "reach" and access of the government and capacitate the government functionaries at the lower levels and expose them to a planning concept, which can take better note of the local needs, aspirations and problems and execute jobs with a greater accountability to the people. Centralization and decentralization may be viewed as the opposite extremes of a single "continuum", neither of which, by itself, would seem to be a practicable choice for any government for any substantial period of time. It is a question of necessity and degree. The choice of direction and of pace and extent of decentralization will depend on the stage of political, economic and social development of the country. One cannot always argue for the "best". In many African countries, a graduated change is called for. In this context, "selective administrative decentralization" viewed as an incremental process holds the key to development.

Political or Democratic Decentralization

Decentralization, as a concept, reaches its acme of perfection when the people are drawn into its fold and are empowered. But when only the elected leaders are drawn into its fold, it is deemed "partial decentralization". When all sections of the population are enabled to participate in the local affairs of a community, then decentralization is said to be "more fine-grained" or total.

Political or democratic decentralization thus signifies the quest for a participative and community approach and the epithet "democratic" only reinforces and underlines the democratic values, purposes and approaches and the style governing it.

The three major components of political or democratic decentralization are : Local Autonomy, Devolution and Public Participation.

Local autonomy should be taken to mean the ability of local communities to govern and serve themselves, to determine their own future and—in practice as well as law—to initiate, integrate and take decisions and actions, with a minimum of outside direction, approval, help or other forms of intervention (particularly by central authorities). It implies an attitude of assertiveness, self-reliance and confidence that the local community knows better where its interests lie and how best to achieve them. But it need not imply self-sufficiency, nor need it mean autarky.[22]

Local autonomy is primarily sought through "Devolution", which, as explained earlier, is the transfer of national government powers, functions and resources to local governments. It is granting decision-making powers to local authorities and allowing them to take full responsibility, without reference back to the central government. For making local autonomy meaningful, devolution should be complemented by deconcentration and other measures. In devolution, Maddick has emphasized the legal aspect. According to him, devolution is "The legal conferring of powers to discharge specified or residual functions upon a formally constituted local authority."[23]

According to Uphoff and Esman, "local autonomy by itself provides little leverage for development".[24] For development purposes, the strength of local government units—in terms of salient functions they perform, the skill and professionalism of local officials, their base of financial resources, and the effectiveness with which they carry out their responsibilities—may be much more significant than their legal status as independent units.

The Balwantrai Committee has made the distinction between delegation of powers and devolution very clear. The report of the Study Team states: "It is not infrequently that delegation of powers is mistaken for decentralization. The former does not divest the government of the ultimate responsibility for the actions of the authority to whom power is delegated; this authority is under the control of the government and is in every way subordinate to it. Decentralization, on the other hand, is a process, whereby the government divests itself completely of certain duties and responsibilities and devolves them on to some other authority."[25] Ocampo elaborates on the various ways in which devolution should enhance the capacities of local governments.[26] These are :

(a) Transfer of more programme responsibilities and resources from the national to the local governments to substantiate the legal duties and powers conferred upon them;
(b) Broadening the range of the programmes and services under their control, so that it is commensurate with responsibility;
(c) Provision of more *productive* revenues in order that the fiscal powers given to them can be effectively made use of and their dependence on the central government can be reduced; and
(d) Enhancing the local institutional capabilities for policy-making and administration so that they can effectively exercise their greater autonomy.

Devolution is thus seen as an orderly transfer of authority, resources and institutional capabilities to local governments. Political commitment to democratic decentralization is a must, if devolution is to become a reality. In its absence, most of the things to implement remain more in law than in practice.

Democratic decentralization is a political ideal and local government is its institutional form.[27] It is premised on advocacies of ensuring basic freedoms, a more liberal and rational sharing of power, and the pursuit of improved well-being for the people under a climate of democratic dispensation. Through democratic decentralization, people are afforded meaningful participation in the process of governance, strengthening of democratic institutions to promote a healthy arrangement of checks and balances, attainment of a certain level of political maturity and cultivation of democratic consciousness. Thus democratic decentralization, it must be understood, is more than holding of elections and tinkering with structures and forms.

The institutional expression of the policy of democratic decentralization in India is identified with "Panchayati Raj". Till recently, the whole structure of the Panchayati Raj system did not have a constitutional backing and it had been left to the whimsicalities of state governments.

This led to the steady erosion of their powers and functions over a period, and for even the elections to them being postponed indefinitely, despite formal legislative enactments at the state level for initially setting them up. An essential step has now been taken through a constitutional amendment (the 73rd Constitution Amendment, 1993), which envisages the establishment of Panchayati Raj institutions as units of local self-government in different states.

Integrating Administrative Decentralization with Democratic Decentralization

Both administrative and political decentralization, in their extremes, are not desirable. The former will lead to excessive bureaucratic control and corruption and the latter to the "withering away of the state". The conceptual differentiation between the two is, however, crucial. But in reality, both must be seen in relation to one another. It should be emphasized in this context that the concept of decentralization is that of a "continuum", rather than a dichotomy; it is a matter of degree rather than an alternative. What is needed in any context is an "appropriate mix" between administrative and political decentralization. This appropriate mix will depend on the socio-economic and developmental context of the particular country.

We may illustrate through a diagram how the false dichotomy of separate "administrative" and "political" decentralization could be integrated. Here we consider a bi-axial system in which "administrative" and "political" decentralization are at the two ends of the continuum along the X-axis, and "centralization" and "decentralization" are at the two ends on the Y-axis. Any system has some internal constraints, which we shall call as "feasibility thresholds". These are shown in the Fig. 1.3.

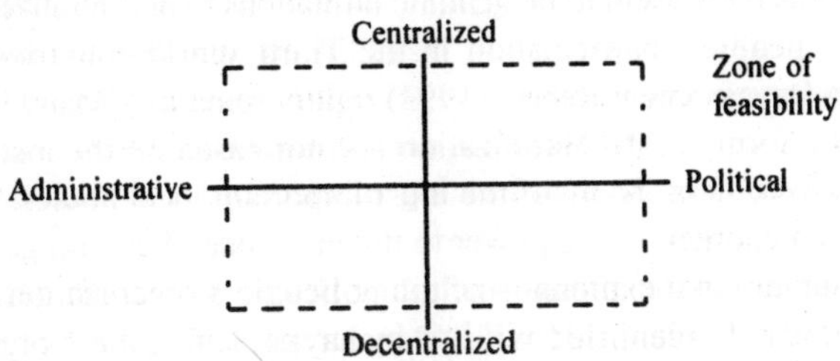

FIG. 1.3 : The Administrative and Democratic Decentralization mix.

The integration of "administrative" and "political" decentralization is achieved through appropriate institutional structures, which will link the bureaucracy and the implementing agencies with the people and their institutions (i.e. local governments and voluntary agencies). Thus an appropriate model of democratic decentralization implies the combination of and cooperation between the official machinery of administration and the non-official leadership and control through the mechanism of local governments.

Rhetoric and Reality of Decentralization

Decentralization, in its ideal and pristine form, with genuine decentralization to democratic structures, has not been realized to its fullest potential, as far as we know, in any part of the globe. The hiatus between the idea, which is undoubtedly noble, and its implementation or realization is disturbingly wide. In most countries, what we find is an extended deconcentration of some administrative functions and powers with limited local participation. In many African countries, which are ruled in a non-democratic way with authoritarian structures, sometimes the bogey of decentralization is raised, but there is hesitancy to extend local autonomy for the fear that the nation may break up. In many other countries, in the absence of democratic structures, local governments lack an effective political power base from which to generate local control over decision-making. Even in some Asian countries, where some progress has been made in establishing suitable institutional mechanisms, the actual decentralization that has been effected is disappointingly short of expectations. Further, many developing countries, which have experimented with democratic decentralization, have not succeeded in drawing the less privileged sections of the society into its local bodies. Decentralization has only further empowered the elites and marginalized the poor. Thus there seem to be genuine limitations to decentralized planning and the people's participation in the Third World countries. The UN Human Development Report (1993) rightly remarks, "Many of the most effective forms of decentralization are not based on the institutions of local government. Some of the most important local bodies, which can serve as a countervailing power to the influence of central governments are voluntary associations—including people's organizations and non-governmental organizations." It is by strengthening these organizations at the grassroot levels that democratic decentralization can truly achieve its ultimate goals.

REFERENCES

1. Lakadawala, D.T., 'Panchayati Raj in Karnataka today : Its National Dimensions, Quoted in *Decentralized Planning and Panchayati Raj* (Proceedings of the D.T. Lakdawala Memorial Symposium), Institute of Social Sciences, New Delhi, and Concept Publishing Company, New Delhi, 1994.
2. Conyers, D., 'Decentralization of Development–A review of literature, in *Public Administration and Development*, 4, 1984.
3. Hicks, U.K., *Development from Below : Local Government and Finance in Developing Countries of the Commonwealth.* Oxford : Oxford University Press, 1961.
4. Maddick, H., *Democracy, Decentralization and Development*, Bombay : Asia Publishing House, 1963.
5. FAO, 'Towards Improved Multi-level Planning for Agriculture and Rural Development in Asia and the Pacific'. *Economic and Social Development*, 52, 1984.
   See also Sundaram, K.V., 'Multi-level Planning, Concepts, Principles and Application to sectoral development'. In Sundaram, K.V. *et al.* (Eds.), *Regional Planning and Development* (Essays in honour of R.P. Misra), New Delhi : Heritage, 1985.
6. Cheema, G.S. and Rondinelli, D.A. (Eds.). *Decentralization and Development : Policy Implementation in Developing Countries*, Beverley Hill : Sage, 1983.
7. Griffin, K., "Economic Development in a Changing World," *World Development* 9(3) : 225, 1981.
8. Sundaram, K.V., 'The Emerging New Development Paradigm : Issues, Considerations and Research Agenda' in Amitava Mukherjee and V.K. Agnihotri (Eds), *Environment and Development—Views from the East and the West*, Concept, New Delhi, 1994.
9. See *Chambers Twentieth Century Dictionary.*
10. Leonard D. White, 'Decentralization' *Encyclopaedia of Social Sciences*, Vol. 5, New York, Macmillan 1959.
11. Meenakshi Sundaram, S.S., *Decentralization in Developing Countries*, Concept Publishing Company, New Delhi, 1994, p. 11.
12. Rondinelli, D.A., J.R. Nellis and G.S. Cheema (1984) *Decentralization in Developing Countries*, Washington, World Bank.
13. Ramachandran, V., 'Report on the measures to be taken for democratic decentralization at the district and lower levels', Vol. I, Government of Kerala, Trivandrun, July 1988.
14. Conyers, Diana "Decentralization : A framework for discussion", in *Decentralization, Local Government Institutions and Resource Mobilization* (Ed.) Hasnat Abdul Hye, Bangladesh Academy for Rural Development, Comilla, Bangladesh, 1985.
15. Conyers, Diana, *Ibid.*
16. Sudhir, Wanmali, *Geography of a Rural Service System in India*, B.R. Publishing Corporation, Delhi, 1987.
17. 'Toward Improved multilevel planning for agricultural and rural development in Asia and the Pacific'—FAO Economic and Social Development Paper 52, Food and Agriculture Organization of the United Nations, Rome, 1990, p. 66.
18. Local finance studies in the Philippines show that 60-65 per cent of the total revenues of most local governments come from external or national government

sources, notably from internal revenue allotments; Only 35 to 40 per cent represent revenues coming from local sources. See Raul P. deGuzman and Perfecto L. Padilla, 'Decentralization, Local Government Institutions and Resource Mobilization–The Philippines Experience' in Hasnat Abdul Hye, 'Decentralization, Local Government Institutions and Resource Mobilization', Bangladesh Academy for Rural Development, Comilla, Bangladesh, 1985.

19. Sundaram, K.V., 'Decentralization of Agricultural Planning for Ghana', January 1992, Report prepared for the Food and Agriculture Organization of the United Nations and the Government of Ghana, Ministry of Agriculture (mimeographed).
20. FAO Economic and Social Development Paper No. 52, 'Toward Improved multilevel planning for agricultural and rural development in Asia and the Pacific', FAO/UN, Rome 1990.
21. Benninger, Christopher C., 'Institutional Strategies for Decentralization', in *The Administrator*, Vol. XXVI, No. 3, July-Sep., 1991.
22. Ocampo, Romeo B., "Toward more authentic Local Autonomy–Premises and Proposals for reform," in 'Papers on Decentralization and Local Autonomy'– Local Government Centre, College of Public Administration, Manila (mimeographed).
23. Maddick, H., *Democracy, Decentralization and Development*, Bombay : Asia Publishing House, 1966, p. 23.
24. Norman Uphoff and Milton J. Esman : 'Local Organization for Rural Development in Asia', Centre for International Studies, Cornell University, Ithaca, 1974.
25. Report of the Team for the Study of Community Projects and National Extension Service, Committee on Plan Projects, New Delhi, Vol. I, 1957.
26. Ocampo, Romeo B., *Ibid.*
27. Iqbal Narain, 'The idea of democratic decentralization', *Indian Journal of Political Science*, Vol. XXI, No. 2.

2

MULTILEVEL PLANNING AND THE TWO-WAY PLANNING PROCESS

Necessity and Trends

The planning process in the developing countries is fast changing in keeping with the emerging new needs, issues, goals and realities of development. Till the mid 1960s, countries were more pre-occupied with macro-economic growth opportunities and laid great emphasis on large scale projects and infrastructural developments. Planning was concentrated at the top and tended to be focused more on strategies of development than on actual spatial potentialities and means of implementation. This inevitably left a wide gap between the plan and ground realities. As inroads into development were made, issues relating to the distribution of investments and the choice of production alternatives in relation to regional and local potentials have assumed great significance. In this context, it has become clear that planning, to be more effective, has to share appropriately decision-making functions with sub-national levels through a system, that is properly adapted to the needs and characteristics of the country involved, and covering the range of regional and local conditions. This implies *multilevel planning*, which essentially involves sharing of planning and policy functions at different sub-national levels and devising mechanisms and procedures for effective flows of information for planning and interaction between and among the sub-national levels. By necessity, it will involve meaningful participation of the people in making the planning process on the whole harmonious, interdependent and participatory and rendering it relevant, authentic and implementable. Country experiences in planning in Asia and Africa reveal that trends along these lines are already in evidence.

Economic realities and the sheer bulk and magnitude of governmental functions in each country have necessitated a certain *deconcentration* process to be initiated during the last three to four decades. This has meant merely breaking the bulk and assigning some duties and functions to the sub-national levels, retaining all powers of planning, decision-making and control at the centre. With changing times and building up of capabilities, many countries are already grappling with the important aspects of mulcilevel planning, i.e. of assigning functions to different tiers of administration along with powers and responsibilities and linking planning and management at the sub-national levels to the central level.

Thus there has been increasing recognition in the developing countries of the need for and the desirability of encouraging multilevel planning. Attempting this kind of planning would involve : (a) decentralization of planning to several discrete sub-national levels; (b) organizing a two-way planning process; (c) the building up of capabilities to plan and implement development functions at each one of the decision-making levels; and (d) managing planning and development with people's participation.

Merits of Multilevel Planning

The major advantages of multilevel planning are fivefold :

(i) It is a logical system and facilitates the sharing of planning and development functions in a rational manner among a number of "actors" at different spatial levels. This enables the actors at the various levels to tackle the problems of their respective areas at sub-national levels with greater understanding and perception. At the national level, these problems are seen as through a ground glass, in a hazy and highly aggregated manner through broad indicators of development. With multilevel planning, however, a sharpened focus is possible and the understanding of problems gains in clarity and content. Consequently, the solution devised also becomes more meaningful and specific from the viewpoint of the area and the community.[1]

(ii) An important objective of multilevel planning is to increase the efficiency of resource use in the economic sectors, increasing their productivity and at the same time ensuring sustainability. For example in the agricultural sector, which is characterized by a diversity of agro-climatic and ecological conditions, centralized planning cannot respond in a flexible and effective manner to the differing potentials, problems and needs of each area. By meeting these requirements, multilevel planning could facilitate the optimum and sustainable use of the agricultural resources.

(iii) Multilevel planning is a cost-effective approach. Since its basis is area planning and development, the linkage effects of development would be maximized and production could take place on the basis of the principle of comparative advantage, thereby promoting area specialization and inter-actional efficiency and thus augmenting the volume and flow of commodities. Cost effectiveness would be increased because production inputs and credit could be channelled to area specific requirements, i.e. according to where they are needed most and where production potentials are great. In another sense also, multilevel planning is a cost-effective approach. This is from the viewpoint of access to information. Multilevel planning with its greater proximity to an area ensures greater access to information. In an optimal system, decisions are taken at a spatial level, where information could be obtained with relative ease, speed, authenticity and at a lesser cost and where responses to interventions could also be spontaneous and effective.[2]

(iv) In the economic development planning practised in every country, multilevel planning will ensure greater equity in the distribution of agricultural and industrial production. It is well known that in the developing countries, the gains of development have tended to bypass the poor and the underprivileged. Multilevel planning, by concentrating development efforts in "manageable" areas and communities, tends to reduce inter-regional and inter-personal disparities, thus ensuring a more equitable type of development. The planning exercise in most developing countries today includes a substantial component of poverty alleviation programmes, which are basically decentralized programmes, requiring detailed knowledge of local conditions. Multilevel planning facilitates the undertaking of these programmes in an effective manner, based on the local assessment of the needs of target groups and aiming at increasing the level of their incomes and employment opportunities.

(v) Among the planning approaches available to the developing countries, multilevel planning is the most effective for involving the people in the planning and development process. It is the surest method to bring the government nearer to the people. Thus the greatest advantage of multilevel planning lies in its ability to reach the people and draw their effective participation in development. This presupposes the establishment of representative bodies at each discrete spatial level, which could be involved in the assessment of area needs, formulation of projects to meet these needs, monitoring their performance and evaluating their impact on the target groups.

Thus the merits of multilevel planning are derived from its ability to discover dormant resources and skills and its endeavour to activise them. To derive the maximum advantages from this approach, it is necessary to be clear about the various conceptual aspects relating to decentralization, linkages, coordination, flow of information and people's participation. These various issues are touched upon in this chapter.

Multilevel Planning : Concept and Principles

According to Chakravarty, multilevel planning "has become all the more important in view of the fact that as contrasted with the earlier argument that investment in material capital holds the key to the structural transformation of a backward economy, it is now beginning to be recognized increasingly that investment in education, health, nutrition, etc., is just as essential for sustained growth with social justice. In some areas, the very nature of the operation involves a larger number of schemes, which cannot always be effectively directed from the top. Hence it becomes essential to devise a system of information flow, and delegation of responsibilities coupled with a suitable provision on the financial side".[3] This statement is quoted here to emphasize the high relevance of multilevel planning for the developing countries.

The heart of the multilevel planning process is the issue of decentralization. It essentially involves the sharing of planning functions at different area levels and devising mechanisms and procedures for the effective flows of information and interaction between and among the area levels as well as for meaningful participation with the people, thus making the planning process on the whole harmonious, interdependent and participatory and the plans themselves geographically relevant, authentic and implementable. This statement, which intends to capture the essence of multilevel planning process, is a long one and implies adherence to many principles, the most important among which are:[4]

(a) Principle of-function-sharing;
(b) Principle of financial decentralization;
(c) Principle of administrative decentralization;
(d) Principle of public participation;
(e) Iteration principle (The relay-rerelay process); and
(f) Principle of nesting and integration of plans.

The above principles are elaborated below.

Principle of Function-sharing

Decentralized planning would be harmonious and effective only when the partners in the planning process are clear about their functions and perform these in a non-competing, non-overlapping and mutually supporting manner. One of the first steps in the multilevel planning process is, therefore, to divide with precision and clarity the total planning functions among the various area levels. This is, in other words, differentiating planning activities according to the territorial levels, where they could most effectively and efficiently be performed. Developmental functions have differing geographic scope. While no developmental activity can be performed in perfect isolation, it is possible to identify activities that can be best performed at particular area levels and also to take note of their linkages with the activities at the other area levels. In this way, an interlinked and interdependent planning process can be established. This is the basic idea in a multi-level planning set-up. The identification of the exclusive planning functions that can be performed at the different territorial levels, therefore, constitutes, the first step of "Functional Decentralization".

Principle of Financial Decentralization

Every territorial level to which particular functions have been assigned must be allocated adequate financial resources to enable it to perform those functions, with some reasonable degree of efficiency. In the planning context, this means that the funds required for the implementation of all the projects in the area are to be directly made available to the agency responsible for planning at that territorial level. While this may sound fair and simple, it is not so in actual practice. It means the establishment of appropriate financial disaggregation procedures, as well as suitable budgeting and re-appropriation procedures. In the administrative sense, it involves a movement away from the traditional procedure of channeling funds through sectoral departments and agencies, which is a vertical procedure, to channelling funds directly to the horizontal area levels in the country. This calls for changing old procedures by removing some powers of control from established centres and creating new centres of power. Such changes are not easy and call for considerable administrative reforms in any country. Financial decentralization also includes an exercise in disaggregation of financial resources from the central level to the other area levels. Here a principle of equity is essentially implied, as interregional allocation of resources must necessarily give weightages to disparities in area development and various criteria of backwardness. Countries that have experimented with financial decentralization methods have initially determined the amount of "divisible outlays" that can be allocated to sub-national levels from the total development resources available at the national level. Then a further breakdown for the various sectors and sub-sectors has been attempted by adopting a formula which gives weightage to different indicators of development. When applying the principle of financial decentralization to any particular sector, the key question will be, which are those planning functions that will remain with the centre and which are those that could be decentralized. The latter will determine the magnitude of divisible outlays in that sector.

Principle of Administrative Decentralization

Decentralization will have no meaning, if it is not accompanied by the assigning of adequate powers and responsibilities to the different area levels to enable them to perform the designated functions, with relative ease and efficiency. This is what is implied in administrative decentralization or "deconcentration", as it is sometimes called. The extent of retention of command with the centre and the extent of delegation of powers to the decentralized levels are matters on which decisions will have to be taken by governments, bearing in mind various factors peculiar to each country situation. No rules can be laid down for the purpose. However, some aspects of administrative decentralization that deserve consideration in a multilevel planning context may be cited. These will relate to changes in the procedures for giving administrative and technical sanctions, procedures for release of funds, procedures for intersectoral transfers and powers of reappropriation and vital departures in matters of personnel control.

Principle of Public Participation

The greatest advantage of multilevel planning lies in its ability to reach the people and draw their effective participation for development. In this context, it is pertinent to mention that there are two views on participation. One is what may be termed the "mobilizing" view, which considers participation as mobilization of the people for the success of development projects. The other view is the "empowering" view, in which the people are empowered to make their own decisions on the planning issues. It is this latter view of participation which is relevant in multilevel planning. In this participatory strategy, the majority of the population characterized by low incomes, low educational levels and restricted or non-existent opportunities are enabled to make their voices heard in forums devised for their participation. Such a mechanism has to be deliberately brought about by effecting suitable changes in the existing institutional framework, which is often dominated by the elites in society. The mechanism so devised also becomes the plan approving or plan authenticating body at the particular area level. At the higher levels, like the national level or the regional level, participation will be more indirect, while at the local level, it will be more direct. Again at the national and regional levels, participation would be of a consultative nature, whereas, at the local level, participation should be seen as both a tool and goal of development, as it serves as a medium of social transformation and as a pre-condition for authentic development.

Iteration Principle

Decentralized planning is not a single-stroke planning operation. It is a relay-rerelay process in which the micro-units, through a repetitive process of interaction, seek continuously convergence to the dynamic path of stable equilibrium for the entire macro system. The different area levels have to act and interact repeatedly, until harmonious planning is achieved. This interaction is achieved through a vigorous flow of information, both top-down and bottom-up. The top-down flows may consist of information pertaining to policies, priorities, targets, guidelines for planning, budgetary information, technical information, coordination directives, review of monitoring and evaluation of projects and suggestions for replanning. Bottom-up flows may consist of data, information on local needs and preferences, area priorities, area targets and problems and constraints faced at the local level. A hypothetical multilevel planning system showing levels, flows and interaction may be seen in Fig. 2.1. In order to bring about this iterative process of inter-

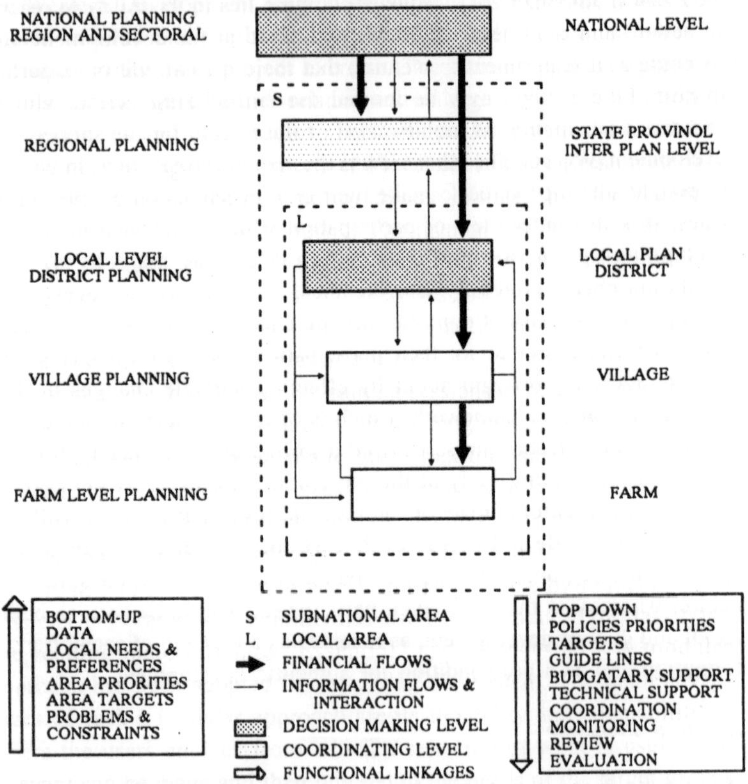

FIG. 2.1 : A Hypothetical Multilevel Planning System showing levels, flows and intreactions

Note: (i) Financial allocation flows directly from national to local level, bypassing the intermediate level.

(ii) Within the local area level, the interaction between district level, village and farm are in all directions.

Source : FAO Economic and Social Development Paper 52 : Toward Improved multilevel planning for agricultural and rural development in Asia and the Pacific, Rome, 1985.

action in the manner envisaged here, an interactive organizational mechanism is required, which can constantly align the plans at the various sub-national levels to the national plan, at each round of implementation. It is in this way that the goal conflicts in multilevel planning are sought to be avoided and harmonized planning ensured. This interactive organizational mechanism would consist of an appropriate planning machinery at each one of the sub-national levels where planning functions are proposed to be decentralized. The structure and composition of this planning machinery is the most crucial in this entire planning process, for it is the apparatus which has to prepare the plans and organize the flows and interactions, both upward and downward. Upon the efficiency of this planning apparatus will depend the entire success of the multilevel planning process.

Principle of Nesting and Integration of Plans

This implies integrating the plans of different spatial levels into a unified frame, so that these plans are harmonized. The integration intended here is a complex one. It would require that the individual plans at the different area levels will be internally consistent and integrated, and so also the overall national plan, into which they fit. If such harmonization is to be achieved, the iterative process of interaction between and among the area levels must become a reality. This should be aided by an effective flow of communication and information, as explained before.

Operational Issues : Organization and Linkages

A policy of decentralization aims, inter alia, to improve on the delivery of government policies, services and development efforts through the local levels of administration and geographical areas, to institutionalize grassroot participation in planning, deciding of their needs and priorities, and actual implementation of their development schemes; and to bring about integration in the functioning of technical departments at the local and regional levels for the purpose of providing the necessary services directly. Building up a territorial and organizational structure for operating decentralized multilevel planning, incorporating the decentralized administrative and technical systems, is, therefore, the basic task. An important consideration in the organizational structure is the number of levels or tiers of decision-making that should be built into the system. A "tall" hierarchy will be "horrendously hierarchical and pyramidal", will slow things down and render development tasks unnecessarily complicated (leading to "implementational paralysis"). Too flat a hierarchy would make functional allocations "concentrated and heavy" at both ends with too short a line of command and operationally not quite ideal, particularly if the country is large in size. Decentralization implies "de-layering" or "down-sizing" to the right geographical size, which will permit governmental, administrative and technical work to move speedily and efficiently, making its presence felt in every part of the country. The popular management "fix-it" formula, quoted in the organization theory is to get organizations "lean, mean and horizontal" i.e. "flatter management structures". In governmental organizations, the question is : How flat should it be? In the multilevel organization system, three types of organizations have to be carefully structured. These are :

(i) Administrative and technical organizations of the government;
(ii) Planning and coordination mechanisms; and
(iii) Participatory mechanisms.

Closely allied to the organizational set-up are the evolving of :

(a) a planning methodology and development procedures (including planning, programming, budgeting, monitoring and evaluation) which harmonize with the decentralized administrative and technical systems;
(b) a legal framework or procedures for the setting-up, directing and facilitating the working of the new systems as well as for directing, providing for coordination and facilitating the working of the related structures, sectoral and project planning, programming, budgeting and implementation; and
(e) laying down the procedures for the effective and complementary functioning of non-governmental organizations.

Administrative and Technical Organizations

The main criteria for the design of these organizations is the "reach" or "access" to the population. Some organizations like the Extension machinery should reach the beneficiary groups, both individually and collectively. In other organizations, the "reach" will depend on the nature of functions and the "load". To achieve a close network of institutional structures should be the goal. But this will be determined by financial considerations and the level of development of the country. In designing a sound organizational set-up, one must take into account and define the *relationship* between line institutions/departments, local administration and parastatal organizations in all their dimensions such as control, accountability, appointments, promotions and coordination.

Planning and Coordination Mechanisms

Since multilevel planning is an integrated operation, the establishment of a planning machinery with coordination mechanisms at all critical levels is crucial to its success.

The planning mechanisms will include a Planning Commission at the national level, a Regional Planning Commission at the regional level and "planning cells" at all critical local levels, including a "village planning forum" at the village level. At all these levels, the organizations should have a team of professionals capable to tackle the technical tasks of planning. This is a theoretical statement. Operationally speaking, in many developing countries, one finds such qualified teams only at one or two levels at the top. The lower levels do not have planning cells with adequate expertise. The major reason given is the paucity of qualified planners in the country and the absence of a systematic planning process, with defined planning functions at each level, which demands the presence of such personnel. When the lower levels do not have the qualified personnel for planning, the upper levels will have to assist them by deputing experts from their own organizations and training the local level personnel. Training is a very essential component in building up the capabilities at the lower level. In achieving the desired goal, the "interaction" among the different levels is very important and that is the essence of multilevel planning.

In order to ensure that an integrated plan is evolved, the setting up of the necessary "coordination mechanisms" is an essential step. This will take the form of inter-sectoral, inter-ministerial and inter-disciplinary committees to be established at all decision-making levels. Where democratic decentralization is in vogue, and elected local bodies are in existence, the elected leaders must find representation in the appropriate Planning Committees. The usual practice is to establish a number of Subject (sectoral) Committees or Task Forces for the formulation of projects and their horizontal coordination in which both elected leaders and officials will be represented. Plan progress review committees with a similar composition may also be established. The budget system developed at different spatial levels can also become a mechanism to support and enhance regional/local integration and interagency coordination of plans and operations for optimum results within a specific geographic area. If effectively harmonized with the decentralized administrative and political structures, the budgeting process will also serve as a mechanism to review, evaluate and monitor government programmes and project activities and performance and relate them with those embodied in the respective area plans. Thus the coordinating role of budgeting is quite important in a system governed by the principles of multilevel planning and development. The planning process, which defines the "actors" and their "activities" in a time-bound frame, determines the nature of the coordination mechanisms and where to place them in the total multilevel planning organizational framework.

Participatory Mechanisms

Decentralized development means not only deconcentration, delegation and devolution of powers within the government, but also the effective functioning of a number of participatory organizations to support, complement and supplement government activities and also to promote a measure of self-reliant development within the community. In a democratic decentralized framework, two types of participation may be distinguished : (1) Participation by the elected leaders; and (2) Participation by various interest groups, functional groups, self-management groups, user groups, etc., in the community. In their institutionalized forms, they constitute a number of what may be called "polycentric" institutions. In the design for a multilevel planning system, both these types of participatior must be institutionalized and structured appropriately at various levels. Thus the structure of a multilevel planning system is quite complex. The kind of organizations that come into play at various levels are indicated in Table 2.1.

Organizations must always interact with their environment. The relationships between organizations and entities in their environment are known as "linkages", which exist in several types. These include downward (i.e. Sector-Projects) linkage, horizontal (i.e. Sector-Sector) linkage and vertical (i.e. Sectoral-Hierarchy) linkage. Linkages facilitate "flow" of information and interaction. In this way, the stage is set for commencing the "operations" in a multi-level system.

TABLE 2.1 : Multilevel Planning System : Mechanisms

Area Level	Planning and decision-making mechanism	Coordination mechanisms	Participatory mechanisms	
			Democratic (Elected)	Community-based
National	Cabinet National Development Council, Planning Commission/ Economic Development Board, Planning cells in the Ministries	Ministry of Finance Inter-ministerial Committees Sectoral Policy Committees	Consultative Committee of Parliamentarians	Interest Groups and other people's organizations at the National level : e.g. Association of Farmers, Women, Backward Communities, Tribals, etc.
Regional	Region/State/Province Cabinet/Executive Council; Regional Development Council; Regional/State Planning Commission/Board; Sectoral Planning cells.	Regional Budgeting office Sectoral Planning Groups/ Committees/Task Forces Programme Coordination Division.	Consultative Committee of elected leaders	Interest groups/People's organizations at the Regional level (as above)
Local	Local (e.g. District) Development Council; Local Planning Office; Village Planning Forum, Village Council (Gram Sabha)	Joint Committee for Planning; Subject Matter Committees	Association of elected leaders in the joint and subject matter committees	Interest groups/ People's organizations at the local level; User groups/Joint Management Committees.

Actions Needed for Establishing a Multilevel Planning Process

From this discussion, it may be seen that multilevel planning is quite a demanding operation and its effective operationalization will depend on a number of parameters. We may sum up the various actions required as follows :

- — Determining the critical area levels in the country to which planning and decision-making functions in the particular sector of activity under consideration could be decentralized.
- — Defining the appropriate planning and decision-making functions against each area level (i.e. function-sharing among levels), so that there are no overlaps in planning among the various area levels.
- — Matching planning functions with adequate allocation of financial resources to the various area levels, so as to enable the performance of those functions in an effective manner.
- — Equipping the area levels with properly staffed planning machinery to perform the designated planning and decision-making functions.
- — Training the planning and development personnel in the tasks of multilevel planning and development.
- — Building up a suitable data base and information system at the critical area levels to support the planning and decision-making activities.
- — Establishing suitable organizational structures for coordination as part of the overall mechanisms for planning devised at the various area levels.
- — Establishing linkages—downward (i.e. sector/component projects linkage), horizontal (i.e. sector—sector linkage) and vertical (i.e. sectoral hierarchy linkage) linkages—for integrated development.
- — Establishing an effective two-way communications network through hierarchical, expert group, status group and friendship group consultations for rapid exchange of information.
- — Instituting regular flows of information, top-down (for policies/priorities, targets, guidelines, finances, reviews, evaluation, etc.) and bottom-up (for data on local needs and preferences, area priorities, area targets, feedback on the implementation of projects and local level perceptions relating to problems and constraints, etc.).

— Delegating various administrative powers and authority to the lower levels to enable as well as quicken the decision-making process at these levels.
— Organizing monitoring on a decentralized basis with evaluation being centralized at appropriate levels.
— Organizing participation at various levels through formal and informal methods so that the needs and aspirations of the people are duly taken note of in the planning process.

The scope of multilevel planning, as indicated in the above discussion, is a process that involves both "top-down" and "bottom-up" approaches. It involves the linking and integration of national planning with the planning at various levels or stages, such as national with sub-national planning and multi-sectoral planning with sectoral and sub-sectoral planning and programming. It always involves the integration of spatial planning, in particular central, with sub-national planning which may include more than one area level, e.g. regions, states, provinces, districts, sub-districts and villages. The plans and programmes at various area levels covering different sectors of activity are inter-linked and coordinated to achieve specific objectives at local, regional and national levels. Thus local level planning, area planning and regional planning are the integral and integrated parts of a multilevel planning process. Decentralization, interaction, linkages and flows are the mechanisms through which it is effected.

The weakest link—the Achilles heel—in the chain of multilevel planning is the local level. In most countries in the Asia and Pacific region, capabilities at the national level have been built up, which is able to transmit planning signals to the local level in terms of objectives, major thrusts, targets, financial allocations and so on. But at the local level, the ability to translate these signals into action has lagged. The major problem is a desperate shortage of planning skills at the local level. "The limited trained manpower has led to a concentration of expertise at the centre, inevitably weakening the capacity at the local level".[5] Talents, in the developing countries, always float to the top. Besides the insufficient number of trained personnel, the local level faces many other constraints, structural, processual and procedural. How to design a local level planning system which will fit existing structures, evolve micro-macro linkages, and transform the officials engaged in routine, implementational roles, decompose the planning process into actionable procedures and enlist the voluntary and willing participation of the local people into planning and developmental tasks is the crux of the matter. In the next chapter, we shall focus on some of these issues.

REFERENCES

1. Sundaram, K.V., 'Multilevel Planning : The Indian experience' in Lata Chatterjee and Peter Nijkamp, *Urban and Regional Policy Analysis in Developing Countries*, Gower Publishing Company, England, 1983.
2. Sundaram, K.V., *Ibid.*
3. Chakravarty, S., 'The Planning Process in India : An Appraisal and a Framework', Planning Commission, New Delhi (mimeographed).
4. Sundaram, K.V., 'Multilevel Planning : Concept, Principles, and some aspects of its application to sectoral planning' in Sundaram K.V. *et al*, (Eds), *Regional Planning and Development*, Heritage Publishers, New Delhi, 1989.
5. Uma Lele, *The Design of Rural Development—Lessons from Africa*, Johns Hopkins University Press, Baltimore and London, 1975, p. 143.

3

SECTORAL DECENTRALIZATION

Sectoral Decentralization involves transfer of substantial decision-making authority from the ministerial headquarters to its field offices. The ministry headquarters would then concentrate on policies on standards and programme evaluation, while the responsibility for operations would pass to field offices. Such reforms would speed up decisions and actions and provide for flexible and timely responses to local needs. They can also facilitate inter-agency and inter-programme coordination in the field.

In this chapter, we shall consider the various aspects of sectoral decentralization, which, in other words, is how "Administrative Decentralization or Deconcentration" is to be organized in each sector of activity. The important principles will be set out and these will be illustrated by considering two major sectors, viz. Agriculture and Forestry.

Administrative Decentralization in each sector is a major structural reform. It cannot be standardized, as decentralized procedures must be designed and implemented by each ministry, taking into account its distinctive requirements. Nevertheless, certain broad principles are common, and these will be stated here.

In the first stage, Administrative Decentralization in any sector of activity has to take place in stages. This is particularly so in the developing countries, because several resource constraints (both financial and personnel) may be present on the one hand, and on the other many preparations must go hand in hand to implement it effectively at the various sub-national levels. It will include the following major steps :

(1) Specific realignment of responsibilities between the headquarters and the field and the statement of detailed procedures for adjusting management responsibilities (i.e. Functional Decentralization for which there will be many bureaucratic obstacles).

(2) Shifts in government-wide financial and tendering rules and procedures, so that decisions and actions can take place expeditiously in the field. Flexibility and Accountability constitute the critical elements in this step.

(3) Reclassification of field positions that are to receive increased duties and responsibilities. This is important, since decentralization of powers is involved and it has to take note of the capabilities of staff at the different levels. The meritorious among the existing staff must be rewarded with promotions. Where necessary, more talented and experienced staff members will have to be deputed on assignment to serve for extended periods in field positions. Special incentives and rewards to field personnel are an essential component of change, as administrative decentralization must be planned as a smooth transition.

(4) Training and re-training of departmental staff both at headquarters and field in the procedures associated with decentralized operations. The field staff have to be trained especially in the methods of programme management that involve meaningful involvement and consultation with local organizations representing the people they are serving. This means cultivating attitudinal change, which is difficult to come about.

Thus administrative decentralization in any sector of activity is a complex process. Because of its complexity, it is best implemented in stages over specified periods of time, as responsibilities and capabilities of staff get built up and are realigned, and staff become accustomed to new procedures.

In view of the "Stages-approach" involved here, administrative decentralization must be seen as a continuum. Its character and content at any particular stage in the country will be determined by several considerations by the bureaucracy and the political leadership. It can be simply nominal, such as opening some regional offices and transferring some responsibilities and power or it can be quite an extensive reform, transferring responsibilities and power to offices located at each level, extending up to the grassroots, and aiming at active involvement and consultations with local organizations. In the latter strategy, the government officials must develop a partnership with people and change their tactics, i.e. to provide the services and responses required of them by the people. Each contributes in his own way to the total development effort, the government contributing funds, supplies, equipment, and technical expertise not available locally, while people contributing information, knowledge about indigenous management practices, perhaps some voluntary labour, funds and locally available materials. In practice, various degrees of flexibility are involved in adapting government services to local conditions and this will depend on the particular situation. In its extreme form, the government's role would be one of facilitating, strengthening and supplementing the combined efforts of all groups in society.

Thus enlightened sectoral decentralization would call for important changes in the way government agencies, especially their field staffs, would interact with the public. In working through village-level organizations, the government personnel will have to give up their traditional command methods of bureaucratic administration and adopt more participatory approaches, demanding great patience and new skills. At the higher level, the government agencies would have to backstop local authorities with technical support, staff training, standards setting and specialized assistance. In short, sectoral decentralization, in the ultimate, would be paving the way for an effective democratic decentralization and preparing their own machinery, including its personnel, for flexibility and responsiveness in administration. But reaching this stage may require a long time—perhaps a decade or more—during which the decentralized machinery is geared and capacitated to take on their challenging roles in participatory democratic decentralization.

In many countries, administrative decentralization has made only a modest progress. The line agencies have been very reluctant to modify their "top-down" approaches to accommodate local preferences. At best, the local authorities are permitted to decide the locations of projects, but not the projects themselves, nor on decisions pertaining to how the projects should be implemented, or whom they should benefit. In many African countries, the sectoral ministries deem decentralization and participation as the domain of responsibility of the Ministry of Local Government (which exists as an anaemic ministry, with no teeth or little or no resources at its command) and go about their own bureaucratic ways of doing things. In quite a few countries, civil servants resist sharing power with local political institutions, on various excuses, the common among them being the poor capacity of the local staff and their lack of accountability.

The adaptation of government programmes to local conditions and the active support of the local community, which should be ultimate goals of the government agencies seeking to decentralize their administration, would be possible only if the local institutions and people are permitted to participate actively in programme choice and programme design. This point cannot be reached until the line agencies become fully decentralized to accommodate local conditions and local needs, without resorting to the long and tedious approvals that must now be obtained from the higher authority at the centre.

Thus administrative decentralization in each sector of activity is a very necessary and essential step towards "Democratic Decentralization", which should be the ultimate goal of any society. In order to move steadily towards genuine sectoral decentralization, therefore, a number of specific measures must be taken. These are :

(1) Each of the line departments should develop and incorporate in its operating manuals specific procedures that delegate to their district staff the authority to make decisions on the spot without referring them for review and approval to department headquarters. Within certain financial ceilings, broad programme parameters and guidelines and government-wide procedures for tendering, accounting and personnel control, the decentralized levels should be allowed to operate after initial programme approvals. They should also have powers to make necessary local adjustments in projects during the process of implementation. The departmental procedural manual should carefully spell out the kind of delegations made and the kinds of information flows needed to keep district offices abreast of the departmental policies on the one hand, and on the other, to keep department headquarters informed of the problems as they arise in the field. More effective monitoring procedures and improved reporting methods should be spelt out.

(2) Field staff re-orientation will have to receive priority attention so that the staff at the decentralized levels are prepared technically and managerially to shoulder the additional responsibilities delegated to them.

(3) Staff readjustment and reclassification, which was explained earlier in this chapter, should receive careful attention.

(4) Decentralized planning procedures must be spelt out in all detail. These will be in the form of indicative guidelines (rather than fixed quantitative targets) and financial requirements that permit rigorous internal and outside audits. In turn, the Ministry of Finance will have to modify its procedures for the release

of funds to approved district-level programmes, in order to facilitate rather than obstruct the implementation of local-level programmes.

(5) Changes in planning methodologies at the regional and local levels : Sectoral decentralization would inevitably mean elaborating the regional planning and micro-level planning methodologies concerning the specific sector and educating and training the governmental functionaries at these levels on the various technical aspects involved in these methodologies. In this way, the planning methodologies and the planning process acquire more sophistication and refinement and the emergence of a planning cadre in each sector is facilitated.

(6) The front-line non-gazetted employees and the paraprofessionals who interface with the public demand particular attention, as they are ultimately the personnel who help shape the people's image of government. They have to be trained not only in technical subjects, but also in the methods of working in a responsive manner with members of the public and their local institutions. Similarly, the capabilities of the local authority staff have to be upgraded so that they are able to handle such important nuts-and-bolts activities as maintaining financial records, making cost estimation for local projects, contracting procedures for supplies and services, record-keeping and so on.

(7) Line Agencies, as well as the local authorities, must share activities with various non-governmental organizations, such as user groups and other organizations, without interfering with their independence and autonomy or seeking to subordinate or politicize them.

(8) Other tasks to be done in the context of sectoral decentralization would include : Establishing a sound monitoring system and building up a training infrastructure. While training may not be a sufficient instrument to change administrative behaviour, it is certainly essential. Trained staff endowed with better insights and skills can bring about changes at all levels of government and increase the efficiency and productivity of government personnel.

From our discussion above, it may be seen that sectoral decentralization is a highly demanding exercise. It implies (a) Structural change,

(b) Procedural changes and improvements, (c) Enhancement of skills, especially among the field staff for administering decentralized activities; and (d) A system of incentives and awards to encourage successful performance.

With the above enunciation of the general principles that are involved, we may proceed to discuss the methodologies involved in the decentralization of the Agriculture and Forestry sectors, as two illustrations.

I. DECENTRALIZATION IN THE AGRICULTURE SECTOR*

The Rationale

The agriculture activity, by its very nature, is a highly decentralized activity. An agricultural plan for any territory cannot be realistic unless it takes due account of the varying ecological requirements in the different areas of a country. Factors like temperature, rainfall, humidity, soil and water resources, drainage, topography and altitude influence the methods used to increase crop and livestock production. Some regions are potentially more productive than others; some with easy access to markets are able to make a headstart, while others, perhaps less accessible, lag behind. Regions with irrigation are able to take advantage of new High Yielding Varieties (HYV) of grain, for example, while those wholly dependent on rainfall may not be able to. Moreover, if regional disparities are to be reduced, the backward region must get some priority attention. Thus agricultural development requirements are area specific.

Elements of Decentralized Approach to Agricultural Development

In a complex sector like agriculture, the Central Government cannot try to do everything. There is a need to decentralize many functions to other entities and the Centre should concentrate on supporting them to perform well. For agricultural development to be effective, many different forms of decentralization may be used. These relate primarily to the methods used by the governments to stimulate and service science-based agri-

---

* This account is based on the author's paper "Decentralized Planning for Agricultural and Rural Development" in Velayudham, T.K. (ed.) : *Challenges Facing Agriculture and Rural Development*, Oxford & IBH Publishing Co. Pvt. Ltd., New Delhi, 1994.

culture—extension services, research, marketing functions, credit, land use, tenure and water rights, small irrigation systems and construction and maintenance of rural roads.

An effective operation of an agricultural extension system requires deconcentration of authority in the hands of field officials, who are close enough to the farmers to be able to make the necessary adaptations, as warranted by the local, natural and ecological conditions. Here the philosophy of decentralization implies that the programme plans will evolve from the bottom, with the extension officials taking note of the local practices and effectively linking them with improved methods and providing the feedback to the research system that will make it responsive to the local conditions.

Similarly, agricultural research stations have to be widely dispersed in the country to enable local trials and farm economics research to be carried out in geographically dissimilar zones. To ensure that more relevant research work is carried out, there is a clear need for planners, extension and research workers and farmers to be in close interaction with each other. This would be possible only when research activities are sufficiently decentralized and vertically integrated and coordinated with an institution, like an Agricultural Research Council, performing the apex functions and providing the necessary technical assistance and guidance to the field stations.

For marketing functions, the needed form of decentralization is to make a multiplicity of smaller business the primary carrier of services, giving farmers control in agri-business activities. A similar movement to the private sector is appropriate for agricultural services, such as curative veterinary care. (Leonard, 1986).[1]

Agricultural credit operations need a decentralized approach. The experiments with small farmer development and poverty alleviation programmes in the Third World countries have demonstrated the need for group lending in which members of a group serve as guarantors on each other's loans. This network of local groups would then be linked to the banking system for its larger savings and credit needs.

Land use, tenure and water rights are the areas for which devolution of authority to local governments is most needed. The appropriate place for such jurisdiction is with small local areas at sub-district levels that traditionally control land use. In the case of many Third World countries, the authority of these traditional entities has been considerably eroded and would have to be re-built by the governments.

The construction and maintenance of small irrigation systems, as well as some common property resource management, are essentially decentralized local affairs, in which group-centred approaches have a considerable development potential. Homogeneous groups of an easily manageable size are more functional and their small scale does not create difficult problems of system maintenance.

Further, in agricultural development, farm-to-market roads are crucial to promote an effective farming system, where a farmer can make a one-day multi-purpose trip to a market centre. In many parts of Asia and Africa, such farm-to-market roads have promoted commercialization of agriculture, raised productive capacity and increased social mobility. In a decentralized agricultural development system, the priority selection of such roads, their construction and maintenance will rest with the local communities/local bodies. This will, by and large, ensure that development is informed by local relevance.

Organizing Decentralized Agricultural Sector Planning : Major Considerations

The above discussion shows that several elements of agricultural development need a decentralized approach. If these various elements are to be handled and coordinated effectively at the different decentralized levels of administration, a viable organizational structure is needed.

> "However, this institution building needs careful watching to avoid unnecessary conflicts of interest and the worst excesses of bureaucracy. Its success is likely to depend on timing—not too hasty or too slow—but taking advantage of gradually increasing numbers of better-trained administrators, nearly always in scarce supply", Mollett, 1984.[2]

The organizational structure for agricultural development will be unique for each country, depending on its existing patterns of governmental authority, the way the civil servants operate, as well as the personal and social characteristics of the people it is to serve. It will also greatly depend on the planning system designed for the country, with its unique institutional and coordination mechanisms for planning, the national planning process operating for the preparation of the perspective, medium-term and annual plans and the annual budget cycle. The planning system is intended to provide an orderly process for anticipating trends and problems, defining objectives and informing public and private decisions in the production, distribution and consumption of food and other agricultural products. In an ideal planning system, the plans that are prepared at different spatial levels—national, regional, district, sub-district, village—will dovetail into each other and get integrated into the overall national planning process and the annual budget cycle. If the planning routines are properly established, the management efforts at the different levels of agricultural planning will tend to get concentrated on strategic goal formulations and problem-solving activities appropriate to those levels.

Basically, agriculture sector planning enables the Ministry of Agriculture at the Centre and other public agencies related to agricultural development to allocate resources, direct activities and deliver services in support of private activities in a coordinated, effective and efficient manner. The broader goals of such an effort could be meeting the basic needs, assisting the economic recovery and growth of the country (by contributing to exports and the earning of foreign exchange) and ensuring environmental quality and social justice. Systematic multilevel planning for agricultural development is imperative for the Third World countries because :

- The agriculture sector meets a basic human need, food as well as animal feed, fibre and other goods needed in industry and trade;
- Agricultural supplies are typically unevenly distributed across the country;
- Prices of agricultural commodities are unstable due to geographic and seasonal variations as well as inelastic consumer demand for food staples;
- As a production sector, agriculture is inherently decentralized and fragmented, being numerically dominated by households as primary producers, and producing a wide variety of commodities with their peculiar natural, technical, social and market requirements; and
- In most Third World countries, 60 to 70 per cent, or even more of the population, depend on agriculture for their living and a predominant proportion of the agriculturists are small farmers, not fully drawn into the market system.

In the above context, a systematic multi-level planning for agricultural development is a tool for rational state direction and co-ordination of the efforts of the various groups and institutions engaged in agriculture, so that it would produce enough food and other supplies at costs and prices that are tolerably reasonable for both producers and consumers.

Demarcation of Agricultural Sector Functions

Introducing a multi-level system of planning for the agriculture sector would mean decentralizing its organization, as well as the planning and development processes, and maximizing the participation of private sector groups. In this context, planning for specifically demarcated functions becomes a serious exercise undertaken at each level with the people's participation. At the same time, an interactive process has to be instituted between different levels. A major task is the demarcation of functions at the different spatial levels. An illustrative list of functions in the agriculture sector planning that could be appropriately transferred to the various spatial levels in the administrative hierarchy (centre, region and district) is provided in Table 3.1.

Planning, Coordination and Participatory Mechanisms

Designing a multi-level organizational structure for agricultural planning and development incorporating suitable planning, co-ordination and participatory mechanisms is a task to be attempted in the context of the prevailing administrative structure in each country. Any new institutional structures that are devised for this purpose must build upon the elements of the existing organizational structure in the country. Some essential features in this regard are as follows. At the national level, an Agricultural Coordination mechanism (Agricultural Coordinating Council or Agriculture Policy Committee) could be set up, consisting of the political heads of all ministries, departments and agencies concerned with agricultural development, to lay down the basic policies, approve development plans and seek to coordinate all activities in the sector. This could be supplemented by a smaller Executive Committee at the official level to carry out the mandate of the policy level committee for specific purposes. Similarly, a participatory mechanism at the national level will also be necessary. It could be in the nature of an Ad Hoc Consultative Committee, composed of representatives of farmers' organizations, national farmers' union, agricultural cooperative societies, etc. At the regional and local levels, similar institutions for planning, coordination and public participation would be necessary. The organizations that are created

TABLE 3.1 : Suggested Demarcation of Functions at Different Area Levels

Centre	Region	District
— Setting agriculture sectoral goals/ objectives/strategies/priorities/targets — Allocation of financial resources to different programmes/projects — Budget and release of funds to para-statals, regions and districts — Agricultural export target and trade policies — Agricultural price and income policy — Interacting with other sectors for bringing about the necessary forward and backward linkages among projects — Drawing up the draft National Agricultural Plan for being integrated into the National Development Plan — Arranging for various inputs as well as production incentives — Food distribution planning — Organizing research — Administering extension services — Administering para-statal organizations in agriculture — Providing guidelines for agriculture sector planning to the regions and districts	— Coordination of district-level activities-overseeing and supervision of implementation — Technical assistance to district-levels — Allocation and release of development funds to the district levels — Technical supervision of agricultural research stations and activities — Backstopping district agriculture activities — Information communication to extension agencies — Monitoring and review of agricultural programmes/projects — Collation of agriculture statistics	— Setting local level objectives in the context of national and regional objectives of agricultural development — Estimation of local production targets for agriculture and allied activities to aid decision-making by the Centre/ Region — Agriculture extension — Agriculture credit — Agriculture implements and inputs — Agriculture marketing, animal husbandry services — Horticulture development — Identification of agricultural projects — Interfacing with people's organizations, and groups at the various sub-district levels and preparing a statement of priority local needs — Identification of credit needs — Collection of statistics: survey, data-feeding to the higher levels.

(*Contd.*)

TABLE 3.1 (*Contd.*)

Centre	Region	District
— Evaluation of programmes/projects; review of audit reports		
— Interfacing with the participatory mechanism at the national level		
— Preparation of annual development programme		
— Approval and sanctions of development schemes/projects		
— Personnel management—appointment, transfer, posting, promotion and other establishment matters		
— Liaison with international organizations		
— Training of trainers, foreign training		
— Agriculture statistics		

must respond flexibly to attitudes and changes in the regional and local situations. Countries have used a variety of organizations to achieve these ends. The technical side of the Ministry of Agriculture itself should be divided according to its functions into different departments. Here, the function should determine the form. Mollett has suggested five groups :

(i) Policy, planning and coordination;
(ii) Research and implementation;
(iii) Education and extension work;
(iv) Direct services and assistance to producers; and
(v) Enforcement of regulations (Mollett, 1984).[3]

After deciding the transferred subjects, administrative and substantive authority should be delegated to the regional and local offices falling within the jurisdiction of the Ministry. These will broadly constitute the administrative decentralization (or deconcentration) measures, which have to fall in place in the first instance, if decentralization, in the true sense of the term, is to follow. Administrative decentralization is, in a sense, creating and strengthening significantly the physical, technical, institutional and human infrastructures at each level of the administrative hierarchy to enable decentralized responsibilities to be effectively and efficiently shouldered.

Decentralized Agricultural Planning Methodology

Coming to the substantive aspects of planning, the present system in most Third World countries is merely a routine annual budget exercise rather than a planning exercise, confined to distributing annual budget ceilings indicated by the Ministry of Finance among different programmes and projects in the districts. At the national level, it is based on setting goals and targets. The major concern is on inputs and a certain order of physical achievements. Under the existing system of planning, the national targets are fixed in the first instance and then disaggregated to the lowest administrative level, which is the district in most countries. The translation of basic needs objectives into the spatial context of the districts, along with its concomitant planning and implementation strategies, programmes and projects, has not been done in most countries. For arriving at the national targets, the data available with the agricultural ministries in Asian and African countries are usually meagre. However, in the light of the available information on resources, natural and human, and about regional development potentials, certain targets are fixed. While doing so, it is stated that some consultations are made with the concerned authorities at the sub-national levels. Such consultations may be formal or informal; they may be a one-time consultation or repetitive in nature; whatever it may be, the Centre is supposed to derive its ideas for target setting from its own studies as well as consultations from below and then firm up these targets, which are then embodied into the plan. These targets are later disaggregated into detailed specific targets for the lowest administrative units (districts) and then passed on to them. It is apparent that this planning procedure runs counter to the concept of multi-level planning. In the latter context, the district's resources and potentials are to be assessed first. Then, based on the understanding of the area, a detailed analysis of the programme options is visualized and conclusions drawn as to how the area can be made to yield its best. Based on such a diagnosis, commodity and other targets are determined and suitable development schemes drawn up to achieve these targets.

Thus, in this procedure, the logical sequence of an analysis is :

> What is the area's potential? What is it that it produces? What are the development options? How can the area be made to produce the maximum output within the available resources?

It is quite clear that if the target and plan formulation exercise follows this procedure meticulously, the agriculture development plan that is drawn up would be more realistic. It is to be noted that such an exercise is a two-way process. In this, central authorities will provide information on the national objectives and the desired level of production for the country as a whole. This will be based on certain macro-economic considerations as well as national priorities, while the lower level authorities will make their assessments as to the feasible targets in the light of the existing potentials and capabilities of their areas. In an ideal multi-level planning system, there will be vigorous interaction among the different area levels as well as "to and fro" flows of information, till the realistic targets are set.

Decentralized agricultural development planning will consist of various steps at the sub-national levels. Broadly, these are :

(i) Review of national objectives;
(ii) Formulation of sub-national level objectives;
(iii) Overview of physical and social features;

(iv) Analysis of agricultural situation;
(v) Evaluation of on-going programmes;
(vi) Analysis of food supply and demand situation;
(vii) Production feasibility : Analysis of constraints and potentials;
(viii) Formulation of strategies and policies;
(ix) Target setting; and
(x) Formulation of programmes and projects.

Key Dimensions of a Decentralized Agricultural Planning System

A decentralized agricultural planning system must concern itself with the following four key dimensions of agricultural development :

— Organizational structure for planning and development administration;
— Planning process organized as a two-way interactive process;
— Organization of agri-support delivery systems; and
— Reach of benefits to the bypassed groups in society, especially small farmers and women farmers.

We have already discussed the first two dimensions of agricultural development. We may now briefly consider the other two dimensions.

Decentralized Approach for Organizing Agri-support Delivery Systems

In order to support the various programmes of agricultural production and meet the demands of farmers, it is necessary to organize efficient agri-support delivery systems in the rural areas, taking into account the uneven distribution of such services and facilities and the problem of optimizing the provision of such services. Apart from the extension service, which was referred to earlier, other major services involved in the provision of agri-support delivery systems are :

(i) Provision of agricultural inputs—seeds, fertilizers, pesticides;
(ii) Provision of credit;
(iii) Provision of storage and warehousing; and
(iv) Provision of marketing.

A number of organizations including public sector agencies, co-operatives and farmers' organizations functioning at the district level provide a variety of the above services, commonly referred to as the "delivery system". There is considerable empirical evidence to suggest that the effectiveness of the government delivery system would be considerably enhanced if a "receiving mechanism" of farmers' groups/ organizations to receive services on behalf of individual farmers is worked out. To the extent that governments avoid the practice of contacting the beneficiaries of a given programme on an individual basis, and consider organized groups as the ultimate points of delivery, problems of coordination at the field level could be minimized. The organization of a coordinated delivery system, appropriately linked to receiving mechanisms, is an important aspect of decentralized agricultural development, as it would promote distributional equity in the rural areas. In fact, one of the criteria for assessing the success of decentralized agricultural development is to examine how the receiving mechanisms are organized and linked to government agencies.

Reaching the Bypassed Groups—A Decentralization Goal

The conventional hierarchical set-up of government, with the Ministry of Agriculture at the top going down to the field level, tends to bypass certain vulnerable groups in society. In the context of the Third World countries, these are the small farmers and women farmers, who constitute a sizable component of the farming community. In a decentralized approach to agricultural development, tackling such problems of inequity must receive the foremost consideration. Such bypassed farmers should be organized into groups. While doing so, it is necessary to take an "empowering" view of participation, rather than the formal "mobilizing" view. When such farmers as a group are empowered, they as an organised group, will be able to see that they derive their due share of benefits from general programmes of development and that these are not cornered by the elite groups. They will also be able to see that the schemes meant for them are vigorously and efficiently implemented, and that the benefits actually accrue to them and not to the non-intended. Their effective association in multilevel planning structures will also help in properly identifying beneficiaries and eliminating official malpractices (Randhawa and Sundaram, 1990).[4]

There are several other problems which decentralized develop ment should address, such as training to build capacity and impart motivational and attitudinal changes for improved decentralized performance. Since decentralization raises expectations of rapid change, a whole host of measures at the planning and implementation levels need to be looked into.

II. MULTILEVEL PLANNING FOR FORESTRY DEVELOPMENT*

Historical trends in the forestry sector planning reveals a context of shifting objectives, which underline the current setting and imperatives for decentralized planning. Traditionally, the forest policy in the developing countries had been guided by two major considerations, conservation and colonial interests. In keeping with these interests, forestry planning and administrative structures to support it had been set-up on a centralized and command basis. Even after independence, this set-up has continued in several countries and the regional and local needs of forests as well as the interrelationships of forest development with the developments in other sectors of the economy were not paid adequate attention. The seventies, which marked the shift in thought from growth to development, also ushered in some new ideas in this sector, such as eco-development and rural development in forestry. The oil crisis starting in the 1970's also lent a sense of urgency to the recognition of the essential linkages between forest development and rural development and forest degradation and rural poverty. With all these changes in ideas, new goals have been added and the prevailing systems of planning and administration in the forestry sector have become obsolete.

The new dimensions in planning are represented by the need to integrate forestry with land use planning to accord importance to environmental, employment and social forestry considerations and generally to dovetail forest planning at all levels with planning for the other sectors of the economy such as agriculture, industry and infrastructure. Forestry planning can no longer afford to remain "aloof" and be done in "ivory towers". The forester is suffering from excessive isolation. This state of affairs needs to be improved by bringing about an interactive type of planning in which he will be enabled to work with other disciplines. In keeping with the changing trends observable in the countries of the Asia and Pacific region, an increasingly decentralized approach to planning and decision-making is called for. This underlines the need for looking at forestry planning in a multilevel planning framework and in a multi-disciplinary perspective.

---

* This account is based on the author's paper "Multilevel Planning : Concept, Principles and some aspects of its application to Sectoral Planning" in Sundaram, K.V. *et al.*, (Eds.). *Regional Planning and Development*, Vol. I. Heritage Publishers, New Delhi, 1989.

The author has made a detailed study of the territorial structure of forest administration and the modalities and practices for formulating and finalizing forestry development plans in a number of countries in the South and South-East Asian realm.[5] These studies point to a number of deficiencies in the planning process in the forestry sector.

Looking at the structures developed in the various countries for forest administration, one feature that stands out is their non-conformity with the existing politico-administrative divisions in the country. This non-congruence of the territorial administration has surfaced as a problem, particularly because a big push is now being given to decentralization of the planning process to the sub-national levels in all these countries. Sectoral planning activities are, therefore, required to respond to such changes. The forest development planning has also to conform to these trends. But there is constraint here for many countries, viz. lack of adequately trained manpower, as territorial adjustments will mean greater deployment of manpower.

Country studies reveal that, in some countries, forest planning follows a project-by-project approach. This is a fragmented approach without providing for adequate linkages in the other sectors of activity. In quite a number of countries, a good framework for decentralized planning exists; but decentralized planning has not been operationalized effectively. Some countries have provided only for a modest delegation of authority and the tendency for centralization of authority persists. In some others, the lack of trained manpower seems to be holding back the implementation of the decentralization scheme. The lack of a sound information system is a major lacuna identified by all the countries. Another characteristic feature of the planning process seems to be the existence of a weak monitoring and evaluation system. In some countries, organizational structures also need suitable revamping. In the Philippines, for instance, it has been observed that development efforts are dissipated through a multiplicity of agencies, pursuing their respective and varied roles which may not be consistent with the national forestry development objectives. In this context, how to achieve the integration of the different territorial organizations has become one of the major issues. In Indonesia, central control versus provincial autonomy has thrown up several issues and problems in planning. The centre has no line authority on the set-up in the provinces, while the provincial levels have no powers to adjust the plan or budget, with the result that delays and monetary losses have become common. The system for planning and control of programmes and budget also operates in a fragmented fashion. All these facts amply illustrate that the present administrative structure for planning in these countries, as well as the planning procedures and processes that have been devised, are not adequate to fully accomplish the planning objectives that have been envisaged for the development of the forestry sector. It is in this context that a justification for a properly ordered multilevel planning structure becomes particularly relevant. In the sequel, we may attempt to provide a certain guidance to thought, indicating the main elements of practice, which underpin a multi-level planning approach in the forestry sector.

(i) **Sectoral Multilevel Planning : Objectives, Limitations and Scope**

Planning for any sector of activity at different levels implies taking of decisions appropriate to each level for future action with a view to achieving pre-determined objectives through the optimum use of scarce resources. This definition has three important components, viz: determination of objectives, limitations in the use of resources and scope of decision-making.

(a) *Determination of Objectives*

The policy-making process applies policy instruments to the target world (the forestry sector, as delimited here) in order to achieve the major national policy goals. The latter in our context are : growth, equity and stability or sustainability.

As against these broad national policy goals, the goal for forestry planning has been stated as follows : "Forestry aims at satisfying the present and future demand for major and minor forest products and for protective and recreational functions, taking into account competing claims for other sectors (mainly agriculture) and the urgent need for creating employment opportunities, particularly in the rural areas" (Nilsson). We may add to this definition explicitly the objectives of social forestry also which are to promote activities that will be primarily planned and implemented by individual farmers or communities to yield products and services for their primary use and benefits as well as for environmental benefits.

The above statement brings out the broad sector-specific goals. In a multilevel planning context, these sector-specific policy goals have to be translated into more concrete objectives, which are area specific and non-overlapping or non-conflicting. This is a very important consideration in order to ensure that planning at the different levels ultimately converges to the same basic national goals. Such objectives would obviously be "country-specific," as these are determined with reference to overall economic policies including foreign trade and balance of payment considerations and the criticality as well as comparative advantage position in forest resources obtaining in each country. While these cannot be generalized for the various area levels, we may broadly note that the accent at the national level will be on securing aggregate production and laying down a firm infrastructural base, including building up of database, personnel capability, studies and research. At the regional level, the emphasis will be on linking and coordinating functions; at the local level, it will be one of securing participatory planning and augmenting the income and employment opportunities of the local population. It should also be noted that as one moves from the national to the local levels, planning changes from the strategic through tactical to operational aspects. The scheme for policy formulation and objectives specification in the forestry sector is shown in Fig. 3.1.

(b) *Limitations in the Use of Scarce Resources*

This is our second component. The resources implied here are : time, talent and financial and material resources.

Time: The objectives enumerated above cannot all be achieved at the same time. While certain things have to be necessarily achieved in a short time, some could be achieved only over a long term and others can be phased out for achievement over a period of years ranging between short and medium terms. Therefore, plan preparation must be broken into its time segments as long-term, medium-term and short-term.

Forest planning has to be done in three contexts, viz. a problem-solving context, a potential realizing context and a regulative context. Here, we are considering the management of a resource, which has a long gestation period. A century or half is sometimes considered necessary for futuristic scenario-building over a long-term. It is understood that Sweden has a 100-year long-term plan. Usually, the argument against adopting such a long period is that there are many uncertainties about economic trends; the assumptions will be on shaky foundations; the picture obtained will be at best dim and hazy, and may not be quite conducive for exercising forethought for causative action. So unless a country has really a strong and stable economic base, it is not advisable

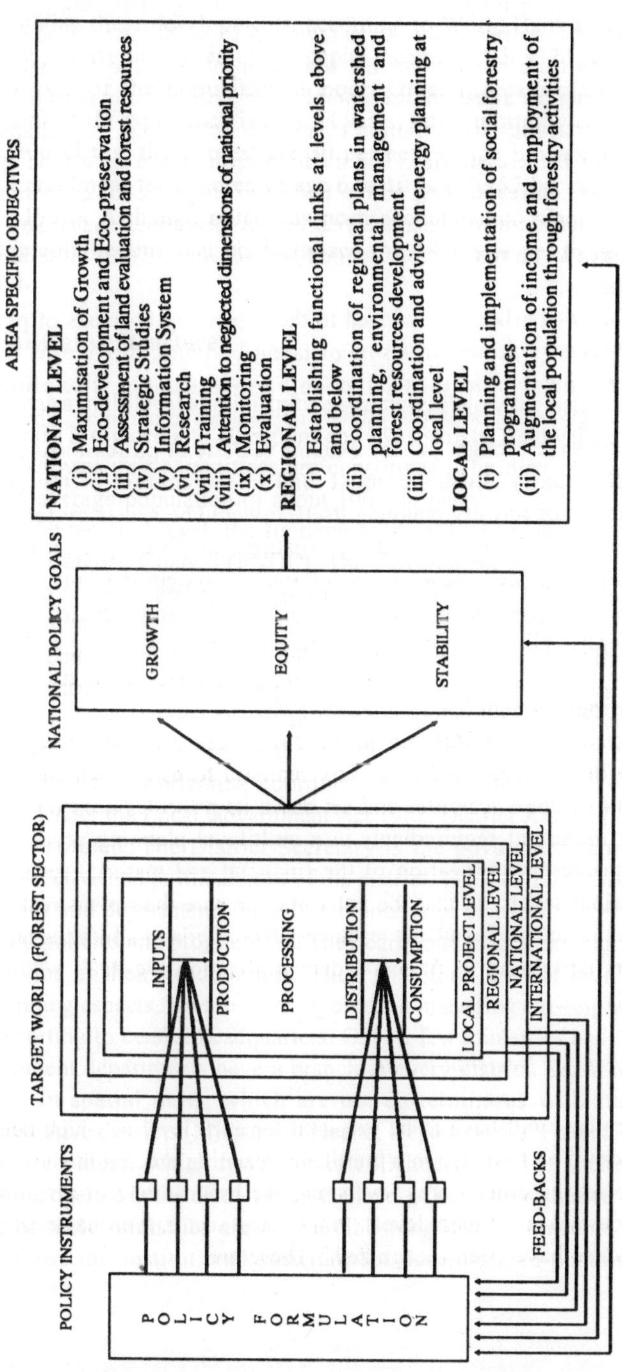

FIG. 3.1 : Scheme for Policy Formulation and Objectives Specification in the Forestry Sector.

to have such a long-term horizon for planning. It is found that in a number of countries in the Asian region, a 15 or 20-year period is adopted, as the time horizon for the long-term plan in the forestry sector. Considering the situation of economic stringencies, exogenous influences and uncertainties in economic trends, this time span is perhaps most suited for these countries. The medium term would be a time span of five years, corresponding to the period of the national economic plan and the short term will be a one-year period. Objectives and targets, therefore, have to be realistically framed and adjusted within these temporal boundaries.

Talent.: Earlier, we referred to the expanding horizons of planning in the forestry sector. In terms of talent-building, this means that the foresters must train themselves in various frontier disciplines and increasingly adopt cross-disciplinary approaches in planning. The country accounts have brought out the extreme scarcity of professional foresters in each country. In this context, and in the context of the growing complexity of forestry planning itself, it would be necessary for forestry to open its doors in its planning organizations to people of other professions—engineers, economists, information system specialists, environmentalists, agronomists, photogrammetrists, hydrologists, etc.—so that an interdisciplinary approach can be followed in planning and managing the forest resources and for solving problems, which are becoming increasingly complex.

Financial and Material Resources: These are undoubtedly scarce in the developing countries. Any realistic forestry plan should take account of these scarcities and set down its priorities accordingly. One of the important requirements in a multilevel planning process is the appropriate disaggregation of the financial and material resources to the various levels, so that the latter may prepare their plans realistically within the limits of available resources. The criteria of allocation and other matters pertaining to financial decentralization are dealt with subsequently.

(c) *Scope of Decision-making*

Forest plans will have to be prepared for each level at which decisions are taken. The first step in a multilevel planning process is, therefore, to decide on the crucial area levels and the broad scope of planning and decision-making at these levels. In the forest sector, four major categories of landuse have been recognized.[6] These are :

— commercial forestry
— community forestry
— environmental forestry
— recreational forestry

Commercial or production forestry is directed at supplying both domestic and national export markets. Its purpose is to meet the requirements of timber and pulpwood. The area levels which will be most concerned with its planning aspects will be the national as well as regional levels. Community or social forestry is that directed primarily at the needs of the local community. As such, the local level will be the most suited for its detailed planning. Environmental or conservation forestry covers cases, where the primary object is either to conserve the natural ecosystem or to restore degraded land. The major thrust areas may include watershed management, soil conservation, soil reclamation, conservation of plant genetic resources and wildlife conservation, usually with multiple objectives. Spatially, these would normally extend over large areas and may be deemed regional in scope. For planning purposes, they could be dealt with at the national and/or regional levels. Recreational forestry will usually enshrine environmental objectives and will encompass all the three levels—local, regional and national. Thus the different components of forest development may be deemed to have varying spatial dimensions as under :

TABLE 3.2 : Spatial Dimentions of Forestry.

Components of Forest Development	Spatial dimensions with which it is concerned			
	International	National	Regional	Local
Commercial forestry	X	X	X	
Community forestry				X
Environmental forestry		X	X	X
Recreational forestry		X	X	X

While the Table 3.2 does reflect the broad spatial scope of the different kinds of forest development activities, it should be understood that it is not to be regarded as a watertight arrangement in a functional sense. The planning tasks or functions are not to be deemed as "cut off" or "closed within" those area levels. For instance, while planning for community forestry will be essentially done at the local level, certain planning tasks will still have to be done at the higher area level, e.g.

allocations, targets, provision of guidelines, etc. What is intended to be conveyed here is that forest development planning as a multi-level planning activity can be delineated at three crucial area levels, viz. national, regional and local, with each unit area level having one or more major responsibilities. The terms, "regional" and "local", will have to be defined according to particular country contexts. A distinction must necessarily be drawn between the federal and unitary structures of government. The former has usually "tall" structures with the "regional" level corresponding to "states" or "provinces", and having a relatively greater autonomy in matters relating to planning and decision-making. Unitary governments, on the other hand, will have relatively flatter structures and will be less complex to deal with.

Broadly, the aspects that call for *centralized* decision-making are : long, medium and short-term goal-setting; the specification of objectives and strategy for different temporal plans; assigning appropriate priorities and weights; setting targets; resources allocations; initiating surveys for land evaluation and forest resources; initiating strategic studies; building up an information system; organizing research and training programmes; sponsoring special programmes for ensuring attention to some neglected dimensions of forestry; monitoring and evaluation of projects and programmes and issuing guidelines including prescription of a time schedule for planning operations to the sub-national levels.

The regional level is, where the top-down and bottom-up planning meet, and the local needs envisaged for the development of the forestry sector are harmonized with national objectives and priorities. Thus, it has a crucial integrating role. A major task at this level is the coordination of functional planning activities operating at the sub-national levels, such as water-shed plans, plans for the rehabilitation of critical environmental areas and industrial forest resource development plans. It will also monitor such programmes and transmit the same to the national level. On the study front, the regional level will be a crucial level, as it will continually have to engage in identifying regional problems and opportunities, delineating development zones and ecological systems and subsystems and generating project ideas. Another important function of the regional level is to do the programming for the social forestry and energy plantation activities at the local level. This would involve both coordination and tendering technical advice.

With the changing orientations that have come about in the forestry sector planning in recent times, participatory aspects of planning have been accorded great importance. Therefore, local-level planning in the forestry sector has assumed great significance. Decentralized planning at this level[7] has become extremely relevant because planning at this level will ensure (a) responsiveness to local conditions, (b) utilization of local resources, (c) direct involvement of local people, and (d) effective integration with other sectoral activities. A variety of planning functions are involved at this level. These include undertaking of detailed resource inventory and forest evaluation, collection of local forestry statistics (as information is best collected and with least cost from the point close to its generation), planning for social forestry (which will include farm forestry, extension forestry and reforestation in degraded forests), forest-based tribal development, forest development with environmental impact specific to local-level planning, recreation forestry, planning for micro-watershed projects within the local area, preparation of forest management plans at the local level incorporating the local needs, preparation of production oriented forestry plans, establishing public participation, involving local institutions and NGO's and monitoring of all forestry projects undertaken at the local level.

One peculiar feature about forestry development is that all planning activities associated with it cannot be performed within a single spatial frame as the basis. Thus while elements such as social forestry including farm forestry, extension forestry, reforestation in degraded areas, recreation forestry, etc., as well as forest management according to work plans (known as departmental forestry) can be ordered on an administrative-territorial basis, subjects such as planning for wildlife conservation, nature conservation, industrial wood plantations, regional recreation and watershed planning have to be carried on within the framework of a "natural unit area" (ecological unit). Thus there are two components in forestry planning, one that can be fitted into the administrative framework of the country (i.e. State, Province, District, etc.) and the other which would call for planning on the basis of natural units that cut across administrative boundaries. The former may be termed "territorial" planning and the latter as "functional" planning. Most governments have entrusted various kinds of functional planning and development activities to separate agencies/corporations/para-statal bodies, which are relatively autonomous. This has been necessary to obtain flexible and responsive management structures to deal with varied types of situations and problems.[8] Also, these organizations have their own specific interests, e.g. meeting the demands of timber, water, recreation, etc. In order both to support the policy objectives and to obtain the long-term resources needed for their activities, it is necessary that these organizations should be linked with the centre. Whatever way the functional planning may be structured, it cannot be conceived of as an entirely exclusive or free-wheeling activity, unrelated to or isolated from decentralized territorial planning. For many crucial linkages that are mutually supportive and economically cost-effective, the two are interdependent. Indeed, for the maximization of outputs in the planning process, both territorial and functional planning must interface with each other, so that the necessary linkages can be provided in the right sequence. For instance, in the case of functional planning for identified special natural unit areas referred to above, several inter-related infrastructural and services planning dimensions (e.g. nursery raising, construction of roads, training of personnel, etc.) would need to be dovetailed and integrated into the formal planning process operating through the administrative territorial system. This task of interfacing and integration has to be achieved through special coordinative mechanisms designed for the purpose at different territorial levels. In the consideration of a multilevel planning framework for the forestry sector, this aspect of horizontal area coordination must receive paramount consideration. The subject of increasing the structural efficiency of the planning process is a sufficiently complex one. For instance, a District Forestry Plan must also take note of the plans for the micro watersheds located within the district territory and must provide for the various linkages required under the plans.

There are three ways of bringing about this integration between territorial planning and functional planning. One is to adopt a "partnership approach" in planning, according to which the functional planning authority may prepare only the strategic plan and parcel out the tactical and operational aspects of planning to the planning authorities at the respective territorial levels. This may be possible in areas like watershed planning, wherein the macro-watershed plan may be prepared by the functional planning authority and the "meso" and "micro" watershed plans can be entrusted to the respective territorial planning authorities.

In the second alternative, the territorial and functional planning in all their dimensions, i.e. strategic, tactical and operational, may be done independently by the respective authorities or agencies. Later, these plans may be sought to be matched or integrated by effecting suitable adjustments. This is, however, a much less satisfactory method. An important principle in multilevel planning is that integration should take place when the plans themselves are in the making and not after they have been made.

The third alternative is to set up a permanent inter-agency coordination mechanism in the planning set-up existing at each level, which meets several times during the plan preparation stage, exchanges plan information and the linkage issues that are involved and effects the necessary coordination. In this approach, it is necessary to deliberately contrive appropriate coordinative mechanisms which will seek to bring about frequent interfacing and better communications and flows of information between and among the different planning authorities at various levels.

Taking into account the varying structural authorities prevailing in different levels, in the developing countries and the emerging needs in a multilevel planning context, an organizational pattern for multi-level planning in the forestry sector is diagrammatically indicated in Fig. 3.2.

The Planning Process : Dynamics

What distinguishes a multilevel planning system from other types of planning activity is its planning process. The planning process here is essentially of a dynamic, inter-acting and integrating character, in which a relay-rerelay process of information operating both upwards and downwards provides the circulatory life-blood and facilitates constant revision and adjustment of plans to accord with the national goals. The basic idea here is that each area level in the multilevel planning framework would prepare its own plans for subjects falling within its geographic scope. Such plans will be internally consistent, but open-ended, meaning that there will be elements or "strands," which need to be linked with the plans of the other area levels. These strands will have to be picked up by the *planning unit* located at each level and knit with those at the other area levels. The planning unit at each area level, therefore, plays a key role, not merely in organizing the planning function within its jurisdiction, but also in interacting with the other area levels and integrating its plans into the plans at the other levels. This is done through a process of interactions and a staged and sequential procedure involving successive approximations. This, in brief, is what the dynamics of the multilevel planning process implies. We may now proceed to discuss the various sequences of this process, so far as the forestry sector is concerned.

The major planning phases and steps involved in the multilevel planning process in the forestry sector are indicated in Table 3.3. The specific responsibilities of each area level have also been indicated in this context.

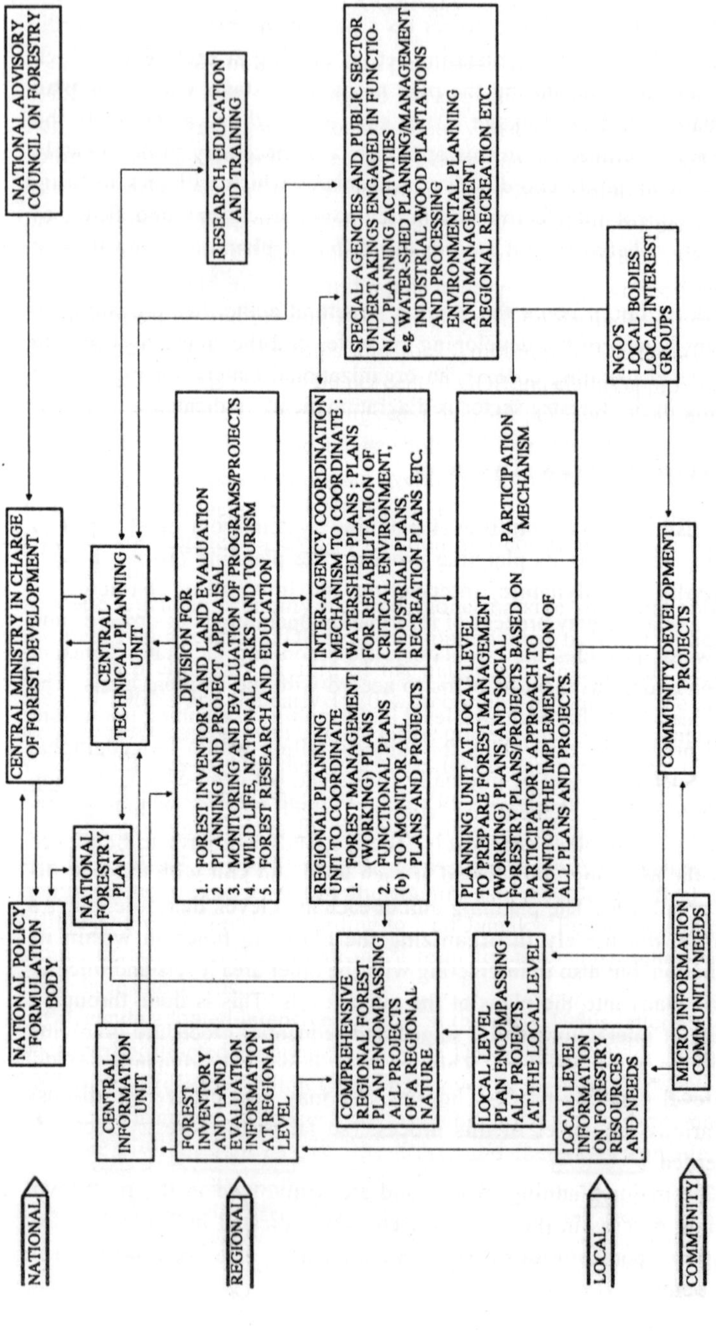

FIG. 3.2 : An Organizational Pattern for Multilevel Planning in the Forestry Sector.

TABLE 3.3 : Phases and Steps in the Planning Process.

Phases	Planning Steps	Responsibility
Strategic Planning	Setting national goals	National Planning Board or Commission
	Making inter-sectoral allocations	—do—
	Setting goals for the forestry sector	Ministry for Forest Development in consultation with the National Advisory Council and the National Planning Board/ Commission
	Laying down the Policy framework for the forestry sector	—do—
	Determining development strategy	—do—
	Determining priorities and targets	—do—
	Deciding on allocations to subsectors and territorywise	Central Planning unit of the Ministry for Forest Development
	Provision of guidelines to sub-national levels and functional planning agencies	—do—
Tactical Planning	Identification of key projects	National and regional levels
	Identification of major support projects	National and regional levels
Operational Planning	Detailed project formulation	Project and territorial levels
	Preparation of Plans—First Stage	National, regional and local levels
	Preparation of plans—Second Stage	—do—
	Finalization and integration of plans	National level
	Monitoring of plans	National, regional, local and project levels
	Evaluation of plans	National level
	Participation of population	National, regional and local levels

In order to facilitate the various planning steps enumerated above, data and information collection and feeding, the undertaking of various surveys, investigations and studies and organization of the necessary inter-actions between and among the levels come as essential operational components. As may be seen, the laying down of a suitable policy framework is a crucial planning step at the national level. The national policy for the forestry sector must incorporate within it a number of vital elements, some of which are :

(a) Policy relating to linkages of the forestry sector with other vital sectors of the economy;
(b) Policy relating to the release of forest land for clearance in a phased manner to ensure a regulated flow of logs together with the maximum possible utilization of the availability of wood supply. In some countries (e.g. Malaysia) this is an important aspect of forest policy;
(c) Policy for the management of forest land designed to maximize commercial returns compatible with the maintenance of environmental values;
(d) Policy relating to the designation and management of biosphere reserves, national parks and wildlife sanctuaries;
(e) Policy regarding forest industries, marketing and prices;
(f) Policy on social forestry and related subjects including public participation;
(g) Policy for manpower planning and training; and
(h) Policy for research.

Within the above policy framework, the various strategy alternatives have to be developed. The methodology for developing such alternatives could range in sophistication from computer models to commonsense value judgements. Malaysia, for instance, has prepared an elaborate economic model for its long-term plan. Whatever may be the method adopted and the degree of sophistication attempted, the premises for the strategy proposed must be clearly laid down. Thus the strategy formulation phase is a very important step in the planning process. Based on the strategy advocated and the goals indicated, each level in the multilevel planning framework then would set about to prepare its plans for the subjects falling within its geographic scope. In each case, three temporal plans are to be drawn up, viz. a perspective plan covering a 20-year period, a medium-term plan covering a five-year period and an annual plan.

Each area level will prepare its plan in five major steps. These are :

(a) Data collection relevant to planning at the particular area level;
(b) Diagnosis : i.e. analysis of the present situation;
(c) Projections of future conditions;

(d) Formulation of detailed strategies; and
(e) Preparation of action plans/projects.

Each step would involve interactions of various kinds—formal and informal—with the levels above and below for clarification of issues, exchange of information and firming up of developmental magnitudes. The interactions may also be visualized as of three kinds : (i) Vertical, i.e. with departmental superiors for obtaining clarifications and guidance; (ii) Horizontal, i.e. with the other sectoral functionaries at the same area level in order to ensure linkages and sequences in the plan; and (iii) Popular interaction, i.e. with the beneficiaries and the public at large in order that the plans may reflect the genuine needs of the population. These interactions may be of different frequencies, as dictated by circumstances and needs.

REFERENCES

1. Leonard, David K., 'Putting the Farmer in Control : Building Agricultural Institutions, In Berg, Robert J. and J.S. Whitaker, (Ed.) Berkeley, *Strategies for African Development*, University of Califonia Press, 1986.
2. Mollett, J.A., *Planning for Agricultural Development*, London and Canberra : Croom Helm, 1984.
3. *Ibid.*
4. Randhawa, N.S. and Sundaram, K.V., *Small Farmer Development in Asia and the Pacific : Some Lessons for Strategy Formulation and Planning.* FAO Economic and Social Development Paper 87, Rome, 1990.
5. The countries studied are : India, Indonesia, Bangladesh, Nepal, Philippines and Sri Lanka. For details, see K.V. Sundaram, "Multilevel Planning Process for Forestry Development in Asia and the Pacific," Working Paper prepared for FAO of the United Nations, August, 1986.
6. FAO Forestry paper 48, "Land Evaluation for Forestry" (FAO, Rome 1984), Chapter 5, p. 36.
7. The term *local level* has to be interpreted for each country. It would depend on the administrative structure in the country.
8. Some examples of shifts away from departmental institutions in order to achieve more dynamic development are : the creation of State Forest Development Corporations in India; State Forest Industries in Thailand and Indonesia; and transfer of the management of some watershed areas and energy forests in the Philippines to the authority responsible for water and energy.

4

DEVELOPMENT FROM BELOW

During the last two decades especially, several new expressions in development planning have increasingly come into usage to signify the different approaches to planning and development. Some of these are : Top-down Planning, Planning or Development from Below, or Bottom-up Planning. Micro-level planning and Multi-level planning. In this context, terms like decentralization, target groups and participation have also received increasing attention. These developments are not without significance. They have followed in response to some changes that have occurred in the orientation and structure of development planning over the years. The thinking and emphasis on development have been changing and planners call this change "Paradigm Shifts". The changes that have occurred in the orientation and structure of development planning are diagramatically illustrated in Fig. 4.1.

The concern about "Development", particularly as it relates to the developing countries, came to be voiced around the 1940's. Since then, the meaning of this term has shifted from time to time in keeping with certain major political, administrative, economic, social and technological changes, as well as certain perceptions relating to income and regional disparities in the developing countries.

The major changes witnessed during the 50's and 60's included decolonization (in a number of countries in Asia and Africa), central control of government functions following independence and a massive effort directed towards national reconstruction and development based on country-specific needs and priorities. These changes have been followed during the 70's, 80's and the 90's by a succession of far-reaching shifts in development orientation, characterized by new thrusts and strategies appropriate to the "developing countries".

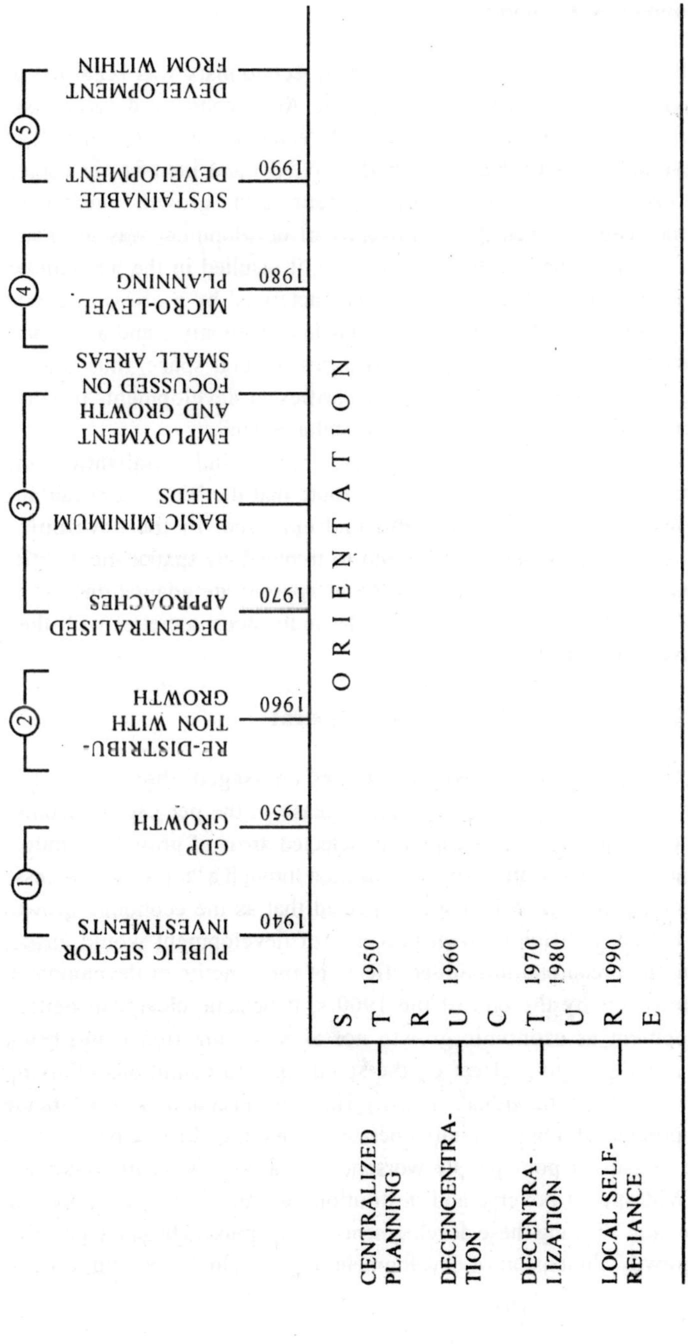

FIG. 4.1 : Changes in the Orientation and Structure of Development Planning.

Development as Economic Growth

Initially, development as interpreted by economists was regarded as synonymous with economic development. Also economic development, for quite some time, was confused with "economic growth," that is, of increase in the Gross National Product (GNP) and income per capita. Sometimes, the two terms "development" and "growth" were used interchangeably. When this philosophy of development was mechanically foisted on the developing countries, it resulted in the well-known phenomenon of a "dual economy," characterized by a growing export sector, distinguished in space as an "enclave economy", and a stagnant traditional sector covering most territories of rural space, thus exacerbating rural poverty, and spatial disparities in development. In some quarters, this was seen as "economic colonialism".

This economic growth game also implied industrialization and modernization, as it was through this route that the West European and American styles of development had emerged. In the developing countries, while industrialization led to tremendous spatial inequalities in development, modernization without appropriate adaptations led to an erosion of the cultural values of the indigenous societies with their negative side effects.

The "Trickle Down Process" of Development

Thus the "economic growth game," as envisaged above, aimed at accumulation of capital through an increase in the per capita incomes and the investment of this capital in selected areas of growth, in industrialization, modernization and urbanization through a "top-down process" of planning and control. It was expected that as the economic growth snow-balled, a "trickle down process" of development would ensue, leading to spread and multiplier effects of the benefits of development.

However, by the end of the 1960's, it became clear that neither development as economic growth nor as modernization could bring about a wide-ranging effect on the standards and conditions of living of the majority of individuals in many Third World countries. The "trickle down process" did not certainly operate. If anything, the relative position of the masses of poor people worsened vis-a-vis that of the relatively rich. Widespread poverty and destitution became visible, tangible and compelling. Viewing these developments, many thinkers began to perceive the "growth" dimension of development, in its exclusive pursuit towards the production of material things, as naive, superficial and unrealistic. In a penetrating analysis of the meaning of development, Dudley Seers characterized it as a mere "web of fantasy".[1]

Growth with Equity Considerations

Following this disenchantment with development, the idea of distributive justice or redistribution with growth was vigorously advocated. As a sequel, a host of issues—poverty, unemployment, inequality (in terms of income distribution, regional disparities, and social inequality) and quality of life came to be regarded as the critical issues to be tackled directly and frontally. The satisfying of certain "basic needs"—nutrition, health, water supply, shelter, sanitation, education and alleviation of poverty—through mobilizing government and foreign aid rather than relying on market forces was considered the major priority in the context of the developing countries.

Following these ideas, new programmatic approaches emerged, among which the Basic Minimum Needs Approach (BMNA), Poverty Alleviation and Employment Generation Programmes for the Rural Poor, Target Group and Target Area (Backward Areas) Programmes, Integrated Rural Development Programmes in different combinations and Development Programmes for Women may be specifically cited.

Concern for Environment

The seventies were thus characterized by governments in the various developing countries experimenting with different policy and programmatic approaches, guided by the shifting emphasis on development thought by the planners. This period also coincided with a sense of concern and anxiety experienced by the advanced industrial countries about environmental pollution and the fear of a rapid depletion of global natural resources. The United Nations Conference on Human Environment held at Stockholm in 1972 gave the first warning signal about the negative aspects of the prevailing development strategies.

Limits of Growth

In 1979, the United Nations Symposium on "Interrelations among Resources, Environment, Population and Development[2] identified the question of consumption problems and lifestyles as one of the most basic sources of conflict in the world. Hence, it stressed that the urgent need, both in the North and in the South, was for exploring alternative patterns of consumption and development that were environmentally sound, socially responsible and less wasteful. This implied limiting the reckless "mining" of natural capital, practising austerity in consumption, reducing wants and caring for long-term prosperity. The Club of Rome talked about "limits to growth". In a further elaboration of the "limits" idea, both an "upper limit" and a "lower limit" (i.e. a minimum and maximum) to economic growth were stressed, implying resource exploitation based on considerations of sustainable resource use, avoidance of environmental degradation in any form and maintenance of an ecological balance at the desired level of quality of life. It was advocated that all countries should specify their growth rates of national product in terms of both minimum and maximum (Sundaram, Chandrashekhara).[3] It has been argued that there are certain viable and attractive technologies, economic structures and lifestyles to which the developed countries and the Third World could move.

These alternatives imply the acceptance of simple material living standards; abandoning the quest for endless economic growth; maximizing regional economic self-sufficiency; employing alternative and intermediate technologies; and adopting cooperative ways of working, wherever possible. "These alternatives constitute a third way. They involve the rejection of the capitalist way with its emphasis on the limitless increases in consumption and waste, its disregard for the poor, and its indifference to any concept of appropriate development."[4]

Sustainable Development

The Brundtland Commission's report in April, 1987, "Our Common Future",[5] became a landmark in development thinking and added further impetus to the governments in the developing as well as developed countries to address environmental issues in their practical country programmes. Sustainable development became the key word, which was defined by the World Commission on Environment and Development as "development which meets the needs of the present without compromising the ability of future generations to meet their own needs". Such sustainable development may mean different things to different countries. To the rich nations, sustainable development may imply preserving for posterity the already high standards of life achieved in their countries. To the poor nations, it may seem a pathway of economic development, which can help to meet the minimum needs of the people without harm to the environmental capital stocks. Initially, the debate on sustainable development came to be centred on issues relating to growth versus environmental conservation, which implied a basic contradiction in thinking. A more exhaustive study of the problem by the Brundtland Commission led to the conclusion that the relationship between sustainable development and the environment is really one of complementarity and interdependence. "What is required is a new approach, in which all nations aim at a type of development, that integrates production with resource conservation and enhancement and that links both to the provision for all, of an adequate livelihood and equitable access to resources".[6] Since poverty is both a major cause and effect of global environment problems, a world in which poverty is endemic will always be prone to ecological and other catastrophes. Thus, economic growth, poverty alleviation and proper management of natural resources are all the mutually interdependent facets of the ultimate development goal, and what is called for today is the achievement of a better balance and closer integration among these objectives. This then is the philosophy of the new development paradigm—that of growth with equity, stability and sustainability.

Structural Changes

Along with changes in the orientation of development planning, we should also take note of the changes in the structure of planning that ensued. During the late forties or fifties, many countries in the Asian region emerged as independent nations. Immediately following their independence, they had to consolidate their freedom and this necessarily meant centralization and control of all government functions. In the field of development, this meant the practice of effective top-down planning. As a result, the top-down planning methodologies evolved. In fact, impressive progress was made, particularly in the early and mid-sixties in the various components of "top-down" planning i.e. in the formulation of macro-economic framework of plans, the design of a national development strategy and priorities, the assessment of resources, investment requirements and gaps, and the coordination of intersectoral allocations. We cannot deny the importance of centre-down process of planning especially in the context of various development constraints, operating in Third World countries. But top-down planning is essentially externally induced and does not take into account regional and area specificities. As the saying goes, you cannot tend a flock of sheep from a camel's back.[7] Top-down Planning is too inflexible and broad, less penetrating and less relevant to the sub-national areas. The resulting development is spotty and uneven. In effect, it tends to be more urban and industrial in nature. The projects tend to be large in nature, thus capital-intensive and dominated by high technology.

Governments have now increasingly recognized that central planning cannot succeed unless there is a matching process of "Planning and development from below". In this case, development is considered as being based on the maximum mobilization of each area's natural, human and institutional resources the primary objective being the satisfaction of the basic needs of the inhabitants of that area. Thus, development from below will be marked by the following characteristics :

— It will be basic-needs oriented;
— It will be labour-intensive;
— It will be small-scale in nature;
— It will be regional/area resources based;
— It will be rural centred;
— It will be based on "appropriate" rather than highest technology.

In all developing countries, "planning and development from below" has acquired a certain connotation and meaning. As a concept, (particularly in the context of poverty alleviation) it means that the intended beneficiaries of development, particularly the weaker sections of the society, must be active agents to plan, generate and manage their own development. They are not merely and passively to receive only the benefits of development handed down from above. On the contrary they have to be active partners in planning, generating and managing their own development.

"Top-down planning", signifying planning at the central level, and "Planning from below," signifying planning at the local level, are not to be regarded as mutually exclusive approaches. Both are necessary. In fact, if development planning is to be scientifically practiced, it has to be done at least at three territorial levels : (i) National, (ii) Regional and (iii) Local. There are subtle differences among these levels of planning in regard to the aim, approach, command, methodology, resources and nature of public participation. Table 4.1 brings out these differences with clarity.

TABLE 4.1 : Planning levels and their differences.

Planning Type	Aim	Approach	Command	Methodology	Resources	Popular participation
National	Economic and Social	Sectoral	Top-Down ↓	Quantitative	National Taxes & Foreign Aid	Minimal Indirect
Regional	Socio-economic & Environmental	Spatio-Sectoral	↓ Integrative ↑	Quantitative & Qualitative	Regional taxes & Devolution from Centre	Maximal Indirect
Local	Socio-economic Human Environmental Grass-roots	Democratic Decentralized Participatory approach	Bottom-Up ↑	Qualitative & Consensus	1. Local Taxes 2. Devolution from National & Regional Governments 3. Community involvement	Maximal Direct

Source :Adapted from R.P. Misra (Ed.) : *Local-Level Planning and Development*, Sterling Publishers, New Delhi, 1983.

"Development from below" with its objectives of growth, equity, stability and sustainability rests on five basic concepts :

(i) Concept of decentralization;
(ii) Concept of area development;
(iii) Concept of participation;
(iv) Concept of sustainable development; and
(v) Concept of integration.

Concept of Decentralization

The degree of "localism" (or freedom to plan) in area development depends on the extent of decentralization of functions, finances and powers conferred on the area by the centre. In most developing countries, the degree of decentralization conferred on the local area is minimal, as powers and funds are controlled from above. This is so far as planning for the public sector allocations is concerned. With the public sector allocations to the regional and local levels now shrinking in many developing countries owing to the "debt crisis" and the adoption of structural adjustment measures, a "self-reliant approach" to development, with the local people's effort becoming a significant component, is now becoming increasingly important. Whatever be the approach to planning, whether confined to the resources provided by the government or through resources generated by the local communities, or by both, the principles of area development are the same. If area development is to emerge as an interdependent local activity, then the local community has to be adequately "empowered" to make its own decisions about development, its objectives and priorities and to have control over the spending of allocations and resources meant for local development. In this context, they should enjoy adequate decentralization of functions, powers and finances.

Concept of Area Development

Development from below has to be necessarily based on a viable unit area, which may be an administrative unit, like a district, or a natural unit like a watershed area. Whatever be this unit area, for development purposes, it should not be regarded as a closed economic unit for planning. It should be noted that many planning issues will transcend the spatial limits of any planning area. Therefore, the planning function has to take note of "external effects" like spatial associations, inter-relationships and complementarities. Indeed this is one of the important principles of area planning or local planning.

Planning at the area level is essentially an attempt to strike harmony in relations among three elements—place (i.e. area), folk (i.e. people), and work (i.e. employment and economy). Each one of these elements has its own set of constraints. Place or area has its constraints in the factor endowments; folk has its constraints in the quantity, quality including skills, as well as the social and attitudinal factor of the local population; work or employment and economy have their constraints in the quantum and quality of utilizable resources of the local area. In the developing countries, there are other constraints also added to these viz. lack of skills and technology and paucity of financial resources for development. These constraints apart, area planning has also to contend with certain conflicts in goals, e.g. efficiency versus equity; long-term growth versus short-term benefits, etc. In this context, area planning is one of resolving the conflicts in a situation full of various constraints and arriving at an optimal solution such that "folk" and "work" are organized in "space", with maximum mutual benefits and minimum mutual conflicts.

Area planning methodology is difficult to set out in a blanket fashion. For any particular country, area planning must evolve its own concept and strategy, building around the unique and indigenous features of the planning area. It must take into account.

- — the resource structure of the area;
- — the stage and level of development;
- — the existing political, social and institutional set-up;
- — the development objectives visualized; and
- — the specific interventionist policies proposed to be pursued.

Further, area planning must be in tune with the problems, needs, perceptions and value systems of the people in the area. It should also take into account the various constraints in the particular situation, like the resource constraints, skill constraints, technology constraints, etc. At the risk of repetition, we may point out that planning from below focused on a viable unit area, such as district, has to be :

- — Area specific;
- — People specific;
- — Problem specific;
- — Rural centred;
- — Basic needs oriented;
- — Labour-intensive and employment oriented;
- — Small-scale related to the capacities of the people;
- — Local resources-based; and
- — Based on appropriate rather than the most advanced technology.

Area planning for the developing countries has to be informed by a "selective approach," and not by a "comprehensive approach". The latter, undoubtedly, has a great appeal for the planner. This is because, in all developing countries, there are serious deficiencies to be met on every front. One would like to have more growth, more employment, more infrastructure and more services. If one could achieve all these at the same time and at the quickest possible time, it would indeed be very good. But as we noted earlier, there are several constraints inhibiting growth in the developing countries. If any planner thinks that he can achieve all these simultaneously and within a small time-frame, it will be only a pipe dream. Thus in our situation, if we try to attempt to do everything that comprehensive planning would demand, our whole planning exercise would be rendered self-defeating, before it has even started. The realistic approach here would be to follow a "Selective development approach". In this approach, "selection" or "prioritization" becomes the "cornerstone" of the development strategy.

A selective development strategy would imply the selection of policies and methods of focusing and concentrating public expenditures within a framework of balanced development. For area planning, the selective strategy implies election between regions, areas, cities and villages; between various sub-branches of the economy; between institutions, enterprises, families and individuals; and between short- and long-run periods of planning and so forth. Thus "selection" becomes one of the key words in area planning. The process of selection is meant to unleash the development potentials of an area. The selected elements are supposed to have some "ignition potentials". They are supposed to trigger, steer and effectuate developments over the area. But this will happen only gradually in the beginning; but later, with the multiplier and linkage effects operating, development would take place more rapidly and more substantially. The process is thus a gradual enlargement of development, a process sometimes referred to as "development based on the Point-Line—Network Principle". According to this principle, development starts at a point, proceeds along a line and then embraces a whole network, signifying a gradual unfolding of the development process.

The second principle in area planning is what is known as the "Reduction Principle". In mathematics, this means modification or simplification or, in other words, a method of understanding a complex idea in terms of its simpler parts or components. In the context of development planning in general, and "Development from below" in particular, "reduction" essentially means reducing the complexity of local planning as a technical exercise, by simplifying methodologies consistent with the availability of skills at the local level. Such reduction is called for in two directions : (i) in the empirical effort that goes into the planning exercise; and (ii) in data collection for planning. As regards empirical effort, this may be reduced by replacing detailed analysis by minimum analysis considered essential for decision-making. A detailed analysis is always time-consuming and also involves more costs. Besides the very best analysis is worthless, if it comes too late for the decision.

At each level of planning, it is possible to decide the minimum analysis that would be required (taking into account the data availability) to meet the plan objectives. As regards data, it has been observed that very often too many surveys are undertaken and too much data are collected that are seldom used in practical planning. The "critical minimum information" needed for each level of planning must be identified and, in this manner, the data collection should be reduced in order to serve the really relevant problems. Thus, it may be noted that the "reduced approach" is an aspect of the theory of *limited rationality*, where the aim is to arrive at fairly satisfactory solutions in a context marked by a number of constraints.

The third principle in area planning is what may be called, "focus". Focus implies concentration and deep thrust in the selected spheres of development activity. "Focus" would be possible only when the planning functions for each level are clearly demarcated, and when there is a clear perception of sound planning procedures.

Concept of Participation

Community or people's participation is an integral part of area development planning. In any planning effort, man becomes both the end and the means for development. As an end, it is an inevitable extension of the national effort and commitment to bring the masses into the mainstream of development process for establishing an egalitarian socio-economic order.

As a means, community participation should subserve the objective of collective self-reliance, which is the basis of all components and aspects of "development from below". Such community participation is of particular relevance to the developing countries to mobilize community resources, to supplement and complement the efforts of the government, and to achieve the goals of area development. Development from below is thus local development resulting from a prudent use of the resources devolved from above and those mobilized from below with the people's cooperation. In Chapter 5, we have discussed a concept called "Development from Within" and have distinguished it from "Development from Below".

Community participation takes three forms :

— Mobilization, in which participation is viewed as a facilitator or a desired plan output;

— Mediation, in which both the government and the people, through their representatives or institutions, are involved in the task of planning and implementation, which is done through a dialectical process; and
— Empowerment, in which the communities are given the autonomy to decide the goals, plans, programmes and projects affecting their development, to mobilize and control their own resources and to implement their development activities.

The last mentioned, i.e. empowerment, is the highest form of participation and is the most desirable for area development planning. Towards this end, people have to be capacitated and their institutions built up and strengthened.

Participation, to be effective, must extend through all levels of decision-making, implementation, benefit-sharing and monitoring and evolution. When participation is "collective, voluntary, bottom-up and self-managing", development tends to build on the inner strength of the human resources and to achieve a desirable level of performance. Grass-root participation in certain specific and unique combinations has resulted in some success stories. In all such cases, the success has been due to the blend or mix of certain unique factors such as the availability of extraordinary local leadership, the close and continuous involvement of a band of dedicated technicians and social workers and, above all, a highly motivated populace. Such a combination may rarely exist. In short, ensuring people's participation in area development is an arduous task. However, the successful stories indicate that the prospects for success would, among other things, depend on:[8]

(a) Involvement of local people in identifying the components of local development projects and the means and mechanisms to implement them effectively. The people's better understanding of their resource base and environment, institutional strength and self-help devices are responsible for this. Local involvement would also facilitate the people's access and command over local resources. The external input could be in terms of financial resources and technological support (including advice); and
(b) People's involvement or participation can be more easily mobilized around any lead activity clearly understood by the local community. The equity gains from such activities may enhance the participation. The formation of user groups and mobilization

> of collective resources are seen as the distinct gains of such an approach. Lower investment needs and lower operational costs emerge as the by-products of activities focused on local participation.

Community participation must be engineered through appropriate people's organizations. Institutions rooted in local community structures have a potentially significant bearing on successful outcomes. To quote Prof. Chakravarty :

> "We must find, along with new technology, newer ways of involving people in the development process. This is a much more demanding job and requires, for its success, involvement of masses of people. While some of it may be organized through the market system, our job as economists and social scientists is to find other organizational possibilities as well. However, some of these possibilities, which exist notably in the creation of rural infrastructure, cannot be treated with centralized methods of planning. By their very nature, they require, as modes of implementation, much smaller units."[9]

Concept of Sustainable Development

Since the publication of the report of the Brundtland Commission, the environmental problems which received some attention by national governments and which have been incorporated into national policies during the latter part of the 20th century, are : pollution control, population planning and energy conservation. But the small-scale and marginal changes that are constantly occurring on our planet, and which have clear local and regional dimensions, have not yet been given adequate attention. All these incremental phenomena may hardly seem important by themselves; but they have severe environmental impacts and, therefore, necessitate more coherent planning. In Decentralized Planning, it is this aspect of environment, which we have to consciously address. The UN Human Development Report (1993) aptly remarks that it is "as important to address the 'silent emergencies' of poverty (water pollution, land degradation, environmental diseases) as it is to focus on the "loud emergencies" (global warming, ozone depletion) that usually dominate the headlines".

According to one view, development became unsustainable because of the collapse of a "co-evolutionary development process," entailing the elements of *knowledge, values, social organization, technology* and *resource system.* Development is a "patchwork quilt" of these elements. Each patch is a complex one. No one way of understanding it is sufficient. A holistic view and a multi-disciplinary approach are needed. It has been argued that development became unsustainable "not simply because the use of hydro-carbons has been destroying the environment, but because there has been a cultural implosion. Value systems have been collapsing. Knowledge has been reduced to Western understanding[10] and social organization and technologies have become increasingly the same around the world.[11] Sustainable development is, therefore, interpreted as a method of returning to the co-evolutionary development process "with the diversity that remains and the deliberate fostering of further diversity to permit adaptation to future surprises". According to Norgaard, the policy challenge of sustainable development consists of finding a path towards a positive social and ecological co-evolution. This co-evolutionary view of development is illustratively shown in Fig. 4.2. In this conception, no system will dominate another; none will provide

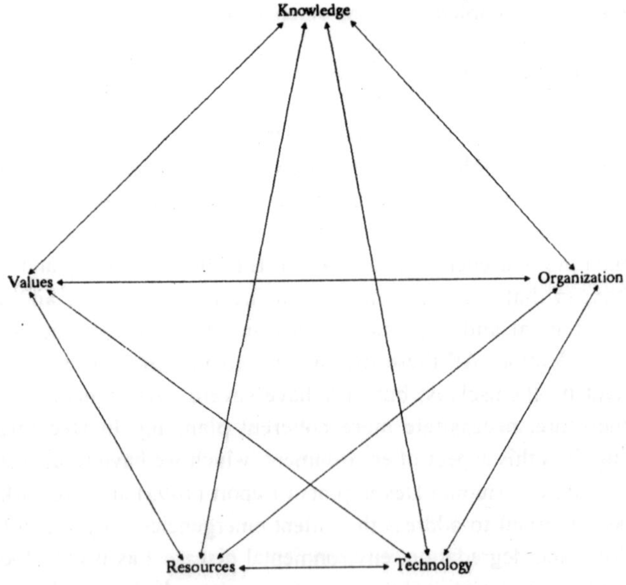

FIG. 4.2 : A Co-evolutionary View of Development.

Source :Richard B. Norgaard, 1988.

a more obvious starting point for understanding the whole, and each can only be understood in the context of the others. This would mean that not only is each subsystem related to all the others, but each is changing and affecting the evolution of the others. In a sound and sustainable development, therefore, with each subsystem putting selective pressure on each of the other subsystems, they "co-evolve" in a manner, whereby each reflects the others. This, in other words, is a holistic view of development, which is nothing new and which has been expressed before in other contexts. However, it needs to be re-stated in the context of sustainable development. In practical terms, the return to co-evolutionary development at the regional and local levels would mean that (a) environmental dimensions should be consciously incorporated into regional and local level planning, and (b) a systems approach to planning should be adopted, in which knowledge, values, social organisation, technology and resources are treated as more or less symmetrical.

In arguing for sustainable development, the moral basis is that the next generation should have access to at least the same resource base as the previous generation. This would mean that a sustainable economy should serve the interests of *justice*. The three types of justice involved here are :

— Justice to people within a generation, i.e. intra-generational justice;
— Justice to people between generations, i.e. inter-generational justice; and
— Justice to nature.

All these three types of justice imply that sustainable development has to be conceived in a long-term perspective and in the context of the following goals :

— Equity (within and between generations, and to nature);
— Survival (durability as well as resilience); and
— Welfare improvement (raising average standards of welfare).

Economic growth and sustaining the environment are not dichotomous issues. Growth is imperative if poverty is to be reduced. What is needed is that the pattern of distribution of growth must change. It must become less wasteful of natural resources and be environment friendly, in both rich and poor nations. This is the sum and substance of the concept of sustainable development. The new models of development must be much more sensitive to people and to nature.

Concept of Integration

The term "integration" is a rather nebulous expression and has been interpreted in many ways. In the context of integrated rural development, as has emerged in many developing countries in recent years, it has been interpreted mainly in two ways. One is the well-known emphasis on inter-sectoral co-ordination, with its elements of inter-sectoral complementarities and internal consistency. In this sense, integrated rural development would comprise comprehensive agricultural development linked to rural industries, subsidiary occupations, tertiary sector opportunities, community services and development organizations. The second way in which integrated rural development has been interpreted is in the sense of an integrated project approach, with the core project as a basic starting point, and then weaving around it all complementarities and linkages, in fact all that are necessary as a support to the core project. Both these approaches—the inter-sectoral approach and the project approach—are partial in scope, and even the limited "linkages" implied in these approaches fail to materialize fully, because of the divided way in which implementation takes place, in the absence of an overarching machinery, which ensures such integration.

Integrated rural development in a decentralized multi-level planning framework would have three dimensions :

(a) Sectoral balance,
(b) Spatial balance, and
(c) Operational balance.

In a given situation, integration within and among these elements is a product of constrained maximization. It has to be achieved within a set of four basic constraints identified in each context. This is illustrated in Fig. 4.3. It may be seen from this diagram that sectoral balance has to be achieved within : (a) national and regional priorities, (b) local relevance, (c) economic efficiency, and (d) internal consistency. Spatial balance has to be achieved, taking into account considerations of (a) location, (b) accessibility, (c) efficiency, and (d) viability/threshold/critical mass. Operational balance has to be achieved in a framework of (a) organization, (b) delegation of functions, (c) management procedures, and (d) personnel systems.

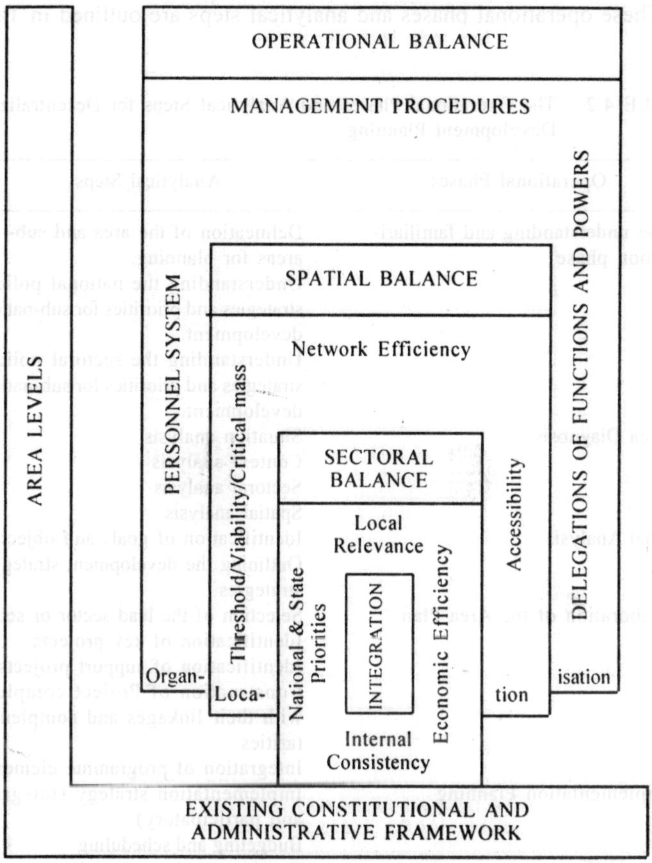

FIG. 4.3 : A Multi-level Concept of Integration.

Source : R.P. Misra and K.V. Sundaram : *Multilevel Planning and Integrated Rural Development in India*, Heritage Publishers, New Delhi, 1980.

The concept of integration, as explained here, seems attractive enough. Nevertheless, in practice, it is a phenomenon difficult to achieve, Some planners call it the "Achilles' heel of planning". It has to be strived in successive stages through a series of "approximations".

Decentralized Planning Methodology

The decentralized methodology consists of a sequence of operational phases and analytical steps.

These operational phases and analytical steps are outlined in Table 4.2.

TABLE 4.2 : The Operational Phases and Analytical Steps for Decentralized Development Planning.

Operational Phases	Analytical Steps
1. The understanding and familiarization phase	Delineation of the area and sub-areas for planning. Understanding the national policies, strategies and priorities for sub-national development. Understanding the sectoral policies, strategies and priorities for sub-national development.
2. Area Diagnosis	Situation analysis Context analysis Sectoral analysis Spatial analysis
3. Goal Analysis	Identification of goals and objectives Outlining the development strategy or strategies.
4. Elaboration of the Area Plan	Selection of the lead sector or sectors Identification of key projects Identification of support projects Construction of Project complexes with their linkages and complementarities Integration of programme elements
5. Implementation Planning	Implementation strategy (Integrated and participatory) Budgeting and scheduling (Implementation scheduling) Monitoring Evaluation

The first phase of this approach is to delineate the area to be planned. This may not arise, where a country had already designated its planning areas in terms of certain administrative divisions. Area/regional delineation may, however, be necessary, when problem oriented area/regional planning is undertaken (e.g. a river basin, a watershed, a backward area, etc.)

The second phase is a very important diagnostic phase. It comprises four kinds of analyses, viz. (a) Situation Analysis, (b) Context Analysis, (c) Sectoral Analysis, and (d) Spatial Analysis.

(a) The *Situation Analysis* phase involves a study of the physical environment in which the plan is to be prepared. It will involve an appraisal of the factor endowments of the area, such as its geographical location, climate, biological resources (flora and fauna), geology and minerals. It will be mostly descriptive with quantitative dimensions indicated, wherever available. The analysis will give an idea of the natural resource potentials and constraints and can also lead to the identification of homogeneous sub-regions, e.g. agro-climatic zones; sub-watersheds etc.

(b) The *Context Analysis* will include an analysis of the existing renewable resources, such as land, water, human resources, economic opportunities and infrastructure. The analysis results in an understanding of the area's development *constraints* and *potentials*. These may vary according to agro-climatic zones or other natural units. A number of stresses are also identified during this step. This step is also sometimes called "Malady-Remedy Analysis". It would involve reviewing the resources of the area and identifying specific problems that are coming in the way of their utilization for development and suggesting the alternative solutions. Finally, a lead sector should be tentatively identified. At this point, some tentative goals should have emerged.

(c) The *Sectoral Analysis* studies the economic activities and infrastructure, social services, and other facilities, and support programmes for the development of social and economic activities. Usually this is done sectorwise and results in a statement of the present levels of development and gaps in inputs required to achieve certain standards of production, to realize minimum levels of quality of life, and to reach basic standards of living. It also results in an understanding of the sectoral opportunities which must be responded to in the identification of development approaches for the area.

(d) The *Spatial Analysis* helps to provide knowledge about the existing level of development in infrastructural facilities and social services in the area and gaps in their spatial coverage and enables identification of a network of Rural Service Centres and Growth Centres.

The present-day trends in development planning suggest that we should add to the above four types of analyses, perhaps, two more, viz.

Gender Analysis and Environmental Analysis. Although, the "Context Analysis" in the above scheme encompasses both these, their separate identity may perhaps serve to underline and emphasize their importance. The broad characteristics of the different analyses are brought out in Table 4.3.

In the third phase of area planning—goal analysis—the basic technique is to derive the goals and objectives from the major problems of the area which are revealed during the diagnostic phase. The *goals* are broad policy statements while *objectives* are specific, time-bound and quantifiable, and are thus subject to being measured. The objectives are spelt out in detail with regard to the desired changes in development.

The fourth and fifth phases deal with the elaboration of the plan and its implementation. It includes various steps like the identification of the lead sector(s), key projects, support projects, visualizing the project complexes along with their linkages and complementarities and finally integrating the various programme elements. For the implementation stage, it involves the steps of spelling out the implementation strategy, budgeting and work scheduling, and then monitoring the progress of the plan and finally its evaluation.

It is to be noted that the steps outlined here mark a departure from the conventional planning approach, which treats all sectors alike without selection and prioritization. In the area development approach, however, the analysis is confined to lead sectors, key projects and support projects. The accent is on making a dent on the perceived problems and on linkages and integration.

Development from Below : Towards Application

In the foregoing paragraphs, we have discussed the various concepts and principles which should govern any attempt at "Development from Below". How these concepts and principles may be applied in the actual planning context may now be gone into in some detail by first considering a hypothetical model and then by examining some field experiments.

In the first place, we may note that "Development from Below" consists of two processes, viz. "Disaggregation" as well as "Aggregation". It is (a) disaggregating the Centre's socio-economic goals to local areas so that locally relevant goals are clearly perceived and planning consistency is ensured; and (b) aggregating local decisions through appropriate institutions at different spatial levels and integrating them into macro plans.

TABLE 4.3 : Characteristics of Area/District Analysis.

Area (District) Analysis

COMPONENTS	Situation Analysis	Context Analysis	Sectoral Analysis	Spatial Analysis
			Development Factors	
BASIS OF CLASSI-FICATION	Natural Factor Endowments (Static Endogenous Factors)	Endogenous Factors (Dynamic)	Exogenous Through National Policies Induced through Regional Interaction Endogenous through Local Effort	Locational Factors; Development Factors.
TECHNIQUES	Qualitative Quantitative	Quantitative Qualitative	Quantitative Qualitative	Quantitative Qualitative
COVERAGE	Geographical Location	Land Resources Water Resources	Programmes, Financial, Outlays, Inputs, Outputs, Targets, Physical Achieve-ements and Problems and	Settlement Hierarchy;

(Contd.)

TABLE 4.3 : (*Contd.*)

COVERAGE	Physiography, Climate Biological Resources Geology Minerals	Human Resources — Demography — Socio-cultural Economic Characteristics of the Area (District) and the Population.	Constraints for Development in Key Sectors: Agriculture Irrigation Animal Husbandry Industry Health Education.	Vertical and Horizontal Linkages; Convergence of Services. Locational Decisions.
OUTPUT	A General Idea of the Factor Endowments of the District; Intra-district disparities; Division into Homogeneous Sub-Regions e.g., Agro-Climatic Zones	Understanding of: Levels of Development (Intra-District Disparities) Potentials and Constraints to Development Identification of Lead sector(s) Formulation of goals.	Understanding of: Level of Development (Intra-district Disparities)-Outputs Potentials and Constraints Sectoral Objectives and Sub-objectives Strategy Options.	Existing Level of Development in Infrastructural Facilities and Social Services; Gaps in Spatial Coverage Identification of a network of Rural Service Centres and Promotion of Growth Centres.

Source : K.V. Sundaram : "What kinds of analytical skills a district planner should possess ?" (Mimeographed, 1987).

The aggregation process must be attempted from the lowest unit area level, i.e. from the village upwards. The planning must be informed by the key objective of "sustainability" along with the other objectives of growth, equity and balanced regional development. As agriculture is the backbone of our village economy, the major thrust of village-based planning will have to be on achieving sustainable agriculture, involving both inter-generational equity and intra-generational equity. Intra-generational equity will aim at giving a fair deal to socially and economically disadvantaged groups. Inter-generational equity will involve attention to the protection of the productive base of agriculture. This implies the use of the basic agricultural assets of land, water, flora, fauna and the atmosphere in such a manner that today's progress does not ruin tomorrow's prospects.[12]

The first step will be the "Resource Inventory" and "Environmental Appraisal".

The resource inventory will be in the nature of a baseline survey of the natural resources potentials and an assessment of the present extent of their degradation. In other words, it is preparing a resource accounting framework. Such a framework will provide the leads to the essential environmental conservation/protection ingredients that should be incorporated into the regional and local development plans. Some aspects of resource inventory analysis with special reference to environmental resources are :

(i) The definition of the nature and extent of the available natural resources, i.e. Resource Potentials;

(ii) The assessment of the nature and magnitude of their current use or consumption levels, i.e. Resource Use;

(iii) An assessment of the ability of the resources to yield, on a continuing basis, without special protection measures, i.e. Resource Sustainability;

(iv) The identification of the extent of degradation of natural resources, i.e. Resource Depletion and Environmental Degradation; and

(v) Alternative strategies or intervention of resource use and estimation of their consequences, i.e. Environmental Impact Analysis.

Resource Inventory and Environmental Appraisal attempted from village level will constitute the basis for preparing the Village Plans. This approach provides the truest picture of the environmental status of the village, because it is based on the most direct method, i.e. the "ground-truthing" itself. It must be emphasized that for fact-finding on the extent of degradation of land and forest resources in an area, the most accurate data could be obtained from the village level rather than from above or through any indirect method.

An essential component of Resource Inventory is "Resource Mapping". The mapable resources at the village level are : (a) Natural resources; (b) Human resources; (c) Infrastructural resources; and (d) Institutional resources. On the cadastral map of a village, these resources are indicated in their correct locations by appropriate mapping techniques. Each kind of resource is mapped separately and then a final integrated map is obtained.

Through resource mapping, we can bring out four major aspects related to resource development planning :

(i) Location of resources;
(ii) Estimation of resource potential;
(iii) Assessment of resource use; and
(iv) Identification of problems and priorities for development projects.

It should be emphasized that in resource mapping as well as in other steps of the bottom-up process of planning, a "participatory approach" is the most crucial aspect. Selected village youth, if properly motivated and trained, can become successful "bare-foot planners". Apart from resource mapping techniques, they should be taught "Rapid Rural Appraisal" techniques, which will help collect the essential data for planning at a minimum cost. Further, when planning is done in this manner, it will instil "local pride" among the youth and will lead to "commitment" on their part to implement the plan with vigour and enthusiasm.

Land, water and forest resources should become the major focus in the village level environmental appraisal. Land degradation and wasteful and improper use of land, water pollution, forest denudation and wasteland reclamation are essentially the problems to be dealt with. Therefore, in a village analysis, resource inventory of the land and water and their use will be the most crucial step. Based on such analysis, it is possible to formulate three types of projects :

(i) Projects designed to directly control the problems encountered on the land, water and forest resources fronts. These could be projects such as soil conservation, minor irrigation works and afforestation;

(ii) Projects for a sustainable agricultural development, designed to increase production and productivity of land without destroying it; and

(iii) Village forestry programmes.

The above projectization based on an analysis of land, water and forest resources constitutes only one component of village development. This is to be supplemented with at least two other stages in projectization.

The second will be projectization meant for providing agri-support services, such as provision of feeder roads, transportation and marketing facilities. The third set of projectization will be needed specifically to effect habitat improvements in the village, such as provision of sanitation, drainage and paved roads, and social infrastructures.

All the above three types of projects (land-based, agri-support and habitat improvement) put together will constitute the "Village Development Plan". The formulation of all these projects has to be based on a participatory approach, in which the various interest groups and other people's organizations must actively interface with the government functionaries, so that the resulting plan satisfies the people's needs and aspirations and their order of priorities. This plan is then broken into certain funding components. The first are those projects which can be executed primarily by the villagers themselves (if they can get organized on a self-reliant basis), which may be called "people's sector". The second are those projects, which can be implemented in the village on a commercial basis through bank loans, which may be called the "bank sector". The third are those projects which can be done with the funds provided by the Government and donor agencies, which may be called the "aided sector". In the last category are those projects which can be done by a combination of more than one of the foregoing methods, which together may be designated as the "combined sector". The village development plan formulated in this manner is then forwarded to the district to be scrutinized, further prioritized and selected and then incorporated into the district plan.[13] This methodology of village-based district planning is illustratively shown in Fig. 4.4.

Development from below based on the approach outlined here is quite a challenging task. It demands not merely sound technical

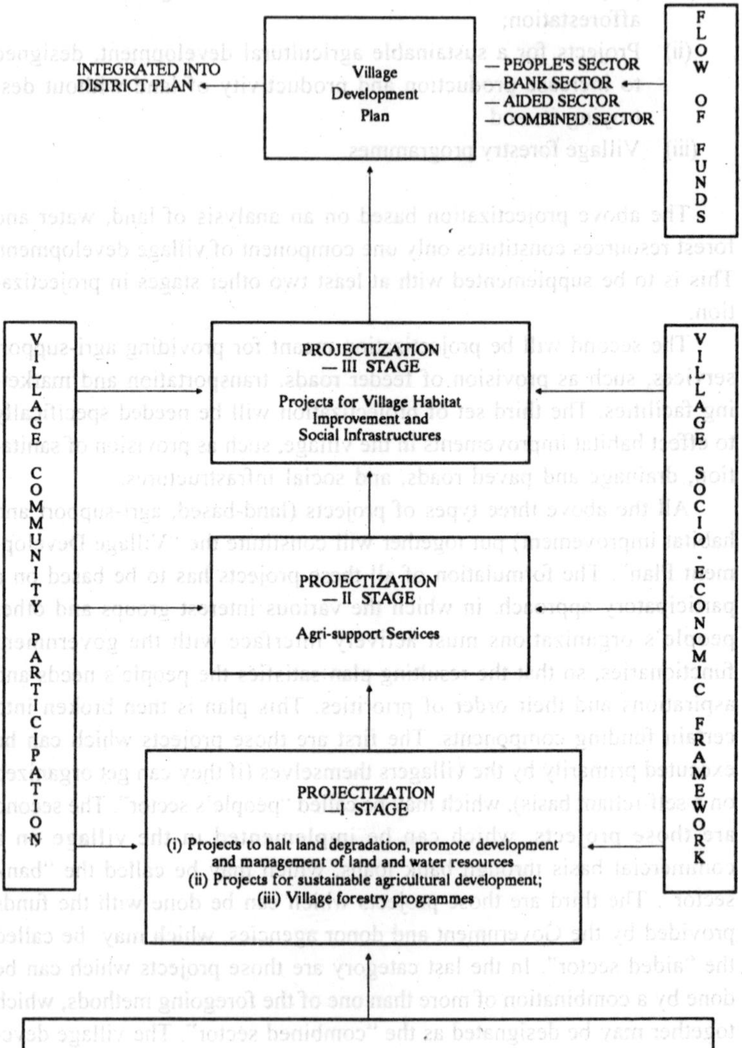

FIG. 4.4 : Planning from Below : An Approach.

knowledge of planning, but also social skills in organizing and mobilizing the local community for planning and resource management. The village-based decentralized planning practised in the district of Midnapore of West Bengal during 1985-86 may be considered as a somewhat modified attempt in this direction.[14]

In the Midnapore experiment, each Gram Panchayat was asked to prepare a "needs statement"—or the most acutely felt problems of the panchayat area (or *anchal*). Each Panchayat Samiti was to (a) prepare a series of maps of the block, outlining the existing facilities, resources and resource use; and (b) with the help of sub-assistant engineers available at the block level, prepare schemes (within a total ceiling of Rs. 1 crore) to meet the most acute problems of each Gram Panchayat (based on the "needs statement" collected by them). Each Panchayat Samiti was also to prepare a statement of the on-going and proposed programme of plan outlay of different departments/authorities in each block. These are then forwarded to the planning authorities at the district headquarters. Then three sub-committees at the district level—a technical sub-committee, an economic sub-committee and a committee headed by the Sabhadhipati—go into action. The technical sub-committee looked into the feasibility and estimated cost/benefits of each scheme. The economic sub-committee arranged all schemes in order of priorities, ensuring the required compatibility of and coordination between different schemes, as well as consistency with the "needs statements" prepared by the Gram Panchayats. The sub-committee headed by the Sabhadhipati himself finally decided the contours of the district plan. An academic institution, Indian Institute of Technology, Kharagpur, was closely associated with the project and assisted in the technical effort.

As may be seen, a major departure of the Midnapore experiment from the hypothetical model outlined earlier lies in the fact that the role of the Gram Panchayat in Midnapore district was merely confined to the preparation of a "statement of needs". On the other hand, in the hypothetical model, the local youth are "capacitated" to become "bare-foot planners" and thus a "nucleus planning capability" is created in the village, which is a permanent asset.

Another experiment called Kerala Experiment initiated by the Centre for Earth Science Studies (CESS) jointly with the Kerala State Land Us Board (KSLUB) and Integrated Rural Technology Centre (IRTC) is a closer approach to the hypothetical model[15] discussed earlier. It is an example of initiating a panchayat-level planning process, leading to sustainable development based on the participatory approach. The activities and linkages of the Panchayat Resource Mapping are depicted in Fig. 4.5. This programme envisaged :

(i) Integrated resource survey and mapping at the panchayat level by involving volunteers (trained for the purpose), panchayat functionaries and earth scientists. While landuse and asset mapping and monitoring of the depth of water table in the open wells are done by the volunteers, organized by the IRTC/ Voluntary Organization or Panchayat, the inferential details (landform, surface materials, geology, ground water, etc.) are documented by specialists;
(ii) Geo-environmental appraisal of every plot of land;
(iii) Blending traditional wisdom with appropriate technology for intervention plans;
(iv) Building up a Land and Water Resources Inventory and Monitoring Group at the Panchayat level to ensure people's continued participation; and
(v) Developing cadastral-based Information System and introducing Geographical Information System (GIS) for micro-level planning and development.

The role of the voluntary organization is to organize volunteers, who are trained by the specialists to undertake this job. A prolonged awareness campaign was arranged in the panchayats for initiating this programme. On the basis of resource-mapping and data collection, the following synthetic, thematic maps on appropriate scales were prepared showing :

1. Landform and erosion;
2. Surface material;
3. Thickness of the weathered mantle;
4. Potential area for water availability;
5. Landuse;
6. Assets; and
7. Environmental appraisal.

These maps were presented in the Panchayat and discussed in detail with the local people and panchayat functionaries. Following this, a socio-economic survey was conducted by volunteers, trained for the purpose.

Then an "Action Plan" was drawn up by collating the Environmental Appraisal Map with other socio-economic and attribute data and by fixing

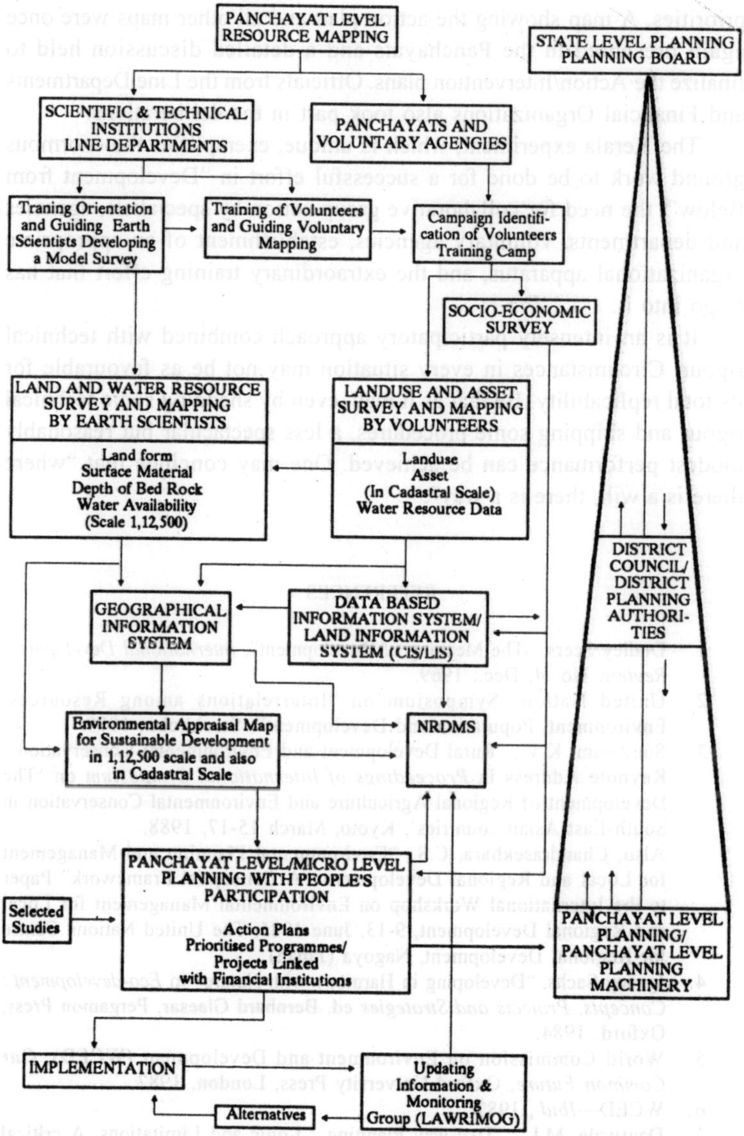

FIG. 4.5 : Panchayat Level Resource Mapping : Activities and Linkages.

Source : S. Chattopadhyay (1993).

priorities. A map showing the action plan and all other maps were once again presented in the Panchayats and a detailed discussion held to finalize the Action/Intervention plans. Officials from the Line Departments and Financial Organizations also took part in the deliberations.

The Kerala experiment, which is unique, exemplifies the enormous ground work to be done for a successful effort in "Development from Below", the need for collaborative group action by specialists, agencies and departments, voluntary agencies, establishment of an appropriate organizational apparatus, and the extraordinary training effort that has to go into it.

It is an intensely participatory approach combined with technical rigour. Circumstances in every situation may not be as favourable for its total replicability. Be that as it may, even by shedding some technical rigour and skipping some procedures, a less spectacular but reasonably modest performance can be achieved. One may conclude that "where there is a will, there is a way".

REFERENCES

1. Dudley Seers, "The Meaning of Development", *International Development Review*, No. 4, Dec., 1969.
2. United Nations Symposium on "Interrelations among Resources, Environment, Population and Development", Stockholm, 1979.
3. Sundaram, K.V., "Rural Development and Environmental Conservation", Keynote Address in *Proceedings of International Symposium* on 'The Development of Regional Agriculture and Environmental Conservation in South-East Asian countries', Kyoto, March 15-17, 1988.
   Also, Chandrasekhara, C.S., "Environmental Planning and Management for Local and Regional Development : A Conceptial Framework" Paper to the International Workshop on Environmental Management for Local and Regional Development, 9-13, June 1985, The United Nations Centre for Regional Development, Nagoya (Japan).
4. Ignacy Sachs, "Developing in Harmony with Nature" in *Eco-development : Concepts, Projects and Strategies* ed. Bernhard Glaesar, Pergamon Press, Oxford, 1984.
5. World Commission on Environment and Development (WCED), *Our Common Future*, Oxford University Press, London, 1987.
6. WCED—*Ibid.*, 1987.
7. Dantwala, M.L., "Two-way Planning : Logic and Limitations, A critical review of Indian experience", Paper to Expert Consultation on Multi-level Planning and the Two-way process in Agriculture and Rural Development Planning", FAO Regional Office for Asia and the Pacific, Bangkok, 1-4, February 1983.
8. Jodha, N.S., *et al*, *Sustainable Mountain Agriculture : Perspectives and Issues*, Vol. I, p. 35, Oxford and IBH Publishing Co., New Delhi, 1992.

9. Chakravarty, S., "Aspects of India's Development Strategies for 1980's", Training Division, Department of Personnel and Administrative Reforms, Govt. of India, New Delhi, July 1984.
10. The idea of "Growth" through technical mastery of nature has been central to Western culture for several centuries. As we push our technologies to produce more and more, we now recognize that both the direct devastation and the unforeseen consequences are becoming increasingly global in nature. Independent of the side-effects, people are increasingly recognizing that the products of new technologies do not necessarily increase happiness.
11. Richard B. Norgaard, "Sustainable Development : A Co-evolutionary view" in *FUTURES*, Vol. 20, No. 6, December 1988.
12. Swaminathan, M.S., "Small Farms and Sustainable Agriculture" in *Sustainable Agriculture in India*, Publication of the Indian Association for the Advancement of Science and Food and Agriculture Organisation, edited by Pradeep Chaturvedi, October 1990.
13. The selection of these projects and their inclusion in the district plan must be preceded by Environmental Impact Analysis (EIA), where necessary and relevant. Such analysis has to be conducted by the District Planning team.
14. Arun Ghosh, "Decentralized Planning : West Bengal Experience", *Economic and Political Weekly*, Bombay, March 26, 1988.
15. Chattopadhyay, Srikumar, "Sustainable Development : Concept and Application—Case of developing countries" in Amitava Mukherjee and V.K. Agnihotri (Eds.), *Environment and Development : Views from the East and the West*, Concept Publishing Company, New Delhi, 1993.
    Also, Centre for Earth Science Studies *et al*, Thiruvananthapuram, "Panchayat Level Resource Mapping—An approach paper" Dec. 1991.

5

DEVELOPMENT FROM WITHIN

As times and circumstances (political, social, economic, internal and external) change, development seeks new directions, orientations and emphases. It is now common knowledge that since the late 1960's and 1970's, the development paradigm has shifted its concerns from growth to redistribution and equity issues and more recently to the added dimensions of stability and sustainability. In keeping with these changing orientations and socio-political contexts of the countries, the nature and type of the planning process have also been changing from time to time. During the 1950's and 1960's, many developing countries of Asia and Africa which attained independence following decolonization adopted a "Top-down planning process" with central control over all government functions. But over time, the shifts in political priorities, new socio-economic realities and the burden as well as the more complex nature of governmental tasks compelled governments to decentralize at least some of their policy formulation and decision-making functions to their sub-national levels.

Since the late 1960's, concepts like "Development from Below" and "Bottom-up Planning" were advocated. Many countries have responded to these developments and adopted multi-level planning procedures with the involvement of people in varying degrees. In most countries, the mechanisms evolved for the purpose are funded by the Central Government and these institutions have over time taken on the characteristics of extensions of state departments without much independent authority or independent financial powers. In this process, the government has also spread its tentacles to all the development sectors of activity at all levels and thus brought the entire range of development functions into the fold of the public sector, including the ones that could be conveniently managed by the local communities. As a result, a "dependency syndrome" has grown, stifling the local and regional initiatives.

Now the national and global context has drastically changed. After decades of steady economic advance, in many countries, development is being thrown into reverse. The explanation is far from simple and it varies from country to country. In most cases, a complex, interlocking set of external, internal and environmental factors are involved. A UNICEF report points out, "For most of the countries of Africa, Latin America and the Caribbean, almost every economic signal points to the fact that development has been derailed. Per capita GNP has fallen, debt repayments have risen to a quarter or more of all export earnings, share in world trade has dropped and productivity of labour has declined." (UNICEF 1988)[1]

New Economic Reforms and their Implications for Local and Regional Development

In India too, our economy is now at the crossroads. Important changes are taking place. We have now moved in the direction of liberalization and market-oriented systems, following the macro-economic crisis in 1991 and the introduction of policy reforms entailing economic stabilization and structural adjustment. What this means, so far as sub-national affairs are concerned, is that the role of the state in local and regional development matters is getting reduced and that of the domain of responsibility of the people and local institutions is increasing. This means that the regional and local communities must now find their own development centres of gravity, in order to respond to the new policy changes that have emerged and which should be reflected in the nature and character of the planning and development responses. It means that the management of the social and economic processes at the regional and local levels, which affect rural production, income distribution, equity, social security and poverty alleviation must now be handled in an increasingly self-reliant manner. A set of new value systems, work ethic and a different development ethos should now evolve to spearhead, energize and mobilize society for the development and management of socio-economic transformation at the grassroot level. This calls for recognizing the discrete spatial levels below the somewhat broadly characterized "local" level. So far as our country is concerned, the local level comprises the following entities :[2]

— District;
— Block;

— Village;
— Household; and
— Individual.

The above hierarchy may further be broadly grouped into two categories.

(a) Area (aggregate of villages) Level : District and Block
(b) Grassroot Level : Village, Household and Individual.

If one were to relate the above categorization to development planning in action, one may hypothesize that at "A" level, where the line agencies have their outposts, the government initiated projects are predominating with a modicum of public participation. It has been the experience in many countries that such projects are often identified at higher administrative levels and people have little or no direct say in their formulation and implementation. Of course, the line agencies as well as individual projects may differ with regard to the degree of mobilizing the villagers' interest in local level planning, enticing their participation, soliciting their contribution and obtaining their back-up support. In any case, in most instances, they are able to elicit passive participation only, and as many evaluation studies have shown, this has been one of the main causes for the ineffectiveness of these projects.

In our view, the grassroots level is the village level, where individuals of the village community closely interact among themselves. At this level, people can initiate projects, which they themselves can handle with the active involvement of their own community and with little or no external support. In such projects, the local participation is genuine and complete. Such efforts will be self-organizing and self-sustaining. The operation and maintenance of such projects are also effectively looked after by the people, as there is a sense of ownership here.

Development from Below and from Within

The above distinction of the Area (group of villages) level and the Grassroots level, with their association with the two categories of initiators of development projects, provides us a new insight to characterize the type of planning that we may associate with each group. Thus, if we may call the type of planning at the "A" level as "Development From Below", we may characterize the one at the "B" level as "Development from Within" (DFW). One may argue that "Development from Within" is also a kind of development from below. But the distinction is subtle, in that it reflects the nature and intensity of the people's participation and relation to government role. Here the distinction that we have made between government-initiated projects and people-initiated projects is significant. It may also be noted that Development from Within is in the nature of "capillary effect", or "Trickle-up" effect, while Development from Below is government controlled, albeit with an element of public participation. In its essentials, DFW is somewhat akin to the concept of auto-centric development propounded by some German scientists.[3]

The reason why we draw this subtle distinction at this point of time is the fact that for our sub-national areas now, the days of "dependent development" must be deemed over. The Central Government, with its preoccupation with macro-economic problems of adjustment and loan repayment, can hardly be expected to find the time and resources to go all out for regional and local development. In this context, the regions (states) and local areas must assume the development responsibilities more and more for their respective areas and must be fully empowered in their tasks. In other words, decentralization, which we have been only loosely "talking about" all along, must now become a vibrant reality with a resurgence of self-organizing abilities by the people and the renewal of a sense of social efficacy. Such decentralization, combined with enhanced opportunities for people's participation, also implies making various institutional arrangements for effective regional and local development, a feat perhaps best done by restructuring and "re-inventing" traditional structures and institutions. This must also be accompanied by a major redistribution of authority, power and financial decentralization. The term "sub-national areas" imply a number of discrete spatial levels. The allocation of appropriate functions, powers and finances to each of these different levels and the development of self-governing institutions for them is a highly complex subject. We do not propose to go into these subject areas. Our limited purpose in this chapter is to discuss some key issues concerned with the concept of "Development from Within" (DFW), which we have cut out as the sphere of action of the people at the grassroots level.

Development from Within—Definition

Development From Within (DFW) has already been advocated as a "survival strategy" for Africa.[4] I have also elaborated the relevance of this concept to "Decentralization of Agricultural Sector Planning in Sub-

Saharan Africa".[5] But we don't limit the concept here to mere survival, which is only a temporary response to a crisis situation and, therefore, a short-term panacea; on the other hand, we see it as a "sustainable development strategy" for the developing countries. It is also not seen here as an isolated rural and local community development effort, but as a vital complement to the concepts of "Top-down development" and "Development from Below", which have already taken root in most developing countries to promote the social and economic development process. Thus DFW is meant to integrate the local initiatives into the larger planning and development efforts of the government.

Development from Within is not a new idea. The seed ideas of this concept are already contained in the teachings of Mahatma Gandhi in India and Julius Nyerere in Africa. There have been other luminaries also like Jaya Prakash Narain, Vinobha Bhave and Ariyaratne (Sri Lanka) who have expounded particular aspects of this philosophy. In broad terms, DFW may be defined as an endogenous development process by which people themselves assume the responsibility to manage their own resources, define their needs, goals and aspirations and make decisions affecting their well-being and sustainable development. Its fundamental aim is to unleash the inner and indigenous potentials of the local community as well as meet their inner urges and preferences for development through self-reliant approaches.

The basic idea of DFW is that development at the local community level has to be self-generated, self-organized and self-sustained. The people of a local community, instead of "spinning their wheels" in seeking action from the central and state bureaucracies or distant governments, must practise self-help.[6] They must apply their resources to productive activity, as opposed to "rent-seeking". The ideas on development must spring from within and must get concretized through local action.

Development from Within would make it possible for local and regional communities to raise more resources for themselves, to assert their own value systems, to have confidence in their own ingenuity and skills and to be less dependent on external agencies for their development. This may sound like autopia, but in the context of the current crisis in macro-economic management, there seems to be no way out excepting to seriously adopt it as the dominant methodology.

If DFW is a concept worthy of practice, how can we go about it? This is a vital question. The answer is not simple, for there are no fixed or precise methodologies or rigid rules for operationalizing it. It is not a normative concept, as the actors here are the individual citizens, who have to come together of their own volition to practise it. In this context, we may only state some general principles by way of guidelines, but may not be able to provide any specific designs.

Localism in Scope and Content

DFW is "localism" in action. What are the kinds of activities which can be promoted through a strategy of DFW? As Prof. Dantwala observes, "Both the scope and content of planning shrinks at each successive lower level of planning."[7] If this is so, at the bottommost level that we are considering, the residuary development functions will be quite limited.

This is not, however, to be seen as a constraint because the local functions that can be performed at this level are, in any case, circumscribed by the technical capabilities of the local people. Normally, the functions that may be performed at this level should be labour intensive using local resources and local know-how, either totally without the assistance of any external aid or with low external input. DFW concretely means using local decisions, local creativity, local raw materials, land, labour and capital for those forms of production that permit local grassroots initiative and innovation and that yields results compatible with local conditions, tastes and culture. There are quite a number of such activities relevant in this context. Broadly the areas where DFW as a strategy and planning process can make a significant contribution to local development are :

- Sustainable agricultural development;
- Natural resource conservation and management;
- Forestry development and environmental protection;
- Social provision :
  - Education
  - Health
  - Rural sanitation
  - Community welfare
- Irrigation and water supply;
- Maintenance of common property resources; and
- Development of renewable energy resources.

More specifically, some activities which fall under the above broad rubric and can lend themselves for a self-reliant approach are :

— Organic farming and manure production (mulching and use of compost);
— Village cleanliness, including garbage removal and drainage;
— Maintenance of village roads, including paving them with bricks;
— Revival of village industries and crafts;
— Education in health and hygiene;
— Primary education;
— Drinking water supply;
— Farm forestry/social forestry;
— Establishment and management of grain golas;
— Construction and maintenance of foot-bridges;
— Construction and maintenance of micro-hydel projects;
— Development of biogas, solar energy and wind energy;
— Waste utilization (bagasse, sawdust, cotton stalks, rice husk, manure);
— Support to informal production units (not only crafts and manufacturing, but also services and trade);
— Revival/maintenance of traditional distribution systems (e.g. periodic markets);
— Protective measures needing group action which increase crop yields; (wind breaks, shade trees, anti-erostive measures, optimization of the tree cover on crop land, etc.).
— Community fodder banks;
— Collection and conservation of run-off water;
— Revival of relevant autochthonous (indigenous) solutions in the agro-ecological and socio-economic spheres;
— Establishment and management of credit institutions like "Grameen Banks" or other indigenous credit arrangements;
— Renovation of village tanks and other water bodies;
— Reclamation of saline-alkali soils;
— Construction and maintenance of small irrigation structures;
— Environmental protection;
— Watershed rehabilitation;
— Construction and maintenance of intra-village and inter-village roads;
— Self-help housing schemes;
— Uplift of the peasantry through cooperative efforts; (transformation of the "small peasant" into a "market-oriented farmer").[8]

— Tribal welfare;
— Women's uplift;
— Human Resource Development.

The above list, formidable in itself in the array of activities in the realm of group action, is only indicative and not exhaustive. Broadly, they fall in the spheres of production, consumption and nature conservation. They constitute a set of some measures to unleash a process of development of production forces with the objective of better satisfying the basic needs of the community and achieving sustainable development. They constitute generally the action areas for DFW.

Development from Within : Key Components

The key components of a concept of DFW are the following :

— Public participation;
— Decentralization and empowerment;
— Self-reliance;
— Self-management through collective voluntary action; and
— Polycentric institutional development.

Some salient features of these components are dealt with in the sequel.

Public Participation

Genuine public participation, where people are at the centre of the development activity, is the hallmark of DFW. But achieving successful public participation in local level development is no easy task. It must emerge from repeated experimentations and trial-and-error. It is inherently an evolutionary process. Activities must proceed from a step-by-step process, allowing for a continuous cycle of learning, observing and doing. It is a progression from passivity to activity and trying to cope with the realities in the human society.

Group action is the basis of DFW. Collective unified action is easier, if the society is homogeneous. However, such homogeneous structures are difficult to come by. Most rural communities are characterized by factions with the clients of local patrons, followers of local leaders, associates of gangs, or members of both formal and informal groups, each pulling in different directions and striving hard to maximize their particular interests. In this situation, a deep understanding of group dynamics and social engineering skills is called for, when seeking to bring them together for collective action.

Decentralization and Empowerment

Decentralization and empowerment constitute the fundamental base on which concepts like "Development from Below" and "Development from Within" can thrive and be operationalized. It has been often emphasized by many intellectuals that if India's democratic polity has to be anchored in truly self-governing units at the level of Panchayats, then there has to be an effective devolution of developmental functions and governmental authority to the different tiers of the Panchayati Raj institutions. With the coming into effect of a recent constitutional amendment, the legislative and executive action of the state legislatures and governments as regards the formation, structure, composition, powers and functions, periodicity of elections and such matters regarding panchayats have been mandated. The states are now expected to bring these bodies into existence within the stipulated one year and enable them to function as effective units of self-government as well as for local level planning and development. The most critical aspect at this juncture is the effective devolution of functions and powers and the devolution of financial powers and resources to the Panchayati Raj institutions in tandem with the functions and responsibilities entrusted to them. Simultaneously, the bureaucratic system must be restructured so that the government functionaries, elected or appointed, become accountable to the people whom they are required to serve. These are essential prerequisites, not merely for establishing a strong Panchayati Raj system, but also for stimulating local initiatives for DFW. Thus, the present seems to be the politically right time to plug in the concept of DFW. One may reasonably hope that the strengthened Panchayati Raj institutions will soon be in place and lend active support to this concept, by providing moral support as well as policy guidance and catalytic stimuli.

Self-reliance

Self-reliance is another key component of the strategy of DFW. Self-reliance, however, only means counting on one's own resources as much as possible and does not mean autarky or total self-sufficiency. It implies the capacity for autonomous decision-making and selective control over external relations. Gandhi may be seen as one of the foremost ideologists and practitioners of self-reliance. According to him, self-reliance starts with the individual (everyone must be his own scavenger), but finds its fullest expression at the level of the "Village Swaraj", "independent for its own vital wants and yet interdependent for many others in which dependence is a necessity".[9] Self-reliance makes possible the efficient and fuller use of local factors and local culture, values and traditions. It stimulates creativity and innovations. Through self-reliance, important positive externalities are internalized. The principal ingredients of a self-reliant approach to development are :[10]

(1) Creating a long-term economic, social and political viability of rural communities. This is done by delineating an appropriate unit consisting of a federation of villages and devolving substantial and effective power to a democratically constituted level of local governance in which the rural poor and the neglected groups will have their due representation.

(2) Providing expanding opportunities for productive work in rural areas, especially for young people and for women, including extractive and processing industries of the rural economy, particularly through small-scale industrial development. The intention is to increase rural incomes by expanding opportunities for productive employment in non-agricultural sectors.

(3) Ensuring continued upgrading and improvement of the natural environment in the following ways :

    (a) Improving basic ecological conditions, including the management of renewable (flow) resources, such as forests and groundwater supplies, the protection of watersheds from erosion and the conservation of common pasture lands;

    (b) Improving agricultural technology including the construction and maintenance of small-scale irrigation systems and appropriate land preparation, such as terracing, land consolidation, etc.

    (e) Improving energy supply including not only the sustained yield management of existing forests and reforestation of denuded areas, but also the use of biogas and solar energy.

(d) Improving the human environment, a comprehensive term that includes not only environmental sanitation, pest control and flood control but also potable water supply and drainage systems, housing, community facilities (assembly hall, sports fields, nurseries for small children, etc.) and physical access facilities (road, radio, television and telecommunication facilities).

(4) Providing for the satisfaction of locally determined basic needs. This signifies an ordering of priorities and identifying certain target groups in order to make them productive by (a) the direct distribution of basic goods and services; (b) raising their real incomes to a level at which they can afford to meet their basic needs; and (c) raising their skills through human resource development efforts. Thus the provision of basic needs is regarded as a moral and reciprocal entitlement.
(5) Achieving balanced rural-urban development;
(6) Establishing linkages with various organizations, both above and below.
(7) Encouraging "Group Action" by establishing healthy cooperative structures to manage production activities and by promoting the organization of functional groups like Farmers' Association, Farm-labour Syndicates, User Groups, Women's Groups, Cooperatives, Youth Organizations, etc.

Self-management through Collective Voluntary Action

Efficient management is a basic prerequisite for all activities. In the context of DFW, what is implied is self-management through collective voluntary action. The emphasis of this form of participation is on developing an overall capability of a community to sustain itself in the present and in the future. Such collective, voluntary, bottom-up and self-management at the grassroot level demands self-discipline or self-rule buttressed by peer pressure. It implies collective leadership and division of responsibilities by the creation of diverse functional groups.

Polycentric Institutional Development

No community is monolithic. It is always differentiated into groups with varying common interests. In this context, what we need are polycentric institutional arrangements for binding, consolidating and unifying the groups and for further promoting their group interests. Such groups will be, in addition to the democratically decentralized institutional structures, such as the Panchayati Raj institutions, which are general-purpose authorities performing the various functions devolved on them. The functional groups that we consider as necessary for operationalizing DFW will be polycentric or non-central institutions, which perform circumscribed functions among numerous jurisdictions, with their own independent rule-making and rule-enforcing authority. They are seen as instruments for collective action in developing and maintaining, for instance, the common property resources and providing various public facilities. They can also be receiving mechanisms, which interact with the government's delivery system and distributing the benefits to the appropriate target groups. They can also be special-purpose groups that provide for, operate and maintain certain small infrastructures like roads, water supply, energy generation, community buildings and irrigation systems. In this way, they serve as mechanisms through which a sustainable infrastructure can be developed. All these collective effort mechanisms need not be established anew. Some of them at least can be developed around existing traditional institutions, which can operate within a broader framework of local self-government. Thus for organizing DFW, the indigenous institutions must be seen as an important source of social capital. In the past, however, we have, in many cases, successfully eliminated this social capital and have created a substantial lacuna in effective local organization.

What we have now to do in the context of rendering DFW operational is to bring about a resurgence of these traditional institutional structures as a vehicle for collective action. Where indigenous informal groups or institutions are still working effectively, it is important to study their design principles and working procedures, as such knowledge will be transferable. In matters of economic and social development at the grassroots level, money is no doubt important; but of greater importance as capital are the organizational ingenuity of a social community and the cooperative work that it can mobilize. Apart from these traditional institutions, wherever necessary, the creation of user groups or interest groups with sufficient autonomy must also be promoted as part of the organizational structure for DFW. Such groups will have a strong, long-term impact, particularly in sustaining small-scale infrastructures. These user/interest groups may be spontaneous responses of the local communities for managing their own affairs or created and supported by governments or agencies for specific projects. In any case, they should be formally recognized and given the right to mobilize their own resources and act independently. Thus, enabling the potential beneficiaries of infrastructure and other types of public goods to organize themselves into polycentric limited-purpose functional groups, with circumscribed governmental authority, should be the topmost priority in the developmental agenda for DFW.

Some studies on user or interest groups have clearly demonstrated that when the users realize that the costs of the operation and maintenance of the projects have to be borne by themselves, who are the beneficiaries, they become highly motivated and try to keep the costs as low as possible and monitor the activities of producers to avoid corrupt practices. In countries like Nepal, where developmental resources are very scarce, the ideas of user or interest groups and self-management enterprises have gone such a long way that even some large-scale voluntary institutional arrangements have come into existence and are functioning successfully. The classic example is the *Chhatis Mauja* (thirty-six villages)—a large-scale, gravity-flow farmer-managed irrigation system, irrigating almost 3,500 hectares of land farmed by approximately 25,000 people in 54 villages.[11]

Now, many donor agencies which are investing in the financing and construction of infrastructure projects are doing so, only when there is firm evidence that those, who are supposed to benefit from a facility, make a firm commitment to maintain that facility over time and have the organizational and financial capabilities to do so. Undoubtedly, the idea of user or interest groups has great potential for the developing countries and the challenges are great. The policy implications here for DFW are quite clear : (a) that we must encourage the beneficiaries into forming "Primary Local Units" or "Provision Units" that can mobilize resources to acquire ownership of small-scale infrastructure over time and assume full responsibility for operation and maintenance, and (b) that we must invest in general institutional facilities that enhance the capabilities of such primary local units. These arrangements may be viewed as a form of privatisation of public services, in other words, market arrangements that have become necessary and must be encouraged by local governments. Normally, when groups of beneficiaries organize to provide a joint benefit by assuming mutual obligations for resource mobilization for joint decision-making, some type of governing authority must be created to ensure that these mutual obligations are met and suitable working rules must be framed.

It is, however, difficult to specify a set of common principles that should guide the formation and working of the organization of primary local units of collective action. For these, there can be no single institutional arrangement. Perhaps, one should study a number of such organizations that are currently successfully operating in the country and draw relevant inferences from them and formulate principles. This is a task for the, Central and State governments in India. "Successful institutional arrangements are usually complex rather than simple and that polycentric institutions that perform relatively well for some types of rural infrastructures have not been successfully fitted into a simple typology".[12] It is not out of place to mention here that some NGOs have applied scientific knowledge to create systems that stay. These deserve to be carefully analyzed for being put to practice. The NGOs which have performed well in this field can function as catalysts to put many grassroot local projects on the ground and make them work productively.

The polycentric institutions that we are talking about here can be of three kinds :

— Indigenous institutions which have proved highly successful over time;
— "User group organizations" sponsored by local and other governments; and
— Organizations like farmer organizations which are self-orga-nized and self-governed.

Indigenous management systems have been particularly recognized to be effective for forest protection and management and for natural resource conservation. Experience in countries like Nepal has shown that such organizations are effective, when operated within the local institutional context. In Nepal, Furer-Haimendorf (1964)[13] noted among the Sherpas of the Khumbu region, the presence of "shingo naua", or forest guards as a part of village organization "in charge of the preservation of protected forests". In many countries, "local forest committees" exist. The idea that the responsibility of using natural resources as well as sustaining them should fall on the same people has now gained widespread recognition. Users and others, who have rights to participate in decision-making about the protection and management of natural resources, should be encouraged and enabled to do so; McNeely and Pitt[14] have argued in favour of adding cultural and social dimensions to environmental planning and management for "conservation from below".

It is noted that cultural norms and values, including religious beliefs, act as control mechanisms, thereby aiding the natural resources protection and management systems.

DFW as a Planning Tool for Sustainable Development

Sustainable development requires local action. The question of how to achieve sustained local action, therefore, becomes crucial for sustainable development efforts. DFW can make a substantial contribution in this area. A scientific approach to deal with the problem is to prepare an indicative micro-level plan at the village level (Eco Development Plan), which can distinguish between the schemes emerging from the village local authority and implemented by the various sectoral agencies and those that are undertaken by the people themselves through polycentric self-management institutions that we mentioned above. The basic elements of such a plan involving active community participation are :

(i) Resource inventory (land, water, biomass); assessment of the extent of resource degradation and optimal resource use.
(ii) Projectization :

   (a) Class I—Projects to halt resource degradation and promote farm development; projects for sustainable agricultural development; village forestry programmes; and programmes for income and employment generation.
   (b) Class II—Projects for Agri-Support Services.
   (c) Class III—Projects for village habitat improvement and provision of social infrastructure.

(iii) Preparation of the Village Ecodevelopment Plan distinguishing between the projects that could fall under "Development from Below" and "Development from Within" and those under different funding arrangements.

This is shown in Fig. 4.4. An innovative project on "Micro level resource survey with people's participation" is currently under way in Kerala State. It is being undertaken by the Centre for Earth Science Studies in collaboration with the Kerala State Land Use Board and other agencies and through the active support of NGOs.[15] Although starting with integrated resources survey and mapping at the panchayat level, it is expected later to lead to a District Development Plan, hope-fully incorporating all the steps and procedures indicated in Fig. 4.4. The Kerala experiment is likely to offer valuable lessons for DFW. Successful DFW by a community would imply : (a) that the community is in full control of the resources in the local area; (b) that it adopts correct resource use; (c) that it avails of the appropriate technology that it can handle; and (d) that it is able to distribute the fruits of development among all members of its community in an equitable manner. All these are implied in the Village Ecodevelopment Plan.

Role of Governments, NGOs and Donor Agencies

DFW does not mean that it can be initiated and sustained totally independent of government support. In fact, government has a great facilitating role to play in this context. It may be in the following directions :

(i) Developing suitable methodologies and guidelines;
(ii) Facilitating group formation and action, establishing codes of conduct for groups and recognizing them as receiving mechanisms for various forms of assistance. (Support to organization development);
(iii) Providing some financial support in the form of seed money or grants; and
(iv) Imparting training on techniques and knowledge for skill development appropriate to the local level and relevant to the context in which people will be organizing their activities.

It should be clearly understood that the government's role is essentially a catalytic one, of stimulating the people to initiate development actions according to their own collectively perceived priorities, aimed at self-reliance. Assuming a too interventionist role will undermine the spontaneous and voluntary processes involved in DFW and should be avoided. What has been said about the role of government applies equally to NGO's and donor agencies, who may be involved in stimulating community efforts at the grassroot level.

Summing Up

To pull together a diffused body of ideas and thoughts presented above, DFW is not a mere abstract idea or philosophical postulate or technical Jargon. It is an aspect of bottom-up strategy, calling for mass action at the local level. It has to be built around the local base, which includes not only local people, but also traditional leaders and indigenous institutions. The basis of this approach is self-reliance. This spirit of self-reliance has to suffuse and permeate, not only the economy as a whole, but all the people collectively and individually. It implies local action in multiple aspects, which works outwards from oneself in a set of "oceanic circles" as Gandhi said. It embraces a lot of Gandhian ideas and programmes. Verily, it is bringing back Gandhi in a big way into local development and adapting his ideas to suit our modern value systems. All these imply far-reaching changes calling for experimentation with ideas, self-help, diligence and cooperation among the people, as well as upgrading the skills of the local people and adoption of new technologies. Human resource development in a big way must, therefore, follow, if DFW is to be successfully operationalized.

According to Peter Oakley *et al*, "it is the Indian subcontinent which has the richest vein of innovative approaches".[16] Here we have many experiments on self-reliant approaches to development, thanks to the dedicated work of a few NGOs and some Gandhian institutions. Their methodological innovations still await detailed study. Methodologies of qualitative processes are often not readily apparent and need a number of key reference points before they become visible. It is necessary to analyze the practice, review the ideas carefully and to see what practical methodologies can emerge from them. Giving methodology a shape and form and preparing guidelines is a big task and must be taken up by the Central and State Governments, by setting up competent study/working groups. The imperatives at this juncture are clear. The urgency is great. There is not much time left for dithering and delaying action.

REFERENCES

1. UNICEF (1988) 'The state of the world's children' UNICEF Publications, New York.
2. In some states of the country, a cluster of villages below the block level designated as the "Mandal" has also been recognized as a planning level.
3. They are D. Senghass and H. Flsenhans, quoted in "Autocentric Development in Peripheral Rural Regions through a strategy of locally integrated economic circuits–Theory and methodology" by Theo Rauch and Axel Redder in *Applied Geography and Development*, Vol. 35, Institute for Scientific Cooperation, Tubingen, 1990.
4. Fraser Taylor, D.R. and Fiona Mackenzie (Ed.), *Development from Within–Survival in Rural Africa*, Routledge, London, 1992.
5. Sundaram, K.V., "Decentralization of Agricultural Sector Planning in Sub-Saharan Africa," F.A.O./UN, Rome, 1993.

6. *See*, "Self-Reliance–A Strategy for Development" by Johan Galtung *et al*, Bogle L'overture Publications Ltd., London, 1980.
7. Dantwala, M.L., "Two-way Planning–Logic and Limitation, A critical review of Indian experience" in FAO document "Expert Consultation on Multilevel Planning and the Two-way process in Agriculture and Rural Development Planning", Bangkok, 1-4 Feb. 1983.
8. Raanan Weitz, *From Peasant to Farmer–A revolutionary strategy for development*, Columbia University Press, New York, 1971.
9. Gandhi, M.K., *Rebuilding our Villages*, Ahmedabad, Navajivan Publishing House, 1958, p.5.
10. Sundaram, K.V., "An alternative Rural Development Strategy : The Self-reliant Approach based on the Gandhian concepts and principles" (Mimeographed).
11. Documented in "Institutional Incentives and sustainable Development—Infrastructure Policies in Perspective" by Elinor Ostrom, Larry Schoeder and Susanne Wynne, Westview Press, Oxford, 1993.
12. Elinor Ostram *et al, Ibid.*
13. Furer-Haimendorf, C-Von, *Sherpas of Nepal : Buddhist Highlanders*, John Murray, London, 1964.
14. McNeely, J.A. and D. Pitt, "Culture : The Missing Element in Conservation and Development" in McNeely and Pitt (Eds.), *Culture and Conservation : The Human Dimension of Environmental Planning*, pp. 1-10. Croom Helm, London, 1985.
15. *See* Centre for Earth Science Studies, "Panchayat Level Resource Mapping—An Approach Paper", Trivandrum, December 1991.
16. Peter Oakley *et al*, "Projects with People–the Practice of Participation in rural development", I.L.O., Geneva, 1991.

6

CHEMISTRY OF MICRO-LEVEL DEVELOPMENT

Decentralized development is a complex phenomenon. There is a chemistry too in it. The word chemistry has two meanings : (i) composition, properties and reactions of substances, and (ii) nature and effects of any complex phenomenon. The latter meaning is relevant to our discussion here. In any close analysis, decentralized development will consist of the following components or ingredients at any spatial level.

(i) Government's delivery systems and various forms of support and assistance (financial, technical and organizational) provided by it;
(ii) Knowledge (scientific and technical);
(iii) Technology (appropriate to the situation); and
(iv) Community cooperation and public participation.

Among these, (i) is a technocratic component, (ii) and (iii) are academic components, and (iv) is a democratic component. In other words, development is intelligently putting together or wisely applying the above "ingredients" in suitable combinations, using appropriate techniques and tools. This combination or Mix may be called TAD Mix. This stands for Technocratic, Academic and Democratic Mix. If the TAD Mix is satisfactory or good, the resulting development will be conducive to success. This is, however, to state the hypothesis in a rather simplistic fashion. In the world of reality, when one seeks to bring together these various ingredients, the reaction that will follow may take different unpredictable turns, as many impeding factors may also come into play. When this happens, it would be necessary to apply appropriate countervailing forces or correctives, to keep the unfavourable reactions under check. This is somewhat analogous to what the scientist does in his chemistry laboratory in his experiments with the reactions of substances.

In the experiments in chemistry, a "catalyst" is used to accelerate "reactions", as a key element. In the world of development too, a catalyst can perform miracles. When we analyze some success stories in development, we also come to the conclusion that at the bottom of a successful experiment, there has been some "catalyst" as the key promoter. This catalyst has always been a human factor. Take any example of a successful development story. In the Comilla model of rural development[1] in Bangladesh, it was Akther Hameed Khan, a highly dedicated administrator turned teacher and social scientist, who played the role of a catalyst. In Tachai in China, where the highest possible yields were obtained with hard work and scientific approach to farming, it was Mao's clarion call for "Learning from Tachai" that moved the masses.[2] The famous Seamaul Undong movement in South Korea[3] was initiated through the dedication of the late President Park Chung Hee and grew into a successful experiment in participatory development. The extraordinary quality of leadership and dedication of an ordinary villager with no formal education, Muhammad Yasin, triggered off the cooperative movement in Bangladesh.[4] In the Sukhomajri experience in India,[5] it was the dedication of a scientist, P.R. Mishra, which brought about the transformation of a village, benefiting the poorest of the poor, arresting ecological degradation in the uplands and reducing the tremendous sedimentation in a lake in Chandigarh (Punjab). There have been many such instances of isolated success stories with their numerous variations all over the world, where a combination of effective leadership, with people's participation and application of science and technology, as well as governmental response, had led to mixed results. It is indeed difficult to replicate such success stories. Nor is it possible to state with precision, from their experiences, what is the best possible combination for success. Nevertheless, they provide some valuable clues in our search for more meaningful development alternatives; at least they indicate some partial solution to problems of local development. Success stories are, therefore, worthy of a critical examination, to bring out those potentially applicable lessons, which could be tried in other situations.

In this chapter, we propose to present a critical examination of a success story of local development in a tiny village called "Kundrakudi" Tamil Nadu.[6] This area study has been included in this volume, because it was studied and documented by this author. It is a good illustration of the Technocratic, Academic and Democratic (TAD) Mix that did help pave the way to a successful development story.

Kundrakudi—A Case Study

Background and Genesis

Kundrakudi is a typical South Indian village in a drought-prone part of the Pasumpon Muthuramalingam district in Tamil Nadu. It is a medium-sized village with a population of about 3,000 (450 families) and an area of about 820 hectares. Nearly 200 hectares of land are cultivated. Forests account for 150 hectares. The remaining 58 per cent of the area consists of cultivable waste land and *poramboke* land. Bulk of the villagers are agriculturists and there are nearly 514 land owners, a majority of whom (89 per cent) belong to the category of small and marginal farmers. The main source of irrigation is tanks and there are 19 such tanks providing irrigation facilities to about one-fifth of the cultivated area. Bore wells supplement the irrigation facilities. One hundred forty-eight hectares are classified as wetland and 345 fall under dry land. The village is covered by a centrally sponsored scheme called the Drought Prone Area Programme (DPAP). The nearest town is Karaikudi, about 17 km. from the village. A National Scientific Organization, called "The Central Electro-Chemical Research Institute" (CECRI), is located in this town.

Temples and holy tanks are part of a typical South Indian village and Kundrakudi is no exception. The village is also the seat of a 500-year-old religious institution called "Thiruvannamalai Adheenam Kundrakudi Mutt." The main aim of this Adheenam is to preach and inculcate the Saiva Sidhanta philosophy of the Hindu religion among the people.

The Mutt is presently headed by His Holiness Srilasri Deivasigamani Arunachala Desiga Paramcharya Swamigal (popularly known as Thavathiru Kundrakudi Adigalar). Sri Adigalar is a great scholar and a powerful orator, and above all a religious reformer with progressive views. He is a follower of Gandhi, an admirer of socialism and a staunch supporter of the cooperative movement.

Sri Adigalar was deeply moved by the poverty and unemployment among the people living in Kundrakudi, and the surrounding villages. He realized that preaching spiritualism to semi-starving citizens would not help propagate the objectives of the religious institution, of which he was the head. He wanted the village to be self-sufficient at least in foodgrains and other essential items. He became convinced that organizing the villagers for collective self-reliance and utilizing the local natural resources of the area in the most optimal manner constituted the essential strategy of rural development. In order to give shape to these ideas, he launched a Village Planning Forum (VPF) in Kundrakudi on 2nd October, 1977, birthday of Gandhi. The main objective of the Village Planning Forum, as envisaged by him, was the achievement of self-sufficiency and eradication of unemployment in the village. In this task, he decided to bring together the three essential actors in the development process, viz. (1) State Government, (2) financiers (represented by the State Bank of India) and (3) a third-party planner represented by the scientists of CECRI for mutual interaction/cooperation in the development process. The idea was to primarily revolve around the government development programmes, modify them according to local requirements and to facilitate their successful implementation by bringing about access to capital (provided through the commercial banks) and the scientific inputs and knowhow (provided by CECRI).

The main aims of the Village Planning Forum, as stated in its constitution, are quite comprehensive, consisting of some 15 items as follows :

1. To uplift the economically weaker sections of the society.
2. To improve the skills of the local artisans.
3. To impart training to the local people for self-employment.
4. To train the local people for leadership through formation of cooperative society, task assignment, participation in discussions, etc.
5. To utilize the available resources in the village for development.
6. To improve the awareness of villagers and to educate them in better health and family welfare measures, sanitation and clean environment.
7. To introduce modern methods of agriculture.
8. To encourage cooperative movements and to train villagers for sheltering the different functions in cooperative societies.
9. To improve irrigation facilities.
10. To improve cattle wealth.
11. To bring the entire wasteland under cultivation.
12. To create an atmosphere conducive to formation of an integrated society free from race, religion and caste differences.
13. To take science and technology to the villages.
14. To improve the academic performance of students in villages.

15. To make the villages self-sufficient in the production of paddy, vegetables, milk, meat and fish.

The Planning Forum is broad-based in composition, with different interests represented in it. Sri Adigalar is the coordinator of the Planning Forum. The interests represented are :

1. Selected village citizens (including women).
2. Presidents, Vice-Presidents and Secretaries of the various co-operative societies.
3. Local industrial interests.
4. Representatives of commercial and cooperative banks.
5. Panchayat Union officials.
6. Scientists from CECRI, Karaikudi.
7. Officials of Agricultural Department.
8. Officials of Animal Husbandry Department.
9. Official of Agricultural Engineering Department.
10. Officials of Education Department.
11. Officials of Electricity Board.
12. General Manager of District Industries Centre, Ramnad.
13. Officials of Khadi and Village Industries.
14. Village officials.

Institutional Arrangements and Planning Process

The Village Planning Forum (VPF) is not a formally constituted organization, such as a registered society, functioning under specified bye-laws and rules. It is quite an informal type of organization, functioning with considerable flexibility, with its own code of conduct and procedures for functioning. On every issue discussed in the forum, "consensus" seems to govern the mode of decision-making. It meets once in a month (every fourth Saturday) to make an assessment of the progress on various decisions taken in its previous meeting and to decide on the follow-up actions.

For the management of development schemes, the VPF has successfully adopted the cooperative form of organization. A number of projects, in and around Kundrakudi village, sponsored by the VPF are run on cooperative lines. The Cooperative Societies Act of Tamil Nadu State governs the functioning of these institutions.

The Kundrakudi VPF formulated the First Five Year Plan, covering the period 1977-82, for the two villages Kundrakudi and Nemam. The monthly meeting of the Forum is an important one in which decisions are taken regarding development schemes that may be taken up in the village. The approach is to assess the potentials for development in various sectors, such as agriculture, animal husbandry, village and small industries, irrigation, etc. Small working groups set up by the VPF go into the aspects of development potential and feasibility in each sector. The Government officials present in the meeting explain to the villagers the various development schemes included in the Government Plans. Villagers, in turn, express their views and the scope for implementing the schemes in selected pockets. Wherever, financial institutions have a role to play, the representatives of the financial institutions (nationalized and cooperative banks) explain the various credit-linked schemes implemented by them and express their opinion as to the feasibility of funding any particular scheme mooted by the VPF. The scientists of CECRI also take active part in the VPF meetings and they explain to the members the potential for development in various sectors of activity and the scientific way of formulating relevant projects. Thus the project ideas get a concrete shape in the VPF meetings. These ideas are then translated into location-specific schemes, indicating the financial requirements, the sources of funding, the organizational arrangements, etc. The monthly meetings of the Planning Forum also provide an opportunity to review the achievements in the previous month under various sectors of development and to decide on the necessary correctives and follow up action, wherever there are slippages. The local perception of problems, as articulated by the villagers, the technical feasibility for development as assessed by the government functionaries of technical departments and the follow-up actions pursued from time to time, helps in the smooth and successful implementation of the schemes. The personal charisma and influence of Shri Adigalar is an important factor in guiding and conducting the deliberations of the meetings of the VPF. Generally, the decisions of the Forum are accepted by all the villagers. The active participation of the villagers, some of whom are unlettered, is an important feature in the activities of the VPF. In the first Five Year Plan, the VPF had set a target of improving the productivity of paddy from 1 tonne to 2 tonnes per acre, through adoption of scientific methods of cultivation. Similarly, they had taken definite decision to improve irrigation facilities through digging of community wells and utilizing the cultivable wasteland in the village. A notable feature of the VPF is its role in channelizing the benefits of Government development programmes to the deserving beneficiaries, without any leakage. Whether it is a community well under DPAP, or distribution of milch cattle or a sheep unit under the Integrated Rural Development Programme (IRDP), the full benefits of the schemes (loan and subsidy) have reached the target groups, for whom the schemes are intended.

Kundrakudi's experience shows the nature and dimension of the development administration problem in the rural areas. In the first place, the choice of the peasants below the poverty line to be helped is not an easy task. It requires a careful survey of the village and considerable verification of facts. When this is done by a body of villagers themselves with no secrecy behind it, then no mistakes are made and no undue favours shown to anyone in particular. But more important than this is the fact that officials entrusted with the administration of any rural development scheme do their job willingly and without succumbing to pressures. This aspect of the problem has been very deftly handled by the VPF. The fact that whoever has been posted to the Kundrakudi area (irrespective of his past) has served his term with a clean record which speaks volumes for the efficacy of the local leadership provided by the VPF in Kundrakudi. The simple fact is that the development objectives cannot be reached or targets hit, unless the way it is to be done is clearly chalked out and followed up through the efficient use of appropriate instruments. Indeed, the role of the Village Planning Forum in Kundrakudi must be understood in the light of these observations.

The VPF was keenly aware of the fact that merely the broadening of economic opportunities alone would not make it possible to bring about the development of the poorer sections of community. It is necessary to find the combinations of other opportunities that would enable different groups among the poor to rise above the poverty line. Based on this idea an industrial development programme has been worked out by the VPF. The project formulation at the village level is totally governed by a meticulous manpower planning concept. While taking each decision as to the choice of development schemes, the concern for the employment of every unemployed youth in the village was a foremost consideration. Thus, while planning for any development activity, simultaneous attempts have been made to fit the unemployed youth in the village in suitable capacities. Thus, the employment plan automatically gets meshed with the development plan for the village. There is no elaborate machinery for effecting the manpower budgeting here. It happens quite autonomously and unobtrusively, with no prodding from anyone or contrivance of any kind. The result is that every village enterprise is manned by local youth, who are well motivated and conscientized. Thus, what we find in the local planning experiment in Kundrakudi is a people's approach rather than a project approach, in which the people are fitted into the project and not vice versa. This is an aspect of humanized development, which we have to note and which, in no small measure, has contributed to the success of the development projects undertaken in Kundrakudi.

Development Schemes and their Relevance

Part of the success of the Kundrakudi experiment may by ascribed to the fact that the Village Planning Forum was able to exercise some thinking as to the choice of schemes relevant to the village and in this way rendered the government schemes both area-specific and people-specific. Since the village lies in a drought-prone area, where the cultivation lasts only for three to four months, other avenues of employment and income have been thought of. This has led to the formulation of the following schemes :

(i) Providing milch animals for the poor villagers;
(ii) Providing sheep units;
(iii) Providing additional facilities for irrigation through community bore wells;
(iv) Dryland cultivation, including development of wasteland through promotion of fodder cultivation, horticulture and sericulture;
(v) Providing employment through agro-based and other industries; and
(vi) Providing training for self-employment.

The utilization of wastelands in the village (about 325 hectares), has been recognized as a priority item in the development agenda for Kundrakudi. The VPF conceived the idea of developing a small orchard in an area of 100 acres by utilizing *poramboke* lands, mainly to demonstrate to the farmers that the area is suitable for horticultural crops.

The project has been a great success. The land here is also being used for nurseries, for producing seeds/seedlings for vegetables, pulses, ornamental plants, flowers and social forestry, in addition to fruit trees.

The orchard has provided employment to about 60 local people throughout the year.

Another important dryland utilization scheme is the cultivation of cashew plantation. This has led to the establishment of a cashew processing unit under the cooperative sector (capacity 120 tonnes). The society has been strengthened further with the production of cashewnut shell liquid-based paints. The society provides employment to 80 members of the weaker sections.

Yet another project aimed at dryland utilization is the Community Well Programme. In Kundrakudi alone, there are 10 community wells. In the surrounding 16 villages, there are 31 more wells. Windmills have been set up at some places to lift water from the wells, thus conserving electricity/diesel. An Agricultural Green Farm Association has been formed and is a registered association, with 40 members to take care of the maintenance and management of the community wells. The Association has 16 representatives from the village and five Government officials. The ultimate aim of the Green Farm Association is to uplift the farmers through full utilization of the community wells, with three crops a year and with modern agricultural techniques.

A sericulture farm and a "Silk Hamlet" are other achievements. A model sericulture farm was set up in 1983 in about 10 acres, for providing training to the farmers and to supply seed cuttings to them. In the first phase, 20 farmers have been trained.

The Silk Hamlet is a novel scheme, seeking to develop mulberry plantations in 100 acres of Government *poramboke* land and settling 100 Harijan (Adi Dravida) families. In the first instance, over a period of three years, the Adi Dravidas will be engaged as workers on a daily wage of Rs. 10 per day. After establishing mulberry plantations, it is proposed to hand over the management to these families, at the rate of one acre per family. A society is proposed to be registered and Government participation will be only in the form of supervising the activities of the Hamlet. Individual chawkie-rearing sheds will be provided to the families by the Tamil Nadu Adi-Dravidar Housing and Development Corporation (TAHDCO). Three bore wells have been set up already and two more are to be added.

The dryland utilization activities in and around Kundrakudi adequately demonstrate the importance of land as a stabilizing force for the rehabilitation of the rural poor.

In the agriculture and non-agriculture sectors taken together, as many as 16 rural industrial units have been brought into existence up to

1984. Since then five more industrial units have been launched. With the development in the small-scale industries that have taken place, Kundrakudi has been able to achieve near full employment. The approach to development has aimed at providing employment to at least one person in a family.

Welfare Activities

In the Kundrakudi style of development, welfare activities have not been lost sight of. The village has a children's park with a library, radio, TV and facilities for indoor games. Besides, there is a ladies club and a youth club. Periodical seminars on health, education, agriculture, animal husbandry, industry and other aspects are organized in the village.

Women's Participation

The women of Kundrakudi have active involvement in the development process. In some of the industries (e.g. cashewnut processing, Nepali loom), a large number of women are employed. Attempts are being made to improve their skills through periodical training. In the Village Planning Forum and the cooperatives also women are represented. Some women, when questioned, freely admitted they had greatly benefited from the development process.

Public Participation

Our visit to Kundrakudi and interaction with various people afforded us a lot of useful insights into rural institutions and people's participation in their own development. Sometimes, people's participation is described as an "ideology without a methodology". But in the case of Kundrakudi, it is to be noted that cooperative development and community organization through VPF constitute the two aspects of its methodology. With these two instruments, it has been possible to reinforce the productivity, welfare and quality of life objectives in the rural development process.

The cooperatives have been organized for almost every enterprise in the village. This is partly because the people of the village are, by and large, poor and everything has to be organized through collective action only. The spiritual leader of the village, who is associated with every activity, has been able to inculcate a sense of discipline and a feeling of reverence among the people for all public sector activities undertaken in the village aimed at the wellbeing of the villagers. They have been told that all cooperative enterprises are to be looked upon as a "trust" handed over to them, which they should manage wisely and carefully. This message, with the trusteeship concept behind it, has gone a long way in ensuring that the institutions that have been built up are managed with responsibility and accountability.

The cooperatives have been promoted, wherever feasible, in order to increase the socialization of wealth and to bring about a wider distribution of benefits. A significant instance that may be cited is the action taken by the VPF in regard to the administration of fishing rights. The fishing rights in a big tank in the village used to be formerly auctioned, a practice around which some vested interests had grown, resulting in the concentration of benefits to a few persons only. The VPF decided to end the practice and took a unanimous decision, to establish a "fishermen's cooperative" in the village and to grant the fishing rights to them. Thus almost every important activity in the village has come into the cooperative fold.

About 10 cooperatives are functioning in Kundrakudi. It is not the fact of setting up the cooperatives or their number that is important. It is the way they function and contribute to development that really matters. In this, as in many other spheres of joint activity, it is the persons who matter. In Kundrakudi, people, who man the cooperatives, are highly motivated individuals. They have been trained primarily on the joint responsibility concept and have been accountable to the VPF. The great achievement of Kundrakudi seems to be this development of local capability among the people to manage with responsibility their own affairs for local development.

The cooperative institutions of the village are not hierarchical structures with a patron-client relationship. On the other hand, these are effective horizontal groupings of small farmers and labourers, operating on the basis of direct participation and serving well-defined common interests. It is well known that only such institutions can ensure loyalty amongst their members and efficiency in the overall performance. These are some of the unique factors in the structure and functioning of the cooperatives that have contributed to their success. Obviously, the cooperative experience here sheds a modicum of light on the alternative ways of organizing the rural community for development. Whether such factors can be replicated in all situations is a moot question.

The success of public participation lies in the extent to which decisions are taken with unanimity. This unanimity has great force in promoting spontaneous and speedy implementation. A number of instances may be cited from Kundrakudi experience to illustrate as to how unanimous decisions were arrived at and executed. They reveal the potency of public participation as a mechanism for problem-solving. The following instances may be particularly highlighted.

1. It is particularly striking that Kundrakudi is free from usurious money-lenders. The cooperative spirit among the people is so great that only informal and friendly give-and-take relationships exist among the people in the community. No private money-lending system exists. It appears that one money-lender—an interloper from outside—came and settled in Kundrakudi village and was indulging in this practice in a clandestine manner. This went on for some time, until a piquant situation arose, when this act came to the notice of the Village Planning Forum. The moneylender started squeezing and tormenting some borrowers for the return of loans, upon which the latter were forced to seek the protection of the VPF. The VPF considered this matter at length and decided unanimously that the money-lender should not be allowed to operate in the village, and ordered him out of the village. This was executed promptly, despite pressure from many quarters. Thus, money-lending as a vocation in the village ceased.
2. Another instance of a bold participatory decision taken by the Village Planning Forum was on the question of the villagers supporting and joining a general resistance movement for the non-repayment of government loans, a movement which had gathered great momentum in the entire State and gripped Kundrakudi as well. The external pressure and the promptings from the opposition parties were quite formidable. On this occasion, the Village Planning Forum, guided by its intelligentsia, took the crucial, extraordinary and bold stand that the people of the village would not join the movement at any cost. They not only took this decision, but also repaid the loan voluntarily and on time, affirming their sincerity and commitment. This incident has gone down in the history of the Kundrakudi Planning Forum as a unique decision and action.
3. As an example of how public participation, and particularly the consensus among the people, could play a significant role in crucial decision-making, we may cite the instance of the election of Panchayat President in Kundrakudi. One of the persons of the

village, who had already been in office for the previous term, was again proposed for a second term. Apparently, there were no wild protests in the VPF meeting against the proposal and this motion was, more or less, carried through by consensus. However, the spiritual leader of the village, who was presiding over the meeting, sensed that there was some hesitation among the members about this decision, although they were not quite vocal about it, for various reasons. So he deferred the ratification of the selection to the next meeting. In the meantime, he discussed the matter outside with a few prominent citizens and came to know that some minor defaults had been committed by the Panchayat President during his previous term of office. While these defaults were not so vital as to disqualify him for a second term of office, yet there was a feeling among the people that he should be made to respect the people's sentiments. Thereupon, the spiritual leader had a word with the President-designate and, in the next meeting, the latter made a statement referring to the particular incident and affirming that he would guard himself against possible lapses of that kind in future. This helped to diffuse the situation and paved the way for unanimous election. This is an incident which shows that public participation can work wonders, not merely for concretizing public opinion on critical issues among diverse interests, but also as a corrective in errant situations.

4. Public participation enables the VPF to call attention to some issues bypassed in project formulation. Repetitive emphasis of such issues in the VPF builds up pressures, ultimately leading to their acceptance by government functionaries. An instance of this kind relates to the expansion of grazing land in the village. While sheep-rearing has been adopted as a scheme under IRDP, the linked programme of establishing sufficient pasture land seems to have been neglected in the government programme. A perusal of the resolutions passed by the VPF showed that this had been repeatedly emphasized in the meetings. During our visit also, a progressive sheep farmer referred to this gap. Since the usual criticism against such schemes is that the lands leased out for this purpose may not be maintained properly by the village, the VPF prepared a specific scheme tying up pasture land development to the scheme of Milk Producers' Cooperative, so that the latter would be responsible for its maintenance. In this way, pasture land development was ensured.

A distinguishing feature of public participation in Kundrakudi is the fact that such participation occurs through all the different stages of planning, viz. pre-planning, action-planning and post-planning stages. Normally, in many participatory programmes, the involvement of people is mainly along implementation and maintenance. The standard procedure is to organize groups at the village level in order to obtain their willing cooperation for the implementation of schemes, planned from above. But in Kundrakudi, the participation goes beyond this approach and involves people directly in various planning tasks, such as the definition of problems, formulation of projects, implementation of projects, evaluation of projects. The implementation and sharing of responsibilities in planning with the government functionaries is accomplished in various ways. This is no doubt a big achievement. But still, in terms of group organizations and mobilizing local resources, more remains to be done. The cooperative and participatory spirit that exists here encourages the hope that it would be possible to develop in this village a bottom-up system of organization for stimulating joint action by viable groups of farmers, imbued with a sense of group-responsibility and spirit of self-reliance, for the performance of integrated land-based management, systematic water management, group credit and development of subsidiary income-raising activities.

Transferability and Replicability of the Kundrakudi Experience

From all accounts, it is apparent that Kundrakudi is a successful story in local-level planning for rural development. If so, the question arises as to what extent it is transferable to other parts of the country. This question, in turn, raises two other sub-questions, viz.: (a) to what extent did this experiment contribute to local development, and (b) what are the factors and conditions that have contributed to its success?

Impacts on Rural Change and Development

The first query is related to the analysis of various impacts of the Kundrakudi experiment upon rural change and development. This analysis should deal with the extent to which this experiment has contributed to capital formation in the rural sector in the form of physical infrastructures, improvement in rural employment and economy, changes in values and attitudes of rural people, fostering of change agents, and promotion of participatory organizations. But since this analysis is based on a reconnaissance study only and not on a total evaluation of the experience in terms of its impact on all the aspects of development, only some partial answers may be attempted.

1. *Impact on Investment*

During the field visit, the Study Team tried to ascertain the total investment that has been made in the area during the period 1977 to 1983, including the extent of mobilization of resources at the local level. Precise figures could not be collected, but it became apparent from the discussions that the contribution of the government is the greatest. As was noted earlier, the Kundrakudi experiment is really an aspect of development in which the local people worked through the government system, relying mainly on government financing. As it very often happens in the case of success stories, it appears that the area has attracted relatively more government investment because of the several positive factors that have induced development in this area. The people's contribution, however, cannot be belittled, as some of the non-economic factors like the extent of self-help and voluntary participation cannot be easily quantified. In other words, it is the government investment plus the people's contribution which has had a snowballing effect on the accelerated rural development which has occurred in the Kundrakudi area.

2. *Impact on the Farmer's Value System*

It cannot be denied that the continued implementation of the Kundrakudi style of development over the past seven years has brought about significant changes in rural communities at the individual as well as organization levels. Although we have not carried out a detailed survey in the area to measure the change orientation that has come among the people—even the reconnaissance visit served to confirm that the people in the area were relatively change-oriented, implying that they were somewhat futuristic in their thinking, were more confident of improvements in their future life and were willing to make vigorous efforts for the realization of these improvements. Our wayside questions and observations revealed that their motivational levels were high. In particular, their positive approach to cooperative endeavour was particularly striking. One may, therefore, conclude that the changes in values and perceptions of the people seem to be a significant factor for success from the developmental point of view.

3. *Impact on Organizational Behaviour*

Organizational changes are reflected both in institutional development and in the participatory behaviour of the village people. In particular, Kundrakudi has contributed to the fostering of community-based development and has thrown up a number of village leaders who have taken up responsible positions in the various cooperative enterprises that have come to be established in the village. These leaders who were interviewed showed that they were moderately educated but were highly motivated and were also imbued with a sense of dedication to promote development. Undoubtedly it is these dedicated personnel who are playing significant roles in organizing and implementing community development at the village level as initiators, promoters, coordinators, educators, advocators and implementors of specific projects. The fact is that the Kundrakudi experience has eventually contributed to the identification and fostering of a certain pattern of village leadership which, in fact, constitutes the source of self-reliant development.

The Village Planning Forum, in particular, has promoted a participatory pattern of interaction between village members and the government functionaries in respect of planning and decision-making, including the selection and implementation of projects in the village. The positive participation in the decision-making process at the village level has also continued during the implementation stages. In this way, it is very interesting to note that the Village Planning Forum has contributed to the development of grassroot democracy in the area.

4. *Impact on the Village Economy*

We could not collect precise details to illustrate how rapidly the village economy has grown in terms of change in household incomes, expenditure patterns and savings. This would require a full-range household survey of the village, which should be undertaken by some agency. The positive features of improvement in the village economy are, however, reflected in the extent of waste-land development, the diversification in terms of landuse pattern and the improvements in agricultural productivity as well as the employment-generation projects that have been started in the non-farm sector. There is no doubt that without the concerted effort of the Village Planning Forum, there could not have been the significant increase in opportunities for non-farm income in the area.

Factors that Promoted Development

The second question to which we may address ourselves is the several factors that have contributed to the success of the Kundrakudi experiment. These include a multiplicity of factors, such as the extraordinary local leadership which has been available, the association of a band of dedicated scientists, who have given proper guidance in the formulation of relevant projects, the establishment of a Village Planning Forum and the single-mindedness and consistency with which it has acted, the intensive local participation in both planning and plan implementation, and, above all, the existence of a moral component of development, which is indefinable and yet apparent in this unique instance.

1. *The Institutional Factor*

The central institution around which all developmental activities revolve in Kundrakudi is the Village Planning Forum. It is the coordinating centre for inter-agency planning and management for local development. It identifies local development projects, gets feasibility studies prepared, monitors and evaluates the progress and effects of projects, maintains a feed-back system with the development agencies concerned and encourages private enterprises and government agencies to formulate development projects for the area. Above all, it is the principal vehicle for the people's participation. In Kundrakudi, it has influenced the performance by governmental functionaries and rendered the government sponsored developmental projects more meaningful to the people, who are the ultimate beneficiaries. Its primary task, as may be seen, is the inter-agency collaboration. It is done in a very subtle, indirect and unobtrusive manner, without raising controversies or rubbing officials on the wrong side. It is coordinating without compelling, and integrating without absorbing or substituting the functions of other agencies. The Village Planning Forum (VPF) has not substituted the functions of any of the line agencies, but has assisted them in the improvement of design as well as of performance. Thus it is the style of its functioning that has evoked the necessary degree of cooperation from government functionaries and other external agencies. Undoubtedly, its composition and way of functioning offer some lessons which may be valid under all circumstances. What its experience suggests is that to coordinate all developmental activities at the local level and to give some leads to developmental agencies as to what is desirable under a given set of circumstances, a local body of informed people is necessary. The idea of a local planning agency is thus quite relevant as an institutional mechanism to match the plan of felt-needs from below, with that of the departmental schemes from above. The Village Planning Forum need not be conceived as *de novo* institution. It may be dovetailed into the existing structures, if found feasible. Any local body functioning in a village and enjoying the confidence of the rural community can incorporate the good features of the Village Planning Forum and transform itself into a planning agency at the village level and perform the functions, which the VPF at Kundrakudi is currently performing. For instance, if a Village Panchayat is functioning in a particular context, it could, by suitably enlarging or modifying its functions, take on the role of the Village Planning Forum. Alternatively, the Village Planning Forum could also be conceived as a separate Committee of the Panchayat, performing advisory planning-and-development coordination functions. Whatever be the structure, as the Kundrakudi experience has demonstrated, it is the method of functioning which is important.

While it can be generally appreciated that local development could be stimulated more effectively through an innovative institution such as the Village Planning Forum, it should also be admitted that its degree of efficacy will heavily depend on the development potential obtaining in a particular context. These contextual factors include such factors as topography and natural resources, the degree of social cohesiveness or divisiveness as well as the nature of the strength of the local institutions and traditions of cooperation and the availability of dynamic local leadership. Considering the marked dissimilarities that exist among areas, it is difficult to lay down a single best organizational design for local development.

To sum up, the Kundrakudi experience suggests that in order to improve the methodology for securing the best results in local development planning at village-level, the following could be posited as necessary steps.

(1) A proper public forum should be constituted, where the rural people will have the freedom to analyze the different approaches to local development and express their felt needs;

(2) After the identification of schemes is done with the consensus of the villagers, their feasibility has to be studied in collaboration with technical personnel; and

(3) After getting a scheme approved by the Village Planning Forum, steps should be taken to dovetail the same into the departmental schemes handed from above. This will require some powers of persuasion to get the schemes accepted and funded from the departmental funds. It is in this context that the local leadership of high calibre is called for.

2. *Local Leadership*

One factor which came up again and again during our discussion for the successful mobilization of local development activities is that of local leadership. As may be seen, the local leadership available in Kundrakudi has some extraordinary features. It only serves to illustrate and underline the tremendous potential of this factor in rural development. Leadership of this kind clearly cannot be expected to be available in every village. However, it cannot be denied that local leadership is essential to guide various developmental activities at the local level, particularly those involving public construction projects, community-run enterprises and cooperative agricultural ventures.

Traditionally in every village, there exists a village chief who holds this appointment on a hereditary basis, although this system is changing in some states. Wherever village panchayats exist, the election system has also thrown up some local leaders. There is a view that the traditional local leaders or the elected leaders are the people who have become entrenched in their positions and hence grown complacent in office. They also usually belong to the elite class. The need for operating an effective cadre of local leaders who would be more enthusiastic and innovative in their approaches and less conservative in their outlook is, therefore, often advocated for a successful rural development programme in some countries. In the Seamaul Undong programme of rural development in South Korea, for instance, a separate cadre of local leaders was created. The government devoted considerable energy to train these local leaders. Through such training of local leaders, an attempt was made to buildup support for local development with emphasis on the virtues of self-sacrifice and the need to guide others by setting a correct example. The training provided little in the way of technical skills, but much by way of generating enthusiasm and confidence in the selected leaders. It is possible that when new leaders are selected and trained in this manner, conflicts may arise between the traditional leaders and the new leaders.

It is argued in the Korean context, however, that a competition between the two types of leaders may often improve the performance of both. From this point of view, it is contended that to have a new leader is not anything undesirable.

Thus, in the matter of developing local leadership, there are different viewpoints and clear generalization about these matters is difficult to pronounce. What makes for good leadership is also a complex issue. One point on which there could be agreement, however, is that a good leader must have a sound knowledge of developmental issues derived either through regular education or through experience. He should be a member of the local community and immensely interested in their welfare. What is even more important is that the local leader should be subjected to periodical training and thus be constantly sensitized to enable him to imbibe more and more education on development issues. Once a decision to have a Village Planning Forum is taken, the question of developing the local leaders and constantly improving their calibre must receive due attention.

3. *The Third Party Planner*

An important component in the success of the Kundrakudi experiment in rural development is an intellectual one, provided by a group of scientists who have assisted the Village Planning Forum with constructive ideas and have been responsible for concretizing many of the suggestions emanating from the discussions in the Planning Forum. This team of scientists constituted what may be called the "third party planner" for the VPF, and filled a vital gap in planning expertise. The VPF, by its very nature and composition, cannot have adequate planning capabilities and expertise on complex developmental issues and may, therefore, require some support from an external agency of this kind.

From the Kundrakudi experience, one may conclude that the assistance from the external agency should be in the nature of a continuous involvement in village development activities (not a mere one-time association). The external agency, offering assistance, should be capable of solving many of the operational problems encountered in plan formulation and implementation. Kundrakudi is fortunate to have such assistance from CECRI, the result of which is visible in the many small-scale industrial projects that have been established in the village. This experience clearly brings out the need for a third party planner to fill a vital gap in the development process at the village level. While few villages may be as fortunate as Kundrakudi, in being able to enlist the support of highly competent institutions, the question for a majority of villages in the country is : how are we to arrange such institutional support?

Wherever professional academic institutions like research institutions, agricultural colleges/universities, engineering colleges, etc., exist, they should be encouraged to offer assistance on a continuous basis to a group of villages in their vicinity. Where such institutions are not available, other institutions such as a local college may be utilized for this purpose. By teaming up their faculty and adopting a multi-disciplinary approach, these institutions can hope to render more effective service in this direction. The task is not so easy. Nevertheless, these alternatives have to be explored.

4. *Attitudinal Change among Government Functionaries*

The objectives of rural development have changed considerably over time. The old stance with the emphasis on "the government decides and people support", must now give place to the idea "people decide and government supports". Many of the studies conducted all over the world have emphasized that local development efforts can succeed only with close involvement of the local people. Participatory planning is a new venture. Government functionaries are still new to the concept and have to learn to work with people and understand the local needs and local specificities. Many rural development programmes are either State or Centrally-sponsored. These State and Central Governments or their agencies have provided guidelines for the planning and implementation of their individual programmes and thus prescribed some do's and dont's. They have also provided discretion to government functionaries to adapt the programmes/schemes in accordance with the local areas' needs and specificities. But in the hurlyburly of achieving the developmental targets within the stipulated time, the lower level government functionaries do not exert themselves to make such adaptations which call for greater understanding and ingenuity on their part and prefer to go ahead mechanically with the implementation of the standard schemes, irrespective of their irrelevance to the local areas. In this context, if a local planning agency comes forward to help with "tailored" schemes, the government functionary is spared much of the intellectual effort and time involved in formal data-gathering and research necessary for "adapting" the schemes to suit the local area. This explains the logic implied in the setting up of local planning forums. In this context, the necessary attitudinal change and partnership spirit has to be cultivated by the government functionary so that he becomes amenable to suggestions and follows the leads provided by the local institutions. One of the ways in which this may be secured is by imparting frequent training to government functionaries in "participatory approaches" to planning and development.

Summing Up

In this case study, we have attempted to provide a catalogue of insights into the factors that have contributed to the success story in Kundrakudi. Re-stated in terms of broad principles at the level of generality, these are :

(a) Building up a responsible and responsive Receiving Mechanism which will be a people's institution for planning and development, to provide a forum for various people to interact and to prepare an acceptable framework for planning;
(b) Ensuring a willing, understanding and adaptive Delivery Mechanism which, in effect, implies bringing about attitudinal changes among the functionaries engaged in development administration;
(c) Bringing into existence a "Think-tank" or "Third Party Planner" which can play both an advisory role in planning on a continuous basis, and a catalystic motivational role in implementation with some degree of involvement (not mere association) in the planning and implementation process;
(d) Identifying a local leader of high personal integrity who is respected by all sections of the people and who can integrate the functions mentioned in (a), (b) and (c);
(e) Ensuring a style of functioning (of the planning mechanism) which will be informed by an informal group-dynamics approach to decision-making and which would be neither compelling nor absorbing in its performance and which would be able to eliminate any conflicts/fluctuations arising during the planning process;
(f) Adopting flexible procedures and consensus-building techniques as well as healthy conventions in the working process;

(g) Devising a network of informal consultative groups outside the regular institutional mechanism for group action which would expand the scope of public participation and also ensure voluntary agency participation; and

(h) Imparting training both formal and informal for the local youth inducted into the development projects to provide both skills and moral qualities.

The principles stated above need to be interpreted appropriately to suit every situation. There can be no fixed rules of the game. Each situation is unique in itself and demands a different approach.

From the foregoing discussion, it may be concluded that the Kundrakudi experiment has succeeded, by and large, because of a particular blend or combination that could be forged by the representatives of the village community with the technocratic functionaries in government and a group of informed and dedicated academic community. The approach here may be termed "Technocratic-Academic-Democratic Mix" (TAD). In other words, a generalization that we may draw from this experience is that a combination of popular participation with an effective local leadership, seeking to work its way through the governmental system, can succeed within certain limitations. It must be realized, however, that the combination does not automatically ensure success in every context. This is to underline the point that the "mix" referred to here is a necessary, but not a sufficient condition for successful development. There are several unique factors in the Kundrakudi context, such as the extraordinary local leadership, the dedicated third party planner and a highly motivated public, which make the problem of replicability of the experience quite a complex and complicated one. In this context, it is perhaps necessary to make a guarded statement as to the replicability and transferability of any experience in rural development. Our view is that exact prototypes of Kundrakudi may—but need not—emerge in every other village. However, if a sincere effort could be made in each context to bring together the three major partners in rural development—technocrats, academics and the people—in the right combination, to suit a particular set of conditions (a blend that is called the "TAD-Mix"), and orchestrate their actions in the direction of planned development, it is likely to go a long way towards improving local-level planning for rural development and result in a better realization of our investments in rural areas.

REFERENCES

1. For full details about the Comilla model of rural development, see 'The Works of Akhtar Hameed Khan', Vols. I to III, published by the Bangladesh Academy for Rural Development, Kotbari, Comilla, 1993.
2. About the Chinese development, there are numerous works—one reference cited here is : Sartaj Aziz, *Rural Development, Learning from China*, The Macmillan Press Ltd, London, 1978.
3. See In Joung Whang, *Management of Rural Change in Korea*, The Seamaul Undong, The Institute of Social Sciences : Korean Studies Series No. 5, Seoul National University Press, 1981. Also Man-Gap Lee (Ed.), 'Toward a New Community Life'—Report of International Research Seminar on The Seamaul Movement, Institute of Seamaul Undong Studies, Seoul National University, 1981.
4. See Jayanta Kumar Ray, *Organising Villagers for Self-reliance : A Study of Deedar in Bangladesh*, Bangladesh Academy for Rural Development, Kotbari, Comilla, 1983.
5. The Sukho Majri experience has been documented in Minoru Ouchi : 'Development Communication and Grassroots Participation in Action'—Experiences in Five Asian Countries—Asian and Pacific Development Centre and Association of Development Research and Training Institute of Asia and the Pacific, Kuala Lumpur, Malaysia, 1987. Also, Planning Com-mission, Government of India, New Delhi, 'Towards Improved Local Level Planning for Rural Development'—Lessons from some experiences, 1986.
6. The Kundrakudi experience was documented by Sundaram, K.V. and Palanidurai, K.V. (Study Team constituted by the Indian Planning Commission) February 1985, at the instance of the former Prime Minister of India, late Smt. Indira Gandhi, who, after going through a press report on the achievements in Kundrakudi, sent a note to the Planning Commission, with the observation, 'This is what I should like for all other villages'.

PART II

ISSUES AND PROBLEMS

"All progress is precarious and the
solution of one problem brings us
face to face with another problem".

—*Martin Luther King Jr.*

INTRODUCTION

The operationalization of decentralized multilevel planning is fraught with several issues and problems. Chapter 7 sets out nine key issues in local-level planning, which are : (1) Defining the degree of "localism." (2) Determining the unit area for local-level planning. (3) Defining the scope of local-level planning. (4) Establishing a machinery for local-level planning. (5) Making administrative adaptations. (6) Training of local-level planners. (7) Effecting programme integration. (8) Mobilizing the finances for the local plan; and (9) Securing public participation. The four tasks in local-level planning are : (a) Resource analysis; (b) Strategy formulation; (c) Plan formulation; and (d) Implementation planning. Each task consists of several steps. It is emphasized that appropriate methodologies have to be devised for carrying out these tasks and steps.

Chapter 8 reviews five case studies on "Local-Level Planning for Integrated Rural Development"—three in India and one each in Nepal and Malaysia—and throws light on the potentials and constraints encountered during the process of planning and implementation and on the relative efficacy of the organizational mechanisms evolved for their operations. Based on the experience from the case studies, some important postulates for the planning of local area development have been set out. These hinge on issues relating to area development, focus on the rural poor, planning methodology, local planning machinery, mechanisms for coordination and integration, or organizational component for effective planning and implementation, micro-macro linkages, people's participation, systematic monitoring of plan implementation, and organized capacitation of the local level personnel for coping with the planning and development tasks. The preparation of appropriate guidelines for planning and the training and re-training of personnel have been particularly emphasized.

A major problem in decentralized planning is the information constraint. Chapter 9 deals with "Information needs and Systems for Decentralized Planning." The large number of micro variables on which data are needed for today's planning include aspects like income, poverty, employment, standard of living, basic services (their access and delivery) quality of life and sustainable development. We also need information about the cultural and behavioural patterns of the people, their asset ownership systems, the way they handle or practise their economy as well as their institutional and organizational capacity. Experience with data and information availability in the developing countries indicates that, generally speaking, the quantity and quality of data and informations decrease as the areal unit changes from larger to smaller. Also, some local level data are low powered and undependable. The chapter discusses the process of designing a data and information system in a multilevel planning context, which involves : (a) The identification of information needs and sources for planning, (b) The identification of data sets that will flow into the system. (c) Computerization, and (d) The establishment of coordinating mechanisms at the national, regional and local levels to effect a continuous and regular flow of information into the system. The point that information structures should match and mesh with the planning structures at the various levels has been emphasized. A "Stages Approach" to transition to the information age has also been emphasized. India, as a case study, has been discussed.

Among the various levels of planning at the local level, planning at the district level is most crucial, as it is the interfacing point for the bottom-up and top-down planning processes, leading to what is termed as "negotiatory or convergent planning". District planning should be guided by a "selective development strategy" and should follow a "step-by-step approach". The district planning methodology in India has unfolded gradually and this substantive methodology could be discerned from the two working group reports of the Planning Commission—Dantwala (1978) and Hanumantha Rao (1982). The various analytical steps for district planning will include : Situation Analysis, Context Analysis, Sectoral Analysis, Spatial Analysis, Environmental Analysis and Gender Analysis. These and other aspects of District Planning methodology are discussed in Chapter 10 on "District Planning Methodologies—Some Reflections". It has been emphasized in this discussion that the "procedural" aspects of a district planning methodology are as important as its "analytical rigour".

The measurement and monitoring aspects of Decentralized Planning have not received much careful attention in planning literature. These neglected issues form the subject matter of Chapter 11. The discussion here revolves around the crucial question of the criteria by which we can compare the degree of decentralization between two different areas.

A framework for analyzing and comparing decentralization among different countries would involve considerations of administration/organization, finance, planning and people's participation. On the question of monitoring, a distinction has been made between *project* monitoring and *plan* monitoring. The latter has to be attempted with reference to the steps, actors and organizational mechanisms involved in the planning process and evaluating the achievements in each context.

Societies grow and develop in historic times. As times and circumstances—social, political and economic—change, development also undergoes some re-orientations. In our current developmental context in India, three major events are influencing the pattern of local development constituting the "current imperatives".

(i) Implementation of the new economic reforms;
(ii) The Burgeoning environmental crisis, calling for systematic environmental management and sustainable development at the local level; and
(iii) Panchayati Raj renaissance, following the passing of the constitutional 73rd and 74th amendments.

The last mentioned development implies the parallel and concurrent march of democracy and decentralized planning and administration, combining both political and managerial objectives. In this context, how the technocratic approach and the political approach should mesh in an interactive, participatory and culturally sensitive planning process to produce a plan that is both technically sound and administratively responsive to the needs, wishes and resources of the local population, has been discussed in Chapter 12, titled "Decentralized Planning in the Context of the current decentralization reforms in India".

7

LOCAL-LEVEL PLANNING FOR INTEGRATED RURAL DEVELOPMENT*

The interest in local-level planning for integrated rural development is growing rapidly in the countries of the ESCAP region, but there is still a wide gap between what the experts have recommended and what is actually practised.[1] A study tour undertaken in India by an ESCAP team in 1979 revealed that the task of operationalizing any concept at the grassroot level was not an easy one and that governments will have to put in a lot of preparatory efforts by way of issuing elaborate guidelines, setting out the methodology of planning in all its details, and by intensely educating and training local-level planners.[2] Local-level planning for rural development implies operationalizing two concepts. One is the concept of Integrated Rural Development (IRD) with its multiple objectives of more production, more employment and more equitable distribution of income. The second is the concept of Area Development, which seeks to apply the IRD concept within a selected locality through establishing a cross functional planning framework and linking the micro-level planning to the macro target setting and planning. Several methodological issues are involved in this operation and national governments are exercising their minds on these issues. Some countries like India have prepared National Guidelines, broadly setting out an approach and providing some instructions for getting about the task of local-level planning. This chapter is intended to highlight some of the critical aspects of local-level planning for rural development. It proposes to set out the key issues and major tasks involved in this exercise and to outline a broad framework within which the methodological problems can be

---

* Keynote paper prepared for an Expert Group Meeting on "Local-level Planning for Integrated Rural Development" held at Bangkok in January 1980 by the United Nations Economic and Social Commission for Asia and Pacific, Bangkok.

handled. It is not to be understood as a "Guideline" or an "Instruction Manual" in any sense of the term, for it is recognized that no uniform pattern of local-level planning for rural development can be suggested for universal adoption by all countries. Each country has to design its own guidelines for local-level planning for rural development, by taking into account its individual.

(i) Stage and level of development;
(ii) Resources inventory;
(iii) Existing political system and institutional structure;
(iv) The development objectives and specific interventionist policies actually being implemented; and
(v) The most pressing needs of the country.

What is attempted here is, therefore, no more than hitting at some high spots and providing a basis for a systematic approach to the problem.

Concept of Local-level Planning

After experimenting with the top-down approach in planning, many developing countries have now come to the conclusion that if development is to have any impact on these countries, it must directly attack the problem of poverty at the grassroot level. That is, the households of the poorer sections of the society should be the target groups for development. With this realization, certain other dimensions in development have also surfaced on the planning horizon. Employment has been recognized as a structural problem which, in most cases, cannot be solved by high G.D.P. growth rates. There are also other objections such as the income distribution, the quality of life and the provision of the basic minimum needs to the rural population, for all of which a decentralized planning approach with its emphasis on "bottom-up" planning is necessary.

The top-down approach to planning not only tended to bypass the rural poor and some social groups, but also some "areas" within a country which had their own unique resource endowments, characteristics and problems. It tended to impose a uniform set of development programmes everywhere, without regard to the variety of conditions existing within a country. It is now increasingly being recognized that spatial justice is as important as social justice in planning and that no country can be planned as a single-level entity. The importance of multi-level planning has been appreciated in several countries. Local-level planning, as a concept, is born of such appreciation.

Local-level planning seeks to look in greater detail into the aspirations and requirements of specific local areas and communities and to take suitable measures for meeting these, so as to take maximum advantage of the local initiative, potentials, capacities and resources. The three essential ingredients of local-level planning are : optimal utilization of local resources, widespread participation by local residents and integrated approach to development. These can best be achieved by adopting an area development approach. Thus, area development is a method of local-level planning and seeks to focus development activity on "manageable areas", in which it can be responsive to the specificity of natural endowment and social order.

The efficiency of local-level planning in any country will depend on the extent of articulation of the multi-level planning process. Where multi-level planning is only feebly articulated, one notes only a mechanical break-up of the developmental programmes to the lower levels without a simultaneous devolution of power and finances to them. (i.e. deconcentration). Where it is highly articulated, there is an effective spatial disaggregation of programmes accompanied by devolution of power and finances to lower-level authorities. (i.e. decentralization).

The tendencies discernible in the changes in orientation and structure of development planning during the past two decades were discussed in Chapter 4. In this context, a reference may be made to Fig. 7.1.[3]

Concept of Rural Development

Rural development (or Integrated Rural Development, as it is called in many countries now) as a concept for planning and executing changes in rural areas is based on the assumption that production increases and social improvements are not mutually exclusive, but on the contrary, are mutually reinforcing. The complementarity between the two is so heavy that development on the one front cannot proceed beyond a point, without a simultaneous or prior change in the other. Another trend in rural development is the special emphasis on the weaker sections of the society, i.e. the rural poor, not merely for improving their level of living, but also to bring about a greater degree of their involvement in the development process. As understood now, rural development has multiple objectives : more production, more employment, more equitable distribution of income and emphasis on the rural poor. Local-level planning is then a tool to translate these objectives into concrete programmes in a local area. The efficacy of local-level planning for rural development will depend on the extent of decentralization of decision-making, planning, administration and budgeting to the local-levels.

A substantial measure of decentralization to the local levels in a country would necessarily involve the strengthening of local level government and other development institutions. The adjustments (i.e. administrative adaptations) needed would vary significantly from country to country. Unless the functional aspects of rural development projects are completely delegated to the lower levels of government, problems would arise with regard to overlapping functions of central and local government departments. Opinion is now almost unanimous on the need for strong planning and executive machinery for rural development at the local levels.[4] Local level planning has the great merit, when it is carried out within "manageable unit areas", as it would enable the identification of the basic inter-relations between the different components of rural development and help in evolving the most appropriate strategy suited to each area. At the same time, local-level management would provide the flexibility needed to modify programmes, as conditions become better understood or as circumstances change. Other advantages of local-level planning for rural development are that it would (a) ensure local participation and evoke local enthusiasm, (b) make local mobilization of resources possible, (c) establish closer correspondence between the resource endowment and potentials of an area and the contents and magnitude of development programmes taken up therein, (d) establish greater complementarity between inter-dependent programmes falling within the sphere of different departments, and (e) obtain feed-back in terms of field level experiences for making the planning process at the other hierarchic levels more realistic and effective.

Despite the vigorous debates on "planning from below" and "felt needs" in the past two decades, it seems that very little actual local level planning has taken place in many countries. The changing policy objectives and developmental compulsions before the developing countries are now quite clear. In this context, the logic of local level planning as the instrument of state intervention for rural development, within the larger framework of multi-level planning, seems almost compelling. This underlines the case for devising appropriate national guidelines for an effective "Local-level Planning for Rural Development" by individual countries, so that some ways of quickly reaching the new development goals and integrating the national planning priorities and the felt needs of local communities (appropriate to each country's context) may be formulated and systematically acted upon.[5]

Key Issues in Local-level Planning

Degree of "localism" in Local-level Planning

One of the questions frequently posed in this context is : How "local" should local-level planning be? It is indeed difficult to answer this question except in a particular country context. The degree of "localism" in planning would vary from country to country, depending on its stage of development and the scale of decentralization. Between the extremes of centralization and decentralization, there are varying degrees of inter-dependency mix and function-sharing between the Central and Local Governments. In most countries, what has been attempted in the name of decentralization is only a mechanical disaggregation of targets and resources to the lower levels (i.e. Deconcentration) involving at best some "delegation", implying entrusting or committing some tasks to the lower level for administrative convenience. In other words, only some form of delegated planning has been attempted. For instance, in Nepal, where planning has been attempted at the district level, it has been merely an exercise in bringing down the State level targets and outlays to district level targets and outlays. There has been no genuine planning exercise at the district level, in the sense of informed decision-making and planning of programmes on the basis of local identification of needs and potentialities. It is the same in India also, where district planning has been attempted in various states. Even in one of the states (Maharashtra), where a comparatively sophisticated form of decentralized planning has emerged at the district level, the exercise conforms more to "district budgeting" rather than to district planning. "The set of schemes which constitute the district plan are those which are not determined by any objective analysis or study, but have been arrived at by consensus in the meetings of the District Planning and Development Council and, therefore, are subjective in nature. They are not organized around any inner logic of their own. They mainly rely on an aggregational exercise based upon the proposals of the department agencies.... Thus, there is very little analytically informed decision-making in regard to the selection of projects in the district plan.[6]

Thus, decentralized planning in its true sense, meaning the assigning of both powers and responsibilities to the lower area levels of a country and rendering the lower territorial levels fully accountable for their activities, does not seem to have been attempted in many countries.

In a highly decentralized set-up, local-level planning would mean that the popular authority (vesting in the rural poor majority) completely takes over the planning functions, including the ordering of priorities and allocation of resources in the local area. In this case, the higher levels of government would simultaneously undertake inter-dependent and complementary planning functions over geographically larger areas, besides providing policy inputs and resources to back-stop the local planning exercise. It may be assumed that all countries are progressing towards this goal of multi-level planning. During the different stages of this evolution, planning at the local level for any country will be characterized by varying degrees of inter-dependency mix and function-sharing between the different levels. Thus, the dynamic character of local-level planning for a country has to be defined taking into account its stage of development, its goal orientation and the extent and magnitude of decentralization to the lower levels.

Unit Area for Local-level Planning

Local-level planning would naturally raise the question about the optimal areal unit which should be adopted as the basis for planning in order to realize the best possible gains. The unit area for any country may be a lower-level administrative unit, like the "district" or a sub-unit of the district, perhaps an electoral division or a cluster of villages or even the individual village itself. Sometimes, it may be a "region", specially carved out for planning purposes. Each of these areas has its own advantages in a given situation.

In the context of local-level planning, it should be noted that the subject as well as the object of planning is the people of the area. Therefore, the unit area of local-level planning must be such that the people become recognizable entities to the planner and not lost as masses without identification. This would mean that the individual household must be recognized as an important unit in local-level planning. One of the objectives of local-level planning is to make each household a viable economic unit. However, in order to sustain the viability of the individual household, necessary infrastructural support has to be provided at the "area" level. Looking at this question from another angle, it should be pointed out that another objective of local-level planning, viz. removal of unemployment could be achieved only when some viable projects can be planned on the basis of available local resources. This would imply that the planning areas selected should contain a range of natural resources within its boundaries. All these considerations would suggest that the unit area chosen for local-level planning should be sufficiently small and close to the people, so that the planner may be alive to their problems, while at the same time sufficiently large, so that there is an adequate natural resource-base for mounting a viable economic plan. Thus, manageability for planning, natural resource availability and economic viability are some essential considerations in the choice of a planning area, and if they could also be matched by relative homogeneity and community of interest within the area, then perhaps, one has hit upon an ideal unit area for local-level planning.

It may be recalled in this context that some countries of the region had, in the past, experimented with the "individual rural community", i.e. the village, as the basis for rural planning. The limitations of the approach were, however, realized very soon. The small rural community was not found to be a viable unit for the planning of many local services, which indeed had to be spread over a wider functional area for various purposes, such as the procurement of inputs, credit, marketing, agricultural extension, education facility, primary health care, etc. The current trend in planning for rural development, therefore, is to look for an area larger than the small community.

ESCAP discussions have revealed that for several countries in the region, the "district" is perhaps the appropriate unit for local-level planning. In countries like India, Pakistan and Indonesia, however, where the districts extend over large areas, the "sub-district" covering a population of about 100,000 (e.g. the "block" in India, "markaz" in Pakistan, and "kacamatan" in Indonesia) is considered more appropriate for this purpose.

Scope of Local-level Planning

Closely related to the question of the unit area of planning is the specification of the subject matter of planning at the local level. The multi-level planning process implies that there will be clear demarcation of planning functions for the various levels, so that there will be minimum of overlapping among these functions. Some of the State Governments in India, which have attempted to place district planning on a relatively sound methodological footing, have defined the "District Sector" and

"State Sector" schemes separately and, thus, earmarked the responsibilities of the respective levels for the planning and implementation of programmes. Fig. 7.1 is illustrative :

State Sector Schemes

- Generation and Distribution of Power
- Major and Medium Irrigation Projects
- Investment in Corporate Bodies
- University and Technical Education
- Professional and Technical Education
- Research and Training
- State and National Highways
- Ayacut Development under Major and Medium Projects
- Ports and Inland Waterways

District Sector Schemes

- Agricultural Production
- Soil Conservation
- Forest
- Fisheries
- Animal Husbandry
- Marketing
- Minor Irrigation
- Ayacut Development under Minor Irrigation Projects
- Primary and Secondary Education
- District and Village Roads
- Health
- Water Supply and Sanitation
- Urban Development
- Welfare of Backward Classes
- Social Welfare

FIG. 7.1 : Demarcation of Functions for different Planning Levels (illustrative).

From the illustrative list, it may be seen that broadly, the domain of the local planning would be : planning for agriculture and allied activities including extension services, cottage and small industries, and the provision of local infra-structure and social services. The range of planning functions at the local level for any country may be determined by the size of the local area and the existing structure of local and development administration in the area. A certain amount of institution-building responsibilities must also be considered as falling within the purview of local-level planning. The official guidelines for block-level planning in India have identified five major components of a local-level plan as under :

(a) Programmes aiming at optimizing the production potential of the area in the various sectors of the economy;

(b) Special production programmes for the target groups in the area in the light of the resource potentials;
(c) Manpower planning and skill development in relation to the production programmes;
(d) A programme for the provision of basic minimum needs; and
(e) Programme for institutional support.

The specification of the area of responsibilities for local level planning will not, however, mean that local-level planning will be an isolated exercise. On the contrary, this exercise must recognize the various linkages and must relate to the plans both from above and below.

Machinery for Local-level Planning

A minimum precondition for local-level planning is the development of an adequate planning machinery at the local level. What should be the nature and personnel composition of such a machinery is an important question. However, no uniform and dogmatic answer to this question is possible. In varying circumstances, different approaches may have to be adopted.

A serious constraint in most developing countries is the lack of availability of suitable technical personnel for undertaking grassroot level planning on a scientific basis. Also the costs involved in setting up an elaborate planning machinery for local level planning may prove to be formidable for most developing countries. In this context, some compromises seem necessary; the feasible alternatives could be adopting a supra-level mobile planning approach or planning by community approach or the Third Party Planner approach. Each one of these methods has its own merits in a given situation.

The supra-level mobile planning approach implies locating the planning organization at a higher level in the multi-level planning framework, and charging it with the responsibility of planning to the lower area levels also. In the Indian context, a Working Group has recommended the creation of a peripatetic planning team at the district level to undertake block-level planning functions also.[7]

"The planning by community" implies preparation of the plan by the local community with minimum governmental assistance. This may, perhaps, be an ideal approach, provided the technical character of the plan is not sacrificed, the plan is internally consistent and the needs of the community are planned within realistic parameters.[8]

The Third Party Planner approach implies entrusting the planning function to a voluntary agency or a technical consultancy organization. The argument for entrusting the function to voluntary agencies is that they have a good rapport with the people and are in a favourable position to secure people's cooperation and participation in local planning and implementation. However, voluntary agencies do not always have the requisite technical expertise for plan formulation. On the contrary, when the task of plan formulation is entrusted to a technical consultancy organization, a technically good document may emerge but it may not fully reflect the popular aspirations and needs and is more likely to run into difficulties during the implementation stage.

The choice of the appropriate method for any country will be dictated by the individual circumstances. Whatever be the nature of the planning machinery, it must be composed of a multi-disciplinary team, having sufficient analytical and integrative skills, for undertaking the task of resource analysis, project formulation, target group planning and monitoring and evaluation. A team of social scientists (economists, geographers and sociologists) combined with some subject matter specialists in agriculture and industry and co-ordinated by a generalist planner would perhaps constitute an ideal team for local-level planning. The exact composition of the team will, however, have to be decided according to individual circumstances[9] in each country.

Administrative Adaptations for Local-level Planning

The establishment of a sound planning machinery at the local level is no doubt important. But this alone will not take local planning very far, unless suitable adaptations are brought about in the system of administration, to remove the dysfunctionality between the existing system and the assigned role of local-level planning. In the developing countries, where an administrative system has entrenched and consolidated itself over a long period going back to the colonial era, the elimination of this dysfunctionality would require a very bold attempt at re-organization from the State level downwards. Perhaps, most countries are already seized of these problems and are taking steps to increase the autonomy of their local-level administration. It is realized, now more than ever before, that if local-level planning is to be effective, the local-level administration must have independent decision-making authority and control over the whole range of rural development activities. The socio-political feasibility of bringing about administrative adaptations would naturally vary from country to country. Nevertheless, it should be emphasized that merely providing a set of technical requirements may not in itself be a sufficient condition for successful local-level planning.

Training of Local-level Planners

A question closely related to the planning machinery is that of training the local-level personnel. Since a team of trained planners is unlikely to be available at the local level, perhaps the most cost-effective option is to undertake large-scale training of the local-level officers themselves, so that their skills can be built up. After an intensive training, these officers could serve the local-level planning organization. They can also function as trainers for providing guidance locally, to officers in individual departments, who are charged with formulating sectoral plans.

"Action training" is the most effective way of imparting training and skills to the local-level planners. There are different variants of the "action-training" technique, which may be adopted depending on the circumstances in each country. In its simple form, it may be in the form of short duration "lecture-cum-exercise-oriented" training programmes. Alternatively, it may be an extended operation of "training-cum-plan preparation", somewhat equivalent to on-the-job training. Many innovative methods of learning may be introduced into these training programmes to render them highly effective.[10]

While on the subject of training, it must be emphasized that in the context of local-level planning, training is not to be confined to the planning personnel alone; it must also be extended to the target groups in the local area in order to :

(a) motivate them sufficiently and make them willing partners in the local-level planning process; and
(b) provide them essential non-formal education of different levels to facilitate rural transformation.

Programme Integration

Ideally, the plan at the local level should aim at a total development approach to the problems of the local area and, therefore, must integrate all programmes sponsored by different agencies, but operated at the area level. In practice, however, the tasks of integrating the plan efforts of various organizations presents a number of hurdles. As it happens in most developing countries today, three sets of programmes seem to be operating at the local level : (i) Departmental programmes operated from the Provincial/Central level, (ii) Local development programmes operated by the local authority (if there is any), and (iii) Special development programmes devised to meet the new development goals operated by Central/provincial/local authorities.[11]

The latter category of special programmes are normally conceived as a "filler" of the missing elements in the sectoral programmes and they require for their success complementarities from other programmes, as they are formulated on the presumption that certain developmental inputs normally precede them. But in practice, neither the complementarity nor the proper sequencing is effected with expediency, with the result that serious development lags occur, making the plans counter-productive.

In the context of the situation obtaining in each country, the official guidelines should identify the problems in integrating programmes at the local level and must offer suitable solutions for bringing about the desired integration.

One of the ways to integrate the various programmes is through the creation of a common executive agency. If the common executive agency is meant only as a co-ordinating body, which mechanically puts together the departmental programmes, which come from above as standard formulations, then it will be actually performing very little planning functions and the resulting local plan would be in the nature of arithmetical summation of departmental programmes. On the other hand, an effective local planning will mean building up plans from below and influencing the investment pattern in the local area, both with reference to programmes and target groups. In this case, the organizational structure has to be very different. The official guidelines prepared for any country must take note of these basic considerations.

Finances for the Local Plan

The ability of a local authority to plan comprehensively for its area would depend on the degree of control it has over the public funds and the development budget. In most cases, government budgets, which operate through sectoral departments, are quite rigid, and do not permit the flexibility needed to enable the local-level planner to make sufficient adjustments in the programmes, in response to local needs and circumstances. It will be, of course, ideal if all investment elements converge at the local level, giving scope to the local-level planner to allocate funds to the various programmes according to local priorities and needs. This, however, rarely obtains in practice. A clean slate and an unfettered freedom to plan will not be normally available to the local-level planner. In this context, the countries embarking on local-level planning must devise their own methods of imparting some flexibility in financial arrangements, so that the local-level planner can operate some funds for implementing programmes that are exclusively meant for the local area. *The Presidential System of Grants* (IMPRES) obtaining in Indonesia and the method suggested in the Indian Guidelines for Block-level Planning[12] may be cited as examples, by which some "untied" grants are provided by the State towards financing of the local area plans.

Public Participation

Local-level planning implies a participative development strategy. In its ideal form, local-level planning would imply entrusting to the local people and their institutions all duties and responsibilities of local-level planning and development, with the government reserving to itself only the functions of guidance, supervision and higher planning. In fact, the local-level planning process is one of working with the local people, most directly affected by facilities and programmes, so that the plan : (i) is more responsive to local needs; (ii) reflects more accurately local perceptions, habits, codes and mores; (iii) produces a sense of local ownership and responsibility; (iv) builds on and reinforces the fabric of the community and its internal structure; and (v) supports the evolution of a continuing on-going structure of local administration by creating a core of people who, having worked to make a project happen, and having seen their ideals become a part of development, would carry their involvement into administration, maintenance and planning for the future.[13]

Involving the "public" would mean involving the appropriate interest groups in the area, for specific tasks of local planning and development. This would mean that the local-level planner must identify the various people's institutions in the area. Since the rural poor, as well as many "interest groups" in the area may not have any institutions of their own, the essential task would be to create the proper atmosphere in which their institutions can grow. "Organizing the unorganized" is a problem fraught with many difficulties. The options open to the local-level planner are limited, but by no means devoid of remedial strength. The strategy would be to buttress the resistance capacity of the poor and reduce their vulnerability to exploitation.[14]

In the context of the individual country circumstances, the question of public participation has to be tackled in different ways. Wherever local institutions exist, they should be brought closely into the local-level planning process by associating them with every step in the planning process. The final plan should also have their assent and approval. Where these bodies are not representative of the rural poor, their composition should be changed so as to get their adequate representation in these bodies.

Tasks of Local-level Planning and Local Planning Process

The guidelines for local-level planning prepared for any country must provide a realistic and operational model of the process through which a local plan may be built up. The formulation of the local plan will naturally follow some steps and sequences. While one may not be dogmatic about them, it is necessary to point out that local-level planning, as a technical operation, will be composed of some well-defined tasks. Simply stated, these tasks will include

Resource analysis
Strategy formulation
Plan formulation, and
Implementation planning

Each one of these tasks may be further broken down into certain steps, which may also be arranged in a certain sequence. Before we go into these aspects, it is pertinent to note that a local-level plan is expected to identify the local development problems in great depth and also enumerate the potential beneficiaries of plan programmes, in order to ensure that the flow of benefits does reach the target groups. Assuming that the objectives of local planning include employment maximization, provision of basic minimum needs and direct attack on rural poverty, these should be suitably reflected in the programmes formulated in the plan.

Keeping the above in view, the steps in the local-level planning process may be enumerated as in Table 7.1.

A critical step in the planning process described above, is the formulation of programmes and project proposals. In fact, all the previous steps may be considered as preparatory and convergent to this step. It would follow from resource analysis and would be basically sector-oriented. However, the area development approach to local-level planning would introduce an important dimension, which would help coordinate sectoral programmes and projects already identified, identify additional areas and set priorities among all of them. The identification of schemes/projects will be essentially guided by local needs, above all the basic minimum needs and priorities among them. Various arrangements are at work in the countries in the region, in order to give the project identification process at the local level an appropriate organizational frame.[15] Projects and programmes identified through this process are usually small and simple with limited scope. They do not require extensive feasibility studies or elaborate cost-benefit appraisals. Often, the annual planning horizon suffices to implement them. For such local projects to be implemented without unnecessary delay and red tape, an arrangement for the allocation of funds to local areas on some untied basis is suggested.

TABLE 7.1 : Tasks and Steps in Local-level Planning.

Tasks	Steps
(i) Resource analysis	Resource inventory Socio-economic bench-mark survey Identification of constraints to development Assessment of on-going programmes.
(ii) Strategy formulation	Identification of goals Formulation of development strategy.
(iii) Plan formulation	Identification of schemes/projects Individual household planning for the target groups Infrastructural planning Locational Planning Employment Planning Institutional Planning
(iv) Implementation planning	Programme integration Programme sequencing Financial programming Programme monitoring Evaluation.

Another point of great relevance in the context of project formulation is the need to dovetail the local-level schemes with the plan schemes formulated from above. Effective coordination in this context will depend on the emergence of multi-level planning techniques and procedures.

Apart from scheme/project identification, the plan formulation phase also involves carrying out some specific exercises for introducing certain other desirable dimensions in local-level planning. Four major dimensions of the exercise will be : (i) Locational planning for socio-economic infrastructures, (ii) Employment planning, (iii) Household planning for the target groups, and (iv) Institutional planning, mainly for organizing the rural poor.

Locational planning is imperative because local-level planning will not merely be planning for the efficient production of goods and services using the local resources to the maximum, but also achieving equity in the distribution of such goods and services. There are various methods and procedures for arriving at proper locational decisions, so that economic and social infrastructures could converge in appropriate combinations at optimum locations, contributing to maximum advantage to the people and the area. The methods will involve the identification of a graded hierarchy of service centres in the area and providing the services according to appropriate distance and population norms.

Special emphasis on employment planning is necessary in order to take stock of the employment situation at the local level and to ensure that the production programmes formulated are also employment-intensive. In this context, the preparation of an annual employment budget for the local area may be necessary, as that would pinpoint the periodical adjustments that will be necessary to meet the supply-demand situation in employment, including the planning of public works programme to the extent necessary.

Household planning for the target groups is yet another important aspect of local-level planning. It would involve the identification of the rural poor on some criteria and preparing household plans for each family and integrating the family plans with infra-structure programmes, including credit planning and delivery of inputs.

Institutional planning, especially for the rural poor, would involve conscientizing them, identifying the vulnerable sections and devising institutions which would close the private exploitation trap with a public support system. All the above steps in local-level planning would present problems in methodology and the country guidelines must provide specific guidance on these issues.

Need for Appropriate Methodologies

The specification of the precise method of going about the various steps outlined above is the task of the individual country guidelines. We may only emphasize in this context that any method advocated for the local level must aim at simplicity, as opposed to sophistication. This is not only because of the fact that the utility of some of the sophisticated exercises in their relation to local-level planning are still in doubt, but more so because, the kind of planning infrastructure, expertise and mechanical data processing facilities available to the local-level planner in the developing countries are at present minimal.

The guidelines devised for each country must, therefore, reflect how the various tasks can be carried out in a manner consistent with the realities of the planning environment in the country. The country guidelines must essentially be a guide to action and must spell out the measures which can be realistically achieved within the existing framework. In this context, they must also specify the allocation of tasks and responsibilities to the field organizations.

Conclusions

To conclude this discussion, we may note that the countries in the ESCAP region are at different stages of development with respect to local-level planning for rural development. This difference, coupled with each country's specific level of socio-economic growth as well as socio-political-economic structure will cause them to go their own ways with respect to planning methods, in order to reach the goals of local-level planning. Nevertheless, it may be possible to recognize at least some universal elements in the local planning approach which may be relevant to all countries. The present chapter attempted to identify these commonalities. In the light of this attempt, some general conclusions may be emphasized here :

(i) Local-level planning is a highly demanding exercise. The prerequisites for its success are a genuine and firm governmental commitment, articulation of the multi-level planning process, provision of clear-cut guidelines as to methodology by the national governments and intensive training of the local-level functionaries.

(2) Planning at the local level must be carried out in a multi-level framework.

(3) The capabilities of planning units at the local level need substantial strengthening. Their role versus all other agencies at the various levels should be clearly defined and the links among them firmly established.

(4) The formulation of a good local-level plan alone is not a sufficient condition for its success. Decisive here is, on the one hand, the existence of an efficient implementational machi-nery, and, on the other, the intensive public participation in the local-level planning process.

(5) Methods and techniques used in local-level planning should be simple and appropriate to the level of expertise and infra-structure available for local-level planning in the developing countries.

(6) Genuine local-level planning would require decentralized administration and local control over resources. The administra-tive system has to suitably adapt itself to make these possible.

(7) Basically local-level planning for rural development is meant to direct all development efforts towards the target groups, i.e. those segments of the population which are below the poverty line. In order to ensure active and direct participation of the rural poor, suitable institutional devices must be made. Also a suitable climate must be established to enable organizations of the rural poor to grow.

REFERENCES

1. See the country papers in "Local-level Planning for Integrated Rural Development—Report of an Expert Group Meeting Bangkok 6-10", November, 1978, United Nations ESCAP.
2. Sundaram, K.V., Report of a Study Tour on Local-level Planning in India (November 1979), United Nations ESCAP.
3. See also DeMan, W.H. and A.D.J. Schaap, A model for incorporating the element of space and some aspects of the basic human needs approach in regional development. *ITC Journal,* Vol. I, 1979, Enschede, Netherlands.
4. World Bank, Rural Development—Sector Policy paper, Feb., 1975.
5. In various developing countries, some efforts have been made to decentralize the planning process or to find some way of merging national planning priorities and the felt needs of local communities. One way is through some institutional arrangement—perhaps in the form of regional planning authorities or co-ordinating committees. The District Development Committees set-up in some States in India is an example. Often such bodies spend most of their time allocating funds received from the Central or State Governments for schemes also received from above. Very little actual local planning seems to take place. See K.V. "Sundaram : District Planning--The Case of Maharashtra". *The Indian Journal of Public Administration*, January-March 1979, Vol. XXV, No. 1.
6. Misra, R.P. and K.V. Sundaram, Multi-level Planning and Integrated Rural Development in India, chapter 7, *Multi-level Planning : The Case of Maharashtra*, Heritage Publishers, New Delhi, 1980.

7. Government of India (Planning Commission) : Report of the Working Group on Block-level Planning, New Delhi, 1978.
8. The Comprehensive Area Development experiment in West Bengal (India) used a similar approach.
9. In India, a Working Group on Block-level Planning considered that the Planning team should consist of a chief Planning Officer and six other technical officers viz. Economist/Statistician, Cartographer/Geographer, Agronomist, Engineer, Small and Cottage Industry Officer and Credit Planning Officer. Later taking various practical constraints into account, the Government of India favoured a three member team consisting of an Economist/Statistician, a Credit Planning Officer and a Small and Cottage Industry Officer.
10. For some innovative experiments in training of local level planners tried in India, See P.H. Vaishnav, "Sub-national" approaches to development planning in India—Implications for training. Paper presented to the United Nations Centre for Regional Development, Nagoya (Japan), Feb. 1980.
11. The achievement of distributive justice, the provision of basic minimum needs, the employment thrust and the target group approaches are all new orientations that have tended to influence the local level planning process in recent years. Normally these new orientations must be reflected in the sectoral programmes operating in the local area. However, experience indicates that this adaptation does not come about quickly. So Governments devise the special programmes in order to accelerate these changes. Such programmes are usually sponsored by the Centre or State Governments.
12. In the guidelines for Block-level Planning drawn up by Government of India, it has been suggested that a certain percentage of the overall State Plan outlay, say 10 per cent, as the State Government may decide, may be annually pre-empted as state assistance towards block plans. This amount may be distributed among the blocks equally, if the blocks are more or less homogeneous in character. If the blocks are uneven, the distribution of state assistance to the blocks may be on the basis of population. See "Guidelines for Block-level Planning", Planning Commission, Govt. of India, 1979.
13. Felicia R. Clark *et al*, "Getting people involved" *International Development Review*, Vol. 20, 1978, No. 1, pp. 28-31.
14. This would need identification of all vulnerable sections of the society and devising institutions, which would close the private exploitation trap with a public support system. See Government of India (Planning Commission)—"Report of the Working Group on Block Level Planning", New Delhi, 1978, pp. 24.
15. Examples are the District Development Committees in India, Village and District Development Committee in Thailand, etc.

8

LOCAL-LEVEL PLANNING FOR INTEGRATED RURAL DEVELOPMENT

Some Case Studies*

A. Case Studies in India

India has had long years of experience in rural development and has tried a variety of approaches, with different emphases, during the last quarter of a century or so. Table 8.1 shows these varying approaches and emphases.

A colossal programme of community development was launched from the very First Five Year Plan, which was designed to transform the economic and social life of the Indian villages. While this programme did build up an institutional framework with a multidisciplinary approach and facilitated the implementation of concrete development projects in respect of improved crop production, cattle breeding, transport, rural industry, public health activity and social education, it was not a complete success in decentralized planning, for many reasons. Its impact on agricultural improvement was meagre, and worse still, whatever benefit it imparted was restricted to an elitist minority. The vast majority of the rural masses, who lacked the requisite resource base and were thinly employed, were bypassed by the programme. Moreover, it bypassed the fundamental problem of land relations and the related power structure in the villages. On the administrative front, co-ordination of activities of the different government departments at the block level proved to be the biggest problem. Above all, the schematic approach which it adopted

* This review of case studies was prepared for UN/ESCAP, Bangkok, in 1979. The case studies covered are three from India and one each from Nepal and Malaysia. They were discussed in an Expert Group Meeting held by UN/ESCAP at Bangkok in January, 1980.

led only to "top-down" planning without initiating a "bottom-up" process in planning.

TABLE 8.1 : Different Approaches and Emphases in Rural Development.

Approach	Emphasis
Rural reconstruction	Village-centred movement based on principles of voluntary effort
Community development	Comprehensive rural development based on ideas of motivation, self-help and self-reliance
Target sector	Intensive development of selected sector or sectors of activity with emphasis on concentrating on areas of comparative advantage
Target groups	Growth with social justice for the weaker sections of the population
Growth centres	Spatial planning and development
Backward area development	Reduction of regional imbalances in development
Minimum needs	Equalization of social consumption
Area planning with full employment	Integrated rural development in an area frame with the removal of unemployment (poverty) as an important aim

The Community Development Programme underwent several changes in emphasis over time, which may be interpreted as the various countervailing measures or correctives applied to the planning process from time to time. However, such correctives, on the whole, led only to piecemeal and fragmented planning rather than to an integrated and comprehensive approach to rural development. The concept of "Integrated rural development and block-level planning", which is being pursued since the Sixth Plan (1978-1983),[1] has emerged from these experiments in the choice of planning interventions.

This programme aims at integrated rural development at the block level to secure fuller utilization of local resources, both physical and human, and to provide full employment opportunities in the area within a specific time frame.[2] It envisages integration of the programmes of agriculture and allied activities, cottage and village industries, socio-economic infrastructure, including the Minimum Needs Programme and the development of human resources. One of the components of the programme is the identification of the target groups, i.e. the beneficiaries, comprising the small and marginal farmers, landless labourers and rural artisans, and development of such appropriate schemes for individual assistance, as would generate increased income from them. In doing so, the prospective beneficiaries were to be selected starting from the poorest of the poor in an ascending scale.[3] The basic idea implied in this component of the programme, i.e. the beneficiary-oriented approach, is already ingrained in the Small Farmers Programme,[4] one of the on-going programmes in India. The new elements are the establishment of various linkages and the task of "integrating" the programme in the agriculture sector with those of the other sectors.

Out of the 5,004 blocks in India, about 3,000 had already been covered by one or more of the special area-based programmes, such as the Small Farmers' Development Agency (SFDA), the Drought Prone Area Programme (DPAP) and the Command Area Development Programme (CADP), each of which had its own particular emphasis. The Integrated Rural Development Programme (IRDP) of India aimed at making the poor productive and "broadening their bases", which would not merely help in solving the problems of the natural environment and resource use, but would also ensure the development of the productive, institutional and social infrastructure in those areas. For this purpose, a phased programme approach was recommended, according to which 2,000 out of the 3,000 blocks with on-going programmes were to be selected for the proposed comprehensive treatment during the Sixth Plan period. In addition to this, the Indian programme sought to cover another 1,500 blocks for the five years (300 blocks each year) in areas which were without special programmes. In all, the target coverage during the Sixth Plan period was 3,500 out of the 5,004 blocks in the country.

The Department of Rural Development of the Ministry of Agriculture and Irrigation of the Government of India, which administered the special area-based programmes in the country, provided some guidelines for intensive development of blocks under the Integrated Rural Development Programme. These guidelines mainly related to the methodology for the formulation of schemes in the agriculture and allied sectors of activity. On the basis of these guidelines, the programme was initiated in all the States in the country. Some progress had been made at the time of this review covering two years (i.e. 1978/79 and 1979/80).

The review revealed that as far as the realization of the policy objective of area planning for full employment was concerned, the progress was somewhat halting. This was attributed to the delay in the issue of guidelines for comprehensive and integrated area planning, the organizational and other bottlenecks associated with transition and the initial teething troubles that had to be encountered, while administering the new programme. In order to spell out the methodology of comprehensive block-level plans, the Planning Commission had set-up a Working Group in November 1977 under the chairmanship of Professor M.L. Dantwala, an eminent economist, which submitted its report in May 1978. Taking into account the recommendations contained in that report, the Planning Commission issued the guidelines for block-level planning to the State Governments.

Any evaluation of field performance has to take note of policy pronouncements and the guidelines framed by the Government to effectuate the policy into action programmes. In this context, the guidelines issued by the Planning Commission have great relevance, as they constitute a statement of intent, against which it is possible to measure the current performance in the blocks. A brief account of the official guidelines highlighting some points is, therefore, necessary.

The Guidelines have envisaged the block-level plan as a seven-year perspective plan (from 1981/82—1987/88), synchronizing with the remaining two years of India's Sixth Plan and the full five-year period of the Seventh Plan. Since the existing block-level set-up is unequal to the task of micro-level planning, both in numbers and in capability, the induction of some expertise in the planning team as well as some administrative adaptations have been suggested. It is proposed that the existing nucleus set up for block-level development be enlarged by the addition of three members—an economist/statistician, a credit planning officer and an industries officer for small and cottage industries. It is proposed to bring all functionaries of the line departments under the control of the Chief Planning Officer, so that effective co-ordination would be possible at the block level. While the brunt of block-level planning will be borne by the official machinery, the guidelines have also envisaged the involvement of voluntary agencies with the necessary experience and expertise, "wherever possible", in both plan formulation and implementation.

The Guidelines have advocated certain essential steps in the local-level planning process, which include undertaking a "base-line survey",[5] assessing the financial resources for the plan,[6] setting-up planning machinery and establishing some co-ordinative mechanisms at higher levels to facilitate the task of integration. The major components of the block-level plan have been specified as :

(a) Programmes aiming at optimizing the production potential of the area in the various sectors, e.g. agriculture, animal husbandry, forests, village and small-scale industries, etc.;
(b) Special production programmes for the target groups in the area in the light of the resource potential;

(c) Manpower planning and skill development in relation to the production programmes;
(d) A programme for the provision of basic minimum needs; and
(e) Programme for institutional support.

It is suggested in the guidelines that while preparing the individual sectoral plans and the final integrated plan, the major objective of augmenting employment for increased incomes, especially for the weaker sections, must be kept in view. In this context, the sectoral planners have been advised to devise projects/programmes which would help augment the duration of employment of the people in their existing occupations. After exhausting all the possibilities of providing employment through production programmes, it is suggested in the guidelines that a special public works programme (e.g. "Food-for-work" scheme) be implemented, if necessary, to provide for transitory unskilled employment.

The official guidelines clearly define the aim, set out the methodology in broad terms and make some reference to the tools, administrative and financial, that are needed to ensure that the plans are executed with optimum results. Nevertheless, they do not go into all operational details. In the official letter forwarding the guidelines to the States, it is stated that while the guidelines cover only "some broad and essential aspects", they may be supplemented "from time to time, as considered necessary" by the Ministry of Rural Reconstruction (Government of India) and elaborated further by the State Governments "by incorporating such modifications as necessary, in the context of the geographical, administrative and other peculiarities of their respective States".

Against this brief account of the official guidelines, we may discuss the case studies undertaken in two States in India, namely, Kerala and Tamil Nadu.

B. Case Study in Kerala

The case study area, Kazhakootam Block in Trivandrum District (area : 133.65 sq.km; population 1971 : 152,781[7]; bounded in the south by the city of Trivandrum.)[8] It comprises seven panchayats, two of them lying along the coast. In terms of working force composition, the primary, secondary and tertiary sectors accounted for 38, 26 and 36 per cent respectively of the total number of workers in 1971. Thus, the block must be regarded as somewhat "atypical", in the sense that agriculture is not so dominant a source of employment and income as in most other blocks. The heterogeneity of the rural economy indicated by the composition of the working force may not, however, be interpreted as diversification, pointing to an affluent economy. This is because the non-agricultural enterprises are not in the organized sector, but fall wholly in the "rural and household industry" sector, characterized by low technology and low productivity, e.g. coir and coir-based industries, oil mills and copra, weaving, bricks and tiles, rice and flour mills.

The block is well-connected by rail and road and is comparatively better endowed in terms of social provision, both education and health care. It has also achieved a fair measure of cooperativization in respect of short-term and medium credit with four service cooperatives, one cooperative bank and as many as 18 branches of commercial banks. In the non-credit co-operative sector also, several cooperatives have come up, e.g. coir, fisheries, handloom and milk, though their performance has been below par.

The Scheduled Caste members account for 11.4 per cent of the total block population and they constitute an indigent group. More than 1,000 households are engaged in fishing, eking out an uncertain and meagre livelihood.

Investigations at various levels reveal that the vast majority of the people are thinly employed. A sample household survey (35 house-holds) undertaken for the case study indicated the income and employment of different family types were differing widely. (See Table 8.2).

IRDP, whose performance has been reviewed in the case study, started implementation in the block in November 1978. The study refers to the operations over a brief period of nine months only (November 1978 to July 1979). During that period, the project had identified a total number of 615 beneficiaries, one-fifth of whom belonged to Scheduled Caste families. The family plans of 562 beneficiaries had already been approved by the District Collector and the approval of others was in the pipeline. The two major categories of beneficiary-oriented schemes undertaken by the project authorities were distribution of milch cows and digging of wells. The physical achievement reported against these schemes was 117 and 53 respectively, which is rated by the State government as a "fairly good performance", as it has served to strengthen the resource base of a considerable number of indigent households in a relatively short period.

TABLE 8.2 : Employment and Incomes of different family types in Kazhakootam Block.

	Family type	Employment	Annual income
		(Man days)	*(Rupees)*
(1)	A typical small nuclear family (agricultural)	100	1,550
(2)	Large, complex agricultural family with subsidiary occupations	175	2,000-3,000
(3)	Handloom family	250	1,800
(4)	Family deriving income mainly from coir-based occupations	300	1,800
(5)	Fisher-folk	Data insufficient for building-up any quantitative assessment of income and employment	

The case study makes an assessment of the contribution of the scheme with reference to seven parameters, namely, identification of beneficiaries, preparation and adoption of family plans, financial assistance, extension and supporting systems, co-ordination with other agencies, follow-up and monitoring, and organization and machinery. The following conclusions emerging from the analysis are worthnoting :

(1) Identification of the eligible beneficiary households was not systematic and exhaustive. There was also no public participation in the selection of beneficiaries. In the rush and preoccupation with financial targets, the overriding priority of the implementing functionaries was on piloting a respectable number of family plans, rather than on a systematic identification of the families.

(2) While the heterogeneous character of the block economy with its different components such as fishing, coir, hand-spinning and weaving or handlooms, called for a separate package of measures appropriate to each, the family plans that were formulated followed a rule-of-the-thumb approach, with a few standard schemes being designed to increase employment and income, particularly of farm families. The scheme formulation appears to have been circumscribed by the range of competence and information available to the Village Extension Officer. In a process of mechanistic simplification, schemes necessitating upgrading of technology,[9] or relevant in the context of diversification of the economy, were sacrificed, as the capacity of the functionaries to innovate was absent. This only serves to underline the difficult nature of the tasks involved in local-level planning and implementation. Unless the functionaries have the requisite competence to handle these problems,

local-level planning will, more often than not, be reduced to a mechanical and often irrelevant exercise. The selection of projects was restricted to bankable schemes only and, as such, they were not necessarily those that conformed to "integrated" development. Thus, the case study has noted that the selective approach to family plans has militated against integrated development efforts.

(3) The special importance of extension and support services, in a programme designed for a group of people that needs them most, does not seem to have been grasped, as these were not simultaneously attended to. The case study notes that there is a clear need for the simultaneous strengthening of the extension machinery and toning up of the support services.

(4) While co-ordination of developmental activities within the concerned departments has been ensured, the co-ordination with other departments and agencies, which has been envisaged in the programme, has not been attempted. Co-ordination has also been not fully effective for want of a district-level or block-level organization.

(5) The voluntary agencies have not been drawn into the exercise.

(6) The study has noted the absence of an organization and machinery, adequate to cope with the task assigned in the context of block-level planning and integrated rural development. The present organization and machinery are inadequate for these tasks. Monitoring and follow-up have not been taken up seriously.

The case study of Kazhakootam block shows that while some intensification of agricultural development has been achieved, which has benefited individual families, integrated development, in the sense in which it was originally conceived by the planners, has not really come about. It has underscored the point that if family programmes are to continue on a self-sustaining basis, then such programmes must be closely linked with the locally available resources for which comprehensive block-level planning is needed.

C. Case Study in Tamil Nadu

The study area, Uthiramerur Block in Chingleput District (area : 420.56 sq.km; population 1971 : 104,200; number of households : 22,241) comprises 127 villages, constituted into 73 village panchayats and one town, which has an urban local body called the "Town Panchayat". The population of the Block has a Scheduled Caste and Scheduled Tribe component, accounting for 26.9 per cent of the total population. Eighty-four per cent of the population is rural. The occupational classification shows : cultivators, 44 per cent; agricultural labourers, 37 per cent; and the remaining 19 per cent in other non-agricultural occupations. The total cropped area of the Block is 73 per cent, of which 27 per cent is double-cropped. Small holdings predominate with the marginal and small farmers holding about 91 per cent of the total number of holdings. Paddy, groundnut, ragi, sugarcane, chillies and gingelly are the important crops, with paddy predominating (71 per cent) the cultivated area. With one primary land development bank, 18 primary agricultural credit societies, 8 weavers' co-operative societies and 48 milk producers' societies and 4 branches of nationalized commercial banks, the Block has a fairly good institutional set-up for disbursing credit for agriculture and allied activities. Industrially, too, the Block is fairly advanced, with one textile mill, 54 rice mills, 14 oil mills, a handloom industry supporting 3,500 persons and other cottage industries. The Block is also well endowed with infrastructure such as electricity, roads and drinking water supply. The democratic institutions in the area are the village panchayats, and the Panchayat Union Council (federation of panchayats), although at the time of the visit of the ESCAP team, the Panchayat Union Council, having been superseded by the Government, was not functioning. Development activities at the block level are co-ordinated by the Block Development Officer, who is assisted by extension officers in agriculture, animal husbandry and co-operation. While the Extension officers are under the administrative control of the Block Development Officer, they are technically controlled by the other departments from where they had been drawn. Two special programmes for rural development are operating in the district, i.e. the Small Farmers' Development Agency (SFDA) programme and IRDP. The implementation of the two special programmes as well as their performance efficiency have been analyzed in the case study.

The SFDA project, being essentially a beneficiary oriented project, involves the following stages in project planning and implementation, namely :

(a) Identification of the target group;
(b) Assessment of their requirements; and
(c) Linking them with the various functional institutions meant for credit, input and services.

The case study analysis revealed that the initial identification of the eligible families was not done systematically, that control and monitoring functions at the field level needed great improvements and that follow-up contacts with the beneficiaries had been neglected. The study traced these inadequacies to an ill-equipped departmental machinery and emphasized the need for organizational and administrative changes in this context. The study has also drawn attention to the lack of area specificity in the schemes adopted, the failure to use resource inventory information for scheme formulation[10] and lack of efficiency in extension services.[11] A definitional ambiguity in regard to "family", which is the unit for identifying the target group of beneficiaries, and the "dual control system" with the small farmers' agency on the one hand and the sectoral departments on the other are also mentioned as deficiencies in the programme.

IRDP, which has been in operation in the Block since April, 1978, seems to have suffered an organizational jolt during the middle of the year. It was initially implemented by the Block Development Officer and his technical and non-technical supporting staff, but in September, 1979, the programme implementation was transferred to the Small Farmers Development Agency. This inevitably impeded the project's momentum.

The project started with the identification of the target group of families in the Block through a survey, based on which an action programme and a financial plan for a three-year period was drawn up. Based on certain assumptions, the effective target group was identified as 13,424 families and their coverage was phased out over the three-year period. The task of linking up each family in the target group with an appropriate economic activity (participation in which will help the family to earn a certain incremental income) was then taken on hand. Thus the tasks actually accomplished in the Uthiramerur Block were the identification of target families and the doling out of the benefits to them in the form of a subsidy on the SFDA pattern. This achievement is very much short of that envisaged in block-level planning in the comprehensive sense. The experience here clearly shows that the integration of the beneficiary-oriented scheme with infrastructure and other supporting programmes was hardly attempted. The discussion also revealed that the field functionaries were not clear as to the precise manner in which integration was to be brought about among the different components of the plan. This is indicative of the lack of adequate preparation before putting through the programme. According to the case study, several operational details had been left to be decided at the local level, which in practice did not work out satisfactorily.

An analysis of the programme content in the plan revealed that about 73 per cent of the outlay had been spent on purchase and supply of milch animals, ploughs, bullocks and sheep. This trend had the unfavourable effect of increasing the market prices of the animals, thereby decreasing the benefit to the farmers. The study has reported that many farmers, therefore, were forced to sell away the animals immediately after purchase, finding it difficult to meet the loan repayment schedule. Further, the linkages with such programmes, e.g. breeding, fodder, etc., were lost sight of, with the result that the programme resulted in an adverse effect on the beneficiaries. Apart from the lack of an organizational pattern conducive to integration among the sectoral activities, the case study also identified the absence of a separate planning machinery for undertaking a detailed planning exercise and the lack of training support to enable the field functionaries to grasp the real content and spirit of the programme as other major lacunae.

A Review of the Block-level Experiments in India

A review of performance at the block level in the two cases examined here shows that while block-level planning on a systematic basis has not yet taken off, considerable experience has been acquired in implementing beneficiary-oriented programmes. The salient features of the methodology in this context are as follows.

The identification of beneficiaries is carried out by village welfare officers, through door-to-door visits, who collect data on family resources and felt needs of activities or materials to achieve increased income and the betterment of living conditions. On the basis of these data, a family plan is formulated by the family itself in consultation with the village welfare officers. The sum total of family plans of the beneficiaries, together with the infrastructural support plan, constitutes the block development plan with its various components, including agriculture and allied activities, village and cottage industries and service sectors.[12] The Block Development Officer, with the assistance of specialists from line departments and a group of village workers, plays a leading role in planning for the block-level development and implementation of programmes.

A proposed activity of the family plan is funded by the Government by granting subsidies, amounting to 25 per cent in the case of small farmers and 33.33 per cent in the case of marginal farmers, the remaining portion to be financed by the commercial banks. The differential rate of interest charged to a poor family earning less than Rs. 3,500 is 4 per cent per annum. As a rule, the individual beneficiary is given the subsidy from the Government in kind only. As a follow-up, the performance of the family plan is reviewed and advice is given, as needed.

The planning process described above has an in-built element of local participation, as the family actively participates in the formulation and implementation of the plan. Further, the Panchayat Samiti, consisting of a body of elected representatives, provides advice and assistance to the BDO and his team of Village Level Officers in the management of block affairs. In fact, the Block Development Committee, a consultative and decision-making body, is formed with the BDO, the Chairmen of the panchayats, representatives of pressure groups and voluntary organizations and district officers from the line departments. At the higher levels, the State Planning Board and District Planning Committees exist. At the State level, co-ordination is effected between the State/sectoral plan and the district/block development plans.

D. A Proto-type Block-level Plan : Ibrahimpatnam Block, Andhra Pradesh

The implementation experience reviewed in the Kazhakootam and Uthiramerur case studies represents action programmes that have started off somewhat on an *ad hoc* basis, without a comprehensive plan to precede or guide them. Quite in contrast, the block plan of Ibrahimpatnam that has been meticulously formulated by a technical team, has not yet got off the ground. It represents a situation where planning is not, as yet, integrated with implementation.

The plan, considered as a prototype exercise, has been framed by the National Institute of Rural Development, Hyderabad, for one of the blocks in Andhra Pradesh, the Ibrahimpatnam Block in Ranga Reddy District. It is claimed that the plan is based on the methodology outlined by the Working Group on Block-level Planning set up by the Planning Commission. The plan combines, in a common plan frame, the merits of sectoral as well as spatial aspects of planning, purposively designed to improve production, to bring benefits of development to the rural poor and to increase employment. The plan has attempted the following seven tasks :

(1) Analysis of the existing level of development in the block area.
(2) Identification of the problems and constraints in the way of development.
(3) Identification of the centres of growth, which can generate and regulate the process of developmental activities in the area.
(4) Assessment of the potentialities of development in the agriculture and allied sectors to propose suitable programmes and optimize growth and generate maximum employment.
(5) Identification of the spatial and functional gaps and to propose infrastructure to support the developmental activities.
(6) Assessment of the employment potential in different sectors in order to propose ways and means of creating full employment conditions in the block.
(7) Integration of all sectoral development programmes into the spatial framework to attain an integrated development of the block area.

The study has started with spatial planning, by identifying the existing and potential centres or focal points of development, on the basis of the movement pattern of the people and their activities in the area. On the basis of this exercise, the block area has been divided into micro-planning units with a central village in each, which would serve as the focal point to generate growth impulses. These micro-planning units are used in the plan as the basic spatial units, where investment could be made and also to take into account the type and quantum of benefit that would accrue to the people in general, and the rural poor in particular. Within these units, the present situation and available potential for different activities have been assessed and future requirements worked out.

The study was based on both secondary and primary data. Secondary data were collected from different offices located at the block as well as the district headquarters. Primary data were collected through questionnaires exclusively designed for the study of :

(a) Village economy,
(b) Household economy,
(c) Artisan economy,
(d) Business and commerce, and
(e) Industry.

In the village studies, the focus was on the small and marginal farmers and landless agricultural labourers. In each major sector of development, e.g. agriculture, forestry, animal husbandry, fisheries, industry, etc. an analysis was made of the existing level of development, the potential for future development as well as the labour utilization and employment potential. Since the focus of the plan was on the development programmes for the weaker sections of rural society, to enable them to augment their family income through provision of gainful employment opportunities, alternative uses of land, water and human resources were examined and certain models evolved indicating the optimum mix of occupations, which would make the household economy of the various poor categories of people viable under different assumptions.

The Ibrahimpatnam Plan is a ten-year perspective plan for the period 1978-1988 and has not merely attempted to reconcile the needs of the area and target groups and individuals in a common plan frame, but has also outlined the organizational changes needed for implementing the plan programmes and increasing their efficiency in implementation. It has emphasized the need for integrating the programmes of the elective body (Panchayat Samiti), the government machinery and voluntary organizations. It has also noted that the task of planning the operational details of the programmes and reviewing the problems in their implementation is not done and has, therefore, emphasized the need for involving the people in the planning function and in reviewing the implementation of programmes. For this purpose, it has suggested the setting up of panels, consisting of extension officers as well as representatives of beneficiaries and voluntary agencies. The plan has also expressed itself against the adoption, at local levels, of uniform schemes based on model schemes evolved at district and higher levels. It has noted that all the target families to be helped for increasing their income above the poverty line require training. Therefore, it has suggested the identification of the training requirements and the formation of a training co-ordination committee to co-ordinate the various training programmes. These various suggestions contained in the plan seem to be quite significant, in the context of the realization that good plans do not by themselves guarantee anything, unless appropriate ways are found to implement them.

E. Case Studies in Malaysia and Nepal

The two Indian case studies discussed have brought out some of the missing elements in local-level planning for integrated rural development.

Since what had been reviewed in those studies was only a programme and not a plan, the need for co-ordination of the programmes in the productive sectors of the economy and their further linking with infrastructural and social development in a reciprocally supportive manner must be greatly emphasized. In addition, the prototype block plan which was discussed illustrates the technicality and complexity of the issues involved in micro-level planning. The other case studies, Malaysia and Nepal, reviewed here serve to emphasize the two vital elements in the local-level planning process, namely, the organizational structure and citizen participation. The need for a permeative planning mechanism, in which people can genuinely participate, has been emphasized in these studies.

The Malaysian case study on the Muda Irrigation Project indicates the methodology of integrated rural development in a selected rice-growing area in Malaysia. Initiated during the First Malaysian Plan (1966-1970), it started primarily as an engineering project involving the construction of physical facilities. Although the major goal of the project was envisaged as promoting more intensive use of land resources by double-cropping, thereby increasing the level of national self-sufficiency in rice production, the concerned agencies, even during the period of physical construction, had begun to question whether the goals of income distribution and welfare were not equally legitimate. It was also soon realized that the physical infrastructure formed only a part of an over-all innovative agronomic package and that a concerted and integrated approach to rural development was necessary to achieve the various goals of rural development. This eventually led to the creation of the Co-ordinator's Office for the project and the replacing of the double-cropping programme into viable irrigation compartments, which made it possible to concentrate scarce resources in different subregions according to a planned schedule. Inter-state problems calling for co-ordinated planning,[12] and the inability of the state governments to finance the project individually, led to the creation of a semi-autonomous organization, the Muda Agricultural Development Authority (MADA), by the Federal Government in 1972. Its creation provided the administrative framework to undertake integrated rural development and to develop the structures by which local-level participation in decision-making could be initiated through the farmers' associations. The changing perspectives of Muda's role as a development agency and in relation to the farming community in general, which is described in the case study, affords useful insights for local-level planning and involvement by citizens. The Muda Phase II Project, which incorporates not only the engineering parameters, but also the agricultural, social, political and economic parameters, also illustrates how agricultural facilities and several dynamic extension strategies should be formulated to ensure active farmer participation. The major extension strategies include the formation of field work groups, revolving around the field neighbourhood concept, establishment of functional linkages between change agents and change recipients, organization of large-scale pilot demonstration projects and the stepping up of existing extension services. The functional basis of the new institutional structure, which links field work groups in irrigation blocks to small agricultural units and the area farmers' associations, has led to the development of a dynamic and commercialized farming community which, in turn, has further potentialities for increased involvement of farmers in local-level integrated rural development planning.

The case study outlines and critically assesses the components of a local-level plan for integrated rural development. In particular, institutions emphasizing the grassroot participation in rural development processes are required, so that any new technology introduced into the area would be economically feasible, physically sound and socially acceptable. The study highlights the important ingredients for successful implementation of the rural development plan which is includes : (a) the formulation of an agronomic package, (b) the establishment of a semi-autonomous body to integrate the various aspects of the development process, and (c) the establishment of an institutional infrastructure consisting of farmers' associations and work groups to promote local-level participation.

Shrestha's study on "Local-level planning in Nepal" lays emphasis on the participatory process for rural development planning and the institutional arrangements that are desired to ensure the full-fledged participation of the low-income groups in the decision-making process in planning and implementation. The crucial issues in local development planning and implementation are discussed with special reference to the Raswa Nuwakot Rural Development Project. The central objective of this approach is to support His Majesty's Government's development strategy, which seeks to balance economic growth with income distribution, provide for more equitable regional development and ensure productive benefit from previous road investment. For this purpose, a detailed investment plan was drawn up and was being implemented through the sectoral agencies as well as the local panchayats. Case studies of three village panchayats have been undertaken to bring out the extent of citizen participation in planning, in implementation of projects as well as in their subsequent maintenance. The case study illustrations point to the following conclusions :

(1) Given the opportunity, the village communities have the capability to plan and implement their own programmes, mobilize their own resources and manage the project on a continuing basis. The case of the reforestation project in the Belkot Village Panchayat is an excellent example of a local self-help effort of this kind. The case also emphasizes that development intervention by the Government has to be judiciously identified, so that it does not cause any negative effect on the local initiative.

(2) The institutionalization of the small farmers greatly helps the planning for local development, e.g. by assisting the poorer people to obtain loans on a group liability basis. The case study of the Tupche Village Panchayat has brought out the importance of the supportive role of local panchayats in the Small Farmers' Programme as well as the effectiveness of the "small farmers' groups" in several areas of social development in the village, such as promotion of family planning and avoidance of unproductive expenditure on social ceremonies. It has also revealed how the transformation of the poorer strata of the village is achieved through "small farmers' groups". The study has drawn attention to instances, where the projects have failed, because of the absence of the involvement of the public in the planning and development process.

(3) Intersectoral consultation and accord are infrequent and ineffective in the planning process in the district. Therefore, there is no integrated planning at the local level. Sectoral planning, which is mostly done at the national level, lacks local focus. In other words, integration as a strategy for the planning and implementation of sectoral plans has not been achieved in practice.

(4) The existing planning procedures for the project are not based on the understanding of the critical ingredients of participation, i.e. participation in decision-making, participation in implementation, including resource mobilization, participation in benefit-sharing and participation in evaluation. There is no permeative planning mechanism in which people can genuinely participate.

(5) The current planning exercises are not based on an objective assessment of the existing situation. Neither officials nor the popular representatives are equipped with the information necessary for it.

(6) Citizen participation in the planning process is now confined to need identification only. In order to actuate integrated planning at the local level, the planning exercise at the village level has to be more than need identification and must be a multi-sectoral endeavour encompassing all the components of planning. This would require considerable training and experience on the part of the village leadership and bureaucracy, and a sustained and integrated support, such as that given to "small farmers' groups" by the project management.

(7) An important area of local planning is the creation and strengthening of an institutional phenomenon, which stands out in the Nepal context as the "user groups", which may be developed as an institution competent to plan, implement, manage and evaluate the project and to generate the necessary resources for it. The Nepal case has also shown that such "user groups" should be promoted within the framework of village organizations. The establishment and nurturing of such an institution should be done as part of the extension and support function to be performed at the district and service centre level and supported by the necessary policy measures adopted at the national level.

(8) While planning activity naturally includes review and evaluation exercises at regular intervals at each of the levels involved, it must be given a special place of importance in rural development at the national level.

(9) Given the stratified nature of the village society, the mere flow of resources to the local level does not necessarily result in their equitable distribution to all segments of local population. The Nepal case study amply illustrates this point.

F. Basic Issues in Local-level Planning for Integrated Rural Development

The performance of local-level planning for integrated rural development reviewed in the case studies can now be summarized with a view to drawing some lessons for the future. It is perhaps necessary at the outset to emphasize the point that the task of local-level planning for integrated rural development is one of enormous complexity.

The case studies have provided some analysis of the constraints and potentials encountered during the process of local-level planning for integrated rural development, of the mechanisms that have evolved to deal with them and of the effectiveness of these mechanisms in improving the performance of the projects. What has been obtained from these analyses is a bundle of insights. In presenting a view of local planning for integrated rural development from these insights, it is assumed that the objective of local planning is to ensure that the rural masses, especially the small farmers, tenants, landless labourers, artisans, etc., will improve their productivity, income and living conditions on a sustained basis. The discussion, therefore, focuses on the following issues, which are closely interrelated.

(1) A planning approach concentrating on a small geographic area seems to be the best way of organizing local-level planning for integrated rural development, as the intensive planning and implementation within a selected locality will help to identify the basic interrelations between the different components of the integrated rural development and evolve the strategies which could be effectively replicated. Area development approach will also help to establish the cross-functional planning framework to link the micro-level planning to the macro target setting and planning. The development experience in many countries (e.g., India and Bangladesh) has demonstrated the usefulness of such an approach in coming to grips with specific problems.

(2) The plan framework of area development should be both comprehensive and in line with resource and administrative capabilities. It is comprehensive in the sense that it takes into account, within the rural space, all the relevant sectors of the economy and uses the interrelationships so as to identify and exploit the linkages and external effects between those sectors. For such comprehensive planning, a method should be evolved through which the objectives can be transformed into action. The planning method should be flexible and adaptable to continuous changes. In the Indian context, the National Planning Commission has outlined such a method in its official guidelines.

(3) Basic in the orientation of the integrated rural development is the focus on the rural poor. The beneficiary-oriented style of planning, involving the identification of the target groups below the poverty line, preparing individual family plans for them and linking them to credit channels is an important component of the IRD programme, as put into operation in India. Planning for the target group and infrastructural development are complementary. In fact, the former can be effective only

when supported by the latter and must, therefore, be preceded by it in the general sequence of implementation. While seeking to tackle the problem of rural poverty, the question of individual versus group approach assumes great relevance. The individual approach is more specific and effective, but time-consuming and costly. In some contexts, it may even be disliked by the people who may be averse to being identified as poor (e.g. Thailand, Sri Lanka).

The group approach, however, may hasten coverage, but would call for considerable effort towards institutionalization of interest groups, although this has a built-in risk that may lead to the monopoly of the dominant group. The decision as to the particular approach for any country will be determined by the circumstances peculiar to it and its level of development.

(4) The systematic planning process at the grassroot level implies the performance of the following technical functions :

(a) Resource inventory and data collection, including analysis of the prevailing levels of development, potential for further development and identification of constraints to development;
(b) Identification of priorities and selection of key programmes;
(c) Project/scheme formulation and the establishment of their spatial and temporal linkages within an integrated framework;
(d) Devising a plan for fuller utilization of manpower resources;
(e) Assessment of the availability of financial resources from various sources; and
(f) Monitoring and concurrent evaluation or parallel audit of development plans and their modification from time to time in the light of experience.

The successful performance of the above functions will demand the existence of a technical planning machinery. In the context of the paucity of trained personnel in the developing countries, the problem of the planning machinery has to be solved in appropriate ways. In India, the block-level planning is sought to be done at least in the initial stages by the district planning organization through a peripatetic planning team.

(5) The selection of appropriate projects/schemes is of crucial importance in local-level planning for IRD. In any scientific approach to this problem, the selection should be preceded by an evaluation of all feasible projects/schemes. To be realistic, the projects/schemes must be grounded in resource inventory information. Lack of area specificity in

the schemes selected and the failure to use the resources inventory information were revealed during the discussion of Indian case studies. In most exercises on local-level planning, project formulation has been reduced to a selection of limited, uniform and standardized sets of schemes. Since the planning agency at the local level is not equipped to find technological solutions, there seems to be no immediate solution to this problem. In this context, the provision of better organizational support to local-level planning for integrated rural development in terms of technical staff to perform the functions of economic programme identification assumes great importance.

(6) The concept of local-level planning for IRD is wider than that of agricultural development or community development alone. It implies a consciously formulated, systematic, multisectoral programme to attain enhanced productivity and reduced poverty. It means *simultaneous* planning of the three sectors of the economy—agriculture, industry and services—at the local level, where development action is taking place. The expression "simultaneous" must be underscored because it refers to the co-ordinated planning of those activities, the result of which will lead to a plan composed of concrete projects for implementation. The case studies, for instance, have revealed that increasing the resource base of the rural poor is no doubt important, but not sufficient.[14] It is also necessary to follow up the whole system of income generation.

(7) Local-level planning for IRD is a highly co-ordinated exercise in two senses. Firstly, it seeks to integrate multiple objectives, namely, more production, more employment and more equitable distribution of income. Secondly, it aims at integration of the low-income segments with the rest of the rural community. How to achieve such integration is the crux of the problem. Lack of built-in mechanisms for co-ordination among the various sectoral departments concerned with local-level planning for IRD is the greatest single problem in the rural administrative system. In the studies reviewed, co-ordination seems to depend purely on the personal relations of the district chief with the departmental heads. It is in this context that the role of a properly conceived micro-level plan assumes great significance. It could well become an instrument for achieving effectiveness in co-ordination. Thus, if a plan of action is prepared in advance, every departmental activity falls in its place and to that extent co-ordination is facilitated. Another way in which co-ordination could be facilitated is by clothing the district chief with adequate authority over the area, by bringing all the line departments effectively under him and

by giving him, for instance, the powers to allocate funds among the sectoral departments, such as is done in Sri Lanka.

(8) One of the glaring external constraints on local-level planning of IRD is provided by the administrative system, which is usually oriented towards sectoral and departmental activities, rather than geared to area development or development of certain target groups. To overcome the difficulties that arise from this conflict, other patterns of organization are thought of, e.g. establishment of special authorities for development. The unique feature of such authorities, as compared with other government agencies, is that their scope of activity is not vertical by function or sector, but horizontal by area. Generally the authorities that have been established belong to one of two main categories : (a) development authorities responsible for planning and for co-ordination between the organs of implementation (e.g. SFDA in India);[15] and (b) development authorities that are themselves entrusted with the responsibility for implementation (e.g. MUDA Agricultural Development Authority in Malaysia). There is no universally valid or generally applicable solution. The administrative structure necessary to ensure the most efficient system of co-ordination has to be evolved separately for each context.

(9) Local-level planning for integrated rural development can succeed only if it is designed for the people and with the people. The real test of local participation is in the share of actual power which rests with the representatives of the local population and especially the poorest among them. The exercise of this power is demonstrated in the process of decision-making regarding the allocation of resources, and planning of the operational details of the plan as well as involvement in reviewing problems of implementation and responsibility for the upkeep and maintenance of projects, etc.

(10) The formulation and implementation of plans for local development require personnel who have received training beyond that of their specific disciplines. Experts in a certain field must learn how to relate the role of their disciplines as an interdependent part of a comprehensive area plan. This requires knowledge of associated fields of development and experience in a team approach to area analysis. Such training enables the planner to maximize his contribution as member of a multidisciplinary team and to co-ordinate integrated development of activities. The training programme should consist of short practical and action-oriented courses combining theoretical lectures with the practical application and demonstrations.

(11) An important aspect for consideration during the implementation process is the provision made for the regular monitoring of the programmes, particularly from the point of view of the impact on the target population. In India, the arrangements made for monitoring the family plans were quite detailed. But the arrangement for monitoring the linkages of family plans with other programmes was not adequate.

(12) One of the vital issues on which clear indications were not available related to the question of the linkages necessary between the local plan and the higher-level planning (e.g. national, including sectoral, and regional planning). This has implications for sustaining the success of the family plans at the local level. While the need for multilevel planning is clear, the procedures and mechanisms for initiating iterative or transactive planning must be evolved in country-specific situations. More in-depth studies are needed in this context.

In conclusion, contemporary development experience in the various ESCAP countries reveals that a fair amount of methodological progress has been achieved through the work undertaken by several national and international agencies and research institutions. There is, however, still room for considerable progress regarding the actual application of such methods in the field. In this context, there is great need for an in-depth analysis of the process of local-level planning in individual countries and for evolving appropriate guidelines. This has to be supplemented by a vigorous programme of training for all those involved in local-level planning activities, both in government and outside.

NOTE

The case studies reviewed here were sponsored by ESCAP in selected rural areas of India, Malaysia and Nepal. They are contained in the ESCAP publication : "The Practice of Local-level Planning" UNESCAP, Bangkok, 1980.

REFERENCES

1. The removal of unemployment and significant underemployment, an appreciable rise in the standard of living of the poorest section of the population and provision by the State of the basic needs of the poor people, have been embodied as the primary objectives of India's Draft Sixth Five-Year Plan, 1978-83. These objectives have been set to be achieved within a period of 10 years.
2. The meaning of "full employment" in this context is neither the provision of full work to all those who are looking for jobs, nor ensuring the full utilization of all available material resources in the local area. It is limited

to the generation of additional employment and the raising of the income level of the identified target groups above the poverty line.

3. This approach of identifying the poorest families for individual assistance has been termed the "Antyodaya approach" in the Indian Plan. According to the programme, about 400 families below the poverty line are to be identified in a block in a year and provided with the necessary support. According to the Planning Commission, the poverty line refers to an individual income of Rs. 62 per month. The case studies have adopted a family income of less than Rs. 400 per month to identify the families below the poverty line.
4. The definition of a "small farmer" in India is one who has less than 5 acres of unirrigated or 2.5 acres of irrigated land. A marginal farmer is one with less than 2 acres of land.
5. The baseline survey is intended to (a) facilitate an assessment of the prevailing situation, i.e. the natural resources and their level of utilization in the area, (b) identify the gaps, and (c) provide a bench-mark against which further development progress can be measured. The resource inventory which is the most important aspect of the base-line survey will consist of an inventory of (a) physical and biological resources, (b) human resources, and (c) infrastructure and institutions. The guidelines have also provided an illustrative list of the information essential for block-level planning.
6. A method of assessing the financial size of a block plan has been indicated. The guidelines have suggested placing at the disposal of the block a certain amount of "untied grants" from the State. This will give some degree of freedom to the local-level planner. Since each item in the budget is determined in advance by the concerned sectoral agencies, the normal budget structure does not provide much leeway for the dynamic process of local-level planning for integrated rural development.
7. The average area and population of a block in India are 600 sq.km and 80,000 to 100,000 people.
8. It is in fact a continuum of the city, "a suburb gradually merging into rural homesteads".
9. For the fishermen in the block, it is the technology for fishing equipment which needs to be upgraded. However, the programme has not applied itself to such problems.
10. Ground-water information had pointed to the scope for digging new wells. But very little has been attempted in the way of minor irrigation works.
11. Project implementation was confined to making available, the subsidy for the needed inputs, without any technical guidance for adopting improved agricultural practices.
12. The linkage of the family plan with the other components was weak.
13. The river basin cuts across two States, Keda and Perlis.
14. For example, by giving a milch animal or two, the small farmers' problem does not get solved. It is equally important to organize an efficient marketing system.
15. SFDA is only a co-ordinative agency, and has to rely on other agencies of government for various implementation tasks. The problems confronting a co-ordinative agency are complex, as it has to deal with a network of relationships both with local agencies of the Government and the various units of local government.

9

INFORMATION NEEDS AND SYSTEMS FOR DECENTRALIZED PLANNING*

Our contemporary society in the Third World countries has witnessed, and is still witnessing, some rapid and extraordinary changes and challenges in various directions—political, administrative, economic, social and technological—which are perhaps far more spectacular in terms of magnitude and impact than any experienced so far during a comparable period of human history. The major changes witnessed during the 1950's and 1960's included decolonization (in a number of countries), central control of government functions and ushering in of a massive effort directed towards national reconstruction and development. This was followed during the 1970's and 1980's by a succession of far-reaching changes in development design and administration. Perhaps, it is more appropriate to characterize this latter period of change as a phase of "development challenges," i.e. challenges that are being thrown up by the very dynamics of development. To meet these changes and challenges, the developing countries are adopting various methods, which include adaptations, adjustments, rationalization, restructuring and even total transformation in government and administration.

It is perhaps better to start this essay by examining how the development scenario is changing in the developing countries and what specific challenges are being faced in the context of the subject of our discussion. The changes, and the challenges experienced here are broadly in the following four directions :

---

* Keynote paper to the "Regional Seminar on Development Information : Policies and Strategies" held in Kuala Lumpur in July 1990, Organized by the Association of Development Research and Training Institutes of Asia and the Pacific (ADIPA).

* Changes in the orientation of planning from a growth-oriented paradigm to one based on growth with equity, stability and sustainability, demanding new planning strategies.
* Changes in the structure of planning from a centralized approach to a more decentralized approach directed towards improved sub-national development planning, characterised by multiple development objectives.
* An enormous need for disaggregated data and information for planning purposes at different levels and also the need to handle and analyze this data with speed and accuracy.
* The revolution in the field of information technology itself, involving the multiple application of micro-technology and optical electronics.

The above development challenges, however, could not be effectively met in most countries, with the result that some notable gaps have appeared between what is obtaining and what is desirable. Perhaps in no area of development planning are these gaps so striking in their manifestations, as in the information sector at the sub-national levels. Here, the present situation is so critical that I would prefer to characterize the problem context as one of an "Information Crisis". This crisis has a historical basis, particularly in the colonial history and the subsequent developments in many countries, which led to centralized control of government functions and the establishment of a "top-down approach" to planning. These political and administrative changes profoundly influenced the structure of development in every sphere of activity.

In the information sector, this resulted in establishing a system of data collection favouring those aspects and activities relevant to macro-level planning, e.g. national accounts—covering national income, savings and investments, foreign trade and the monetary system. Such data, as generated, were at a rather aggregated level with, of course, a fair degree of sectorial disaggregation suited to planning at the national level. With the changes that have now come about in these countries, necessitating the introduction of decentralized planning characterized by multi-objective approaches, the network of development planning information "systems" established earlier has demonstrated its irrelevance and non-utility to the changed context. Governments in the developing countries are struggling with the existing structure and organization of data and information systems, and are seeking to adapt it for meeting the new needs of planning-related data at the sub-national levels. However, in many countries, these changes have not come about quite satisfactorily. What is perhaps needed now is a total reversal of the earlier system and its substitution by consciously designed (networks of) planning information systems suited to a multi-level planning context. In fact, the nature and degree of transformation called for in the information sector to cope with the emerging needs of planned development is the major preoccupation of this paper. As we go along in this discussion, the problem of how to bring about the requisite degree of transformation in information provision activity, in the technical, technological and organizational directions as well as in country-specific contexts will be commented upon. The changes taking place in a dynamic planning context in India will receive special attention in the latter part of this paper.

Decentralized Development Planning: Critical Issues in Change and Transformation

Our point of departure here is Decentralized Planning or Multilevel Planning, in the context of the new orientations or strategies that are emerging, to make planning and development increasingly attuned to the structural, demographic, economic and social characteristics peculiar to each country and areas within a country. This essentially involves the sharing of planning functions at different area levels and devising of appropriate mechanisms and procedures for the effective capture, processing and "flows" of detailed information, interface between and among the area levels, as well as interaction for the meaningful participation with the people. All such arrangements are intended to make the planning process at the various spatial levels, on the whole, harmonious, interdependent and participatory and the plans themselves geographically relevant, authentic and implementable.[1] What is very significant about multi-level planning is that it is a technical exercise as well as a management and negotiation process. Decision-making here is based on a "participatory or negotiated planning approach",[2] which means that such decisions are not made on a unilateral or even bilateral basis, but are the result of "negotiations" among a number of concerned parties. In the information context, this means that we have to reckon with not one, but several information users and often several distinct needs. Taking these varied requirements into account, we now need data and information at different spatial levels of aggregation and disaggregation. Particularly in the context of the changed planning orientations and strategies, we now need data on a large number of micro variables, touching on a wide range of distributional and equity issues—income, poverty, employment, standard of living, basic services (their access and delivery), quality of life and sustainable development—either on a universal or on a large sampling frame basis. Further, as decentralized planning is increasingly area as well as people specific, we need to know more about the cultural and behaviour patterns of the people, their asset ownership systems, the way they handle or practise their economy as well as their institutional and organizational capacities. It is only with such knowledge that we can plan for feasible technological packages for their benefit, provide systems of support facilities and services to backstop their economy and make appropriate organizational and institutional arrangements to facilitate their development. This is one aspect of our data and information need, i.e. the need for more information, more authentic information and micro-level information, which so far has not been effectively captured by our traditional statistical machinery in the various countries. Experience with data and information availability in many developing countries has indicated that, generally speaking, the amount of data decreases as the areal unit changes from larger to smaller. Also some local-level data are low powered and undependable.

Thus decentralized sub-national planning, cutting across a number of hierarchical levels, would result in the introduction of a planning process, which may be seen as increasingly information intensive as well as information selective. In this context, not merely has the need for data and information at disaggregated levels grown tremendously, but also the need for some extremely specialized and specific information in relation to the new development strategies. It is to be emphasized here that while these data and information needs have been, by and large, perceived and identified by planners and administrators, the information provision activity itself in many countries is yet to respond fully and appropriately to the varying perceptions of development planning and to the different strategies that are being sought to be introduced from time to time.

The problem today is not merely one of proper identification of data and information needs for different levels and stages (or phases) of planning. This, no doubt, is an important item in our agenda for discussion and will be considered in the latter part of this paper. With the need to collect an increasing volume of information, and the need to use this information for performing a wide range and depth of analyses for planning, there has also surfaced data handling and processing problems, which developing countries can no longer ignore. There is also a speed or time factor implied here, because the decentralized planning process is a *time-bound* activity. Here the plans have to be prepared according to a time calendar (often specified in legislations pertaining to the particular area level) and integrated with each other, and ultimately with the budgeting/allocating machinery of the government and submitted *in time* for authentication and approval to the appropriate authority in accordance with the democratic traditions and practices prevalent in particular country. So there is a rigid time frame to be adhered to in all planning-related activities. This means that the processes of data collection/updating, transformation, processing and analyses for planning have to respond with speed and commitment to conform to this time frame. This "time squeeze" is a factor that has to be carefully understood. It, more or less, sets a limit to the nature and volume of data and information to be collected, the ways in which these may be collected, the kind of processing and analyses for planning that may be performed, and the kind of compromises that may sometimes be necessary.

It is here that we have perhaps to pay some attention to certain concepts like "critical minimum information" and "reduced analytical approaches" for planning. All these are closely linked to some concepts like the concept of "limited or bounded rationality" (i.e. not trying to know what is not worth knowing), the concept of "appropriate imprecision" (i.e. not measuring more precisely than needed), and techniques like "rapid rural appraisal", "key informants approach", "successive approximation", "progressive learning", "learning through transects",[3] etc., which are now and then raised and discussed in several forums today, with a view to getting over or lessen the "nightmare" of data collection and the "tyranny" of statistical analysis.

The increased speed and accuracy needed in the processing of large quantities of information for decentralized planning could be met by the developing countries through an intelligent application of the rapidly advancing information technology, based on computers and telecommunication advances. These developments in information technology have placed at our disposal tools that can quickly collect, store, process and transfer data and information of all kinds. Indeed, the developing countries cannot afford to ignore these developments, because what we are dealing with here is nothing less than a powerful "technological avalanche", which is unstoppable because of its innate dynamism and also because of the economic conditions of today's international marketplace.[4] The problems before the developing countries, therefore, are :

how to match these two needs, i.e. the users' needs and the need to take advantage of the potentials and capabilities of the information technology and how to benefit through the innovative approaches of data and information handling and processing.[5]

If we accept the contention that the information challenges of the developing countries are to be met through a rigorous assessment of critical minimum data and information needs and the intelligent application of information technology, one must be prepared also to effect some necessary degree of organizational and administrative changes and also to modify the strategic planning process, as necessary, so as to incorporate information technology as an explicit and major support to decision-making for sub-national level planning. Changes in organization needed to support the new information technology have been termed as "orgware" by Nijkamp and de Jong.[6] While the changes implied in "orgware" are indispensable to achieve maximum benefits from the technology, in a multi-level planning context, they are to be preceded by the establishment of what this author would like to call "multi-level information structures". In the dynamic system of multi-level planning, the planning authorities at different spatial levels have to continuously act and interact with each other, before firming up decisions on programmes and projects. If this is to be dealt with efficiently, data and information for planning must flow up and down and in all directions. These flows cannot happen automatically, unless specific institutional structures are created for that purpose and procedures established for the direction of the flows. Thus one major step in the innovation needed in the context of the application of the new technology is to establish suitable *Information Structures* to match the *Planning Authority Structures*. In other words, what we need at this stage of transition is the establishment of a system, which will effectively link the users of information with those engaged in providing that information.

In the changes and reorganization that have to come about, I consider the establishment of these linkages as of crucial importance. Without such linkages, the operationalization of decentralized planning in many countries has tended to become less effective, as available data for planning have not consciously related themselves to the users' (i.e. planners') needs. In fact, in many countries today, both "Authority" and "Information" Structures are not only weak, but also "Unmatched". Further, such changes as are being introduced in many countries are merely responding to symptomatic deficiencies, as opposed to planning and managing more fundamental changes, which is very much desired.[7]

In this context, we would like to place great emphasis on the organizational changes that are called for—in particular, for the matching of information structures with planning authority structures. These two types of structures have to match and mesh and mutually complement each other, if decentralized planning activity is to become realistic and effective. There are different ways in which this coordination can come about. One approach may be to build the information structures into the planning authority structures themselves. Alternatively, if they remain separate, some consultative mechanisms may be established for interaction and understanding. In some countries, the planning and statistical personnel are brought into the same "Economic Service" for career development. Thus they move freely across planning and information provision jobs, thus bringing about the required coordination and understanding.

Current State of Art on Data and Information at Sub-national Levels

Several critical observations have been made in regard to the present state of art on the data and information obtaining at sub-national levels in the developing countries. The picture is sometimes confusing. In the mainstream debate on data inadequacies, some points which have been emphasized are :

— Paucity of data, referring to lack of data, sometimes called "under-information". This is specially in regard to primary data relating to income, consumption, employment, housing, health or nutrition behaviour.

— Conflicting data, with the existence of multiple estimates of the same phenomenon in the files of different ministries or in the files of different divisions of the same ministry, providing different estimates.

— Irregular data, referring to lack of a definite periodicity or timeliness in the availability of information.

— Imperfect data, referring to data of doubtful validity.

— Irrelevant data, referring to the existence of abundant data on some aspects that are strictly not necessary for planning.

— Insufficient data, referring to gaps in information, either in terms of spatial coverage, or subject coverage, or both.

— Incoherent data, referring to information which does not relate to each other.

One view that has been expressed is that in many countries, there is adequate data with numerous agencies and the problem is one of selecting the "best data set" and coordinating future data collection on systematic lines. According to an assessment, "the rural problem is not one of insufficient data, but one of an abundance of imperfectly veracious data".[8] Proponents of techniques like Rapid Rural Appraisal (PRA) assert that :

— Too much data is collected;
— Irrelevant data is collected;
— Late and inappropriate results are produced; and
— In data collection, there is too little/no participation by the local people.

In the above context, less adherence to long and costly formal surveys, resort to more informal and participatory approaches to data collection and reliance on local insights have been advocated.

On the other hand, countries which have embarked on local-level planning and decentralized programmes of the poverty alleviation type find themselves seriously hamstrung by lack of adequate data pertaining to several micro-variables. Even in countries, which have established a regular National Sample Survey Organization (NSSO), the data and information that are collected are often inadequate to meet the requirements of local-level planning, e.g. India.[9] On some aspects, like employment for instance, data have been found to be inadequate for rural manpower and employment planning. Apart from quantitative data, decentralized planning has to rely a lot more on some important qualitative information on the ordinal scale.

Particularly on some important aspects like socio-economic behaviour, intra-generational aspects of development, some aspects of development like indigenous development practices, development impact and development monitoring, the qualitative information is very relevant. Such qualitative information is usually contained in the several formal field studies undertaken by various agencies. But there is no systematic means of "extracting" such information and providing them to the planning bodies for the meaningful analysis and interpretation of development problems. Several suggestions are being made to overcome such problems, e.g. suggestion by UNRISD for the setting up of "socio-economic observatories" in rural areas in order to obtain periodic data on socio-economic changes.[10]

In a heterogeneous context, where different countries are developing their decentralized planning systems in different ways, it is difficult to generalize whether the present data and information available for planning is adequate or inadequate or in what respects or directions, they should be supplemented and how (i.e. the methods of survey/ data collection). The data problems listed here (lags, snags, gaps, inadequacies, etc.) need country-specific assessments and solutions.

A Conceptual Base for Deriving Data and Information Needs

Data and information are essentially tools or means to planning. In this context, their potential roles are :

- For problem definition, measurement and analysis;
- For inventorying and decision-making;
- For evaluation of plans, programmes and projects; and
- For orienting planning to people's perspectives (not merely to planner's perspectives).

To meet the above planning-related purposes, various types of data and information will be required. They could be spelt out or derived conceptually by adopting some rational approaches and building into them relevant considerations.

To elaborate such a conceptual base for the derivation of the data and information needs, four distinct levels for planning may be assumed, viz. regional, local, community and household levels.[11] For each level, the data and information requirements may be derived through a combination of four major approaches, in which the key determinants are :

- Goals/sub-goals and Policy Areas (sectorwise and programme-wise);
- Scope of Planning Functions;
- Programmes/Projects included in the plans; and
- Methodology/Techniques used for planning.

The identification of data and information could be further aided and refined by two other considerations, viz. the various planning stages (pre-planning, action planning and implementation planning) and the major planning tasks or steps involved in each one of these stages. The rationale and approach indicated here for the identification of data and information requirements would call for very meticulous work in its actual application. Some illustrations are available.[12]

Information System and Information Technology : Current Applications

While the term "Information System" may refer to any apparatus or method, which allows the transfer of information between producers or sources and users of information, in the modern context it is used in the sense of sophisticated technology and computerization, with its components of human actors (users and staff), information, information processes (i.e. relating one information element to another), data, data processes (i.e. processing of data) and hardware (equipment). Statistical and other information processed and presented in readily usable form, no doubt, greatly assists in advancing both the planning process and its supporting analyses. In the planning context, an information base that is oriented towards both "problem finding" and "solution finding" is essential. All these would suggest that an information system has to be purposive. In a multi-objective framework like decentralized planning there could be, therefore, a number of information systems, which, however, must relate to each other. For meeting the data and information requirements for multilevel planning, the information system may perhaps be conceived in two broad contexts : (i) as a non-specialized general purpose system, which could be utilized by a heterogeneous group of users concerned with policy-making and planning at the regional and local levels (i.e. a policy and planning-oriented information system). This can handle the planning tasks of *diagnosis* (i.e. problem identification) and macro-framework building for the plan (i.e. the setting of goals, strategies, priorities and targets), which constitute the first stages in a planning cycle; and (ii) as specialized, individual action-oriented systems, focusing on specific requirements (i.e. designed for sectoral planning and other specific planning orientations). For this, we must start with identifying the various programme/project segments associated with each sector of planning and their objectives. Then we should design the information system appropriate to that segment of planning. A Geographical Information System (GIS) would also fall in this special category, dealing with spatial data set, the sources for which may include field surveys, air photography, remote sensing, satellite imagery and existing maps and records.

As for the use and application of modern information technology for planning purposes, the progress in the developing countries is quite slow and uneven. What has been achieved in most cases are incomplete inventories of some baseline data and the automation of routine, record-keeping applications, primarily in finance and revenue raising services. Some applications for planning have been attempted in a few countries, e.g. China, India, Thailand, Nepal, Sri Lanka and Indonesia.

This shows that the application of information technology to planning related tasks is in very formative stages of development in the developing countries of the Asian region. The attempts made so far are piecemeal and selective and not designed to cover the entire spectrum of planning activities at the various levels. In order to take advantage of the potentials and possibilities thrown up by the new technology, and introduce it in a big way in a comprehensive and wide-ranging context, it would be necessary for these countries to establish some essential prerequisites as follows :

(i) Establishing a reliable collection of data at the sources and imparting knowledge as to how to feed these into the system;

(ii) Installing micro-computers for performing specific planning and analytical tasks at various spatial levels and networking them with the mainframe computer, thus establishing a viable communications network in the country;

(iii) Developing a suitable software to handle the variety of planning problems;

(iv) Building up a sound personnel base, with experts conversant not only with the technical side of their equipment, but also with the methods of handling the vast volume of statistical materials; and

(v) Sensitizing or rendering the top policy experts in government, particularly in the ministries of finance and planning, knowledgeable about the potentials of the new information technology and information systems.

Transition to Information Age

Towards a "Stages Approach" and a "National Information Policy"

Overcoming the numerous existing constraints and establishing the above prerequisites at one stroke would be a tall order for the developing countries. In this context, a search for feasible solutions and making some compromises seem necessary. Perhaps a useful approach could be a "blending" of old and new technologies and a gradual adoption of the new technology. Proceeding in a *modular,* way i.e. staged in steps. In this case, the new information technology will not suddenly replace, but slowly supplement existing technologies. Such an approach would be in response to the various existing constraints in the developing countries and would ensure :

(i) A smooth transition from existing to new technology;
(ii) The optimum utilization of existing equipment and skills;
(iii) Possibilities of upgrading equipment in case of growing demand;
(iv) A wide diversity of outputs to meet all types of needs; and
(v) The possibility of step-by-step progress in establishing equipment to allow for staggered investments and training

In the context of the adoption of the new information technology and preparing themselves for the transition to an information age, in which the emphasis will be on evolving an end-user and decision-support information systems, developing countries have to proceed with much caution, deliberation and care. Quality control, technical competence and systems compatibility are important issues associated with the implementation of the new technology. A blind imitation, in our euphoria for innovation and change, may result in unnecessary data duplication and inconsistencies. It is necessary to take a clear view of the "planning task environment" as a whole in the context of each country, and then decide the way in which information technology can be applied. Which of the key areas of planning should receive the first and foremost attention (i.e. identification of the strategic information system opportunities), what organizational structures and related procedures should evolve, as information systems are developed, are important questions for decision-making. These are essentially policy issues. What is clearly indicated at this moment of transition, therefore, is a "National Information Policy", which incorporates information technology as an explicit and major component of the policy, and spells out the "what, where and how" of the adoption and utilization of the new technology in the country's development context, particularly the emerging "planning task environment". Two recent international conferences—at Kawasaki (Japan) and Visakhapatnam (India)—ended their deliberations with a "declaration", calling upon the developing countries to adopt explicit policies for the information sector. My reliable knowledge is that no country has, as yet, come forward with a national policy declaration on this subject. This shows that countries are moving towards the information age in a "policy vacuum", which is a risky venture and a dangerous portent. The best that can be done at this moment will be to make a very strong reiteration and lay emphasis on this strategic need, so that the developing countries can build up a reliable, scientifically sound and coordinated data and information system, avoiding the mistakes and costs associated with their haphazard development.

The Case of India

Changing Information Scenario for Development

Now I discuss the present state of art on data and information system in India. The Indian case is particularly interesting, because the country has relatively a rich acquisition of planning-related data and information at sub-national levels and has made some striking adaptations and adjustments in its administrative and organizational structures for data collection and dissemination, in response to several policy and programme changes that have been initiated, particularly during the 1970's and 1980's. Being a country of vast sub-continental dimensions. (Area : 3.3 million km^2 Popn : > 700 million), federal structure (twenty-four states and eight centrally administered territories), heterogeneous population (differentiated in terms of castes and economic classes) and development experience representing a wide spectrum of approaches to development, planned in the framework of individual projects and regional and area programmes, the data and information requirements here are indeed stupendous and varied. India has also a vast reservoir of scientific and technological manpower, with the result that the technical personnel constraints that usually inhibit technological advances in many developing countries do not pose a serious problem for India. However, efforts to harness the science and technological capability towards innovations in the information sector had barely started during the Seventh Plan period (1985-1990) and is now gathering momentum. It cannot be overemphasized that the next phase of developments in India is going to be in the direction of a revolution in information technology, involving extensive applications of the new technology in a wide range of planning and development contexts.

In considering the data needs in the Indian context, the development approaches, strategies, policies and programmes that are adopted at the sub-national levels constitute a crucial consideration.

Soon after Independence, the country addressed itself to some essential tasks. These included :

1. Conversion of the law-and-order system of administration into a welfare and development oriented system;
2. Building up of popular institutions at the grassroot level, which could motivate the masses into identifying themselves with the national development efforts;
3. Co-ordination and streamlining of the technical services, which under the traditional administrative system had been working in isolation from each other and from the people; and
4. Generation of development oriented local leadership suited to the changing circumstances.[13]

Following the experimentation with community development programmes, central intervention continued in rural areas, trying to give programmatic content to the various problems thrown up from time to time in the form of special programmes. These special programmes impinging on local areas (districts, blocks and villages) have created the need for a tremendous volume of disaggregated information, touching on various micro-level aspects. Simultaneously, since the Seventh Plan period (1985-1990), a major thrust or emphasis in planning is being directed towards decentralized district planning and in creating a responsive administration aimed at changing the power structure in the countryside. Thus the point that we would like to emphasize is that the changes in the orientations of planning at the sub-national levels, leading to a plethora of special programmes, the vigorous push towards decentralization and the changes in the institutional aspects of rural development have brought to surface the numerous data lags, gaps, inadequacies and inconsistencies at the regional and local levels, and equally the necessity to quickly process and analyze this data for planning and monitoring tasks. The developments that are taking place in India in the information sector have to be viewed in the light of these changes and are intended to cope with the requirements of the present development situation, particularly decentralization.

Existing Database and Organization

In countries like India, it is important to realize that the data and information system has evolved as part of the administrative organization of the country. Now that it is serving the needs of administration as well as development, it cannot be overemphasized that in a dynamic development context, organizational flexibility is one of the foremost requirements.

In the developments that took place in India during the 1960's and 1970's, with the emergence of several new "differentiated" area-specific and target group-specific programmes, a number of new agencies with their own organizational structures within the district/division were created, leading to the development of pluralistic planning and development structures and increasing the problems of coordination and integration. These "differentiated" structures are now yielding place to "integrated" structures, with the formation of a new agency at the district level—the "District Rural Development Agency" (DRDA). Simultaneously, with such organizational integration, a multi-level planning process has emerged, which views planning as an inter-linked activity. This has served to emphasize effective data and information flows between and among the different territorial levels and the establishment of organizational and communication linkages among them, so as to facilitate reciprocal interaction, exchange, cooperation and resolution of conflicts. Against the desired organizational changes as envisaged above, we may now examine the nature of the existing database and how it is organized. For the purpose of this analysis, we may classify the data and information into seven major categories : (1) Geo-based information; (2) Socio-economic information; (3) Special purpose information : (a) special programme-wise; (b) sector-wise; (4) District level Information; (5) Sub-district-level information; (6) Village level information; and, (7) Household level information.

(i) *Geo-based Information*

This consists of information with spatial dimensions or locational distribution. Such spatial data are of the following kinds. (See Table 9.1).

It may be seen from Table 9.1 that the various geo-based data and information on natural resources are scattered among numerous agencies. At present, the updating and flow of this information is irregular and spatially unintegrated. Such regular updation and revision of natural resources data is now possible, thanks to the advancements in satellite imagery, remote sensing and computer sciences, which have revolutionized the data acquisition and processing methods in this context, cutting down the time and increasing the precision. In order to use the natural resources data meaningfully for planning purposes at the different spatial levels, it is necessary to ensure a joint and interrelated presentation of the resources information. In this context, the building up of an "integrated resource information system" on a scientifically established database is emphasized. The next phase of development in regard to geo-based information in India has to be an "integration and consolidation phase", intended to bring together the various raw data generated by the various agencies for numerous applications, after paying due attention to the question of standardization and compatibility. This would mean carrying out the required degree of processing and analysis and converting the raw-data into meaningful information that can be readily used by the Planning Agencies for various development purposes. The Survey of India and the National Remote Sensing Agency will have a crucial leading role in this respect.

The Survey of India is an important apex organization, with its counterpart in all State Governments and together with the National Remote Sensing Agency (NRSA), which is a more recent development it is today in a position to provide "integrated" information for planning at decentralized levels. The Surveyor General of India had drawn up a blueprint to develop a common datbase, using multi-disciplinary groups for integrating spatial data, including statistics, maps and aerial photographs (including space imagery, as relevant) and computer graphics for generating alternatives.[14] It envisages a multi-level effort with a National Level Task Force to coordinate and standardize procedures and monitor the programmes. Under this scheme, the geodetic and resources information generated through the various Central Agencies would be passed on to planning teams at the state level, where these teams will be organized to process the information according to districts, using micro-computers and computer assisted mapping systems.[15] The scheme is shown diagrammatically in Fig. 9.1. The Surveyor General's proposal is to be seen in conjunction with a recommendation made by an important

TABLE 9.1 : Geo-based Information

	Type	Data elements	How available	Source
1.	Information contained in geodetic and topographic surveys.	Physical features, rivers, settlements, general landuse, transport links and selected basic community facilities.	Maps covering the whole country with uniform scales 1:M 1:250,000 1:50,000 1:25,000	Survey of India
2.	Detailed information contained in cadastral surveys.	Physical boundaries; land ownership information by small unit areas; detailed urban information—residences, landuse, utility services etc.	Cadastral maps ranging in scales from 1:5000 to 1:500	Survey of India, State Survey Departments, State, Town and Country Planning Departments.
3.	Information thrown up by natural resources surveys.	Geological information: minerals; forest resources; soils; landuse; water resources; geophysical information.	Both as maps on different scales and in the form of quantitative and qualitative information.	Geological Survey of India; Forest Planning Offices; Soil and Landuse Board; Water Resources Directorates of the Central and State Govts.
4.	Climatic data for weather stations.	Temperature; rainfall; atmospheric pressure; winds; cloud cover; etc.	Tabulations of values at specific places.	Meteorological Survey of India.
5.	Thematic maps of the country and region.	Various development information suitably portrayed in analytical maps.	Usually in scale: 1:100,000 or 1:200,000.	National Atlas and Thematic Mapping Organization (NATMO).
6.	Remote, sense mapping with the assistance of satellite imagery and airphoto interpretation.	(a) Updation of natural resource inventories on a regular basis; (b) Monitoring changes in landuse and vegetation cover and their environmental impact.	As black and white products; false colour composite products; black and white TM products; false colour composite TM products and paper prints.	National Remote Sensing Agency (NRSA).

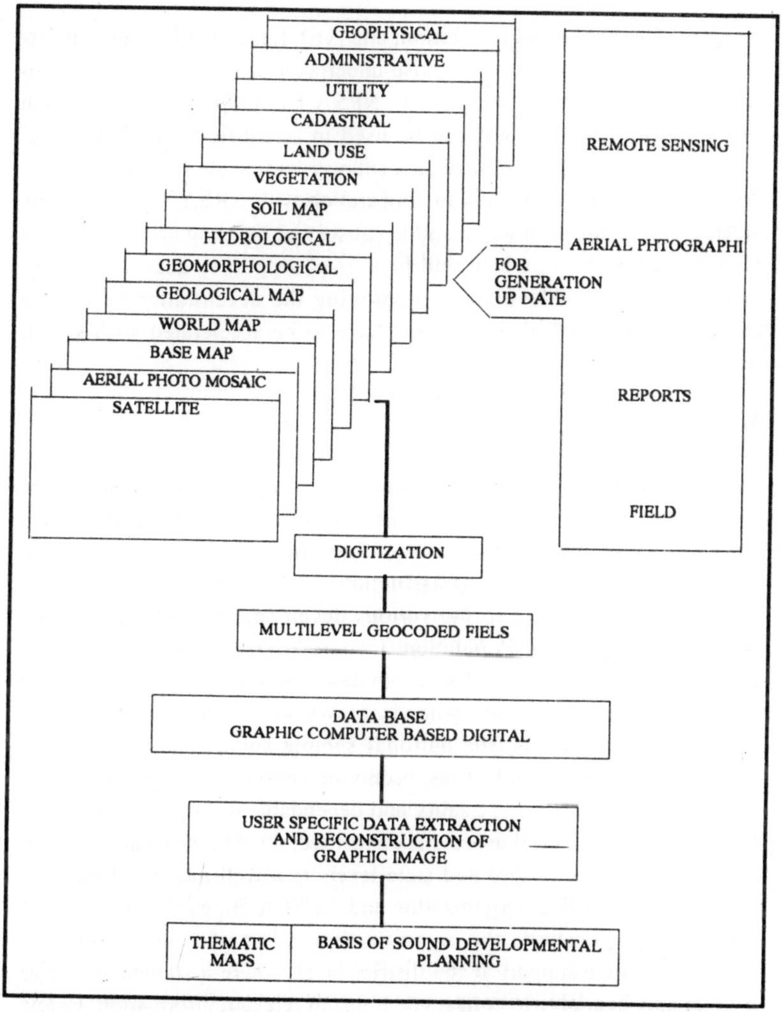

FIG. 9.1 : Scheme of a Data Base for Scientific Development of a Region.
Source : Major General Aggarwal, *An Integrated Scientific Approach to Rural Development* (Mimeographed).

Working Group on District Planning appointed by the Indian Planning Commission,[16] which has emphasized that for every district in the country, the following seven thematic maps should be prepared : (i) Geological; (ii) Groundwater; (iii) Soils; (iv) Forest; (v) Existing Land

Use; (vi) Optimal Land Utilization; and (vii) Integrated Resource Information. In a demonstrative exercise undertaken for one district—Karimnagar District in Andhra Pradesh—NRSA has prepared a set of such maps and indicated how it can be used in scientific district planning. The replication of this exercise on a country-wide scale should be undertaken by the Survey of India in cooperation with NRSA. Developments steered in this direction will result in substantial building up of integrated resource information, which will be a great support to decision-making at the sub-national levels. For improving the decentralized planning methodologies, such developments have to be accelerated with speed, commitment and decisiveness.

Socio-economic Information

Information in the socio-economic domain covers a wide range of human, social, economic and employment aspects, information on basic services and community facilities, besides information relating to production, technological, financial, infrastructural and institutional aspects of development pertaining to the various development sectors. For some basic information, e.g. Population, Income, Consumption, Agricultural Infrastructure, Industrial Establishments and Employment Market Information, periodical information is thrown up by various organizations. The population census, the national sample survey, the agricultural census, the census of industries, economic census and labour statistics, which provide fairly good quality and dependable information. So far as information on sectorial aspects is concerned, the data provision activity is organized at the central and state levels in a well-integrated manner. The Central Statistical Organization and the State Bureaus of Economics and Statistics constitute the organizational pillars of such information. These have their support at the district level, where a statistical officer is invariably available to collect and transmit relevant information. Below the district level, at the level of blocks (a group of about 100 villages), there is a Block Development Office, in which is posted an official designated as Progress Assistant, who maintains development information pertaining to the block. At the village level, the revenue officials maintain all relevant information and as the revenue system in India is very well organized (a British legacy), all the basic data required are available on a systematic basis (every year updated in a routine manner). The organizational structure with vertical and horizontal levels of integration may be seen in Fig. 9.2. In point of time, the state bureaus are a later development and their organizational growth occurred with the generation of an increasing volume of development data at the sub-national levels in the wake of the emergence of special area-specific and target-group-specific programmes and new emphases given from time to time to district and block-level planning in the country. These developments took place during the 1970's and 1980's and it is during this period that several state governments made concerted efforts to build up their economics and statistical bureaus, to bring about the required vertical and horizontal integration of data at the different spatial levels. These developments are still not complete. There is much streamlining yet to be brought about to establish regular "flows" of information from the numerous programme agencies and special-purpose authorities and vice-versa. There is also the need to strengthen the linkages between planning authorities at the district and block levels and the statistical bureaus. Further, the diffe-

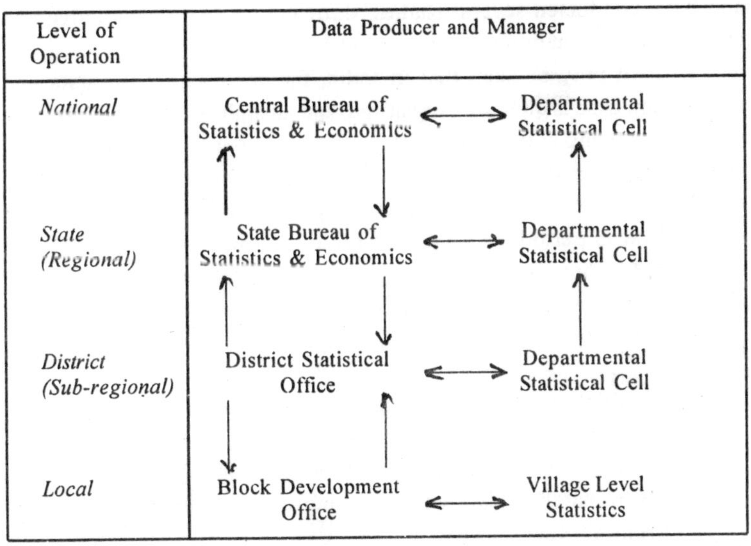

FIG. 9.2 : Vertical and Horizontal Levels of Integration of Socio-economic Statistics in India.

Source : Routray, J.K., *Data Base : An Aid to CIS Application for Decentralized Micro-level Planning in Developing Countries—Indian Experience.* Paper presented in the International Conference on 'Geographic Information Systems, Application for Urban and Regional Planning : A State-of-the-Art Review', organized by the United Nations Centre for Regional Development, Nagoya (Japan), Jakarta 3-6 October, 1989.

rences in methodologies adopted for computation of certain essential information, like the state income estimates at the central and state levels, have led to discrepancies in estimations between the different sources. Now coordination mechanisms have been introduced to reconcile these differences. In some states, the bureau of economics and statistics and the planning service at the state and district levels have a common cadre of personnel, with the result that coordination has become easier. The situation in this regard varies from state to state. Nevertheless, there is acute consciousness in every state on the need for the consolidation as well as the vertical and horizontal integration of data and information at the different spatial levels. An important point to be emphasized here is that the statistical machinery at the state level has shown the resilience and flexibility to adapt, assimilate and to respond to the dynamics of development in the country and to the challenges that are thrown up in this context. Not only this, the bureaus function not merely as data collection agencies, but also as instruments of social and economic surveys and have conducted several studies, throwing up both quantitative and qualitative information of various kinds.

Thus, it may be seen that in India, the socio-economic data and information base is quite well organized, and an agile and flexible structure which is growing at the state level is effectively performing the bridging and coordinating function. Not only are data and information relating to all major variables available on a fairly reliable basis, but also such information is periodically updated (cutting down the decay rate) and maintained to provide data systematically on a time-series basis. Nevertheless, there are still some problems associated with the currently available database in India. Routray[17] has listed the following problems :

1. Multiplicity of data management institutions;
2. Neither need specific nor adequate;
3. The quality of data and question of reliability;
4. Non-matching data sets on a common theme between two different sources;
5. Discrepancy in geographical area for the level of data aggregation;
6. Inconsistency of data in relation to time and areal units;
7. Weak vertical integration of the data sources and organization;
8. Non-adoption of common format/data structure for district and sub-district level within a state for basic information;

9. Non-availability of some basic data because of unnecessary restrictions by the data managers; and
10. The data organizations (mostly government departments) orient very much to fulfil the data needs of the government administration rather than maintaining data objectively needed for universal use of planning, development, monitoring and evaluation.

Special Purpose Information

In India, several special-purpose area-specific and target-group-specific programmes have been launched since the 1970's to assist the development of certain types of backward areas and backward groups. Examples are the Integrated Rural Development Programme (a poverty alleviation programme), programmes for the drought-prone areas, tribal areas and hill areas, the small and marginal farmer's programme, the command area development programme, employment programme, etc. For the effective planning of such programmes, in-depth data and information are needed in problem-specific and target-group-specific contexts. The problem-specific data may comprise both natural resources inventory data as well as data on human resources. The target-group programmes need information at household level. Thus both primary and secondary data are to be collected. For the planning and implementation of many of these special-purpose programmes, new organizational structures have been created. These organizations have generated a lot of programme-specific data. The problem has arisen in handling the voluminous data and processing them, as needed. Computerization and use of micro-computers in this context has become indispensable and some interesting developments are taking place in this direction. This will be discussed later in this chapter.

District-level Information

As noted earlier, the major thrust in planning in India is now shifting to district and micro-level planning. In this context, much thinking has gone ahead to visualize the data requirements, their availability in various organizations and the significant gaps yet to be filled through fresh surveys and other means.[18]

Keeping in view the planning functions at the district level, "the critical minimum" information (to avoid over-collection of data and "data graveyards") necessary for planning and decision-making have been identified. This consists of data and information covering all those areas defined as the "District Sector", plus such background information as may be helpful in their meaningful interpretation. Such data and information have then been arranged under certain meaningful analytical rubrics under six data sets as follows :

(i) Natural resources data set
(ii) Demographic data set
(iii) Agro-economic data set
(iv) Socio-economic data set
(v) Infrastructure data set
(vi) Data inputs from primary surveys.

Besides the data and information indicated in the six data sets above, detailed information about on-going development programmes and their achievements will be necessary. These are particularly indicated when new developments, like zero-based budgeting, are being introduced at the state level. Besides the statistical information, some maps intended to reveal the spatial relationship among the various developments have also been suggested.[19]

Sub-district Level Information

At the sub-district level, the Block (a cluster of about 100 villages), has emerged as an important developmental administration unit in India, with democratic decentralization also established at this level through a people's organization, called "Panchayat Samiti". A sub-district level organization like the block has an essential role in bringing about balanced spatial development, eliminating intra-district disparities in development and enabling closer public participation in development. Of late, the thinking has emerged in some states that even the block is a large unit for planning at the sub-district level, and a smaller unit named as *Mandal* (a cluster of about 15-20 villages) will be more appropriate for this purpose. Some states, e.g. Karnataka, and Andhra Pradesh, have already adopted such a unit for sub-district level planning. Probably developments, such as this, would be desirable in all the states, as it will lead to the emergence of a viable unit for micro-level planning, which would enable the better functioning of the government delivery system on the one hand and the building up of effective people's receiving mechanisms on the other. Currently, the data and information machinery at the block level, which is centred on one multi-purpose official--the Progress Assistant functioning under the Block Development Officer—has proved to be a very unsatisfactory arrangement, as the Block Office has become an overloaded apparatus of development administration, with the proliferation of several development agencies at the sub-district level and the operation of a plethora of poverty alleviation programmes. In this context, a revamping and energizing of the sub-district level data and information has become imperative in many states.

Village-level Information

As noted earlier, because of the existence of a sound revenue machinery in the states of India, extending from the collector at the district level to the *patwari* (known by different names in the various states) at the village level, the land records, and information pertaining to the primary sector (agriculture) are available in the villages on a fairly satisfactory basis. The development information at the village level is available with the extension machinery. To enable the essential village-level information to be compiled systematically, the village Index Card system has been introduced since 1982. Many states have adopted this system and some are also taking steps to computerize the village-level information. The village level again is an area, in which more innovative changes can be introduced, to render the collection, maintenance and flow of information more systematic and organized.

Household-level Information

With the proliferation of special-purpose and area-specific and target-group specific programmes, micro-level planning has become data-intensive and reliable and authentic data at household level (with particular emphasis on "Profile of the Poor") has become an urgent necessity. Such data are now being collected through special household surveys designed for each individual programme. A lot of data and information are also being generated during the monitoring of these programmes. The handling and processing of all these voluminous data is posing serious problems. Further, the micro-level data relating to the beneficiaries of several poverty alleviation programmes have to be maintained carefully "over time", to monitor and study the behaviour of these households after initially crossing over the poverty line. For the efficient collection, storage, processing and retrieval of such data, the use of the new information technology is particularly indicated, as it will bring speed and sophistication in the analytical process. Developments in this regard will be discussed in the sequel.

Development of Information Systems

In the field of information technology, many important developments are taking place in India. These are still in various stages of trial and experimentation (i.e. pilot research and development stage) and evolution, although some programmes are past this stage and have entered a stage of operationalization on a country-wide scale. The four major directions in which the current efforts are focussed are :

1. Development of an integrated geographic information system (NRDMS Project);
2. Computerization of Rural Information System (CRISP);
3. Developing an Urban and Regional Information System (URIS); and
4. Networking all districts in the country through a system of computers and satellite, for efficient multi-level planning and management called "District Information System of National Informatics Centre" (DISNIC).

It is interesting to note that all the above-mentioned efforts are directed towards the establishment of decentralized information systems and are mutually complementary. The consolidation, integration and unification of these efforts may take a long time. Nevertheless, by themselves, they seek to cover certain distinct components of the planned economy in stages. In a vast country like India, where the pace and pattern of any development effort is bound to be uneven among the states and a "unified approach" is difficult to implement, technological developments must necessarily come about in "stages and steps". This is what is happening. A brief account of the state of art in this respect has been attempted below.

Development of an Integrated Geographic Information System

This is an attempt to develop a computer-aided spatial-oriented database for data storage, retrieval, dissemination and analysis as well as the economic aspects of planning. It is called the Natural Resources Data Management System (NRDMS). It is intended to generate area-specific profiles of natural resources and socio-economic parameters and decision-support models for micro-level planning. The databases store information on attributes, location (geo-coordinates) and time—the primary constituents for generating dynamic resource profiles of an area. Under the NRDMS project, pilot data bases have been set up in nine places located in eight States with different geo-environments.[20] For extending the project throughout the country, Aggrawal's blue-print[21] approach referred to earlier is quite relevant.

Computerization of Rural Information System (CRISP)

Attempts to introduce a decentralized information system, to make the planning and implementation of the rural development programmes more effective, started during the Seventh Plan period (1985-1990) by the Department of Rural Development, Government of India. The idea was to gradually make it a major component of district planning. The Department has developed a comprehensive system of monitoring and concurrent evaluation of major programmes of rural development. The emphasis is on a strong database and feedback on the implementation of the programmes. Computers are being installed in all DRDA's, based on the experience of pilot project on Computerized Rural Information System (CRISP). CRISP became operational in 1988.[22] States are developing a technical support organization as a nodal agency to take over the ongoing process of software enhancement, training of staff and general technical support to DRDAs.

In the various states of India, computerization is also extending into certain other selected areas. But the developments in information technology are uneven across the states. A state like Rajasthan, for instance, has set up during the Seventh Plan period (1985-1990) a Directorate of Computer as the nodal agency for coordinating all developments. This has ushered in a new era of information technology application in a number of government departments and autonomous bodies. Madhya Pradesh has computerized the collection of land records and settlements. Thus a database has been created to record every detail to a piece of land—name of the holder, crop patterns, tenancy details, irrigation details and land utilization details. Any individual, on paying a nominal fee (Rs. 10), can get a copy containing every detail of his land. Thus the computers are heralding the information revolution in the country.

The right mix of technology and tradition continues to be a debatable issue.

Development of an Urban and Regional Information System (URIS)

This is a development initiated by the Town and Country Planning Organization of the Union Ministry of Urban Development with the assistance of UNDP. Installation of hardware, development of software and training are the major components of the project. It is being sought to be operationalized with the active assistance of the State Town Planning Departments. Data entry forms have been standardized, which are sent through the state governments to the district headquarters and from there to various agencies for collecting information. URIS is still evolving and trying to tackle the various administrative and coordination problems.

District Information System of National Informatics Centre (DISNIC)

The National Informatics Centre (NIC) under the Planning Commission is the most important organization in India, which is in the process of accomplishing a very challenging task of "networking" all districts in the country through a system of computers and satellite for efficient multi-level planning and management called the District Information System of National Informatics Centre (DISNIC). NIC has established an inter-city network in Delhi called NICNET (National Informatics Centre Network). NIC is expected to facilitate through this network (NICNET), the fulfilment of long-felt information gap for the planning agencies and provide decision-support information for economic and social development, programme implementation and project monitoring.

During the first phase of development during the Sixth Plan period (1980-1985), NIC formed an inter-city network of 20 minicomputers and 80 terminals around a Cyber 170/370 main frame system. It also acquired and installed four large main frame systems, NECS-1000 at Bhubaneswar, Pune, Hyderabad and New Delhi. Since then, the system has been extended from time to time. For the Eighth Plan period (1990-1995), it is envisaged to strengthen NICNET further by installing 7,000 earth stations and another 3,000 for special groups like banks.

As of 1989, 238 out of the 422 districts have been brought under NICNET. Each of these districts has got a District Information Office, with PC super AT with four terminals (300 M-bytes hard disk, 8M-bytes onboard-memory and a heavy duty printer). A NIC satellite-based network links each of these through a "controller" type earth station in New Delhi to their respective state units. The micro-earth station provides two ports and has a data transmission speed of 1,200 bytes per second and a receiving speed of 9,600 bytes per second.[23] The state units located at the state capitals are in turn linked to mother earth station located in Delhi.

Thus a massive country-wide computerized network with an impressive hard-ware build-up has been achieved under DISNIC. This is now to be followed by the development of the District Information System consisting of three major aspects, viz:

(i) A Monitoring Database;
(ii) An Administrative Database; and
(iii) A Socio-economic Database.

The data components under each database have been worked out by involving concerned departments at district, state and central levels. Studies have been conducted for identifying the input parameters required at both micro and macro levels in all the sectors for decision-support system. Twenty-six sectors are proposed to be covered to start with.[24] NIC has set up the District Informatics Centre at all the district headquarters, with fully trained officers and staff, consisting of one District Informatics Officer and one District Information Assistant to manage the District Centre. The necessary hardware/software has been made available at the District Informatics Centre. These centres are supported by a core group of scientific/technical professionals of NIC in the State Capital. All the officers and staff in the District Informatics Centres have been fully trained by NIC. Simultaneously, NIC is also taking steps to train the field staff of those organizations and agencies, who are capturing the data in the field, in modern techniques of data capture, data entry, data reconciliation, querying databases and in the use of information analysis techniques. When this phase is completed and DISNIC becomes fully operational and effectively linked to the district planning process, it will be one of the most important application areas of information systems, realized on an extensive scale and functioning as a multi-level planning and management system.

From the foregoing account, which indicates the evolutionary trends in the development of computerized information systems in India, we may now consider in broad perspective the likely future developments.

In my view, the future developments will be in two parallel directions of systems integration. These will be : (a) the full-fledged development of the Geographic Information System (GIS), which will come about through a logical expansion of the NRDMS project on the lines envisaged by Aggarwal. Hopefully, the Urban and Regional Information System (URIS) will be linked to this development; (b) In the second major likely development, NICNET and DISNIC will become operational and while doing so, they will integrate CRISP and play a significant role in strategic planning at all levels. It is also possible that development of information systems may encompass certain other aspects of development planning, e.g. Environmental Planning.

Notwithstanding a simple statement as above, these developments along with the integration as envisaged here should not be construed as a natural, inevitable and easy process of change. In fact, the challenges that will have to be faced in this context of systems integration will be many. It is in this context that the formulation of suitable policy guidelines by the government, to guide the information systems and information technology along the desired path of change, is very essential.

Towards an Integrated Organizational Network

Building up a scientific database and information system for an effective decentralized planning and management is a task which is full of difficulties and challenges. Any system that is built up has to integrate natural resources data with socio-economic information on the one hand, and data and information on beneficiaries with those relating to infrastructure and economic activities on the other. It has also to be integrated with the planning process operating at the different levels and finally it has to be integrated with the planning process operating at the different levels and with the higher order areal units in the hierarchical planning system of the country. The Indian case, set out here, shows that the growing demand for data and information in the context of decentralized planning have been, by and large, met through effectively manipulating the existing data sources and organizations. This is now again to be integrated into the organizational structures that are emerging in the context of the developments in information technology. Lastly, these information structures have to match and mesh with the planning structures at the various levels, a point which we emphasized in the very beginning of this chapter. We would like to emphasize this point again in our concluding remarks, as this organizational linkage is very crucial. In the context of the changes that are occurring, the following organizational elements need to be intermeshed :

1. The traditional statistical system in the country, which is changing and adapting itself to the new orientations and structures of development planning.
2. The modern computerized information systems and networks that are evolving in the wake of the new developments in information technology.
3. The new planning structures that are evolving, together with their counterpart people's organizations at the critical administrative levels to support the planning process and the participatory approach implied in this development.

An integrated organizational network comprising the above elements, in which they can mutually and effectively interface and interact, leading to a narrowing of the gap between users' needs and suppliers' provision, will ultimately lead to an improved decentralized planning. How this may be achieved in the Indian context is indicated illustratively in Fig. 9.3. But the identification of data and information needs and organizing their collection and processing in compatible structures alone are not enough. The entire spectrum of changes envisaged here has to be carefully visualized and implemented in appropriate stages through a well-conceived "National Information Policy".

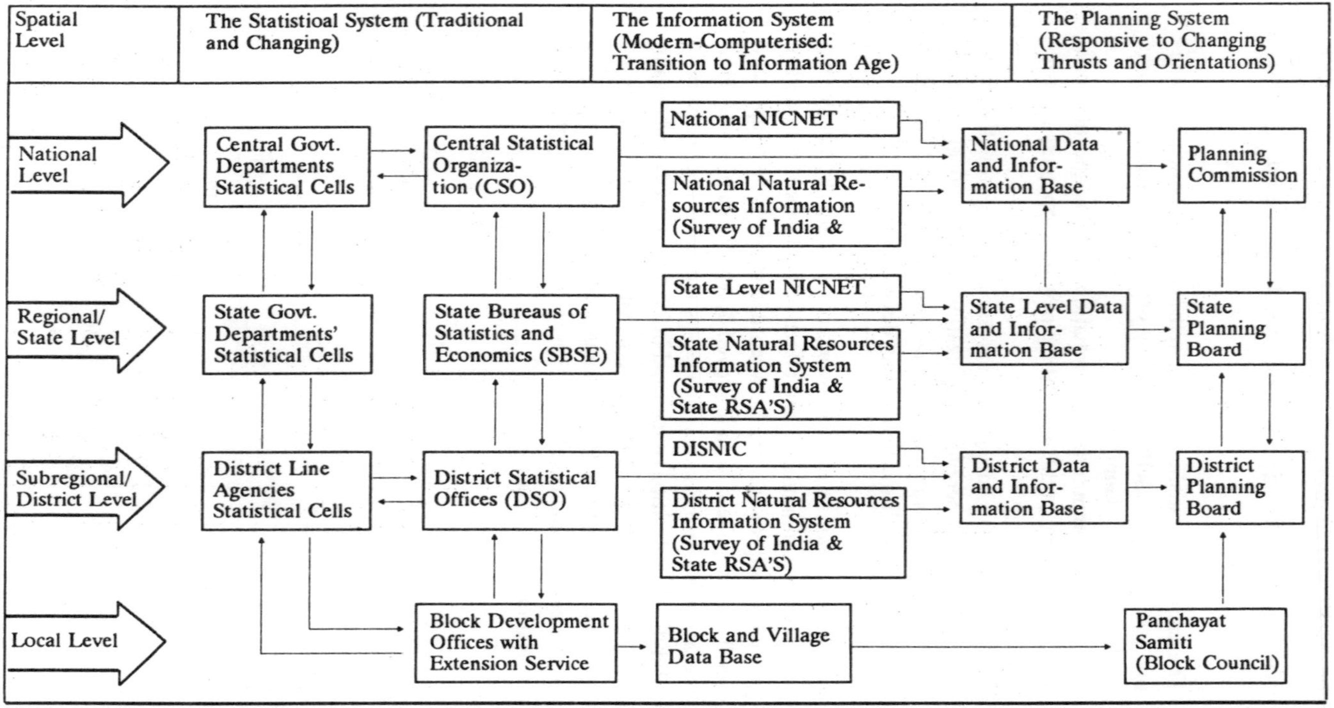

FIG. 9.3 : An Integrated Organizational Network for Improved Decentralized Planning.

NICNET = National Informatics Centre Network.
DISNIC = District Information System of National Information Centre.

REFERENCES

1. For an account of the principles of multi-level planning, see K.V. Sundaram : "Multi-level Planning : concept, principles and some aspects of its application to sectoral planning" in *Regional Planning and Development : Essays in honour of Prof. R.P. Misra*, Edited by K.V. Sundaram *et al.*, Heritage Publishers, New Delhi, 1990. Also, K.V. Sundaram "Multi-level Planning, The Indian Experience" in *Urban and Regional Policy Analysis in Developing Countries*", (Ed.) Lata Chatterjee and Peter Nijkamp, Gower Publishing Co. England 1983.
2. Sundaram, K.V., *Data and Information Needs for Sub-National Planning*, Key Note Paper to the UNESCO International Seminar on "Information System for Sub-national Development Planning", Visakhapatnam, India 16-20, December, 1985.
3. For an introduction to the philosophy, approaches and methods, now known as Rapid Rural Appraisal (RRA), *see* "Proceedings of the 1985 International Conference on Rapid Rural Appraisal, Rural Systems Research and Farming Systems Research Project", Khon Kaen, Thailand, University of Khonkaen, Thailand.
4. Sundaram, K.V., "An Integrated Approach to Training for the Establishment and Use of Information Systems for Sub-national Development Planning", *Regional Development Dialogue*, Vol. 8, No. 1, Spring 1987.
5. Sundaram, K.V., "Changing Data and Information Needs for Agricultural Planning : The challenge for the developing countries", in *Information System for Government and Business : Trends, Issues, Challenges*, United Nations Centre for Regional Development, Nagoya, Japan, 1988.
6. This refers to the organization structure for using knowledge, information and opinions in a coherent way. It would need a clear division and coordination of tasks among operations staff, heads of data processing departments, administrative personnel and decision-makers. Permanent arrangements for monitoring and evaluation is also an essential part of "orgware". *See*, Peter Nijkamp and Wouter de Jong, "Training Needs in Information Systems for Local and Regional Development and Planning in Developing Countries", *Regional Development Dialogue*, Vol. 8, No. 1, Spring 1987.
7. Christopher, C. Benninger, "New Institutional Systems for Enhanced Regional Planning and Management" in *Regional Planning and Development*, (Ed) K.V. Sundaram *et al*, Heritage Publishers, New Delhi, 1990.
8. Lata Chatterjee, "Quantitative Analysis for Regional Policy in Developing Countries : A response to data scarcity" in *Regional Planning and Development, Essays in honour of Prof. R.P. Misra*, Edited by K.V. Sundaram *et al*, Heritage Publishers, New Delhi, 1990.
9. The author found that when block level (micro-level) planning was introduced in India, the yield data available through crop-cutting experiments by the National Sample Survey Organization could not be effectively used, as the size of sample was too low and could not capture the reality at the block level.
10. United Nations Research Institute for Social Development, *Measurement and Analysis of Progress at the Local Level by Wolf Scott*, Geneva, 1979.
11. The specific levels for any country must be suitably defined in the context of its existing administrative structure.

12. The application of the "Goals/Policy Areas Approach" in regard to a specific policy intervention like improving food and nutrition has been illustrated by Rossmiller and Johnson (1978). FAO has, in one of its publications, indicated how the "Planning Techniques Approach" can be used for identifying the data and studies required for agricultural development planning. See K.V. Sundaram, "Changing Data and Information Needs for Agricultural Planning : The challenge for the developing countries" in *Information Systems for Government and Business; Trends, Issues, Challenges,* United Nations Centre for Regional Development, Nagoya, Japan, 1988.
13. K.V. Sundaram, "India—Development Experience" in *Rural Development—Capitalist and Socialist Paths,* Vol. 4 (Ed.) R.P. Misra, Concept Publishing Company, New Delhi, 1985.
14. *An Integrated Scientific Approach to Rural Development* by Major-General Aggarwal, Survey of India, Dehra Dun. (Mimeographed).
15. It is said that the map of the future may not be the traditional printed map. It could be a magnetic tape on which digitized data duly structured is stored and a hard copy is obtained only when needed.
16. Government of India, Planning Commission : Report of the Working Group on District Planning, May 1984.
17. Routray, J.K., "Data Base : An aid to GIS application for decentralized micro-level planning in developing countries–Indian experience"–Paper presented to the International Conference on Geographic Information Systems organized by the United Nations Centre for Regional Development, Nagoya, at Jakarta, October 1989 (Mimeographed).
18. Data and information gaps identified at the district level are those relating to (a) income and consumption levels of the population, (b) employment and unemployment, (c) technology and productivity, (d) inflows and outflows of goods and services; and (e) district income estimates. Activities have been initiated in the various states to tackle these data gap problems. For monitoring, some states have also brought out special publications on "District level indicators of development".
19. Government of India, Planning Commission : "Report of the Working Group on District Planning", May 1984. The author served as Member-Convenor of this Group.
20. Midha, R.K., "Note on Natural Resources Data Management System (NRDMS) in *Report of the Committee of the Study Group on Information Gap*, New Delhi, 1989.
21. Major General Aggarwal, "An Integrated Scientific Approach to Rural Development", Survey of India, Dehra Dun (Mimeographed).
22. Government of India, Department of Rural Development, Ministry of Agriculture : Annual Report 1988-1989, p.7. For an in-depth report on CRISP, *See* "Information Technology and Rural Development : A New Harvest", in *PC World India*, May 1989.
23. Vinod Kumar, T.M., *District Information System—The State-of-the-Art*, (Mimeographed), School of Planning and Architecture, New Delhi, January 1990.
24. "A note on DISNIC" in *Report of the Committee of the Study Group on Information Gap*, Planning Commission, 1989, New Delhi.

10

DISTRICT PLANNING METHODOLOGIES
Some Reflections

Three new thrusts in the development strategy have become relevant to our sub-national development efforts and their methodologies. These have become important in the context of the dynamics of socio-economic change. It is important to have a realistic appreciation of this dynamics, so as to be clear about the nature, content, strategy and methodology of development that should now inform District Planning and below. The three new thrusts are :

(1) Liberalization and other market-oriented policies that are influencing our macro-economic perspectives;
(2) The sustainable development strategy that has become a paramount issue of our times; and
(3) The self-reliant strategy that is becoming increasingly relevant to our local-level development efforts.

Our methodologies for local-level (district level and below) planning should naturally take note of these new developmental thrusts.

In the first place, planning methodologies have to be understood only as an integral component of state policy. In keeping with any changes in state policy, the planning methodologies will also have to change. This contextual, dynamic and flexible character of the planning methodologies is one point which should be emphasized. It would mean that no planning methodology can be deemed static or perfect for all time. Planning methodology is a continually changing phenomenon, its parameters being :

— The Socio-political context and macro policies;
— The newly emerging thrusts in development planning;

— The level of knowledge and the basic and contributory skills possessed by planners;
— The level of sophistication in technology and the planning process; and
— The time available for analysis in a *time-bound* planning process.

India's economy is now at the crossroads and some important changes are taking place. It is now moving in the direction of market-oriented systems and restructuring itself for better integration with the international economy. It is a movement from state-regulated and state-dominated systems to the market economy. It is a result of what is called the "Structural Adjustment Process". What it means, so far as sub-national affairs are concerned, is that the role of the state in local and regional development affairs is getting reduced and that of the domain of responsibility of the people and local institutions is increasing. This means that the regional and local communities must now find their own development centres of gravity, in order to respond to the new policy changes that have emerged, and which should be reflected in the nature and character of the planning and development responses. It means that the management of the social and economic processes at the regional and local levels, which affect income distribution, equity, social security and poverty alleviation must now be handled in an increasingly self-reliant manner. A set of new value systems, work ethic and a different development ethos should now prevail, to spearhead, energize and mobilize society for the development and management of socio-economic transformation at the grassroot level. So far as the planning at the local levels is concerned, such as the district and sub-district, these changes call for an intensified effort towards what may be called "Development from Within".

It follows from this, that if this new development ethos should guide and determine the crucial issues of the content, techniques and methodology of District Planning, the roles of the different actors in the District Development Planning process should also be reassessed and seen in a new perspective.

Apart from the emerging new thrusts in development, a District Planning methodology should also be concerned with the following elements :

1. Approach;
2. Strategy;

3. Content;
4. Structure, Process and Stage of Development; and
5. Analysis : Steps and Tools.

Approach

It is now time, particularly in a context in which the Panchayati Raj institutions in our country are being revitalized, that we seriously seek to operationalise a *negotiatory or convergent planning approach* at the district level.

Ideally, a decentralized development process is initiated from the grassroots, which originates from certain local initiatives (sparked off by both internal dynamics and external stimuli) and engineered through "local organizations", and culminates in a "demand for resources" from the centre. Simultaneously, the government operates through its decentralized delivery systems and supply resources of various kinds, which include provision of government grants and loans, material inputs and technical assistance. These resources, coupled with the locally generated resources and those that are provided by the NGO's and other external agencies (e.g. foreign aid), constitute the total supply of resources to the local (district) level. The matching of this "supply" with the "demand" for resources to meet the development needs articulated by the people constitutes the essence of local-level planning. This is achieved through a process of interfacing and negotiation at the crucial administrative level, which is the District, where the top-down and bottom-up processes converge. While this would be ideal, in reality the planning process does not operate in this manner. Some progress has no, doubt, been made here and there in some states such as West Bengal and Karnataka, but even in these cases, the systematic conveyance of experience and analysis from the lower to the higher levels in a multi-level planning structure is extremely disjointed and unsatisfactory. In this context, the effectuation of satisfactory micro-macro linkages is an aspect of the District Planning methodology, which must be deemed as extremely important.

While considering the "Approach to Planning", we should pay due attention to some neglected dimensions in our development. One of them is the question of sustainable development. Earlier, ecology and environment were aspects, which were taken for granted or considered peripheral. Even after environmental awareness emerged in many developing countries, the actual task of introducing explicit environmental considerations into development planning and activities and thus "planning environmentally" on a scientific basis is only emerging in slow and halting steps. When the importance of environmental considerations came to be felt, governments and donor agencies like the World Bank confined their attention to only certain specific projects. This took the form of Environmental Impact Assessments and certain corrective measures were added to a plan, as a "technical fix" or additive. Soon it was realized that such a "project and additive approach" addressed only symptoms and not the root causes. The wisdom has now dawned that the ecological dimension of development is area-wide in scope and has regional and local characteristics, which demand not merely intervention in individual projects and programmes, but also in well-conceived regional and local strategies for managing development on a sustainable basis. So the district planning methodology should interweave into it concerns for ecological and environmental aspects, as part and parcel of the District plan, like the warp and woof in a tapestry.

Another neglected dimension in our development planning, which has now been increasingly recognized as important, is the role of women in development. Women exercise crucial multiple influences on population growth dynamics and on the health and nutritional status of their children and households which, in turn, affect population growth. Women are also increasingly acknowledged as the real managers of local environmental resources, since most of the gathering of fuel, water, fodder and wild products for subsistence is done by women. Gender analysis, therefore, should constitute an important component of the overall analysis in district planning.

Selective Development Strategy

Then there is the vital component of *strategy*, which should guide the methodology in District Planning. Here, it will be realistic to adopt a "selective development" strategy, which implies rigorous prioritization to select "lead sector(s)" and "core projects", to impart an initial trigger or "kick" to the development process. It involves the selection of policies and methods of focusing and concentrating public expenditures within a framework of balanced development. It also implies selection between regions, areas, cities and villages; between various sub-branches of the economy, between institutions, enterprises, families and individuals; and between short and long-run periods of planning and so forth.

Stages Approach

Studies made on decentralization indicate that it cannot be achieved through a "one-shot approach" and must unfold as a gradual "step-by-step" approach. A Working Group on district planning set up by the Indian Planning Commission has recommended a "Stages Approach" to decentralization for the different states in the country.[1] A World Bank Working Paper states, as one of the principles for achieving successful decentralization, "Plan small, expand incrementally". Successful small efforts can be expanded incrementally as personnel and organizations attain greater skills and capacity to plan and manage development activities. So, in the methodology for district planning, it is necessary to state clearly how the decentralization process is proposed to be advanced in steps; what will be accomplished in each step and how it will be followed up in future.

My experiences in some Asian and African countries leads me to the conclusion that in situations where there is no planning machinery at the district level and, therefore, the capabilities for planning are weak and the "Structure-Process-Stage" prerequisites are rudimentary, the first steps towards District Planning should be taken through pilot experiments as "demonstration exercises". Later, through training and capacitation, such experiments should be carefully planned to "spread and multiply" in other areas. In such contexts, the higher spatial levels in the multilevel planning hierarchy, endowed with greater capabilities and planning expertise, should shoulder all the burden of technically back-stopping the planning efforts at the lower levels. While expanding the pilot project experiments, they could be done so in a "cluster of districts", located in different ecological environments, so that the pilot experiments could become "proto-type" plans suited to different environments leading to their demonstration and spread effects on a large scale.

Content

In the case of district planning, the term "methodology" is applicable in the following substantive contexts :

1. For preparing the resource inventory and "Profile" of the district.
2. For identifying the lead sector(s) and strategies for planning.
3. For assessing the needs of the people and in preparing a "prioritized" statement of needs.

4. For formulating projects.
5. For assessing the intra-areal disparities in development and allocating resources accordingly.
6. For assessing the inter-sectoral linkages, when selecting and putting the projects in order.
7. For the appraisal of the on-going and new projects.
8. For monitoring the progress of projects and plan performance.

In all the above matters, some planning techniques are involved to secure some degree of "analytical rigour". But as important as "analytical rigour" are matters of a "procedural" nature. In fact, for the purpose of operationalising district plans, the procedural aspects are more important than even sophisticated techniques. The procedures are, therefore, very much a part of the District Planning methodology.

Structure, Process and Stage of Development

Methodology also depends on the three determinants, viz. Structure, Process and Stage of Development of the country. Structure implies institutional configurations. Of chief interest in our context are those related to planning, coordination and participation. They constitute a cluster of operations and how well they are performed in their institutional contexts, individually and collectively, depends on the linkages that are instituted among them.

The term "Process" refers not merely to the planning process operating—wether, only a "Top-down" or a two-way planning process—but also the functional, financial and administrative aspects of deconcentration from the centre to the periphery, that determines the degree of success of the decentralization process. It also includes the interactional and iterative procedures that make the process dynamic. "Stage" refers to the net result in the operation of the "Structure-Process nexus" and is the sum total of achievements in a decentralized set-up. In other words, it constitutes a measurement of decentralization.

Methodologies Advocated Earlier

The previous experiences in district planning in India have thrown up a lot of lessons in methodology which have considerable validity. The earliest among these is the 1969 guidelines of the Planning Commission.[2] This seminal document set out a five-step methodology which consisted of the following :

1. Drawing up a broad statement of prospects, objectives and priorities, called "Preliminary Framework".
2. Preparation of a "Revised Framework" of prospects, objectives and priorities based on consultation with the local bureaucracy and elected representatives of the public.
3. Laying down the guidelines for the long-term perspective of development as well as the integrated strategies for short-term planning.
4. Plan formulation, which itself consists of :

   — Regionalization of the district
   — Assessing existing levels of development
   — Working out the development strategies for each sub-region and identification of schemes and projects relating to the central and subsidiary economic activities on the one hand and the infrastructural and support services needed on the other, and

5. Plan finalization and communication.

In the late 70's, a Working Group for Block Level Planning was set up under the chairmanship of Prof. Dantwala[3], which set out a seven-step procedure or planning phases to block-level planning as follows :

1. The Acquaintance phase;
2. The Resource Inventory phase;
3. The Project Identification and Formulation phase;
4. The Employment Planning phase;
5. The Spatial Planning phase;
6. The Credit Planning phase; and
7. The Coordination and Implementation phase.

In the early 80's, a Working Group on District Planning was set up by the Planning Commission[4], which visualized the planning methodology in four distinct phases :

— The Pre-planning phase
— The Planning phase
— The Implementation phase; and
— The Monitoring and Evaluation phase.

During the Pre-planning phase, certain vital prerequisites were emphasized for district planning. For the planning phase, a nine-step operation was stipulated as follows :

1. Formulation of the major objectives of the district plan;
2. Collection and compilation of data for district planning;
3. Bringing out the profile of the district in relation to the basic objectives;
4. Formulating the main strategy and thrust of district planning;
5. Analysis of the on-going programmes and projects with reference to the strategy outlined above along with the proposals regarding.

    (i) The time phasing or sequencing of the on-going programmes and projects;
    (ii) Proposals for reducing inter-block disparities;
    (iii) Assessment of unemployment/underemployment and proposals for manpower planning and budgeting;
    (iv) Inclusion of new projects and plans;
    (v) Interlinkages between various projects and programmes; and
    (vi) Organization and management in terms of plan operations to ensure that no implementation gap exists.

6. Assessment of resources for allocation to various programmes and projects.
7. A statement of physical and financial components of the district plan.
8. Statement of the spatial dimensions of the district plan.
9. Relationships and links between the district plan and regional and state development plans.

Taken together, the three seminal reports mentioned here have covered different aspects of the district planning methodology. These are unexceptionable and quite valid in any discussion on the subject. In some respects, however, they may be lacking or have gaps and need a sharpening of focus in relation to contemporary thrusts.

One gap is in regard to the lack of adequate appreciation of the participatory aspects of district planning and spelling out of the nature and extent of public participation as well as its institutional aspects, and how to weave these considerations effectively into a district planning methodology, so that it is sufficiently responsive to people's needs.

The second is in respect of the techniques and tools of analysis which should inform the district planning methodology.

In the first place, negotiatory planning will become a reality only when the two-way process of planning becomes a reality and the necessary planning, co-ordination and participatory mechanisms for this purpose are established and the planning procedures standardized and crystallized in a time-bound planning process operating through all levels.

It is in this context that the reduced approach has great relevance. The reduced approach has to evolve in two directions, viz:

1. In data collection, processing and analysis, the techniques should be absolutely "simple"—not more than codified commonsense—in view of the logistic and staffing difficulties in the Third World countries.
2. The number of planning steps should be minimal, so as to speed up the process of planning and reduce the complexity of the planning task.

In India some specific methodologies have evolved for district planning over the years in a few states, which are sometimes spoken of as models (e.g. West Bengal, Karnataka). Amitava Mukherjee[5] has made a comprehensive review of all these methodologies and the inquisitive reader is referred to his three volumes on this subject.

Analytical Steps

So far as the analytical steps are concerned, we have not yet standardized them. But with the experiences gone through, the steps have become clear. When this author was engaged in preparing a training module for Decentralized District Planning for Nepal, all the various analytical techniques needed for district planning were synthesized under four major rubrics :

1. Situation Analysis;
2. Context Analysis;
3. Sectoral Analysis; and
4. Spatial Analysis.

The details of the above analyses are outside the scope of this book. In the present context, we only emphasize that these are minimal and necessary. Each one of the analyses, however, has to be conducted through appropriate techniques to bring out the relevant information for planning. These techniques could be simple or sophisticated, qualitative or quantitative, depending on the nature and extent of sensitivity of the data and the skills and technical competence available. One cannot be dogmatic about techniques. It is better to leave the aspect of techniques as open-ended. While all these types of analyses and techniques are necessary, they are not sufficient. They have to be supplemented by "perceptions" afforded by disciplines like Social Anthropology. The planning process is always dynamic and our methodologies have also to change to be in tune with the times. In the new emerging context, the District Planning methodology should also incorporate three new dimensions.

(i) The methodology should now focus on "Development from Within", which means greater accent on self-reliance.
(ii) To the above four kinds of analyses, two more should be added. These are :
  (a) Environmental Analysis, and
  (b) Gender Analysis.
(iii) Reduced approaches must be used in data collection and analysis and in the planning steps and procedures.

The conventional methodology should incorporate the contextual and strategic elements and should also include some missing dimensions and continuously modify itself to the dynamics of our times. In this way, the District Planning methodology would become more realistic and relevant.

In the viewpoints expressed here, the details of the methodology have not been gone into. These details become relevant only when applying the methodology in particular contexts. It should also be emphasized that there is nothing like a single, straight-jacketed, invincible, water-tight and all-embracing methodology. Methodologies should be dynamic and flexible, matching the capabilities of those who plan. When methodologies are rigid and water-tight, they become counter-productive. The essential function of a methodology is to provide a mental machinery for dealing with a large variety of data and interpreting them into something which has a "meaning". There is no reason why we should not have, at our disposal, several alternative methodologies, which provide different ways of interpreting chaotic data into sensible information.

Tools of Analysis

As for tools of analysis, it is better to have a nice range of tools, amongst which we may find something suitable for whichever situation we find ourselves dealing with. Thus, while the broad methodology should be a logical framework, ranging from resource inventory to analysis, strategy formulation and project identification, the detailed methodo-logy about techniques of analysis should be a flexible one. It should be something like a powerful battery or tool-box, from which we can, more or less automatically, pick up the hammer or the mallet, the screw-driver or the chisel, the plane or the spoke shave, according to the task in hand. For, we should remember that we are discussing a field, which is very free and open-ended—free for the planner to make mistakes as well as free for him to produce very fertile new insights. Here we are confronting a "problematique", a challenging situation which is to be met in a flexible and free manner, taking into account the available planning capabilities and skills, the temporal constraints in the planning situation and the logistical support services that are available to the planner.

Some Constraints in District Planning Methodologies

In District Planning, we work with policy-makers, planners, implementers, community leaders and representatives of the public and interest groups, in order to arrive at more rational and widely acceptable policies, plans and programmes. Here time is of the essence. This is because district planning has to be linked to the overall two-way planning and implementation process and has to be integrated into the state budget. In such a planning context, time is always a constraint.

Secondly, what is important about development planning methodologies is that *they should work,* i.e. they should be intensely operational, and must lead to the speedy preparation of the plan and have the desired impact on the area and the people. I am reminded of Moynihan's words :[7]

> "The great questions of government have to do, not with what will work, but what does work. The best of behavioural sciences would in truth be of no great utility in a genuine political democracy, where one opinion is as good as another and where public polices emerging

from legislative-executive collaboration will constantly move in one direction, then another following such whim, fashion, or pressure that seem uppermost at the moment. What government and public most need to know in the aftermath of this process is, whether there was anything to show for the effort, and if so what. Causal insights of the kind that can lead to the prediction of events are interesting and absorbing, but they are hardly necessary to the management of a large open political system; all that is needed is a rough, but hopefully refined, set of understandings as to what is associated with what".

Communication of Methodologies

If methodologies are to influence plan-making at the district level, they ought to be communicated effectively, i.e. in an understandable way to the district planners. What good is a methodology if it cannot be understood by its users? Thus communication strategies need to be a part of the planning methodology. These communication strategies will include :[8]

— Impersonal communication through guidelines and circulars;
— Personal communication through training programmes or organized meetings;
— Effective communication through some interesting forms, such as through videotapes, films, slides, or transparencies; and
— Illustrative communication through some case studies in which the application of these methodologies is attempted.

Conclusive Comment

Methodology for decentralized planning at any level for any country bristles with several problems and is dependent on many factors. The specific country context, the data availability, the nature of the planning process operating and the capability of the personnel involved in planning are all relevant issues. It can be rudimentary or sophisticated, narrowly focused or broadly designed, straightforward or complex. It can employ minimal or extensive quantitative analysis. More than all these, it will be related to the objectives of planning at the particular level and in the particular country. The author is reminded of a quotation from *Alice in Wonderland* by Lewis Caroll :

Would you tell me please, which way
I ought to go from here? said Alice.
That depends a good deal on where
you want to get to, said the Cheshire cat.

REFERENCES

1. Report of the Working Group on District Planning, Government of India, Planning Commission, 1984.
2. Guidelines for District Planning, Government of India, Planning Commission, 1969.
3. Report of the Working Group on Block Level Planning, Government of India, Planning Commission, 1975. Also Sundaram, K.V., Poverty Alleviation in Rural Areas through Employment creation–Implication of Block Level Planning and other methodologies, *Manpower Journal*, Vol. XIV, No. 4, January-March 1979.
4. *Ibid.*, Planning Commission, 1984. Also Sundaram, K.V., Planning below the state level : Policies, Strategies and Methodologies, *The Indian Journal of Geography*, Vol. XIII, No. 1, 1978.
5. Mukherjee, Amitava, *Methodology and Database for Decentralized Planning*, Vol. 3 (Parts A, B and C), Heritage Publishers, New Delhi, 1991. Also Amitava Mukherjee 'Methodologies in Decentralized Planning : A Survey', *Annuls of the National Association of Geographers* (India), Vol. II, Nos. I and II, December 1992.
6. For a standard work on analytical techniques on local-level planning, see, Avrom Bendavid Val, 'Regional and Local Economic Analysis for Practitioners' (New and Expanded edition), Praeger, 1983. Also for some applications, see Training Manual on Decentralized Planning (District Level)–8 Modules, Agricultural Project Services Centre (APROSC) and Food and Agriculture Organization of the United Nations (FAO/UN), November 1990, Nepal.
7. Moynihan, D.P., "Maximum Feasible Misunderstanding : Community, Action in the War on Poverty". New York, The Free Press, 1969.
8. World Bank Staff Working Paper No. 581 by Rondinelli, D.A. *et al.*, "Decentralization in Developing Countries—A Review of Recent Experience", World Bank, Washington, 1983.

11

DECENTRALIZATION
Measurement and Monitoring

Decentralization is a continuum and its level of attainment at any point of time in a country will be determined by many factors. Thus it is a dynamic variable. When someone says that the Philippines is more decentralized than Indonesia, by what criteria and standards does such comparison hold good? Similarly in a federal structure like the USA or India, when we compare one state with another in regard to the degree of decentralization, what measures should we employ for making such comparisons? Whatever be the criteria, the measurement of decentralization is basic or fundamental to any study or evaluation of decentralization, i.e. to understand the effects of greater or lesser decentralization. In this chapter, the various approaches to formulate criteria by which we can compare the degree of decentralization between two different areas have been dealt with.

Smith[1] mentions the following criteria for a broad analysis :

1. Functions or tasks of decentralized institutions.
2. The extent of taxation permitted to local authorities.
3. Field administration, i.e. the level of decentralization within field hierarchies, and the frequency with which field officers have to refer matters to central headquarters for decision.
4. The extent of delegation, measured by the extent of jurisdiction delegated by the centre.
5. Expenditure—the level of local expenditure as a proportion of total public spending.
6. The number of hierarchy levels in the administration.
7. The extent of financial dependence of the local body, e.g. the ratio of local government revenues to total government revenues.

8. Personnel—the extent of the centre's control on the selection and deployment of local personnel.

In each of the above eight components of measurement, there are several tricky issues involved. Generally speaking,"'delegation", by which the governmental tasks or functions are transferred to the field offices, is deemed to be a lesser degree of decentralization rather than devolution, which is "the legal conferring of powers to discharge specified or residual functions upon formally constituted local authorities".[2] But there are quite a few problems involved in the measurement of decentralized functions and tasks. Sometimes, the centre takes over functions, which might otherwise be the responsibility of local governments. And even while considering "delegation", it must be remembered that the same function is split up in the form of different tasks among different structures and jurisdictions. Thus the distribution of localized functions and tasks between different structures of decentralization must be analyzed in great detail, to distinguish the purely central tasks (such as audit and inspection) performed by field offices from those which might have been devolved. In a multi-national comparative analysis, it is the "range of decision areas" of local governments that matters. Local legislations may sometimes vaguely indicate a broad range of responsibilities to local governments; but when it comes to reality, the local governments may be doing relatively little. In such cases, a mechanical across-the-board comparison based on a study of legislations alone may not reveal the whole truth. More indepth investigation on how the system actually functions will be necessary.

When it comes to local finance, the powers given to the local bodies for raising revenue from their own sources is what really matters, more than the subventions from the centre. While considering the decentralization of powers in this context, it is not merely the proportion of revenues that are locally raised, which is of course an important measure, but also the latitude and flexibility permitted to the local authorities to increase the local tax rates in keeping with the growth of the economy and the rate of inflation which matters.

In considering "Field Administration" as a measure of decentralization, one has to compare the nature of delegation (managerial, administrative) of responsibilities from the headquarters and how the authority is exercised. The frequency with which field officers have to refer matters to central headquarters for decision is a critical measure. While considering the exercise of authority by the field officers, the extent of jurisdiction delegated by the centre matters. Here, the distinction between "control" and "influence" is important. The greater the number of local decisions, which are centrally influenced rather than controlled, the greater the decentralization. The pattern of controls and influences at the disposal of the centre varies with the system of decentralization obtaining in each country. The details of each pattern have to be studied in-depth, before making a judgement as to their impact on the overall level of decentralization.

The level of local expenditure as a proportion of total public spending is a useful measure of decentralization, if the aim is to compare states or a single political system at different stages in time. The greater the proportion of total public spending incurred by local governments, the greater the decentralization.

The structure of the hierarchical set-up also influences the level of decentralization. Some are of the view that a multi-tiered system is more decentralized. On the other hand, the organization theory considers the flatter management structures, which increase productivity and efficiency, as an efficiently decentralized system. Obviously, more research is indicated to find out how the structure of the hierarchy influences the degree of decentralization. For a lower-level local authority, is it less time-consuming and easier to obtain approval from its immediately higher level rather than from the centre? As a wag once put it to this author, during one of his tours to a sub-district in an Indian state, "It is easier and quicker to obtain approval from a Deputy Secretary in the Central Government, than from an official at the district or regional level, to whom the powers are decentralized". Much depends upon what is the degree of delegation of powers to the various layers of decision-making and the attitudinal behaviour of the individual officer and his commitment to decentralization.

Financial dependence or independence is often considered as a proxy for decentralization. But it depends on the control over the funds that are decentralized. A local authority, receiving a high proportion of its local revenues from central grants, need not necessarily be deemed as less decentralized, if the funds come as block grants and the local authority enjoys the freedom of discretionary spending, as it deems best under its circumstances. Here, it is the degree of local autonomy which is the critical measure. Thus, it is the viability of financial "dependence" which decides the measure of decentralization.

Personnel and the degree of control which the local authorities have on them is another important index of decentralization. It is usually assumed that a local authority is less decentralized, when all its control over the staff is with the centre. The decentralization is said to be inadequate, so long as the staff are not totally loyal and accountable to the local authority. Considering the various factors that determine personnel management, for local bodies, usually a "unified" system of personnel management is considered the best arrangement, in which the senior staff are drawn from a local government cadre and the junior staff are employed by the local authority itself. But in many countries, the "integrated" system prevails, in which the senior personnel are from the centre who are seconded to the local authority. In such cases, the rele=vant question would be what proportion of total public servants are the employees of central agencies. In any case, the measurement of decentralization has to be with reference to the system of personnel management prevailing in the country.

The various indices of measurement suggested above have all due relevance with reference to the particular context. Any judgement in regard to the status of decentralization must be taken after a careful analysis of each context and intelligent interpretation. Since both political and administrative systems vary considerably from one country to another, a multi-national comparative analysis becomes a complex subject. A country may appear to be more decentralized with respect to one criterion, while with reference to another, it may be less decentralized. In this context, how do we give weightages to the different criteria and arrive at an overall judgement? This is again tricky and no prescriptions may be given, which will be valid under all circumstances. In this, as in many other areas of investigation in social science research, the researcher has to face the problem in all its complexities, and arrive at a proper value judgement.

In an FAO document, Materne Maetz and Maria Quieti[3] have elaborated a framework for analyzing and comparing decentralization among different countries. They have based the framework based on the following four questions : What is the type of decentralization? At what stage of development is it? What is the extent of government commitment to decentralization? What are the responsibilities of the major development actors under decentralization? The framework is divided into four parts, viz. :

(i) Administration/organization, i.e. the extent of deconcentration and delegation, along with government commitment and the stage of evolution reached by decentralization.

(ii) Finance, i.e. the analysis of financial devolution and delegation.
(iii) Planning, i.e. the way the planning process is organized with the various "actors" and "steps" and the institutional mechanisms in place.
(iv) People's participation, i.e. the extent to which NGO's and various people's organization participate and influence planning and decision-making.

They have framed a series of meaningful questions, the answers to which help in analyzing the extent of decentralization. It is in a tabular form (See annexure to this chapter) with four columns, viz. Item, No, Yes and Remarks. The No/Yes columns are meant to help define each point or question, which can then be elaborated further under "Remarks". Maetz and Quieti have adopted a "weighting technique" to measure the four aspects of decentralization and then to arrive at an overall judgement of the degree of decentralization in the country. The weighting is subjective and cannot be helped. But even then, the systematic, step-by-step procedure involved here may lead to a sound value judgement, which is something much better than mere a hunch or guess work. If the analysis is sufficiently in-depth and the understanding of the researcher is good, the resulting evaluation is bound to be reasonably sound.

An alternative to the FAO approach is to institute a detailed survey of the present state of decentralization, deconcentration, devolution, delegation and public participation in the administration of the country. Such surveys are usually undertaken by the government of a country when they want to introduce reforms in decentralization, after assessing the bottlenecks in the decentralization process. In Bangladesh, for example, a detailed study on decentralization and the people's participation was undertaken in 1983[4] by the National Institute of Public Administration (NIPA) at the request of the Bangladesh Ministry of Planning. The study involved not merely literature survey, but also an opinion survey using 24 types of questionnaires and interview schedules and covering a total of 6,293 respondents. The Indian Government sets up Committees/Working Groups from time to time to make similar assessments, in which a number of experts participate. Similarly in other countries too, such evaluations are done either by entrusting the study to a reputed institution or by constituting Committees/Task Forces/Working Groups at government level. The purpose in such exercises is somewhat different, though it may involve assessment/measurement of decentralization.

Monitoring and Evaluation of Planning Process

The monitoring of the planning process is something different from programme or project monitoring. In plan monitoring, we consider how the planning process operated, whether the plan objectives were achieved and whether the plan as a whole benefited the people (which kind of people) and what problems were faced during planning and implementation.

Decentralized Planning is a *process*. So the major thrust of Monitiring and Evaluation (M&E) here is : (a) How the process was conducted; (b) the gap between what was visualized and what was obtained, i.e. between aspirations and reality. In every country, this gap is huge; and (c) In decentralized planning, there are some Key Steps, Key Actors and Key Instruments. During the process of monitoring, we have to inquire as to how these generally functioned. In order to understand the methodology, we may discuss these issues in the context of a specific country, where the planning process and procedures have been clearly spelt out. The country chosen for illustration is Nepal.

The Decentralization Act of 1982 and the Working Procedures framed under it in Nepal have spelt out 17 Key Steps in the planning process. These are :

1. Preparation of Guidelines and Budget Ceiling.
2. Preparation of Village Profiles and District Profiles.
3. Aggregating Village Profiles into District Profiles.
4. Internal Resource Estimation.
5. Preparation of Budget Estimate.
6. Resource Allocation.
7. Approval and Despatch of Information on Resource Allocation.
8. Identification of Local Need-based Projects.
9. Preparation of Village Plan.
10. Approval of Village Plan.
11. Technical Assistance to Panchayat and Wards for Project Preparation.
12. Preparation of Sectoral Plans.
13. Consolidation of Sectoral Plans.
14. Analyze Village Plans and Despatch for Approval.
15. Prepare District Development Plan for discussion and approval.
16. Amend and approve plan as required.
17. Integration of District Plan into National Plan.

Taking note of the above key steps, we may specifically inquire into : what specific problems were encountered at each step.

Whether such problems were :

(a) Structural, i.e. the way the planning process had been structured along with the various institutional mechanisms.
(b) Procedural/administrative, i.e. concerned with the procedures prescribed.
(c) Concerned with the human factor, e.g. capability of personnel;
(d) Concerned with financial inflexibility or inadequacy.
(e) Whether any "time squeeze" was felt while going through these steps.
(f) What output or outputs emerged from each Key Step?
(g) Whether the output was in accordance with what was originally envisaged?

Key Actors in Decentralized Planning

In the Nepal context, one may identify nine Key Actors having distinct roles in the planning process. These are :

Officials

1. District Level Officers/Sectoral Officers (District Chiefs).
2. District Office Assistants.
3. Ilaka Level—Line Agency Officers.
4. Village Development Committee Secretaries.

Non-Officials

5. District Development Committee Members.
6. Village Chairmen/Vice-Chairmen.
7. Ward Chairmen and Ward Members.
8. Members of Users' Groups.
9. Whole Village Population.

In order to monitor and evaluate the activities of key persons, we may raise a number of questions pertaining to different aspects of their roles and performance. The following are indicative :

— Did they understand their roles and act accordingly so as to advance or push the decentralization process at each step?
— What problems or difficulties the Key Actors (each one of them) faced and how these were resolved?
— What was the output of each Key Actor?
— How did the Key Actors mutually complement and supplement each other's roles?
— Were there confrontations/personality clashes among the Key Actors? If so, how were they resolved?
— Is it the lack of clarity in their respective roles that led to these confrontations?
— Is it possible to devise a rating scale to adjudge the performance of the various actors? (This helps to design the training programmes suited to their needs.)
— Did a partnership approach prevail among the Key Actors, particularly between the officials and the non-officials?
— What kind of clash of loyalties (vertical and horizontal) did you notice among the Key Actors (particularly in relation to line agency officials) in the performance of their duties? To what extent such clash of loyalties contributed to the short-comings in the decentralization process?
— Did the Key officials demonstrate their willingness to be *accountable* to the elected functionaries in their actions?
— Did the Key line agency officials demonstrate a healthy team sprit? Did they accept the coordinating role of the Local Development Officer (the Chief Coordinator) and cooperate with him? Did they adequately dialogue with the local leaders? Did they make themselves accessible to the local population? Did they collaborate with and encourage Users' Groups? Were they able to move closely with the people and motivate them?
— Did the key non-officials :

(a) Understand their roles;
(b) Exhibit the necessary development orientation;
(c) Believe and respect the planned way of doing things as against ad-hocism;
(d) Evince interest in dialoguing and discussing with the officials and then take decisions in a rational and objective manner? (For this, one has to list each major decision taken and analyze it carefully.)

(e) Look upon officials (bureaucracy) as partners in the development game or enemies or obstacles to their way of doing things?

(f) Show sufficient eagerness to participate in the planning process and contribute to the implementation of projects?

Key Instruments in Decentralized Planning

There are several key instruments in decentralized planning. These are :

A. Key Ministries and Line Ministries (Agencies)

— Did they give resource projection and guidelines to the District Panchayats *in time*?
— Did they backstop the District Panchayats from time to time with technical assistance?
— Did they undertake review and inspection of the on-going projects and programmes in the districts?
— If so, how frequently? What steps were taken by them to see that the observations made by them during these reviews and inspections were acted upon and suitable course corrections were applied?
— What do you think should be the role of the regional offices of the Key Ministries/Line Agencies in backstopping the planning activities at the District, *Ilaka*, Village and Ward levels? (The regional offices are important and if they play an effective role, the quality of the planning process will greatly improve.)

B. Sectoral Planning Committees

— How frequently did the sectoral planning committees meet during the process of the formulation of the district plan?
— What was the nature of discussions during the meetings of the District Planning Committees? (For this purpose, the minutes or proceedings of the meetings should be gone through.)
— Did the sectoral planning committees prioritize their projects and schemes? How was this done? (a) by consensus or (b) purely by technical/planning considerations as advocated by the technical line ministries? How were individual preferences weighted against collective decision-making?

C. Joint Planning Committee

— How many times did the Joint Planning Committee meet?
— How did this committee perform its tasks of scrutiny and appraisal?

(a) Did it only mechanically assemble the sectoral plans and forward them to the District Panchayat and later to the District Assembly for the final approval?
(b) Did it look into the forward and backward linkages in each sectoral plan and examine whether these were appropriately provided for in the other relevant or related sectoral plans? (This is a process of instituting consistency checks and is the means to arrive at an integrated District Development Plan.)
(c) Did it fully debate the prioritization attempted by the District Line Agencies and satisfy itself that these priorities were in accordance with the local area specificities and needs?
(d) What was the degree of consensus among the members of the Joint Planning Committee?

D. District Development Committee and District Assembly

Planning

— Whether these bodies examined the plan forwarded to them by the Joint Planning Committee from the point of view of whether the proposals included therein were relevant to the felt needs, identified problems and the existing potentialities of the district?
— Whether they examined the setting of physical targets and resource requirements, including locally mobilized resources from the point of view of realistic achievements?
— Did they examine the calendar of operations for annual activities for implementating the programmes and projects and satisfy themselves that : (a) the time schedule was in order; and (b) that the activities themselves were in accordance with the people's expectations relating to the materialization of benefits?
— Did they examine the statement of benefits that are expected

from the proposed projects and investments and see what proportion of these benefited the following groups :

(a) The rural poor and the disadvantaged sections of the society; and
(b) The general public, including all economic classes and interests.

— Did they examine specifically whether the local goals and objectives implied in the district plan are generally in conformity with the national development goals and objectives?
— Did they specifically address themselves to the enhancement of the level and coverage of the social services, particularly education, health and environmental management? (This is very important because, if these cannot be adequately met from the government's allocation of resources to the district, effective ways and means must be devised to raise local resources of the order that may be necessary.)

Implementation

— M&E should clearly provide statements to the District Panchayats and District Assemblies on the following :

* How much money was spent against allocations on particular programmes and projects?
* How judiciously this money was spent? (infructuous investment and the reasons therefor should be specifically brought out).
* What benefits were actually realized from the investment?
* Inventory of projects and the stage of their implementation. (at the time of review.)
* Examination of the effectiveness of projects. (at the time of review.)
* Examination of the projects from the point of view of whether they are being followed (implemented) strictly in accordance with the time schedule.
* Whether the physical achievements are in accordance with those envisaged at the time of project formulation.

* Whether or not the people are being benefited by the projects, as envisaged during their formulation and initiation.
* Did these bodies examine whether the inputs were delivered on time?
* Whether the inputs resulted in the intended outputs and effects?
* Whether their communities are actually heading towards an improvement of socio-economic conditions?

Plan Integration

The litmus test of a successful plan is how well it is integrated. Integration is a complicated task. It is necessary in the first instance to comprehend the full meaning of integration and the basic principles underlying the integrated approach to area development. These principles may be broadly stated as follows :

1. The very nature of the process of area development and the size of the problem of framing economic and social progress in rural and urban areas in a particular area, say, a district, require that action be taken on several fronts simultaneously and not independently of each other. Hence, programmes of agriculture, minor irrigation, soil conservation, grassland development, roads, education and training, health and nutrition, community development, etc., should not be planned and implemented each in isolation and without consideration of the implications that development programmes for one area might have for the other.
2. The concept of the integrated approach in the context of area development means an "integral" approach in the sense that it is a highly structural and systematic exercise in which each of the components in the system can be understood as important and appreciated for the part which they play individually and collectively. In this sense, the concept of integration differs from the "hormonization" of plans or the "cooperation" of various agencies or even the "administrative co-ordination" of existing plans and programmes.
3. Integration is not something which could be manipulated at a final stage by pruning something here or increasing something there, but must come as a conscious exercise carried on right from the time of inception of an idea/scheme through its completion.

4. The concept of integration implies establishing proper linkages, complementarities and sequences among various programmes and sectors and envisaging development in its totality.

Plan integration has to be examined from the following angles :

1. Multilevel integration, i.e. whether the district plan has been effectively dovetailed into the plans at the higher and lower area levels.
2. Sectoral and inter-sectoral integration, i.e. whether the programmes and projects in the different sectors, sub-sectors and between one sector and another have been consistently adjusted in a cohesive and unified manner to attain a structural balance in the plan. These consistencies will be of different kinds. (They are not specifically gone into here.)
3. Sectoral—spatial integration, i.e. whether the location of specific activities is given due and proper attention and spatial overlaps have been avoided.
4. Rural-urban integration, i.e. whether the plans of urban local bodies have been integrated with those of the villages.

Participation

Since decentralization is essentially a participatory approach, participation should be measured on the following lines :

(i) Who are those that participate? (Name all the institutions—Local Authority, NGO's. various polycentric institutions, cooperatives, etc.)
(ii) How did they participate in the following areas?

  (a) Decision-making for planning : data processing; determination of societal goals; allocation of resources; identificition and formulation of projects; assessment and prioritization of needs; formulation of options, etc.
  (b) Implementation process—through voluntary association in the execution of plans, programmes and projects; through assisting in resource mobilization, management and maintenance of projects;

(c) In ensuring the rational sharing of benefits of development. This may include identifying the beneficiaries of projects; organizing them for common purposes; making their voices heard in the appropriate quarters for any needs that have not been met, or any problems that have not been resolved, etc.

(d) In assisting in monitoring and evaluating plans, programmes and projects; and

(e) In educating the public about the plan and its benefits.

The problems faced in each of the above steps should be stated.

Some Concluding Observations

To conclude this discussion, measurement and monitoring implies some quantitative assessment of outcomes. In the case of decentralization, the outcomes encompass numerous variables, all of which are not susceptible to statistical measurement. For measuring and monitoring the quantitative outcomes of decentralization (its tangible objectives), adequate techniques are available. Decentralization as a qualitative process (e.g. behavioural elements), however, presents us with more difficult conceptual problems. When some quantitative technique is used for this purpose, it would probably only capture one dimension rather than the variable dimensions of the change occurring. A technique like "social impact analysis" is sometimes advocated. Here again, the notion of "impact" suggests a straightforward one-directional cousality resulting from decentralization and can ignore many others. A broad spectrum of "Indicators" may perhaps be more appropriate. But the use of indicators ultimately implies "interpretation", which may be somewhat subjective. Peter Oakley et al[5] sum up these dilemmas in measurement and monitoring as follows :

Quantitative Aspects

Measurement ⟶ Judgement

Qualitative Aspects

Description ⟶ Interpretation

REFERENCES

1. Smith, B.C., *Decentralization, the Territorial Dimension of the State*, London, Allen and Unwin, 1985.
2. Maddick, H., *Democracy, Decentralization and Development*, Asia Publishing House, 1963.
3. Materne Maetz and Maria G. Quieti, 'Training for Decentralized Planning—Lessons from Experience', Food and Agriculture Organization of the United Nations, Rome 1987.
4. Shaikh Maqsood Ali *et al.*, 'Decentralization and People's Participation', National Institute of Public Administration, Dhaka, 1983.
5. Peter Oakley *et al.*, Projects with people : The practice of participation in rural development, ILO Geneva, 1991.

ANNEXURE

A FRAMEWORK TO ANALYZE DECENTRALIZATION

Item	No	Yes	Remarks
1. *Administration/Organization*			
Creation of a local planning capability			
Creation of a local planning cell (pluridisciplinary)			
Decentralized planning and implementation procedures developed			
Central-level high-power committee to coordinate decentralization			
High calibre staff transferred to local-level			
Accountability of government staff to local-level authority			
Staff performance assessment made at local-level			
2. *Finance*			
Resources earmarked for decentralization			
Funds allocated to local-level			
Criteria to allocate funds to local-level			
Existence of untied funds			
Power to levy taxes given to local authority			
Incentives provided for local resources mobilization			
Financial accountability of government officers to local authority			

Item	No	Yes	Remarks
3. *Planning*			
Scope and content of local-level planning defined			
Attempt to train and/or provide technical backstopping to local planners			
Local planning authority decides at least on location of projects			
Sectoral targets for the local level exist			
Sectoral targets prepared at local level			
Targets organized and presented in a sectoral plan (standard format).			
Existence of a database at local level			
Existence of a local level M&E cell			
Possibilities of intersectoral planning			
Partially integrated multisectoral planning at local level			
Fully integrated multisectoral planning at local level			
Projects formulated at local level			
Village plans formulated at village level			
Intra-district balance consideration			
Possibility to modify content and costs of projects to a certain extent during implementation without referring to the national level			
4. *People's Participation*			
Local planning authority includes government officials only			

Item	No	Yes	Remarks
Local planning authority includes a mix of government officials and local leaders			
Local planning authority includes political leaders only			
Local planning authority also includes various interest groups and NGO's.			
Actions to promote people's participation			
Local planning authority legally established			
If planning prerogatives are legally established			
People participate in terms of Labour/finance			
People participate in management of projects			
People are consulted during the planning phase : —by survey —by participation in assemblies and forums			

Source : Materne Maetz and Maria G. Quieti—*Ibid.*

12

DECENTRALIZED PLANNING IN THE CONTEXT OF THE CURRENT DECENTRALIZATION REFORMS*

Societies grow and develop in historic times. As our times and circumstances—social, political and economic—change, development also undergoes some reorientation. In this context, certain new issues and imperatives emerge. In our current historical context, one may perceive at least three major developments, which have their impact on local development affairs. These are :

(i) The passing of the Constitutional (73rd and 74th) amendments, which are now being followed by appropriate enactments by the states. As a result of the 73rd amendment, the district below the state level has been now constitutionally recognized as the third stratum in the politico-administrative hierarchy. This should be considered as a big leap forward, as it pushes democratic decentralized development to the district level;

(ii) The implementation of the new economic reforms has indirectly meant somewhat reduced state-level assistance to local areas and hence the necessity to opt for increasingly self-reliant approaches in local-level planning and development; and

(iii) "The Environmental Crisis", which is the outcome of an economic, structural crisis, has become more significant and is now gaining increased attention, calling for systematic environmental management and "sustainable development" at the local level and above.

---

* Based on a paper presented to the National Conference on "Emerging Trends in Panchayati Raj in India". National Institute of Rural Development, Hyderabad. Nov. 29-Dec. 1, 1994.

All the abovementioned imperatives underline the need to move towards an alternative model of development that is more decentralized, more democratic and in better tune with the resource potentials, problems and needs of the regional and local communities. The Panchayati Raj institutions are being revived and there is a resurgence of interest in District Planning. This renaissance marks the beginning of a new watershed in our progress towards a more democratic order. It gives rise to the emergence of the vision of a New Society, which may be characterized by the following features :

(i) The functions and powers of the government will be shared willingly by the state and the bureaucracy with the sub-state levels;
(ii) There will be no ambiguity about the respective roles of the bureaucracy and the local government institutions. The two would march hand in hand towards the common goal;
(iii) It will lead to the emergence of local leaderships without let or hindrance;
(iv) It will lead to empowerment of the people, not merely of the elites, but also of the weaker sections of society. Thus there will be the widest scope for participation;
(v) Local government institutions will be established with sufficient local autonomy and will articulate the indigenous and collective wisdom of the people and the community's desires and needs in the exercise of planning and decision-making; and
(vi) Numerous grassroot level institutions will emerge such as Users' Groups, Collective Self-Management Groups, Joint Management Groups and various interest groups, who will actively participate in the local-level planning and development process.

The above vision of the New Society is indeed utopian and reminds us of Rabindranath Tagore's vision of "heavenly freedom", commencing with lines "where the mind is without fear". But this glorious vision does not last long and soon gets blurred when one begins to reflect on the past failures of the Panchayati Raj institutions, which were once resplendent with hopes. The nagging pessimism and persistent doubts in this context are :

(i) Will this second Renaissance of PRI's yield anything more hopeful and more valid?

(ii) Will the transition to a decentralized democracy be smooth and painless?

(iii) Will the grassroot democracies be able to cope with the various demands on them, particularly with those on the policy and planning front?

Decentralization tends to disturb the existing equations and brings about new equations in the power structure between the elected functionaries (at different layers) on the one hand, and the appointed executives on the other. Decentralization also affects the relations between the different tiers of development administration—both vertical and horizontal. Political power, financial allocation and the images of development functionaries and elected members are now in a vortex of change. At the people's front, there are lofty expectations. In the current trends, one may see popular perceptions in most advanced states, though not uniform, yet which seem to be crystallizing into some directions, particularly regarding the institutions and process of decentralization. Taking note of these changes and the people's aspirations, it is now necessary to devise a carefully designed Decentralized Planning System.

All the above-stated imperatives call for a reorientation of the objectives, process and institutional structure of local-level planning. In this context, a conceptual or analytical framework for the design of the organization for decentralized planning and the orchestration of the planning process is necessary. The main purpose of this chapter is to help provide such a framework.

Panchayati Raj System and Decentralized Planning Implications

Decentralized Planning in the current context implies the parallel and concurrent march of democracy and decentralized development administration. Therefore, it must address itself to both managerial and political objectives. The managerial approach involves the practical aspects of setting up of the appropriate planning and co-ordination mechanisms and the working out of organizational procedures, such as the reporting system and budgetary procedures and the training and re-training of personnel "involved" in decentralized planning and implementation. The political objectives are those designed to legitimize decentralized planning in the eyes of the general public as well as particular interest groups, whom specific programmes are intended to benefit. They are generally objectives related to public participation, usually expressed in terms of various phrases, such as "Bringing power to the people". "Involving the grassroots" or "Bringing government closer to the people", etc. The decentralized planning, involving both managerial and political objectives, is inevitably complex and has to be designed carefully, taking into account the many factors and interests involved and the political nature of the planning process. Thus in the context of the Panchayati Raj System, decentralized planning implies that the technocratic approach and the political approach should mesh, in an interactive, participatory and culturally sensitive planning process, to produce a plan, that is both technically sound and administratively responsive to the needs, wishes and resources of the local population.

Local Level : Definition

The Panchayati Raj System, in India, consists of three tiers, viz. Village Panchayat, Block Samiti and Zilla Parishad. Thus three unit areas are involved—the village, the block and the district. All these three unit areas are subsumed under the definition of "local level". Thus the local level itself is a multilevel system. Planning for such a system involves the adoption of multilevel planning procedures and effecting suitable micro-macro linkages, so as to integrate local-level planning into the state and national levels of planning.

Decentralized Planning is not a single-stroke planning operation. It is a relay and re-relay process in which the micro-units, through a repetitive process of interaction, seek continuously convergence to the dynamic path of stable equilibrium for the entire macro system. The different area levels have to act and interact repeatedly, until harmonious planning is achieved. This interaction is achieved through vigorous flows of information, both top-down and bottom-up. The top-down flows may consist of information pertaining to policies, priorities, targets, guidelines for planning, budgetary information, technical information, co-ordination directives, review of monitoring and evaluation of projects and suggestions for re-planning. Bottom-up flows may consist of data, information on local needs and preferences, area priorities, area targets and problems and constraints faced at the local level. A hypothetical multilevel planning system showing levels, flows and interaction may be seen in Fig. 2.1 in Chapter 2. In order to bring about this iterative process of interaction in the manner envisaged here, an interactive adjustment mechanism is required, which can constantly align the plans at the various sub-national levels to the national plan at each round of implementation. It is in this way that the goal conflicts in multilevel planning are sought to be resolved and harmonized planning ensured. This interactive adjustment mechanism would consist of an appropriate planning machinery at each one of the sub-national levels, where planning functions are proposed to be decentralized. The structure and composition of this planning machinery is the most crucial in this entire planning process, for it is this apparatus which has to prepare the plans and organize the flows and interactions, both upwards and downwards. Upon the efficiency of this planning apparatus will depend the entire success of the multilevel planning process.[1]

Decentralized Planning Principles

Local-level planning, viewed as multilevel planning, will be based on three major principles : (1) Principle of function-sharing or Functional Decentralization; (2) Principle of Financial Decentralization; and (3) Principle of Administrative Decentralization.

Functional decentralization means indicating with precision and clarity which functional activities are to be decentralized and what powers over each activity are to be decentralized. Accordingly, the relevant authority and powers have to be decentralized to each area level by the state government. The specifications of functions should be clear-cut and not in very broad and vague terms, as has been done in the 11th schedule of the constitutional amendment. The mere indication of sectoral responsibilities in global terms like agriculture, industry, health, education and so on will not do. The meticulous sub-division of each responsibility is necessary, because it is usual for any one sectoral activity to be divided between the national, state and different local levels. Thus to take the example of education, one needs to consider different types of education service (primary, secondary, tertiary, vocational, etc.) and different types of functions with regard to each kind of service (day-to-day administration, location of new schools, curriculum design, teacher training and so on). The actual division of functional activities and, in particular, the degree of detail required will depend very much on the actual situation prevailing in each state and the state's degree of willingness to part with powers. The Panchayati Raj Acts have listed a number of items and one has to examine these closely to find out the degree of clarity and ambiguity if any in these lists.

Financial Decentralization

The devolution of financial powers and resources to the PRI's in tandem with the functions and responsibilities entrusted to them constitutes the most crucial aspect of decentralization. The State Finance Commissions must now act with speed and specificity and decide, after reviewing the financial position of local governments, on the devolution of functions and additional responsibilities to them. In this context, they should also decide about questions like the sharing of revenues and taxation powers to local bodies as well as the powers to borrow, subject to a limit, from the state government and financial institutions. While the larger question of Centre-State financial relations yet remain to be settled, this should not become an excuse for the states to delay the devolution of functions and finances to the local bodies.

Administrative decentralization or "Deconcentration" is an essential prerequisite and will decide the extent of powers to be decentralized to the lower levels. There are three main categories of such powers to be considered. These are : policy-making powers, financial powers and powers over personnel matters. Policy-making powers can be law-making powers or executive powers. Financial powers, about which a mention was made earlier, are powers concerning revenue and expenditure. Personnel powers are those relating to the appointment, promotion, transfer and discipline of staff and their accountability. All these will not be gone into detail here. But it should be noted that decentralized planning will fail to get off the ground or may be seriously delayed, if these vital elements are neglected or their importance not recognized.

Concepts : Development from Below and Development from Within

Local-level planning is based on two concepts, viz: "Development from below" (DFB) and "Development from Within" (DFW). The distinction between the two is subtle. They are variants of participatory development. The difference lies in the nature and intensity of the people's participation and in the government's role in the formulation of projects. "Development from Below" is, by and large, a government-initiated planning venture with a modicum of people's participation. The projects initiated by the sectoral departments belong to this category. In the case of "Development from Within", the projects are basically initiated by the people. It is an endogenous development process, triggered off by people themselves through "capillary or trickle-up effect". Here, the people themselves assume responsibility to plan and manage their own development with their own resources (financial and personnel). It is an activity that is self-generated, self-organized and self-sustained. In this type of development, the people of a local community define their own goals, needs and aspirations and make decisions affecting their well-being and sustained development. The projects that are planned by a local community, with the "un-tied" resources coming to them from above and the resources that are generated within by the local community belong to this category. In the context of the implementation of the new-economic reforms, the relative role of the state in local and regional development matters is getting reduced and that of the domain of responsibility of the people and local institutions is increasing. In this context, DFW holds the key to local development.[2] It will be the right tool to unleash the inner and indigenous potentials of the local community and the basis for action to realize their inner urges and preferences for development through self-reliant approaches. DFW would make it possible for local communities to raise more resources for themselves, to assert their own value systems, to have confidence in their own ingenuity and skills and to be less dependent on external agencies for their development. Panchyati Raj bodies must use this concept in a big way to generate increased local resources and undertake an enlarged development effort.

Negotiatory Planning

Decentralized planning is a negotiatory planning process, in which the different "actors" involved in the planning process interface, dialogue and determine matters relating to resource allocation and the projects to be implemented. Ideally, it is initiated from the grassroots and originates from certain "local initiatives", which are sparked off by both internal dynamics and external stimuli, and engineered through several local organizations and interest groups. These local bodies throw up several project ideas, which represent the wishes and desires of the local community and which constitute a "Demand" for resources by them. Simultaneously, the government and its development agencies work out the feasible level of "Supply" of resources of various kinds, such as the provision of government grants and loans, material inputs and technical assistance. These sources, coupled with the locally generated resources and those that are provided by NGO's and other external agencies (e.g. foreign aid), constitute the total supply of resources to the local level.

The matching of this "Supply" with the "Demand" constitutes the essence of decentralized planning. For arriving at the "matching", the two major actors in the planning game, viz. representatives of the government and of the people, must meet and vigorously "negotiate" the quantum and content of the local-level plan. Thus the plan is arrived at by participatory consensus. The interface takes place at the district level. Thus local-level planning is a process of certain top-down and bottom-up initiatives converging at the district level, resulting in a development effort that meets the people's needs within the framework of national objectives and available resources. This is shown in Fig. 12.1.

Development Framework

(a) *The District Level*

For operationalizing decentralized planning, the organizational set-up at the district level and below, as well as its way of functioning (both processual and procedural), should undergo some radical transformations. The development structure at these levels must have the necessary degree of operational flexibility, with all development departments acting in unison (and not in isolation) and enjoying a certain degree of freedom to rapidly respond to local-level requirements. In the organizational set-up, the local people must have adequate opportunities to interface with the local administration and articulate their needs, which would mean a certain degree of institutionalization of people's participation. These general principles are already ingrained in the Panchayati Raj system of local bodies at different levels. The legislations enacted by the various states have also made provisions for the setting up of various committees under the local bodies. From the point of view of decentralized planning, the District Development Committee (DDC) is a crucial development mechanism. It will consist of elected as well as nominated representatives. Their constitution, as stated in the various Panchayati Raj legislations, suggests that they would be big and unwieldy bodies. They would serve primarily as deliberating and policy guideline-setting bodies. For day-to-day decision-making, however, smaller Executive Committees are to be constituted under them. For undertaking the technical task of formulating the development projects and placing them before the local authorities for their consideration, several subject-matter committees should be constituted. Such arrangements seem to have already been spelt out in several state Panchayati Raj legislations. The various project proposals emerging from the subject-matter committees may have to be

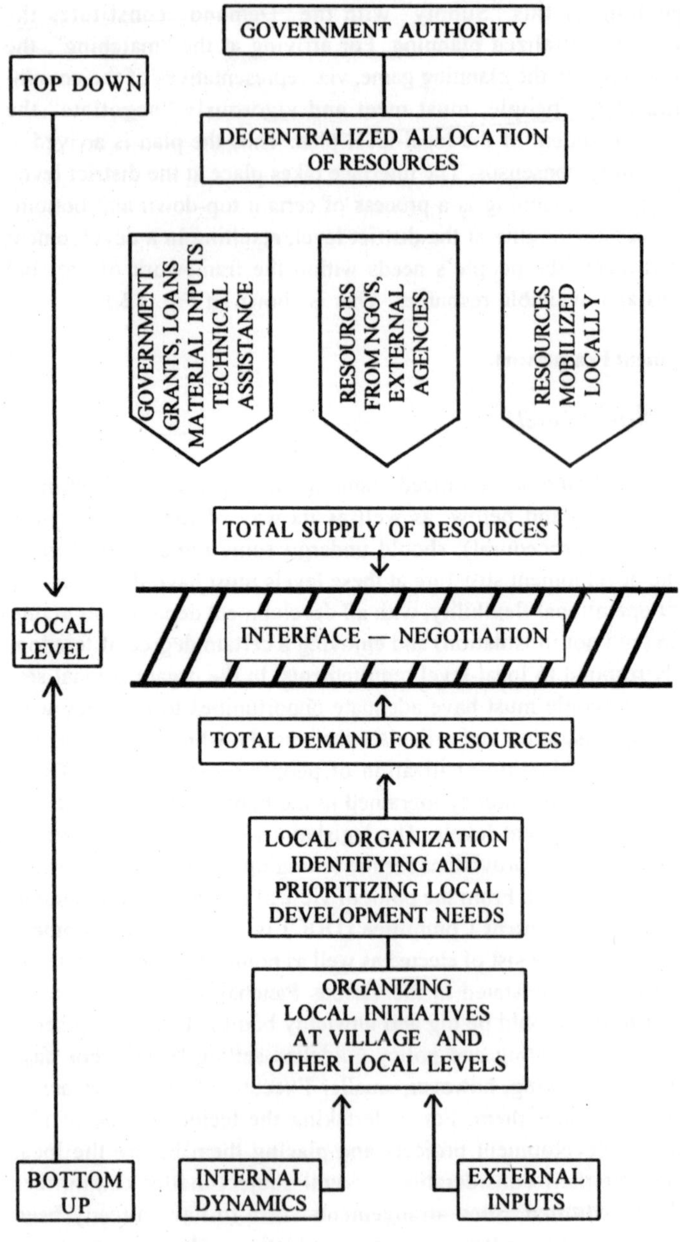

FIG. 12.1 : Micro Planning Process.

further pruned and whittled down, as necessary, to fit them into the available kitty of financial resources for development. This task may be done by the Executive Committee, before it submits the proposals for approval to the District Assembly. Alternatively, this task may be done by a specially constituted "Joint" or "Coordination" Committee.

In short, the District Development Committee and its subject-matter committees, together with a suitable coordination mechanism, constitute the major elements of a District Development Organizational Framework.

(b) *The Block Level*

All line departments and agencies are supposed to have their outposts at the Block level. They will prepare their own plans according to the guidelines received by them from their vertical departments. However, it is proposed that as the key centre for planning and coordination at this level, a new institution, called the "Block Planning and Development Training Centre" (BPDTC), to be regarded as the symbol of the new renaissance should be established. It would be a focal point, where the officers would coordinate departmental activities with each other as well as with the elected leaders. It will be the focus not only of planning and co-ordination, but also of training for village officials. It has to be the new symbol of local government. The idea here is somewhat similar to the "Thana Training and Development Centre" conceived in the Comilla model of rural development in Bangladesh in the late fifties and early sixties. In the words of Akhter Hameed Khan, the person who innovated this experiment, "Now our Government said that it had changed its orientation (from the colonial system of administration). It wanted rural development. Therefore, it was necessary to build a new symbol, and this symbol was to be the 'Thana Training and Development Centre'. It was to be much bigger than the old police station (Thana) building. But it was to be by the side of a police station deliberately—to put the police station in the shade. It was to be much bigger in physical dimensions and also administratively, so that every department could put one of its officers as a representative in the same building, and all these officers could work in coordination".[3]

The BPDTC can have under it a few "subject-matter committees" to formulate project proposals. Such committees have already been proposed in many state Panchayati Raj legislations. But the most important feature of the BPDTC is the positioning of some technical personnel in the Block, with planning expertise to assist in the preparation of the development plans at the Block and Village levels. It may be recalled that the Dantwala Working Group, appointed by the Planning Commission in 1978,[4] recognized the absence of planning expertise as a major hindrance to Block level planning and recommended a "peripatetic team" of experts from the district level, to go round and prepare the Block-level plans. This measure was suggested as an interim solution, till such time as the blocks themselves were able to build up their own competence in planning. More than 15 years have passed since this recommendation was made and one would have hopefully expected the Block levels to have been sufficiently strengthened. But, we all know that this recommendation has not been implemented and that nothing has happened at the Block level. However, this is not the time to repent but to learn from past failings and move ahead. The BPDTC has been deliberately suggested here to overcome this problem and to ensure that the necessary planning expertise gets into place at the Block level. In the present Panchayati Raj context, this idea has to be ruthlessly followed and implemented. The BPDTC will not only coordinate the sectoral planning proposals, but will also scrutinize the project ideas emerging from the numerous villages in the Block and prepare a consolidated "statement of needs". The departmental proposals and statement of needs will then be debated by the Block Samiti and the final set of proposals emerging from these discussions will be forwarded to the Zilla Parishad.

(c) *The Village Level*

In our scheme of decentralized planning framework, the village is the pivotal area, wherein public participation can find its boldest articulation. It is also at this level that sustainable development can be meaningfully operationalized by the people themselves, who are in daily contact with their soil, water and forests, thus in a position to handle their ecosystem in a balanced way, without damaging it. In terms of planning, the villages will be the agencies to throw up a lot of primary data and information for planning. They will also articulate the felt needs of the people, which will be helpful in setting proper priorities among investment proposals. The project ideas from the village level should emerge from a number of what we may call "polycentric institutions", which will be autonomous, non-hierarchical and informal, in which people with similar interests can come together and contribute to solve their own problems. These are "collective self-management groups" such as different occupational groups, rural workers' associations, associations of backward communities, women's groups, user groups, beneficiary groups of specific programmes, Joint Forest Management Groups, cooperatives and such other interest groups. Since such groups do not automatically come into existence, a deliberate attempt should be made to form such groups and lay down some procedures for their effective functioning. Nepal has done this for "user groups" by laying down the procedures in the Decentralization Act itself.[5] In an ideal set-up, the polycentric institutions should be linked together with the higher-level organizations and expertise at the block and district levels for effective integration. "The most productive approach is to try to draw on the respective strengths of both the educated class and the rural population in a two-way collaboration".[6] Undoubtedly, leadership is required at both the levels. With the state providing the necessary direction, support and protection, the local leaders can blossom into effective planners. No serious attempts have, so far, been made to bring village people effectively into the planning, decision-making, monitoring, and implementation process, except in some success stories.[7] The Panchayati Raj system should now systematize the procedures for this experiment and turn village-based planning into reality.

The organizational framework for planning at the village level should be as follows. The apex body should be the "Village Panchayat". The "Village Assembly" or the "Gram Sabha" will be its general body. Under this body, a "Village Planning Forum" (VPF) consisting of representatives of various "Interest groups" and the village officials may be constituted. The VPF may also constitute some "subject-matter committees" under it. The project ideas emerging from these committees and the various "poly-centric institutions" mentioned above should be pooled together and considered by the VPF, which should order these proposals into a set of priorities and then forward them to the block level. Obviously, since the village will not have all the planning expertise, the village proposals will be in the nature of a catalogue of needs. The task of prioritizing them and projectizing them with estimation of costs should be done either at the block level or by the village itself with the assistance and guidance of the block staff. Since the BPDTC will have a strong arm of training under it, one should hope that, in course of time, all the village officials will get trained in the various tasks of plan formulation and will be gradually enabled to prepare reasonably good village plans themselves. The institutional framework for planning at different local levels may be seen in Fig. 12.2.

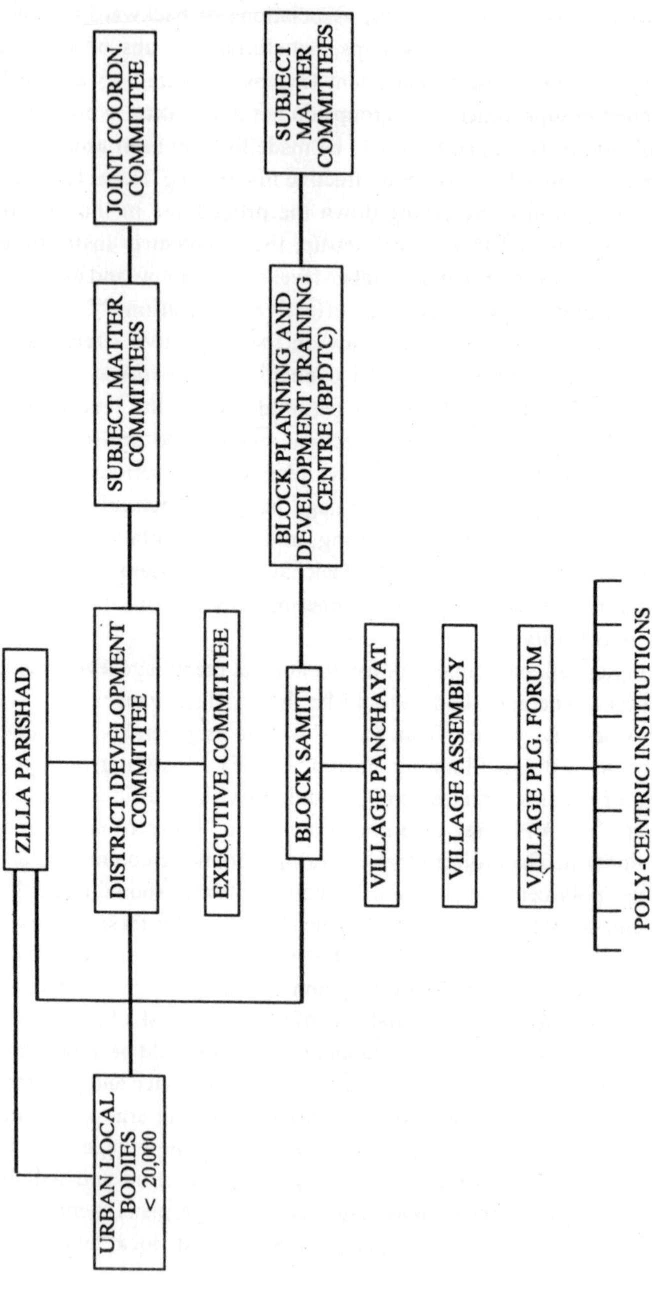

FIG. 12.2 : The Institutional Framework for Planning.

Some Other Issues

In our discussion on the organization for an integrated set-up for decentralized planning, we have not touched upon two other major issues. These relate to the rural-urban relationships and the preparation of the decentralized budget.

The decentralized planning set-up should not disregard the hierarchy of urban centres which provide the various services to the rural areas. The small towns are part and parcel of the countryside and should form an integral part of the rural planning system. Several committees set up by the Government of India, particularly the rural-urban relationship committee (1969)[8] and the Working Group on District Planning (1984)[9] have warned against regarding rural and urban areas as dichotomous entities and have made specific recommendations for integrating the small towns into district planning. In our present context, it is recommended that the planning of towns with less than 20,000 population should fall within the ambit of district planning. In this way, urban-rural linkages can be taken into account and effectively interwoven into the district plan.

Guidelines for the preparation of the District budget and reappropriation powers should be outlined by the State Government. The State Panchayati Raj legislations have made some reference to these points. An important consideration is the format of the District Budget. It should consist of three components reflecting the different sources of funding. These are : (1) Projects funded by departmental funds; (2) Projects funded by shared revenue, government grants and other forms of aid; and (3) Projects that are self-financed, including those financed with bank loans, under "Development from Within". The capital projects should be separately indicated.

Planning Cycle and Planning Process

At each unit area level, there is a "planning cycle" to be gone through and a time-bound "planning process" to be adhered to. The "planning cycle" may be conceived in eight steps (see Fig. 12.3) as follows :

1. Assessing the planning environment, which means taking note of the environmental and socio-economic-cultural peculiarities.
2. Data collection, using rapid rural appraisal techniques, where necessary, and Data Analysis for bringing out the problems and potentials of the area.

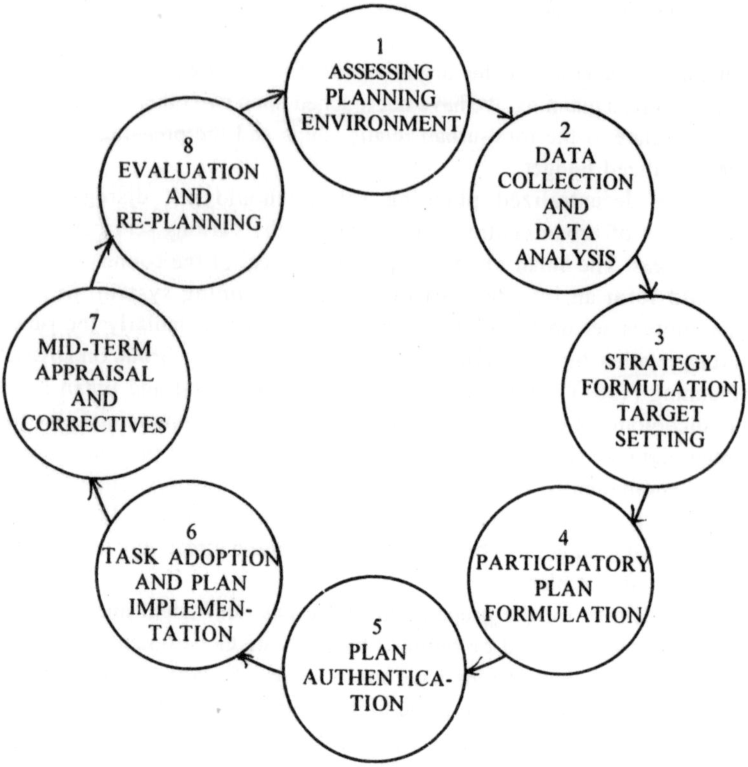

FIG. 12.3 : Planning Cycle—8 Steps.

3. Strategy formulation and setting realistic targets for the plan.
4. Participatory plan formulation.
5. Plan authentication and linking the plan with the plan at the next higher level.
6. Task adoption and plan implementation.
7. Mid-term appraisal and making corrections.
8. Evaluation and re-planning.

The "planning process" will be a time-bound activity, ultimately tied to the budget preparation at the state and national levels. Since our financial year is from April-March, the planning process should start from the beginning of the previous year and end with the budget preparation in February of the next year. It should start with the Planning

Commission and the sectoral ministries at the centre, and the state planning departments and the sectoral departments at the state level issuing the guidelines setting out the framework of objectives and major thrusts for the plan and indicating the cut-off dates for the submission of plan proposals by the various planning levels. The Finance Ministry should indicate the order of financial outlays for the plan sometime during the middle of the year. But irrespective of this, the planning exercise should commence at the various levels soon after the guidelines are issued, based on certain assumptions. Some corrections could be applied later to conform to financial limits. The orchestrating of the planning process and ensuring the micro-macro linkages in a federal country like India is not easy. It has to be systematically laboured. For successful local-level planning, the entire series of "plan operations" must follow a rigid time schedule, so that the State Planning Board can have enough time to "negotiate" with the districts and finalize each district plan and then incorporate the same into the state budget. There are numerous "actors", who play a distinct role in the planning process. These actors are the various institutional mechanisms at different levels that we have outlined in this paper. The time limit for "operations" by each actor should be meticulously worked out and strictly adhered to. Otherwise, a plan may go haywire, without cohesiveness, complementarities and linkages. The "plan of operations" may be indicated through a chart with the "actors" along the column and the time limit along the row.

Summing Up

In this chapter, we have discussed as to how we may decentralize the decision-making process within the framework of national and state policies and promote local institutions. This involves :-(a) devolution of appropriate powers and finances to institutions of local government administrative delegation for increasing responsibility for decision-making in development activities as well as in their implementation and evaluation; and (b) Promotion of people's organizations and strengthening their participation in development activities.

In our view, the addition of a new stratum of government with freedom to devise its own instrumentalities has offered a fresh opportunity to the states in the country, to innovate action in regard to the strengthening of local governments through various institutional mechanisms. This opportunity should not be missed.

REFERENCES

1. Sundaram, K.V., Multilevel Planning : Concept, principles and some aspects of its application to sectoral planning : in Sundaram K.V. *et al.*, (Eds.), *Regional Planning and Development.* Heritage Publishers, New Delhi, 1989.
2. For a fuller exposition of the concept of 'Development from Within'. See Sundaram, K.V. 'Development from Within—A rethinking on an alternative development path in *Asia-Pacific Journal of Rural Development*, Published by CIRDAP, Dhaka, Bangladesh, Vol. IV, Nos. 1 and 2, July-Dec., 1994.
3. Akhter Hameed Khan, "My understanding of the the Comilla Model' in *The Works of Akhter Hameed Khan*, Vol. II, published by the Bangladesh Academy for Rural Development, Kotbari, Comilla 1993, (p. 172).
4. Report of the Working Group on Block Level Planning, Planning Commission (Govt. of India), 1978.
5. Sant Bahadur Rai, "Planning and implementation with users groups' in *Planning with People—Decentralization in Nepal*, Sant B. Gurung and Prodipto Roy. Orient Longman Ltd., Hyderabad, 1987.
6. Uphoff, Norman, "Problems inhibiting achievement of broader people's participation" in *People's Participation in Rural Development in Nepal*, Kathmandu, APROSC (1978).
7. The case of Kundrakudi in Tamil Nadu Documented by this author for the Planning Commission is one instance. See 'Towards Improved Local Level Planning', Planning Commission, Govt. of India, 1986.
8. Report of the Rural-Urban Relationship Committee, Govt. of India, Ministry of Health, 1969.
9. Report of the Working Group on District Planning, Govt. of India, Planning Commission, 1984.

PART III

COUNTRY EXPERIENCES

1. India
2. Nepal
3. Ghana
4. Uganda

And thou wert still a hope, a love
Still longed for, never seen.

—*William Wordsworth*

INTRODUCTION

In Part III of the book, are presented four case studies—two from Asia and two from Africa, which are intended to review the application of decentralization policies in particular country contexts. These country experiences serve to indicate how ineffectively decentralization policies are being implemented in the developing countries and what a tremendous gap exists between the theory and practice of decentralization.

Among the four countries, India has had the longest history of experience with decentralization policies than the others, extending over a period of nearly half a century. Here the decentralization policy has followed different impulses and taken several routes. Being a federal country, the states have moved at a different pace towards decentralized development and one finds quite a few interesting models for planning. The chapter on India provides an interesting illustration of the Maharashtra, Gujarat, Karnataka and West Bengal models. Currently, much emphasis is being paid in India to improve the database as well as the techniques for district planning and to enhance the capabilities of the field functionaries in decentralized planning.

In Nepal, decentralization efforts were commendable during the 1980's, particularly after the promulgation of the Decentralization Act, 1982 and the rules framed under it in 1984. However, the implementation of decentralization policies has suffered in the past because of the absence of bureaucratic will, imperfect planning mechanisms, weak institutional structures and the highly individualistic approaches to local development followed by the donor agencies and more recently due to the political uncertainties, which the nascent democracy is currently facing.

Nepal's experience underlines the fact that good legislation is a necessary but not sufficient condition for decentralization and policy continuity at the national level is a *sine qua non* for the effective and efficient implementation of decentralization policies.

In sub-Saharan Africa, which is in a debt crisis with many countries bogged down with structural adjustment and economic recovery programmes, one finds only a feeble articulation of decentralization policies.

National consolidation is the main focus, which is also reflected in the form and content of decentralization at the sub-national levels. Some structures like the District Development Committees exist in many countries, but these are dominated by central control and there is very little local autonomy. At the district level and below, serious inadequacies in logistic support, housing, transport facilities, office accommodation, etc., hamper the effective decentralized functioning of the governmental system. Even in the important sectoral ministries like Agriculture and Industry, the planning process is mainly concentrated at the national level. The two African countries—Ghana and Uganda—discussed in the book show that in these countries, most prerequisites necessary for decentralization have not been met and what we find are only some "weak forms" of decentralization. In the present situation characterizing most sub-Saharan African countries, only a gradual and incremental approach to decentralization is the answer, which would mean pushing ahead with the administrative aspects of decentralization in the first stage and paving the way for the democratic decentralization, which may follow at a later stage.

The experience with decentralization policies in the developing countries shows that it has always been a seesaw movement between the centre and the local government. Decentralization is thus sometimes one step forward, later two steps backwards. It seems to be a game between challenge and response. Sometimes, certain functions were given to the local governments under public pressure, but later were taken away from them for some reasons. In practice, the functional relation between the higher government and local government has always tended to tilt the balance against local government. In some countries the aggressive role of the central government on the plea of improving the functioning of social services has led to the loss of local initiative.

The critical lessons that we learn from the country experiences in Asia and Africa cited here are :

(1) Attention to certain prerequisites of decentralization is basic and fundamental;

(2) Decentralization has to be pursued as a gradual, incremental process; and

(3) Decentralization must be consistently and continuously pursued, without major shifts and set-backs.

13

DECENTRALIZATION
Asian Experiences

1. INDIA

India (Area : 3.29 million km^2; population in 1991 : 846 million) is a sovereign democratic socialist republic. It has a federal structure with 25 States and 7 Union Territories. Below the State are Districts, Blocks (Sub-district consisting of about 100 villages) and Villages. The Constitution of India has defined the division of functions between the Centre (Union) and the State through a specific listing of Union, State and concurrent subjects. Till recently (1993), the local government institutions (Village Panchayats and above) were creatures of the State Legislatures and their existence and functions depended on the decisions taken by State governments from time to time. However, a constitutional amendment (Seventy-third Amendment) which came into effect from April 24, 1993, has sought to ensure the establishment of local self-governments throughout the country as an acknowledged third tier of the government. The State governments are now taking steps to restructure, reinforce and revitalize the grassroot institutions as an organic part of India's polity. This has ushered in another phase of decentralization in India.

Decentralization : Shifting Scenario

Planning in India commenced in 1951. Since then, several initiatives have been taken by the government to strengthen local-level planning. The decentralization policy adopted by the government, however, has placed different emphases at different times, with the result that planning and development at the sub-national levels have "followed different impulses and taken several routes".[1] As we look back in retrospect, at the various policy shifts that have taken place on decentralization, we may distinguish at least five different phases of change that have left their varying imprints on the local-level planning and development. Table 13.1 seeks to capture these changes :

TABLE 13.1 : Different Phases of Change

Phase	Period	Major changes
I.	1950-60	The transition from a law and order Administrative system to a Welfare and Development-oriented system. The Community Development phase.
II.	1960-70	The Panchayati Raj phase.
III.	1970-80	The Special Programmes phase. The Block Level Planning phase.
IV.	1980-90	The District Planning phase (IRD Programme & Employment programmes).
V.	1990—	The Panchayati Raj Renaissance phase : Emergence of new issues and imperatives.

Phase I : 1950-60—The Community Development Phase

At the dawn of freedom, the idea of Gandhi's self-reliant "Village Republics" permeated the thinking. This prompted the Community Development movement "to cover a wider plan for development of village life in all its aspects".[2] The programme, which was implemented through the National Extension Service, was initially launched in 55 blocks and then rapidly expanded its coverage. It combined welfare aims and social and economic change through self-help and self-reliance techniques. In the euphoria of exultation that characterized the community development movement in the beginning, it was envisaged that at the local level, the enthusiasm and aspirations of the people would be translated into constructive programmes of development through community action. But this did not happen. The programme was directed from the Centre, without adequate infrastructural support and financial and technical (human) resources and failed to evoke popular participation. One of the basic problems was that it envisaged a multi-purpose approach. In an underdeveloped economy, struggling with its serious resource constraints, such an approach, with its multi-sectorial components directed at a wide spectrum of the rural population, could not make much headway. It raised certain basic issues of great practical import—about the appropriate balance between the development of food crops (i.e. productive activities) and provision of social services; between Central direction and grassroot involvement; and between precision in planning and flexibility in implementation. There was necessity to give a sense of direction to the approach to rural development. This led to the devising of a more "all purpose approach", with its concentration on the more demanding aspects of economic development, viz. the increase in agricultural production. Thus the multipurpose approach yielded place to a limited purpose approach. The Community Development movement failed because of other reasons also. The "schematic approach" which it adopted led only to "top-down" planning without initiating a bottom-up process of planning. As the movement became bureaucratized, the adoption of practical and specific solutions to local problems was inhibited. Later, a high-level committee under Balwantrai Mehta observed that one of the least successful aspects of C.D. work was its inability to "evoke popular participation".

The period 1950-60 comprised two plan periods. The First Five Year Plan (1951-56), besides emphasizing on community development and extension services, also stated that "District Plans are always essential, but they may gain in value, if they are also part of well-considered regional plans".[3] However, as a review of the plan admitted, not much progress could be made in giving local bodies the sole responsibility in implementing development programmes envisaged for them in the district plans.[4]

It was in the Second Five Year Plan (1956-61) that the idea of decentralized planning was rigourously addressed. This plan talked at great length about the planning at the State level and district level. The precise scope and content of the three-tier planning process was clearly stated in the Second Five Year Plan document as follows :

> "When planning is undertaken on a national scale, a careful view has to be taken as to which programmes should form part respectively of the national, State and district plans. Among the factors that have to be taken into account are—
>
> (1) the level at which the activity can be undertaken with the necessary technical and administrative resources;
> (2) whether the activity is limited to a particular area or has significance for a wider area, so that it should form part of a larger inter-connected plan; and
> (3) the extent to which public participation and cooperation is called for in implementing the programme or augmenting its scope and influence.

On these considerations, the Central Government has to undertake the main responsibility for the development of major industries, the railway network, national highways, and overall coordination in various fields of development such as irrigation and power, large and small industries, etc. There are other projects which are best planned on a State basis, as, for example, irrigation and power schemes of medium size, road transport services and surveys for drawing up minor irrigation programmes." (para 19, Chapter VII)

> "A district plan would include programmes prepared on a territorial basis for villages, groups of villages, talukas, extension blocks, municipal areas etc. and also programmes to be executed within the district, which are derived from departmental plans formulated at the State level". (para 21)
>
> ".....in different sectors of the State Plan, programmes or schemes, in which local participation and community action have a special contribution to make, are to be separated out and shown as constituents of the plans of districts". (para 22)

In fact, in a huge democratic country like India, decentralization of planning from the national to sub-national level, that is, the State level was almost axiomatic. A large number of schemes and programmes were such as could be taken up and implemented only at the State level, while the national level confined itself to laying down the national priorities consistent with its goals and objectives and providing for the necessary infrastructure for their attainment.

Although the second plan document talked about District Planning, this was not really attempted. The plan document only generated some thinking on the concept of district planning and its rationale.

Phase II : 1960-70—The Panchayati Raj Phase

In January, 1957, the government appointed a Study Team under the Chairmanship of Balwantrai Mehta to study and report on the working of Community Development Projects and the National Extension Service. The same team was entrusted with the investigation into the reorganization of the district administration. The team submitted its report by the end of 1957.

The historic observation of the Balwantrai Mehta Report (1957) is worth noting : "So long as we do not discover or create a representative and democratic institution which will supply the local interest, supervision and care necessary to ensure that expenditure of money upon local projects conforms with the needs and wishes of the locality, invest it with adequate power and assign to it appropriate finances, we will never be able to evoke local interest and excite local initiative in the field of development".

The Balwantrai Mehta team recommended the setting up of a three-tiered Panchayati Raj system with elected democratic bodies at the village and block levels and entrusting these bodies with planning and development activities. At the district level, it recommended an advisory coordinating body under the Chairmanship of the District Collector with the Presidents of the Panchayat Samitis and Members of the State Legislature and Parliament and District level officers of important departments as members.

Following this report, Panchayati Raj institutions were established in a number of states with such local changes as were considered necessary; with these changes, the administrative structure was as depicted in Fig. 13.1. It may be seen that at the district level, although the Panchayati Raj institutions were established, they did not constitute a separate level of government. Many functions were bifurcated and fragmented with the decision-making and accountability scattered among State Departments and their field agencies and finally the not so important statutory local bodies, as concessions to democracy and local self-government.[4A] These local bodies functioned with varying degrees of powers, autonomy and efficiency. By the end of the 1970's, these institutions declined. According to the Asoka Mehta Committee (1978), these institutions seem to have passed through three phases : the phase of ascendancy (1959-64); the phase of stagnation (1965-69); and the phase of decline (1969-77). According to Vyas, even at its peak in the early 1960's, it gave no meaningful slant to local-level planning. "Thus, even when local-level government had ostensibly been strengthened through popularly elected representatives, planning at the block level and below was performed just as before, by the disaggregation of Central and State plans to districts and blocks. No Panchayat Samiti (at the block) and Zilla Parishad (at the district) adequately developed an overall development profile for its area. When these institutions engaged themselves in any planning activity, it consisted simply in aggregating demands of various kinds, . . . euphemistically called 'felt needs'. . . . Decisions on these demands were generally taken in the Panchayat Samiti or Zilla Parishad meetings in a hurried and summary manner, with the discussion dominated by a few political heavyweights. . . . At higher levels, State and Central authorities generally took development decisions, which were *uniform* for all blocks. . . . Lower level units were often given detailed guidelines for targets as well as for programme implementation".[5] The States of Maharashtra and Gujarat were departures, where a three-tier structure, with the first point of decentralization at the district level, was organized. Here the Zilla Parishad came to constitute a separate level of government, bringing under its canopy all the development departments at the district level. The District Collector was relieved of developmental responsibilities and a separate senior officer was entrusted with these responsibilities. To that extent there was a distinct improvement in the capacity and effective functioning of local district governments. In a later development, in both these states, the planning functions were entrusted to a separately constituted body under the Chairmanship of a Minister of State. This body was called the District Planning and Development Council (DPDC) in Maharashtra and District Planning Board (DPB) in Gujarat. The justification given for this separation was that apart from the activities of the Zilla Parishads and Panchayat Samities (which were limited to such schemes or programmes that were entrusted to them under the Act), there were many others, such as the programmes of the various financing institutions, urban local bodies and statutory Corporations/Boards constituted by the State Government, which had to be coordinated. Later, similar set-ups also emerged in Uttar Pradesh and a number of other states.

In 1977, the government appointed a Committee headed by Asoka Mehta to review the existing situation regarding democratic decentralization in the States and Union Territories and the working of the Panchayati Raj institutions and to make suitable recommendations for reorganizing the Panchayati Raj system and removing its short-comings and defects. The Committee recommended a two-tier structure, with the district as the first point for decentralization below the State level. Below the district level, it recommended that development management could best be achieved by grouping a number of villages to constitute "Mandal Panchayats". It recognized the existence of other tiers at the block (Taluk) and village levels in some states and suggested gradual conversion to a two-tier system in such states.

Thus the period 1960-70 is an important phase, so far as local-level planning is concerned. The Panchayati Raj institutions were experimented in several states and an institutional set-up for planning at the district level, as well as some important procedures for district planning

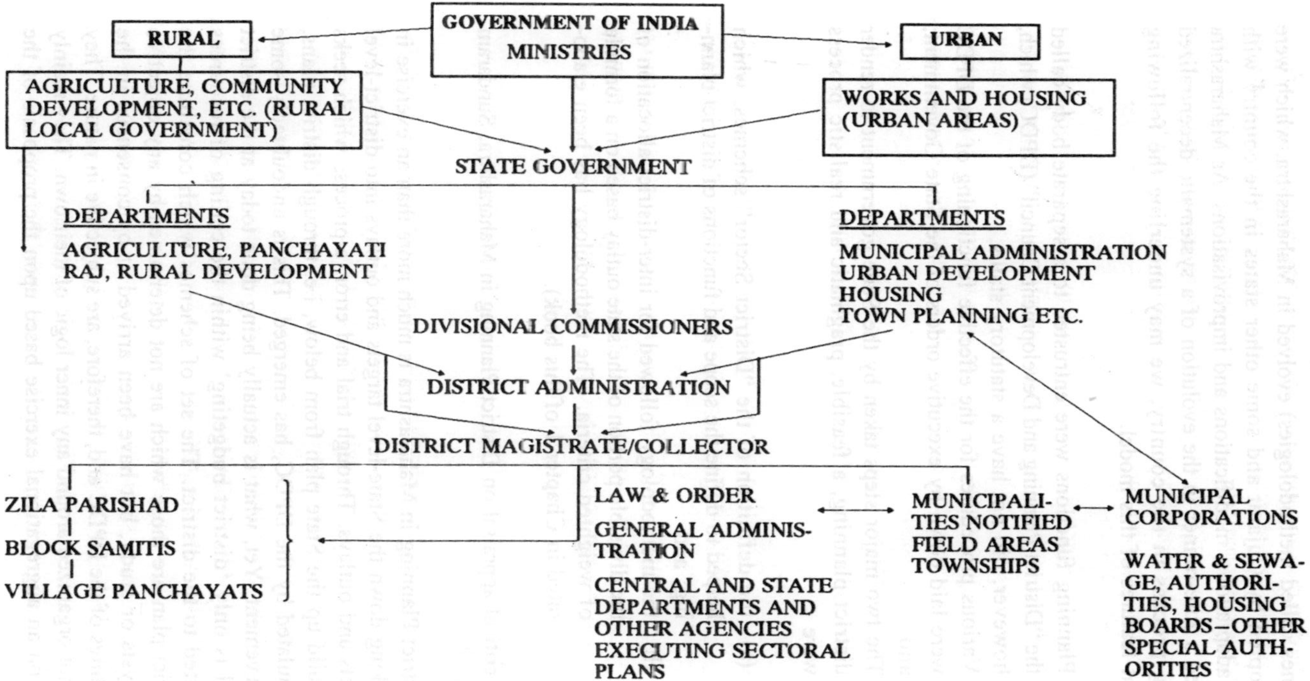

FIG. 13.1 : Administrative Structure (1970's).

Source: Deva Raj, Multilevel Planning and Local Government Structure, *Indian Journal of Public Administration*, Vol. XIX, No. 3, July-Sep. 1973.

(sometimes called methodologies) evolved in Maharashtra, which were later adopted by Gujarat and some other states in the country with suitable adaptations, modifications and improvisations. As Maharashtra is deemed a fore-runner in the evolution of a systematic decentralized planning process in the country, we may underline the following important features of this model.

(i) Planning functions were entrusted to a separate body called the "District Planning and Development Council" (DPDC) which, however, did not have a statutory status;

(ii) Various procedures for the effective functioning of the DPDC were laid down by executive orders of the State Government; and

(iii) The two major steps taken by the State government to render district planning, a feasible, pragmatic and realistic process were :

  (a) the definition of the "District Sector" schemes, which helped to define the scope and functions of district planning; and

  (b) the methodology followed for inter-district allocation of the divisible portion of the state outlay based on a formula of weighted criteria. (The methodology has been elaborated in Chapter 1 of this book).

In a critical appraisal on District Planning in Maharashtra, Sundaram observes :[6]

> "District Planning in Maharashtra is much more than an exercise in breaking down the State-level targets and outlays into district-level targets and outlays. Through trial and error, a process which seeks to build up the State plan from below, i.e. through district plans, formulated by the DPDC, has emerged. This is undoubtedly some achievement. Yet, what is actually being done today at the district level is only 'district budgeting' within the ceiling of resources allotted to the district. The set of schemes which constitute the district plan are those which are not determined by any objective analysis or study, but have been arrived at by consensus in the meetings of the DPDC and, therefore, are subjective in nature. They are not organized around any inner logic of their own. They mainly rely on an aggregational exercise based upon the proposals of the

departments and their agencies. The district plans, therefore, may not answer the rigorous tests of internal consistency, inter-sectorial complementarity, or criteria of efficiency. The district planning staff do not conduct any studies on their own or project alternative plans or do any impact analysis or evaluation of on-going programmes. Thus there is very little analytically informed decision-making in regard to the selection of projects in the district plan".

Phase III : 1970-80—The Special Programmes Phase

In the history of planned development in India, the Fourth Plan period (1969-74) may be seen as a significant "watershed". In keeping with the global trends since 1969 (when the meaning of development came to be questioned and changes in the orientation and structure of planning came about),[7] certain vital departures, both in the planning process and in the content of planning were introduced in India too. The most important change was in relation to the devolution of plan funds to the State level. Earlier, planning at the State level was heavily influenced by a system of Central assistance (of loans and grants) to States tied to specific schemes. Accordingly, State plans were prepared by "putting together standard schemes for each department or each activity, schemes known to be acceptable to the Planning Commission, in such a manner as to attract the largest amount of assistance that the State or the department can obtain from the Centre".[8]

This system of disbursement of Central assistance to the States was changed during the Fourth Five Year Plan (1969-74) in favour of a method of block allocation, based on certain objective criteria (which later came to be known as Gadgil Formula) in the form of 30 per cent grant and 70 per cent loan irrespective of priorities or schemes adopted by them in their plans. This initiated a first stage of decentralization of the planning process from the National to the State level in a realistic sense. Since then, the State governments in the country have been building up their own machinery for planning at the State level and improving their planning methodologies.[9] Simultaneously, by the end of the 1960's, there was a growing disenchantment with the strategy and thrust in rural development planning, which tended to marginalize the rural poor and certain backward areas in the country from deriving reasonable benefits from development programmes. This led to the introduction of "special programmes", with focus on weaker groups and areas. This author has, therefore, labelled this period 1970-80 as the "Special Programmes Phase".

A plethora of special programmes were introduced in the plan. These included :

— The Pilot Intensive Rural Employment Project (PIREP)
— The Small Farmers Development Agency Programme (SFDA)
— The Marginal Farmers and Agricultural Labourers Agencies Programme (MFAL)
— The Drought-Prone Areas Programme (DPAP)
— The Command Area Development Programme (CADP)
— The Tribal Areas Development Programme (TADP)
— The Hill Areas Development Programme (HADP)
— The Minimum Needs Programme (MNP).

Thus the programme emphasis in rural development shifted to "Target-group" and "Target-area" approaches. This inevitably meant some organizational and institutional innovations as well as the strengthening of infrastructure for scientific research and technological services. Soon, this "organizational pluralization" led to problems of integration with the growth potential of the region, keeping the target group and area specificities fully in view. Prof. Gadgil rightly observed, "Our economy does not have resources to give employment for the sake of employment. Employment opportunities have to be integrated with the path of development". In a critical analysis of the trends in rural area development planning during this period, Sundaram observed that the special programmes were "on the whole, piecemeal and fragmented rather than integrated and comprehensive".[10] Some evaluation studies made of the special programmes, including the PIREP schemes, revealed that there were large gaps between the declared aims of policy and their actual achievement, particularly in the areas of unemployment and poverty. It was felt in this context that the approach should be through an area-by-area assessment of the potentials and problems and a matching of the manpower resources with the development of natural resources. A Development Block was considered the appropriate unit for this kind of area planning. This would imply the identification within this area of activities suitable to the particular area and capable of absorbing local labour surpluses. Such an area planning also implies a closer involvement of the people in both the formulation and implementation of development plans. This is the concept of "Block Level Planning for full employment" which was advocated and it was expected that government agencies, in association with voluntary agencies, will draw up and implement such Block-level plans. In furtherance of this approach, a Working Group on Block-level planning was appointed by the government under the Chairmanship of Prof. M.L. Dantwala to prepare guidelines for Block-level planning.

The group recommended an elaborate block-level planning system. It noted the absence of a planning machinery, with some expertise in planning at the block level, and recommended that a peripatetic planning team from the District would lend technical support to the preparation of block-level plans. It also suggested the involvement of academic institutions and competent voluntary agencies in plan preparation. Subsequent to the Working Group Report, quite a few block-level planning exercises (about 300 in all) were carried out in the States. An evaluation study sponsored by UNESCAP of two block plans—Kazhakootam Block in Kerala and Uttiramerur Block in Tamil Nadu—showed that achievements fell very much short of expectations. Integrated development was hardly attempted. (See Chapter 8 of this book for details). However, before the block-level plans prepared in the States could be operationalized, there was a change of government at the Centre in 1980. The Draft Sixth Plan (1978-83) was dropped by the new government and a new Sixth Plan (1980-85) was adopted, which shifted the emphasis on local planning from the block to the district level. Thus the Indian decentralization policy has changed from time to time. No single idea or policy was pursued to its logical conclusion, with the result that decentralized planning and development in India has always remained an unfinished development agenda, with frequent shifts in the policy from time to time.

Phase IV : 1980-1990—The District Planning Phase

This period is covered by the Sixth (1980-85) and Seventh (1985-90) Plans. The special programmes were continued with new ones being added. The Integrated Rural Development Programme was introduced in 1979 by merging the earlier target group programmes. The National Rural Employment Programme (NREP) was launched in October, 1980, replacing the earlier Food for Work Programme. The Rural Landless Employment Guarantee Programme (RLEGP) was launched during 1983-84 with the objective of improving and expanding employment opportunities for the rural landless labour with a view to providing guarantee of employment to at least one member of the household up to 100 days in a year and creating durable assets for strengthening the rural infrastructure.

The subjects of decentralization and district and local planning came under intensive discussion in most States. Gujarat launched a new phase of Decentralized District Planning on November 14, 1980. This is an improved version of the Maharashtra model. It provided for district plan outlay in three parts, viz. (1) Outlay for normal district schemes; (2) Discretionary outlay against which the District Planning Boards can select the schemes which they consider useful, having regard to local needs; and (3) Incentive outlay to be allocated against the funds raised by the district. The State earmarked 35 per cent of the State Plan outlays, on an average, for district-level schemes. Eighty per cent of this district plan outlay was disaggregated and apportioned among the departments at the State level. The balance 20 per cent was given for discretionary (15 per cent) and incentive (5 per cent) outlays. The discretionary and incentive outlays constitute the "Un-tied funds" placed wholly at the disposal of the District Planning Boards. This was an innovation which evoked considerable popular enthusiasm at the district level.

This period also saw the enactment of comprehensive new legislations for decentralization in some of the States, the notable among them being the Karnataka Zilla Parishad, Mandal Panchayat, Gram Sabha and Nyaya Panchayat Act 1983 and the Andhra Pradesh Mandala Praja Parishads, Zilla Praja Parishads and Zilla Pranalika, Abhivardi Mandals Act 1986.

A notable step taken by the Central Government to push the decentralization process was the setting up of a Working Group on District Planning under the Chairmanship of C.H. Hanumantha Rao in 1982. The Working Group submitted its report in 1984.[11]

The Working Group on District Planning emphasized that District planning should be conceived as a single holistic operation (and not as a fragmented operation among many agencies) in which all individual sectorial programmes and projects would be harmonized into a unified planning activity. With such a concept of District Planning as the background, the Working Group has detailed the various arrangements necessary for rendering the district planning process effective, including the various prerequisites that should be met, the institutional arrangements that should be devised and the essentials of planning methodology that should be followed. Noting that the states differed widely in their performance as well as experience relating to decentralized district planning, it has advocated a progressive or "stages approach" to be followed for moving steadily towards decentralization over a definite period of time. The three stages are as follows :

Stage I Phase of Initiation : Establishing planning procedures; determining functions and powers to the district level; disaggregating outlays between the State and district sectors; evolving criteria for inter-district allocation of plan funds; and strengthening planning capabilities at the district level.

Stage II Phase of "Limited Decentralization" : Bringing within the purview of district planning certain sectors of activity like the Minimum Needs Programme, agriculture and allied activities and all target-group oriented planning; granting extensive delegation of powers to the district level.

Stage III Final Stage : District Planning will encompass all district sector activities; A set of wide-ranging administrative, financial and decision-making powers will devolve upon the district and a high level of popular participation will be sought to be achieved.

The year A.D. 2000 or earlier was set as the time limit for achieving the final stage and certain essential prerequisites were specified. These are :

(i) Existence of political will and commitment;
(ii) Setting up of District Planning body in each district;
(iii) Setting up a suitable machinery for planning in each district;
(iv) Clear demarcation of planning functions;
(v) Disaggregation of plan funds and devolution of financial resources;
(vi) Delegation of administrative powers;
(vii) Evolution of new patterns of political and bureaucratic behaviour;
(viii) Ensuring public participation at all stages in the planning process; and
(viii) Training and retraining of personnel.

In March 1985, another Committee was appointed under the Chairmanship of Dr. G.V.K. Rao to recommend the administrative arrangements for rural development and poverty alleviation programmes.[12] This Committee again emphasized that district plan should not simply be the district segment of the State Plan, involving a mechanical disaggregation of the State Plan Schemes. It should be the product of a well-conceived and well-debated exercise, taking note of the local aspirations and local needs. It made the following recommendations :

(i) The Zilla Parishads should assume all planning functions at the district level;
(ii) In order to consider the district plans and integrate them into the State Plan, a "State Development Council" should be set up;
(iii) At the Block level, the Block Development Office should be upgraded, with its Chief Executive being raised to the status of a Sub-Divisional Officer;
(iv) Since the present block area is too large for micro-level planning, a cluster of 10-12 villages called "Mandal" with a population of about 15,000 should be considered as suitable for such planning;
(v) At the village level, an organization like the village planning forum should be constituted to facilitate improved local-level planning for rural development;
(vi) The District Planning bodies should be given substantial "untied" funds to enable them to take up small schemes to meet the local priorities, needs and aspirations;
(vii) At the district level, a separate senior officer called District Development Commissioner (apart from the District Collector) should be appointed solely in charge of development functions; and
(viii) The pluralistic institutional structures at the district level should be rationalized to avoid overlaps.

The recommendations of the two committees mentioned above mark significant milestones in local-level planning. They have provided major guidelines to the states to revamp their planning arrangements below the state level.

In late 80's, some state governments innovated in various ways, by experimenting with different methodologies for promoting the development of democratic institutions and securing a greater measure of participation by the people at the local level. Among these experiments, those of Karnataka and West Bengal deserve a closer look. Sometimes, these are spoken of as "Decentralization Models". We shall attempt to hit at some "high spots" of these experiments here.

The Karnataka Model[13]

This is based on the Karnataka Zilla Parishads, Taluk Panchayat Samities, Mandal Panchayats and Nyaya Panchayats Act 1983, which received Presidential assent on July 10, 1985. The model came into being during 1987 and functioned for a full term of five years thereafter. The Act had provided for two elected tiers of decentralization, viz. the Mandal Panchayat and the Zilla Parishad. But operationally, there were five different layers in the system. These were : (1) The Gram Sabha; (2) The Mandal Panchayat; (3) The Taluk Panchayat Samiti; (4) The Zilla Parishad; and (5) The State Development Council. Each tier in the system enjoys relative freedom and is organically linked with the others. The State has retained over the Zilla Parishads only the power of dissolution for excess or abuse of their powers, persistent default in or incompetence to perform their statutory duties. Reconstitution by election is mandatory within six months. In respect of Mandals, the Zilla Parishad has similar powers plus the power to approve the annual budget and the power to suspend any resolution or order of the Mandal or its officers. To secure speedy and inexpensive justice in civil and criminal matters of a relatively minor nature, Nyaya Panchayats have been envisaged under the Act. However, a conscious decision was taken by the Government of Karnataka to bring Nyaya Panchayats into effect, five years after the commencement of the Panchayati Raj System. But this did not happen as the decentralization process was interrupted by a change of government. The Mandal Panchayat's financial resources consisted of allotments by the government or the Zilla Parishad, proceeds from tax on buildings, entertainment, markets; levy of water rates, etc. The Zilla Parishad's financial resources consisted of the amounts transferred to the Zilla Parishad by appropriation from out of the Consolidated Fund of the State; all grants, assignments, loans and contributions made by the State Government, all levies and penalties paid to or levied by on behalf of the Zilla Parishad, etc. Zilla Parishads did not have powers to levy taxes or cesses, but had powers to raise their own resources by borrowings, investments and remunerative assets. They retained all accruals from income-generating schemes, which were transferred to them by the State Government.

For the transfer of resources among the districts, the State Government adopted a certain criteria for giving relatively higher share to the backward areas/regions. This involved 12 indicators with weightages accorded to each (see Annexure I). Similarly, for transferring resources from the Zilla Parishad to the Mandal Panchayats, a certain criteria with appropriate weightages was adopted involving five indicators : viz., Population, Area of Mandal, Dryland Area, Agricultural Labour Population and Per Capita Resources raised. A 10 per cent weightage to the resources raised by the Mandals was given, keeping in view the need to encourage them to perform better in mobilizing resources.

A significant feature of the Karnataka model is the adoption of a "Calandar of Operations", to link up the grassroot level planning with the planning above. The "Planning Calendar" was as follows :

July 15 : Adopting the tentative size for the State's Annual Plan for the next year beginning April 1.

July 25 : State Government's Planning Department indicates to the Zilla Parishads and Mandal Panchayats the financial ceiling within which their annual plan should be formulated for the next year.

Aug. 15 : Mandal Panchayats to send their plan proposals to Zilla Parishads after convening Gram Sabha meeting in each of the villages within their jurisdiction.

Sept. 20 : Zilla Parishads to send their draft District Plan to the State Planning Department and the other concerned heads of departments in the State Government.

Sept. 28 to Oct. 25: Discussion with individual Zilla Parishads on their draft plans by the State Planning Department for achieving consistency and integration of District sector with State sector schemes/plans.

Nov. 10 : Government/State Heads of Departments to consolidate these proposals and build them into the State's draft plan. The same is sent to the National Planning Commission.

Jan. 15 : Approval of the Planning Commission to the State's plan, after discussion with the State representatives.

Feb. 25 : Finalizing the State's plan budget in the light of the Planning Commission approval to the State Plan and finalizing the district plans of the Zilla Parishads accordingly.

Mar. 10 : Presentation of the State budget to legislature along with the link document giving scheme-wise, sector-wise and Zilla Parishad-wise outlays.

The interface of the Zilla Parishads with the State Planning Department is a noteworthy part of the whole exercise. In meticulously evolving the various procedures for decentralized planning, the Karnataka model has gone far ahead of other States. As the then Chief Minister of the State observed. "It was a great experiment, a revolutionary step."[14] The Karnataka Model was implemented for five years, i.e. till 1992, after which the Government changed. The new Government introduced a three-tier system of Panchayats under the New Karnataka Panchayat Act 1993.

The West Bengal Model[15]

West Bengal is a State ruled by a leftist government. Here the experimentation with decentralized planning started with land reforms. It is claimed that after the accomplishment of land reforms, the poorer farmers now have an effective control, either through ownership or permanent operational control, over more than 75 per cent of the agricultural land. The major thrust of Decentralized Planning was on the following :

(i) Provision of adequate non-land inputs to the small and marginal farmers (who constituted the bulk of the land-owning class), through an appropriate mix of chemical and bio-fertilizers and choice relating to cropping patterns;

(ii) Making rural service centres play their legitimate role in supporting agriculture through location of services and marketing;

(iii) Using simple technology, as in irrigation, that would make fuller use of local labour and local resources; and

(iv) Going step by step in giving powers of planning and implementation to the Panchayats. Two schemes that were given to begin with were the Food for Work and the Integrated Rural Development Programme (IRDP). In the IRDP, the choice of beneficiaries was done by the Panchayats very seriously. An evaluation revealed that the choice of beneficiaries was 100 per cent correct. As IRDP is a credit-linked programme, in order to ensure collection of loans. "Repayment Melas" (Repayment Fairs) were organized.

The organizational structure for Decentralized Planning consisted of a District Planning Committee at the district level and a Block Planning Committee at the block level. The Chairman of the District Planning Committee was the Chief of the Zilla Parishad (called Sabhadipathi) and its Member Secretary was the District Magistrate. In addition to the

District Planning Committee, a general deliberative body called the District Planning Coordination Council was constituted comprising the members of the District Planning Committee plus the MLAs and MPs. The District Planning Committee is the executive operative arm of this body.

At the Block level, the Block Planning Committee is chaired by the Block Panchayat Chief (i.e. Panchayat Samiti Sabhapati) and the Block Development Officer is its Member Secretary. The chiefs of the Standing Committees of the Panchayat Samiti, the Gram Panchayat Pradhans and the block-level officials are the members.[16]

The State made a clear separation in the budget between the State level and district or below level schemes. A little more than 50 per cent of the entire State budget is devolved down to district or below even as regards decision-making about allocations. Thus the district knows what are the schemes under its jurisdiction and what funds are available. From the total funds received at the district level, about 70-75 per cent is distributed across the blocks on the basis of certain criteria. As for the planning procedures adopted, Arun Ghosh[17] gives a description of these in the case of the district of Midnapore, in the planning of which an academic institution—Indian Institute of Technology, Kharagpur—also played an advisory role. The procedures were as follows :

(i) Each Gram Panchayat was asked to prepare a "needs statement";

(ii) Each Panchayat Samiti was to : (a) prepare a series of maps of the block, outlining the existing facilities, resources and resource use; and (b) with the help of sub-assistant engineers available at the block level, prepare schemes to meet the most acute problems of each Gram Panchayat (based on the "needs statement" collated by them);

(iii) Each Panchayat Samiti was also to prepare a statement of the on-going and proposed programme of plan outlay of different departments/authorities in each block;

(iv) The block plans consisting of the "needs statements" and the schemes drawn up with the help of sub-assistant engineers, were then forwarded to the planning authorities at the district headquarters;

(v) Three sub-committees were constituted in the district to go through the block plans. They are : (a) A technical sub-committee which looked into the feasibility and estimated costs/

benefits of each scheme; (b) an economic sub-committee which arranged all schemes in order of priorities, making sure of the required order funds and the coordination between different schemes as well as the consistency with the "needs statements" prepared by the Gram Panchayats; and (c) A sub-committee headed by the Sabhapati to decide on the contours of the district plan and the block plans; and

(vi) A credit plan was also prepared and appended to the District Plan.

Arun Ghosh also gives an account of the District Plan prepared for Burdwan district for the year 1985-86. It was in seven volumes.

Vol. I Gives, after a brief introduction, the methodology and the administrative arrangements, the profile of the district (basic data), district plan outlays and sectoral plans, a credit plan for the district and a perspective plan for the district.

Vol. II Devoted to maps delineating the basic features of the Burdwan economy.

Vols. III to VII Deal with the five sub-divisions of the district.

Phase V : 1990- —The Panchayati Raj Renaissance Phase

During the last year of the Seventh Plan (1985-90) one more employment programme was added in addition to the National Rural Employment Programme (NREP). This is called Jawahar Rozgar Yojana (JRY). While NREP is a wage employment programme, JRY is a self-employment, subsidy and bank loan-oriented programme.

Currently, the Eighth Plan (1992-97) is in operation. Unlike the previous plans, it is an indicative plan and lays considerable emphasis on the involvement of people in the process of development. It says : "The attitude of passive observance and total dependence on the government for developmental activities has become all-pervasive. It has to be altered to a pro-active attitude of people taking initiative themselves. In the process of development, people must operate and the government must cooperate".[18] After the Directional paper to the Eighth Plan was approved by the National Development Council, the latter set up a Committee under the Chairmanship of Chimanbhai Patel in 1992 to make recommendations on "Micro-Level Planning and involvement of people at grassroot level". The Committee emphasized the strengthening of the planning machinery at sub-state levels and recommended sharing of expenditure on technical staff by the Central Government to the extent of two-thirds at all levels of state and sub-state. It also emphasized substantial training of staff at the relevant levels for micro-level planning. It observed that for decentralized planning to succeed, decentralization of authority and funds are not enough by themselves. There has to be consensus to that end and a will to carry it through. Even when powers and functions are given up, often something is held back for parallel implementation through competing agencies, creating situations of potential conflict. It recommended the kind of programmes and activities that could be entrusted to micro-level planning and suggested non-government organizations to get involved to a great degree in micro level planning, providing technical expertise and carrying out institution building among the people on a pilot basis in selected blocks. The Committee also recommended formation of village development committees, involvement of youth in "Shram Dan" and giving a fair trial to the concept of "Sarvodaya Yojana".[18A]

A bold initiative taken by the Central Government, so far as Democratic Decentralization is concerned, is the passing of the 73rd amendment of the Constitution in 1993, which has sought to ensure the establishment of local self-governments throughout the country as an acknowledged third tier of the Government. Some salient features of this amendment may be seen in Annexure II. Following this, the Panchayati Raj institutions are being revived and re-invented. A Renaissance Phase for the Panchayati Raj institutions has begun and this ushers in a new era of decentralization in India. It poses many challenges as well as offers many opportunities. The coming years will tell how the democratic decentralization process in India fared during the "Renaissance Phase".

Decentralized Planning Experience in India : A Synthesis

A historical review of different developments relevant to local-level planning was attempted in the foregoing paragraphs. Now an attempt will be made to pull the threads of this analysis, so as to hit some high spots of India's experience in decentralized planning.

Notwithstanding the constitutional lacuna that existed before the 73rd constitutional amendment, there has been quite a substantial experience of decentralized planning in the country. Some states have articulated their own methodologies for decentralized planning with innovative ideas. There is, however, no single and uniform pattern of decentralized planning, which can be trotted as the Indian model of decentralization. What one really finds here is a mosaic of varying patterns and different hues that offer diverse methodologies and numerous lessons along with a warning for "cautious optimism".

In the earlier phase of planning era after independence (1947), the planning activity, by and large, remained centred around the Union (Central Government) and the States. Since the 60's, the planning orientations changed distinctly in favour of greater decentralized effort. During 1960-70, the establishment of local self-government institutions (called Panchayati Raj Institutions) under the Government's democratic decentralization scheme was vigorously promoted. The euphoria did not last long and these institutions declined during 1970-80. Now again they are being revived, as they have now been given the constitutional back-up. Since 1965 the Central Government has initiated several decentralized programmes in the nature of "target area" and "target-group" oriented programmes under a scheme of "central and centrally sponsored programmes" to ensure that developments did not flag in certain neglected areas. Some of them still continue. In fact, there is a plethora of anti-poverty and employment-oriented schemes operating from the centre. These have been sometimes criticized as "top-down approach". Hegde observes, "Except for schemes of national importance, which would benefit all the states, none of the other schemes should be treated as centrally sponsored schemes. These schemes must come from the people themselves and they must be called "village-sponsored schemes".[19]

To really promote decentralization at the level of states, the Central Government has taken the following five major steps :

(1) The Centre issued detailed guidelines for formulating District Plans in 1969.
(2) The Centre has been providing special financial assistance to the States since 1972 for strengthening the planning machinery at the state and district levels.
(3) In 1982, the Centre through a "Working Group on District Planning", provided up-dated and detailed guidelines covering all aspects of District Planning. The prerequisites that must be fulfilled by the State Governments for initiating decentralized planning on sound lines has been particularly stressed in these guidelines.

(4) In 1993, the Centre amended the Constitution, introducing Part IX in it, which elaborates the structure, composition, elections to and scope of powers of Panchayats at the District, intermediate and village levels. The eleventh schedule added to the Constitution lists the subjects under which powers and functions could be given to Panchayats at District/Intermediate/Village levels. The constitutional status now accorded to the Panchayat bodies is expected to check the States from tampering with the life of these institutions, as has been the case so far. This will facilitate them to function as instruments of vibrant and viable rural local self-government and acquire the capacity to learn, to respond, to change and to mobilize better participation by the people in managing their own affairs.

(5) The task of training functionaries at three levels—officials at the sub-district level, officials at the district level and non-officials/elected representatives at both district and sub-district levels—has been given much prominence since the 80's. The training of trainers is being conducted at the national level.

The various initiatives taken by the Centre were reinforced by experiments at the state level, which have thrown up specific methodologies on various aspects of planning from below. The 1970's is the age of methodologies. We have provided a few glimpses of these varied methodologies. Maharashtra and Gujarat in the western part of India have been fore-runners in operationalizing district planning. Maharashtra innovated in the late '60s by devising a formula based on some managerial criteria for district allocations from the State's "divisible pool", which was pegged at 40 per cent of the total development funds of the state. Gujarat in the 70's refined this procedure by providing a 'modicum' of "un-tied funds"—placed at the sole discretion of the local bodies for meeting their perceived needs. In both these states, elected local self-government institutions (Panchayati Raj Institutions) existed and were performing "agency functions" for implementation of specific development activities devolved on them by the State Government. But planning was deliberately kept out of their jurisdiction and placed with institutional structures called "District Planning and Development Councils". Initially, Maharashtra and Gujarat experiments were a great success. But after some time, contrary pulls affected the process of decentralization. In Maharashtra, for instance, the state originally decided to allocate 40 per cent of the total plan funds at the state level to the district. Later, the state started making inroads into district outlays by introducing a component called "State sponsored District Sector Schemes" and diverting funds from the district outlays to the State. This resulted in a gradual shrinking of the proportion of the District sector allocation.[20] Arun Ghosh remarks, "Perhaps their (i.e. Maharashtra and Gujarat) very success spelt their demise. The MLA's and MP's, even the State Cabinet, felt disturbed and uneasy at the growing signs of a shift in the centre of power and authority in these two states. For the fact remains that nobody really likes to shed power; and the bureaucracy successfully played upon the fears and misgivings of the State Government leaders. With time, therefore, the role and the authority of the Panchayats receded into the background, and the role and authority of the bureaucracy—backed by the Ministers, MLA's and MP's—increased. The planning process in Gujarat and Maharashtra thus gradually came to be decentralized only in name, not in substance".[21]

Thus it may be seen that the decentralization process never runs smooth. It oscillates back and forth. Sometimes, the forces of centralization assert themselves and cause serious set-backs. Coping with such set-backs becomes a serious problem in the developing countries. For instance, the Indian Government which took a bold initiative to push decentralization in the States, by amending the Constitution in 1993, came up with a scheme in 1994, of allocating a sum of rupees one crore to each Member of Parliament to be devoted to development projects that will meet the needs of their constituencies, a patently retrograde step which threatens or dilutes the decentralization process. Obviously, the M.P's will opt for prestigious projects, which will ensure them their votes. The experience of Pakistan (quoted in the U.N. Human Development Report 1993) is a pointer in this regard.[22] Further, one may just imagine as to what will happen, if the states in the country are to follow suit and provide such constituency funds to each M.L.A. The local authorities will be left with little or no funds to plan for their areas. All these point to the fact that there are 'limits' to decentralization in all developing countries. Prof. Dantwala observes : "The more one thinks about India's planning process, as it has evolved . . . , the more aware one becomes of the limits to decentralization. The limits are of three types : political, administrative and technological. One can assume that the political and administrative obstacles can be removed through better understanding and open debate. That the obstacles are removable is not questioned, though it would need much more than good sense to remove them".[23]

In India, structural-functional aspects of local self-government and integration with the planning process has received much attention in the 1980's in some states. The southern State of Karnataka ushered in a new era of democratic decentralization in 1983 with an integrated set of Panchayati Raj institutions. All the development departments and agencies of the district were brought under the purview of the elected representatives and "organizational pluralism" was remarkably reduced, facilitating the integration and consolidation of the efforts and resources of development departments and the element of accountability of bureaucrats to the elected representatives of the Panchayati Raj institutions was introduced. A complete separation of the development and regulatory functions at the district level was made and both planning and implementation were brought under the purview of the elected representatives at the grassroots level. Similar innovations were also made in the State of West Bengal. (We have earlier discussed the Karnataka and West Bengal models of decentralization in this chapter.)

Thus over the last two decades, considerable progress has been made in India in the direction of Decentralized District Planning. Issues like the need for district plans and the prerequisites for district planning, which dominated the discussions during the 70's and even early 80's, are no longer the current subjects of debate, showing that decentralized planning has made a permanent imprint on the national psyche. Discussion has now shifted to finer issues of instruments, such as techniques of analysis, more integrated structures, achieving better integration of activities and programmes and linkages, instituting a multi-tiered training system and building up of information systems. The broad framework for decentralized planning is now deeply entrenched in the country. The finer details are being debated upon.

In other words, the focus now has shifted to the actual task of drawing up a district plan, using the kind of capabilities that are available at the district level. The planning staff at both state and district levels are now fairly competent to tackle the planning tasks, thanks to the continuous assistance provided by the Planning Commission through a scheme of strengthening of planning machinery. (Through this scheme, Central assistance was provided to the extent of two-thirds of the expenditure on planning staff at the state level and 50 per cent of the expenditure on planning staff at the district level.) Over the last 50 years, several methodologies of planning at the district and sub-district levels have also been evolved. Amitava Mukherjee[24] has critically analyzed all the major methodologies, starting from Gadgil's methodology down to the ones evolved by Misra and Sundaram in three published volumes, which is worthy of study by all District Planners. Each of these methodologies has their merits and demerits. Despite the existence of all these methodologies, the task of preparing a reasonably sound District Plan that will be based on resources (natural and human) appraisal with the proper choice of priority schemes, which are internally consistent and integrated vertically and horizontally with their overall objectives consistent with the national objectives and are prepared with the close participation by people at all levels and within a framework of temporal perspectives (annual, medium- and long-term) poses difficult challenges—technical, managerial and participatory. Before the commencement of the Eighth Plan (1992-97), the Planning Commission made some attempts to have some pilot plans prepared, so that the methodology followed in them could be commended for adoption by other districts as well. This involved the preparation of plans for five districts under the guidance provided by the National Institute of Rural Development (NIRD). In spite of a systematic effort aimed at, nothing worthwhile emerged from these exercises. Out of the five plans, one of them, that of Nasik District in Maharashtra, was deemed a better exercise. Arun Sinha reflects on the reasons why we have not been able to make much headway in the area of district planning. His observations are :[25]

- "Even when it is not so obvious, there is lurking reluctance on the part of Governments and their sectorial heads to devolve sufficient authority—administrative and financial—to the planning bodies at the district level;
- There is lack of effective coordination at the district level between various agencies involved in the planning exercise. Often, there is no arrangement for systematic integration of planning perspectives of different sectorial agencies operating at the field level. This applies even to the vertical integration between the responsible functionaries at different levels. The planning aspect tends to be neglected;
- Institutionalized arrangements, for seeking consultation with various participants in the planning process, are either not well established or not sufficiently encouraged and developed. Hence, despite the use of planning techniques, a lot of subjectivity, even selfish arbitrariness, creeps in taking decisions. The planning aspect thus becomes a casualty. What is more,

on the rebound, it breeds cynicism amongst the core planning personnel;

— There is lack of trained staff both in terms of numbers and adequacy of training. Training deficiencies are often noticed in the acquisition and mastering of necessary skills and techniques. The inculcation of right approach and attitude towards planning also requires attention. To promote planned way of thinking, it is necessary that a proper querry system should be developed, analytical skills of the planning personnel sharpened and they should also be trained to assimilate and integrate seemingly different points of view, display responsiveness and cultivate a habit of exploring options. A planner must also be able to persuade others to his way of thinking. Communication skill is, therefore, equally necessary. Above all, training must bring home the importance of the planning aspect of one's work;

— A very elaborate methodology may stifle whatever little initiative and efforts may be possible, by a limited number of staff. In some cases, non-availability of planning staff poses a serious problem. For instance, in the Hill Areas, there is usually shortage of staff. Complexities of methodology should not be allowed to become a pretence for not doing planning;

— While planning, sufficient attention is not given to the realities of resource constraints. The "need" factor or the importance of a particular sector, in relation to other, motivates the prescribing of higher and higher allocations. Financial constraints at this stage are relegated to a secondary position. However, by the time District level plans are firmed up and integrated with the State level plans, resources re-emerge as the overall constraint and quite often drastic re-adjustments have to be worked out. The deleterious side effect of this kind of re-adjustments is that the initial overenthusiasm for planning turns to scepticism about its utility. This feeling, basically due to uninformed thinking about the true character of the planning process, has in reality greatly impeded the effective operationalization of district planning;

— At the district level more than at any other level planning and implementation are almost visibly aligned. The planner is acutely aware of the realities of implementation. It is, therefore, necessary that the budgetary mechanism for the release of funds should be so devised that it supports the cause of planning rather than weakens it. Though not strictly a part of planning methodology, this is an important factor which should be sorted out if the cause of planning is to be advanced; and

— Finally, district level planning is essentially a reflection of the belief that it is a step forward in the direction of bringing the planning process within the reach of the local people. If so, the people must also show interest in it, support it and ensure that it prospers. Unless, therefore, an enlightened pressure group develops or is developed, the success of the district planning exercise will always be at the mercy of people who may not be interested in it. Planning methodology should, therefore, give considerable attention to developing a sustaining force within the district, which would help ensure operationalization of district plans".

There have been no rigorous impact analysis of the decentralization policy in the various States in India so far. But one study done by Srivastava[26] in Maharashtra State may be referred to. This study has attempted to assess the impact of decentralization policy on government bureaucracy. According to this study, "the non-officials, by and large, appeared to be satisfied with the functioning of the bureaucracy at the district and block levels. . . . At present, the bureaucracy, to a normative extent, has accepted the supremacy of elected representatives and has been giving due attention to the advice and suggestions rendered by the elected representatives. By accepting the superiority of people's representatives, the bureaucracy has tended to be more responsive to the people. The officials also felt that the initial stalemate over the question of who had the 'upperhand' in the exercise of powers between officials and non-officials no longer exists. There have been frequent purposeful consultations between the two wings, helping each other in achieving the developmental objectives and the decision-making power is being shared by elected representatives and bureaucracy".[27] When questions were put to the rural poor, it was noted that "the bureaucracy often consults them, whenever possible accommodates their point of view and indeed tries to give preferential treatment to the rural poor".[28] The study has concluded that "the cumulative impact of decentralization policy on the socio-economic development of the rural poor has been satisfactory. It has increased the participation of the rural poor in the development process, their bargaining power has increased, it has facilitated equitable distribution of benefits and has helped promote capabilities of weaker sections to take up a leadership role. These were no less achievements when compared to the situation prevalent before the onset of decentralized system".[29] It must be remembered that the situation as portrayed here is that of a state which is much advanced and progressive in regard to decentralization and cannot be deemed to be representative of India, as a whole. Even in the case of Maharashtra, the study notes that if we compare the achievements with the length of the decentralization process, the pace of change must be deemed "sluggish and slow".[30] This finding only reiterates our conclusion that for the decentralization process to register a sizable impact in any developing country, both political will and continuity of the policy over a long period are essential.

In the light of the Indian experience in decentralization, it may be observed that in spite of the many impressive achievements made so far in the country on the institutional and methodological fronts, there still remain many aspects on which the progress towards decentralization seems limited and halting. The major constraints are in the areas of political will, bureaucratic willingness, local capabilities, public participation and accountability. Undoubtedly, we have "miles and miles to go" in decentralization. One is tempted to conclude that decentralized multi-level planning in India is "still a hope, a love, still longed for, never seen" (William Wordsworth).

2. NEPAL

Nepal is administratively divided into five development regions, each of which is divided into two to five zones, which are further sub-divided into districts. Each district is also divided into nine Ilakas (clusters of villages). The lowest level of administrative unit is the village. There are 5 regions, 14 zones, 75 districts, 29 Town Municipalities and 4,023 villages.

Nepal had a highly centralized politico-administrative system prior to 1951. Since the sixties, the country has made several attempts to decentralize the powers and functions of the government to the lower echelons and elected local bodies. A partyless panchayat system was introduced in 1962. During 1960-70, several Committees and Commissions were constituted for studying and recommending decentralization of political and administrative powers. However, their recommendations were not seriously implemented and the results of decentralization experiments were far from satisfactory. In the eighties, following the promulgation of the Decentralization Act 1982, some concerted efforts were made to operationalize decentralized district planning. But the progress of decentralization was interrupted in 1990, after a revolution, when the Panchayat system was abolished and a multi-party system introduced. The new Constitution also made it clear that the new government will pursue a policy of involving the people in the development administration of the country through the implementation of decentralized policy.

After the elections in May, 1992, local governments were reestablished and the decentralization process started making some headway. There was a change of government in 1994 and again another in 1995.

With the above background, we may now analyze the evolution of decentralized democracy and the status of decentralized planning in Nepal.

Decentralization in the Sixties[31]

According to the provision of the Constitution of Nepal of 1962, the decentralization of power and people's participation in the political process are important dimensions of the administrative and political reorganization of the country. The series of reforms introduced in the sixties sought to make administrative units smaller (thus increasing their number from thirty-five to seventy-five) so that administrative services could reach the people. The Local Administration Act of 1965 authorized district Panchayats to look after all development activities in the districts. Under this Act, the district Panchayats were constituted with an elected chairman and an official, the chief district officer (CDO) as the secretary of the Panchayat. This system, however, did not work satisfactorily, as conflicts arose between the CDO and the chairman of the district Panchayat. This plan repeatedly ran into difficulties because of the reluctance of civil servants to part with power, on the one hand, and the alleged lack of accountability on the part of the elected leaders, on the other.

Decentralization in the Seventies

A more elaborate attempt was made when a District Administration Plan (DAP) was implemented in 1975. The major thrust of this reform was to bring about a unified and strong district administration. The following measures were taken :

(i) The district-level departments of the Central Government were designated as the constituent sections of a unified district office;
(ii) The planning for all sectorial programmes was to be initiated at the local level, some starting at the village level and others at the district level, and an integrated document called the District Development Plan (DDP) was to be prepared each year in each district with the intent of making them the basis for resource allocation;
(iii) Several subject committees (called Coordinating Committees) were formed of district panchayat members and concerned technical officials to enlist people's participation in decision-making for all development programmes in the district; and
(iv) The CDO was to be the coordinator of all development programmes at the district level and to function as the executor of district panchayat decisions, with adequate discretionary power vested in him.

Although DAP was in existence for close to a decade, it did not become fully operational, mainly for the following reasons :[32]

(i) The departments and ministries concerned tended to go slowly in entrusting supervisory and coordinating role over their programmes and personnel at the district level to the CDO;
(ii) District-level personnel were inadequately trained in project analysis and local-level planning and were not equal to the task of drawing up coherent district development plans; and
(iii) Planning in most of the sectors was done separately at the national level. These nationally set quantitative targets were later disaggregated and handed down to individual districts. The planning of programmes on the basis of a local identification of needs and potentials still remains to be fully implemented. Only in the case of rural works, locally identified projects constituted an important basis for central and local resource allocation.

To complement DAP, the Government came up with another approach called the Integrated Panchayat Development Design (IPDD) to provide stronger inter-sectorial coordination. Extensive institutional mechanisms were to be instituted for this purpose through a chain of coordinating committees at various levels, starting from a cabinet sub-committee. Another provision in the design was the establishment of service centres, nine in each district. Despite the comprehensive nature of provisions in its design, the IPDD did not appear to have achieved much, mainly because of the indifference of the line ministries.

Decentralization in the Eighties

His Majesty's Government of (HMG/N) made a bold initiative during the eighties and made some important efforts towards decentralization during the eighties. In 1981, the Ministry of Local Development was renamed as the Ministry of Panchayat and Local Development (MPLD). The position of the Secretary to the District Panchayat was upgraded to officer of class II level and designated as Local Development Officer (LDO), who took over development functions from the Chief District Officer (CDO). Simultaneously, a number of donor-aided decentralized programmes were initiated during this period. An accelerated Basic Needs Programme (BNP) was initiated from June 1987.

The most important event is the promulgation of the Decentralization Act in 1983 and the rules framed under it in 1984. It was a "product of hard thinking, enormous exercises at district and national levels and deliberation of a series of workshops. Even quite a number of foreign experts were involved in drafting the Decentralization Act. It took almost two years for drafting by-laws of 1984".[33] In the opinion of this author, it is undoubtedly a very well drafted document and can be a model Act for the developing countries. It spelt out three decision-making bodies for decentralized planning.

(i) The National Planning Commission (NPC) to set development priorities and provide guidelines for the District and Local Level Panchayats;

(ii) District Panchayat Assembly to approve all district development projects; and

(iii) The Village Panchayat to decide on the planning and implementation of the village-level projects.

The Act has laid down a time-bound and elaborate planning process involving some 17 actors and about 20 steps. It is a combination of top-down and bottom-up processes. The planning process starts with the preparation of guidelines and budget ceiling by the National Planning Commission (NPC), which communicates them to the districts. At district level, the District Panchayat makes an estimate of its own resources, as well as the resources available to the Village Panchayat and adds them to the funds coming from the Centre most of which are sectorially earmarked. The District Panchayat allocates them to the various *Ilakas* (service centre areas) and issues guidelines on how they should be used. This is done on the basis of central guidelines and on an analysis of the District Profile. The remaining part of the resources from the Centre is provided as a lump sum to the district. The District Panchayat has to allocate at least 50 per cent of this lump sum to the Village Panchayats and provide guidelines on how to use them. The remainder may be used for district level projects. Once all this information is available, planning starts at the lowest level, the ward, where the population identifies, formulates and prioritizes projects with the help of village/ilaka/district level officials. These projects after selection and approval by village bodies are consolidated into a Village Plan. The village plans, in turn, go to the district level where additional selection may take place. They are then, together with the District projects, included in a District plan, after approval by District bodies. Finally, the plan has to be approved by NPC and the funds for implementation given by the Centre are made available to the District Treasurer. Detailed normative formats have been developed for the plan, project description and the district profile.

At the Central level, two committees were established : Decentralization Task Force and Decentralization Evaluation Committee. Under the Act, all district-level offices are part of the District Panchayat Secretariat.[34]

The top-down and bottom-up processes of Decentralized Planning and the Decentralized Planning and implementation structure, as visualized under the Decentralized Act, may be seen in Figs. 13.2 A, 13.2 B and Fig. 13.3.

The district development plan will be in accordance with the policies determined at the national level and communicated to the district through the various sectorial ministries. The Decentralization Act lays down the following six priorities for the district development plan.

(a) Projects which provide direct benefits to the general public and which fulfil minimum needs;

(A)

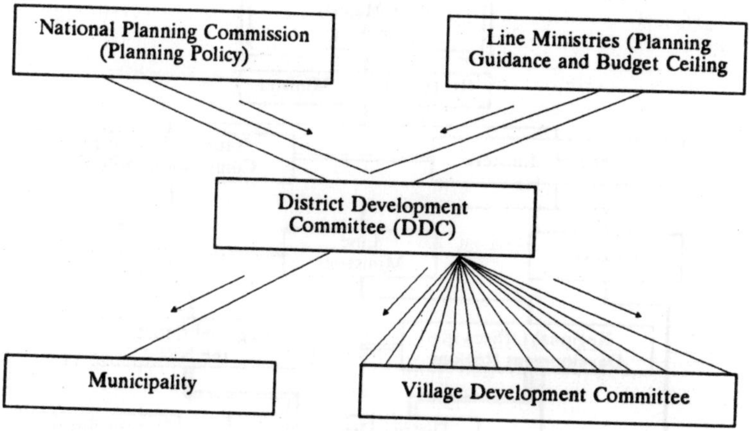

(B)

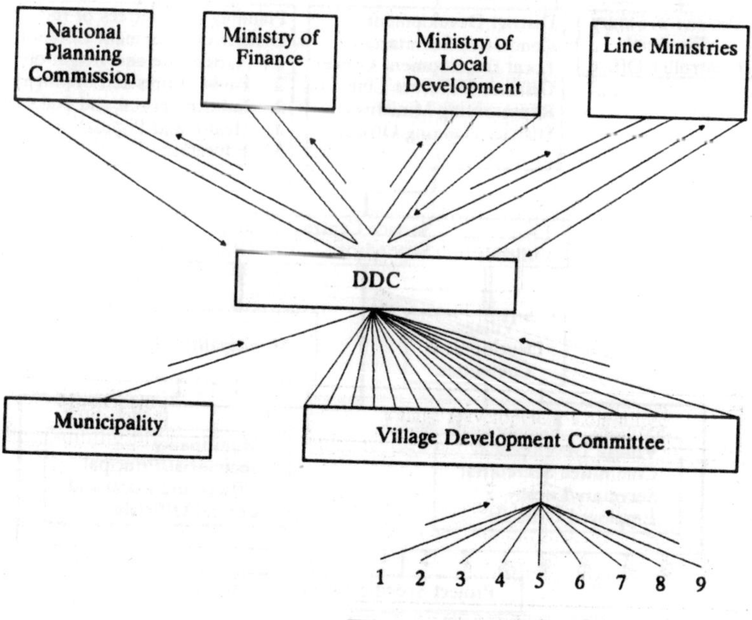

FIG. 13.2 : (a) Top-Down Process under Decentralized Planning and (b) Bottom-up Process under Decentralized Planning.

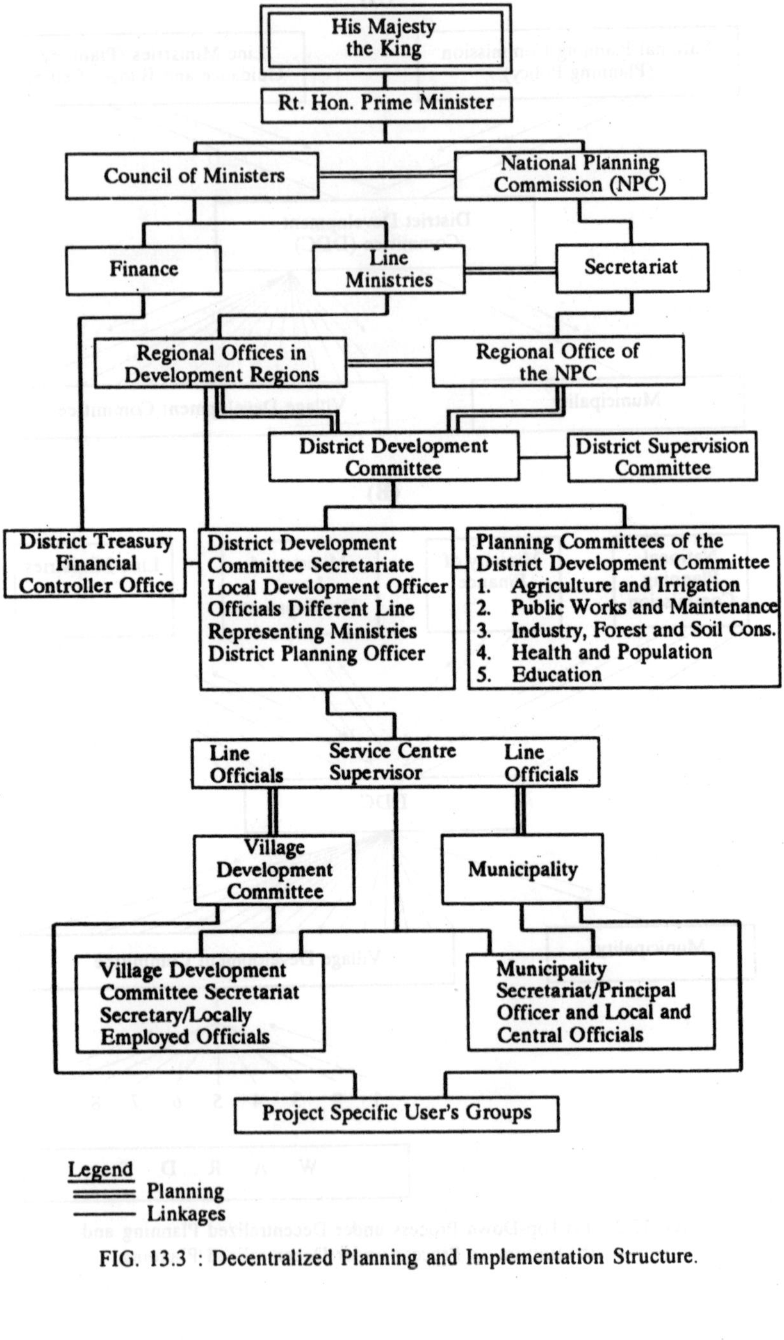

FIG. 13.3 : Decentralized Planning and Implementation Structure.

(b) Projects which help in increasing agricultural production;
(c) Projects which can be implemented through local resources and skills;
(d) Projects which help in increasing productivity and employment opportunities;
(e) Projects which have been assigned priority in national level plans; and
(f) Projects which help to protect the environment.

The district development plan is supposed to evolve through an elaborate committee system. Five subject committees are proposed to be set up for this purpose, one each for agriculture and irrigation, works and maintenance, industry, forest and soil conservation, health and population, and education. These committees are themselves expected to base their plans on suggestions received from village and town panchayats. Besides the subject committees, two other important committees have also been envisaged. One is a Joint Committee for the coordination of planning, to bring together the proposals of the subject committees. Another is a District Supervision Committee, which will have a threefold function : (a) that of supervising the district development plan; (b) that of ensuring a certain measure of economy and fiscal discipline during the course of implementation; and (c) that of initiating appropriate action in the event of any errors being detected in execution. Both committees are to be chaired by a national panchayat member (MP) hailing from the district. In his absence, the chairman of the District Panchayat will preside over such meetings.

Another important aspect of the legislation is the requirement that each district be divided into nine *Ilakas* (blocks) and in each of them, a service centre would ordinarily be established as the organized focal point for all government and parastatal services, to promote a self-sustaining development process in the villages. Thus rural-urban integration has been provided for and a growth centre strategy has been advocated. The Decentralization Act provides for a strong organizational structure that is not only well coordinated, but is also permeative in nature. It is geographically dispersed so that it can provide the necessary assistance and information to panchayats from close quarters on a continuing basis. This is the rationale for the creation of service centres.

A unique aspect of the Decentralization Act 1982 is that the concept of target groups as beneficiaries of a project are clearly identified and defined as "Users Groups". Clause 19 of the Act spells out the composition of Users Committees, their functions, responsibilities and rights. Such provisions have attempted to safeguard the interests of the target groups and have thus decentralized the whole planning process by encouraging a greater degree of spontaneous participation by the people. Nepal has a number of successful Users' Groups for various types of projects, such as Drinking Water Schemes, School Buildings and Irrigation. One may conclude that generally speaking, Nepal has done quite well in promoting people's participation.

The Decentralization Act was an ambitious venture and sought to bring about the very structure which could not be established in previous attempts, namely, the establishment of a unified strong development administration in the district under the political executive.[35]

Decentralization Programmes

During the period following the seventies, a number of donor-assisted Integrated Rural Development Projects were initiated in Nepal. Table 13.2 provides an idea of the projects and their coverage.

TABLE 13.2 : Integrated Rural Development Projects in Nepal (IRDP—Status).

	Project	Districts	Phase I	Phase II	Phase III
1.	Rasuwa-Nuwakot	2	1976-1983 1984-1985	1985-1993	
2.	Integrated Hill Development Programme (IHDP)	2	1974-1980	1980-1985	1985-1990
3.	Sagarmatha	3	1978-1985	1986	
4.	Kosi (KHARDEP)	4	1977-1979	1979-1985	
5.	Mahakali	3	1980-1985	1986-1990	
6.	Rapti	5	1980-1985	1988-1996	
7.	Karnali-Bheri	3	1981-1985	1985-1990	
8.	Dhading	1	1983-1985	1985-1990	
9.	Seti	5	1986		
10.	Mechi Hill Irrigation and Related Development Programme	3	1986		

Source: Amatya (1988).

Many evaluation reports of the IRDPs emphasized the need for integrating the rural development programmes having different focus with the planning at district and local levels. After the decentralization scheme came into force in December 1984, the preparation of periodic plans for the Seventh Five Year Plan was initiated at village and district levels. Although the plans appeared very crude, the process of planning at grassroot level was initiated. Over the years, it was expected that the IRDPs will cease to be "planning from above" and an "ivory tower" operation and will form part of the district plans.

On the experiences of Decentralized Programmes, Amatya observes :

> "All the IRDPs were designed at the centre and the bureaucratic approach of HMG/N officials as well as the foreign experts appeared dominant in the whole decision-making processes. Although invariably all the project reports referred to the needs of raising the rural poor, final decisions were made at the centre. The rural people or even local institutions like district and village panchayats did not have much to say in the decision-making. The needs and priorities of the rural people were visualized by HMG officials and programmes were implemented by district line agencies. It was only at the implementation stage, the local contribution in the form of labour or materials was sought. Voluntary labour was easily mobilized and, in some cases, it was partly paid or covered under 'the programme of food for work'."

Some people saw voluntary labour mobilization for public works as exploitation of the rural poor people (Pradhan, 1985).[36]

An important point to note is that donors often tended to bypass the district-level planning and implementation process on the excuse that it would impede the speedy progress of their projects and that their programme had a multi-district focus. After the operationalization of the Decentralization Act started, HMG began to address the need to restructure the government in order to devolve more authority and more staff to the field. This process was accelerated by the introduction of the Basic Needs Programme (BNP) in June 1987. A reorganization of those line ministries charged with BNP implementation was initiated. Functions were consolidated (e.g. all irrigation programmes were brought under a new Irrigation Department); a new Ministry of Housing and Physical Planning was created. The Ministry of Panchayat and Local Development was streamlined and was made the lead ministry for decentralization. It shed its direct implementation functions, so that it may concentrate on its principal role as coordinator of the line ministries at the local level.

Despite all these positive moves towards decentralization, the predisposition and capacity of district-level staff to share authority with local communities was obviously limited by the centralist orientation of their own parent departments. A reluctance to delegate authority to mid-level management and to the field was characteristic of the higher-level administration. According to a UNDP report, a "hoarding of discretion" at the centre was common, whereby "public administration... is overloaded and overcongested at the centre and consequently underutilized and unresponsive in the field". Bihari Shrestha calls this situation. "The paradox of a highly competent but normally non-performing bureaucracy".[37]

FAO Involvement in Decentralized Planning

To make decentralization a success, both institution-building and capability-building are essential. The latter is more important, because even after the institutions have been built up, skilled and capable personnel are necessary to make these institutions "work". In Nepal, the Village Panchayats and District Panchayats were grossly lacking in the capability to formulate projects and plans due to lack of information and shortages of trained personnel. In these circumstances, FAO assistance was sought for capability building among the government functionaries. An FAO assisted project (with Swiss funding) commenced in 1983. For the first five years, the emphasis was on imparting skills to middle-level personnel through training in project formulation and monitoring and evaluation. A training section was built up in the Agricultural Projects Services Centre (APROSC), an autonomous institution sponsored by the Ministry of Agriculture. In the second phase of this project, which commenced in 1988, the emphasis shifted to Decentralized Planning. During this second phase of project, this author played a crucial role in this project as Project Co-Manager and Chief Technical Adviser. The accomplishments during this phase consisted of strengthening the training section in APROSC for decentralized planning, working the technical methodology for district planning, preparing a comprehensive training manual for the training of trainers and operationalizing training for district planning.

The effort to build-up a methodology for District Planning in the Nepal context was started in 1985-86, as a pilot training-cum-technical assistance cycle, which was implemented in one of the districts in the Western Development Region of Nepal, i.e. Tanahun district.

It was conceived as a partnership endeavour, with the district officials, the Agricultural Projects Services Centre (APROSC) and the FAO—all joining together and contributing their mite to a common cause. The district officials constituted the primary planning team. APROSC acted as a planning Aid Team, training the district officials and providing technical assistance for district planning. The expatriate experts of FAO acted as a catalyst in the whole process, providing training of trainers and technical backstopping to the APROSC team. In order to secure the support of government officials at all levels, a High Level Steering Committee (HLSC) was constituted under the chairmanship of a member of the National Planning Commission.

The Tanahun district experiment provided on-the-job training to the district officials and enabled them to prepare the plan for the district. It also enabled APROSC to prepare a first draft of training materials for district planning. Later, the threads were picked up in 1988 by FAO experts, in association with the APROSC technical team, to refine these training materials further in the light of the many changes that were initiated by HMG/N and to bring out a comprehensive training manual on Decentralized Planning. The first insights into the district planning methodology were derived from the Tanahun experiment. Broadly, this methodology consisted of the following steps

* Preparation of a Physical Resource Inventory of the district. This step requires an inventory in each Panchayat which will then be aggregated at *Ilaka* (a cluster of villages) and district levels. In the Panchayat inventory, both the Panchayat Chairman and Secretary will be actually involved. This will be done after appropriate training in data collection.
* Preparation of resource inventory maps.
* Identification of local needs and priorities with people's participation.
* Evaluation of needs against resource potential.
* Final discussion with people.

The Tanahun district experience at least served to highlight three major lessons of the tripartite partnership approach.

(i) That a tripartite partnership approach to district planning helps to operationalize the district planning process with a modicum of technical competence;

(ii) That it helps to identify the available database and to outline a broad and feasible methodology for district planning in the context of the various constraints in the situation; and

(iii) That it helps to make an assessment of the training needs and the types of planned training interventions needed to enable the district functionaries to acquire the skills, knowledge and attitudes they require.

The Tanahun experience also revealed that more such action research type of pilot projects are needed in different agro-climatic and socio-cultural environments to gain better insights into the diverse technical aspects of planning methodologies as well as participatory planning strategies.

The Tanahun experience, besides training the district team and helping the district to prepare a plan, also enabled APROSC to prepare a first draft of training materials. These needed considerable refinement and systematization before they could be turned into a comprehensive training manual. This task was attempted during the second phase of the project. For the first time, a comprehensive Training Manual for Decentralized District Planning in 8 modules, with case studies, readings and training exercises was prepared.[38] The Manual was first prepared in English and then translated into Nepali language. A detailed plan for organizing training programmes was under way, when one of the most noteworthy political, social and economic changes overtook Nepal. The Congress and an alliance of Marxist parties mounted a campaign to bring down the Panchayat system. With the promulgation of the democratic constitution of the Kingdom of Nepal, 1990, the partyless Panchayat system was abolished and the multi-party system was introduced. The first elections were held in May 1992 and the Congress party came to power. Following this event, local governments were sought to be revived and new legislations were enacted in 1992, providing for a wide range of powers to District, Municipal and Village Governments. The major features include :

- Three separate Acts for village, municipal and district governments.
- Direct election at the village and municipal level.
- Indirect election at the district level from among those elected in village or municipality.
- Procedures (monthly meetings with 50 per cent quorum requirement) and functions (education, health/family planning,

agriculture, irrigation, forestry, drinking water, public works, social welfare) were clearly specified in the Acts.

— Central government bureaucrats were assigned to work with local government.
— Local governments were given powers to hire staff from their own resources.
— Governments at all levels were provided substantial specified revenue resources and districts and municipalities were given authority to develop others.
— District governments were given authority to borrow funds.
— Governments were encouraged to collaborate with NGO's and to form sub-committees, including NGO representatives, intelligentsia and social workers.
— Village Governments to have limited non-formal judicial authorities; they can receive complaints about disputes over private land, public property, wages, prices etc. and attempt to effect conciliation.
— District governments can levy fines on law-breakers.
— Local governments can be suspended or dissolved, but only after a public hearing and parliamentary review.

The new government started working on a Local Development Programme in the context of Decentralization. The National Planning Commission laid out the following six areas for focusing attention.[39]

1. Review of existing laws and regulations.
2. Improvement in the information system of local bodies.
3. Arrangement of training for officials of local bodies.
4. Definition of the Centre's role for the development of local bodies.
5. Creation of a financial resource base and improvement of the local bodies.
6. Arranging technical assistance to local bodies.

However, the above decentralization strategy could not make much headway, as the Congress government was overthrown in 1994. Fresh elections were held in late 1994 and a Communist government took over. Again, this government was thrown over and a new government has taken its place. Thus the decentralization programme has received severe jolts and set-backs.

To sum up, decentralization has been shifting its gears in Nepal. After the revolution in 1990, sustained development has been a challenge. Some degree of institutionalization of democratic institutions has taken place over the years. According to one assessment, "the major barrier is an under-performing of an overpowerful bureaucracy, that is reluctant to surrender any of its privileges and power".[40] This may be one constraint. But there are many other constraints as well, such as the inadequacy of the database, the excessive departmentalism and poor inter-organizational linkages and dearth of trained staff. In the sphere of resources, the main problem is the very high dependence of the district on HMG/N resources. This dependence automatically limits the autonomy and the power of decisions of the local political bodies, particularly when the use of the HMG/N resources is directed by a set of strong constraints".[41] Decentralization has still a long way to go in Nepal.

REFERENCES

1. Vyas, V.S. *et al.*, *Decentralized Planning in India*, Oxford and IBH Publishing Co., New Delhi, 1985.
2. Report of the Grow More Food Enquiry Committee, Govt. of India, M/o Agriculture, New Delhi, 1952.
3. The First Five Year Plan of India, Planning Commission, Chapter VIII, p. 140.
4. Review of the First Five Year Plan, Chapter XVII, p. 309-310, Planning Commission, May 1957.

4A. See Deva Raj, "Multilevel Planning and Local Government Structure", *The Indian Journal of Public Administration*, Vol. XIX, July-Sep. 1973.

5. Vyas, V.S., *et al.*, *Ibid.*
6. Sundaram, K.V., 'District Planning : The Case of Maharashtra', *Indian Journal of Public Administration*, No. 1, Jan.-March 1979, pp. 57-73.
7. See Dudley Seers, 'The Meaning of Development', *International Development Review*, No. 4, Dec. 1969. Also Dudley Seers 'The Meaning of Development', *International Development Review*, No. 3, 1977.
8. Gadgil, D.R., 'District Development Planning' Kale Memorial Lecture, 1966, Gokhale Institute of Politics and Economics, Poona.
9. Report of the Committee to review the existing administrative arrangements for rural development and poverty alleviation programmes. (CAARD), Planning Commission and the Department of Rural Development, Ministry of Agriculture, Govt. of India, December 1985.
10. Sundaram, K.V., 'Some recent trends in Rural Area Development Planning, in R.P. Misra and K.V. Sundaram (Ed.) *Rural Area Development : Perspectives and Approaches*, Sterling Publishers (Pvt) Ltd, New Delhi, 1979.
11. Planning Commission, Govt. of India, 'Report of the Working Group on District Planning, Vols. I and II, 1984.

12. Report of the Committee to review the existing administrative arrangements for Rural Development and Poverty Alleviation Programmes. (CAARD), Planning Commission and the Department of Rural Development, Ministry of Agriculture, Govt. of India, Dec. 1985.
13. For full details of the Karnataka Model, see Meenakshi Sundaram, S.S., *Decentralization in Developing Countries*, Concept Publishing Company, New Delhi, 1994.
14. Ramakrishna, Hegde, 'Local self-government in Karnataka : Planning from Below' in *Decentralized Planning and Panchayati Raj* (Proceedings of the D.T. Lakdawala Memorial Symposium), Institute of Social Sciences, Concept Publishing Company, New Delhi, 1994.
15. This account of West Bengal model is based on two published papers : (i) Ashim Das Gupta : 'Panchayati Raj and Decentralized Planning in West Bengal in *Decentralized Planning and Panchayati Raj*. (Proceedings of the D.T. Lakdawala Memorial Symposium), Institute of Social Sciences, New Delhi, published by Concept Publishing Company, New Delhi,1994; (ii) Arun Ghosh, "Decentralized Planning, West Bengal Experience", *Economic and Political Weekly*, March 26, 1988.
16. Das Gupta, Ashin, *Ibid*.
17. Ghosh, Arum, *Ibid*.
18. Eighth Five Year Plan (1992-93), Government of India, Planning Commission, July 1992. Preface, p. (iii).

18A. Report of NDC Committee on 'Microlevel Planning and involvement of people at grassroot level, Planning Commission, New Delhi, April 1993.

19. Hegde, Ramakrishna, Local Self-Government in Karnataka : Planning from below', *Ibid*.
20. Sundaram, K.V. and Palanidurai, K.V., 'The Challenge and Response to Decentralization—The Indian experience, an overview', in *Decentralization : Area Development in Practice in Asia*, Harvey Demaine and R.E. Malong (Eds.), Asian Institute of Technology, Bangkok and Institute of Social Studies, The Hague, 1987.
21. Ghosh, Arun, 'Decentralized Planning : West Bengal Experience', *Ibid*.
22. 'Human Development Report 1993' UNDP Published by Oxford University Press, Bombay, 1993, p. 74.
23. Dantwala, M.L., "Two-way Planning : Logic and Limitations—A critical review of Indian Experience", paper to Expert consultation on Multilevel Planning and the two way process in Agriculture and Rural Development Planning held at Bangkok 1-4 February 1983, F.A.O. Regional Office for Asia and the Pacific, Bangkok, May 1983.
24. Mukherjee, Amitava, *Methodology and Data Base for Decentralized Planning* (with special reference to District Planning in India), Vols. I to III, Heritage Publishers, New Delhi 1991.
25. Arun, Sinha, 'Methodology of Operationalizing District level plans' (mimeographed).
26. Srivastava, K.B., "Impact of Decentralization on Rural Poverty in India", Paper presented at the Expert Consultation on "Impact of Decentralization on Rural Poverty (Asia)" held at Bangkok 17-20 September 1991, sponsored by Centre on Integrated Rural Development for Asia and the Pacific and Division of Human Settlements Development, Asian Institute of Technology.

27. Srivastava, K.B., *Ibid.*
28. Srivastava, K.B., *Ibid.*
29. Srivastava, K.B., *Ibid.*
30. Srivastava, K.B., *Ibid.*
31. For a good historical analysis on Decentralization in Nepal, see Bhoj Raj Ghimire, *Decentralization, A Historical Analysis* in *Planning with People—Decentralization in Nepal* Sant B. Gurung and Prodipto Roy (Eds). Orient Longman, 1988. Also S.D. Pant, *Aspect of Decentralization in Nepal*, Research Centre for South Asia, 1989.
32. Yadav, R.P. and M.P. Kafle, 'Development Planning in Nepal', Paper to the Expert Group Meeting of Development Planning at District Level, Kathmandu, Nepal, Oct. 24-Nov. 1, 1980. (mimeographed)
33. Amatya, S.L., *Rural Development through Decentralized Planning*, East-West Centre Association, Honolulu, March 1988.
34. Materne Maetz, Nepal, Case study in 'Training for Decentralized planning—lesson from experience, Food and Agriculture Organization of the United Nations, Rome, 1987.
35. "Toward Improved Multilevel Planning for Agricultural and Rural Development in Asia and the Pacific" FAO, Economic and Social Development Paper 52, Rome, 1985.
36. Amatya, S.L., *Ibid.*
37. Shrestha, Bihari K., "Decentralization, Basic Needs and the Makings of a responsive bureaucracy in Nepal", *Administration and Management Review*, Vol. No. 1, December 1987.
38. For full details about the Training Manual and Courses of Training organized in Nepal, see 'In-service Training for Decentralized Planning at District level : Content, Techniques, Analytical Tools and Curriculum Building : Experience of Nepal—Chapter 19 in this book.
39. Upadhyay, Shrikrishna, 'Implementing the Decentralization Strategy in Nepal. (Mimeographed)
40. Calavan, Michael M., 'Local Government and Central Bureaucracy : A crucial nexus in Democratic Nepal' (Mimeographed).
41. Shrestha, Raj Krishna, "Impact of Decentralization on Rural Poverty in Nepal"—Paper presented to the Expert Consultation held at AIT, Bangkok 17-20 September 1991. Jointly Sponsored by Centre on Integrated Rural Development for Asia and the Pacific and Division of Human Settlements Development, Asian Institute of Technology.

ANNEXURE-I

INDICATORS AND WEIGHTAGES FOR DISTRIBUTION OF PLAN OUTLAY IN THE KARNATAKA MODEL

A. For Zilla Parishads

Indicators	Weights (%)
1. Population	50
2. Backwardness in agriculture as measured by the value of agricultural output per hectare	5
3. Backwardness in Irrigation as measured by the proportion of Irrigated Area to Net Area Sown	7
4. Backwardness as measured by the value of Industrial Output.	5
5. Backwardness in Communications as measured by Road and Railway mileage per 100 sq.km. and per lakh of population	5
6. Backwardness in Financial infrastructure as measured by size of population served by each commercial and cooperative bank.	2
7. Backwardness in Medical and Health Facilities as measured by the number of hospitals per 1000 population/bed population ratio.	5
8. Backwardness in Power Supply as measured by the proportion of villages electrified	5
9. Problems of the Weaker Sections :	
(a) as measured by the proportion of SCs/STs in the population	2
(b) as measured by the proportion of landless agricultural labourers	2
10. Special Problems of Malnad areas and Drought Prone Areas :	
(a) as measured by the area under forest :	2
(b) as measured by the rural population of Drought Prone Areas.	2
11. Literacy Percentage	5
12. Performance in Family Planning Programme	3
Total	100

B. Criteria for Determining the Share of the Mandal Panchayats within the Zilla Parishads

	Indicators	Weights (%)
1.	Population	50
2.	Area of Mandal	15
3.	Dryland Area	15
4.	Agricultural Labour Population	10
5.	Per Capita Resources Raised	10

Note: A 10 per cent weightage to resources raised by Mandals was given keeping in view the need to encourage Mandals who perform better in mobilizing the resources. A similar incentive was not provided for Zilla Parishads, since they did not have taxation powers.

ANNEXURE-II

SALIENT FEATURES OF THE CONSTITUTION (SEVENTY-THIRD) AMENDMENT ACT, 1993

Until this Constitution amendment was made, the formation, structure, composition, power and functions, periodicity of elections and such matters regarding Panchayats were entirely the responsibility of the States (Legislature and Government). With the coming into effect of the Constitutional Amendment, the legislative and executive action of the State legislatures and governments as regards Panchayats will have to be in accordance with the provision of Part IX of the Constitution. The features of Part IX of the Constitution are :

Structure of Panchayati Raj

(1) Except in specified tribal and hilly areas, there shall be in all States and Union Territories, Panchayats (by whatever name called)

(a) At the Village and District levels in the case of States/Union Territories with a population not exceeding twenty lakhs; and
(b) At the Village, Intermediate and District levels in all other States/ Union Territories. The jurisdiction of the Village, Intermediate (Block, Mandal, Taluk, etc.) and District level is to be determined by the State Government/Union Territory administration concerned.

(2) *Composition*

State will provide by law for :

(a) Direct election of Panchayats at each level;
(b) Representation of Chairperson and of Village Panchayats in the intermediate or district Panchayat, as the case may be;
(c) Representation of the Chairpersons of village or Intermediate levels at the District level, as the case may be;
(d) Representation of MPs, MLCs as provided in Part IX;
(e) All members of Panchayats, directly elected or otherwise will have a right to vote in the meetings;
(f) The election of Chairperson of Panchayat at Village level either by direct election or from among members;
(g) The election of Chairperson of Panchayats at the intermediate or district level only from among the elected members;

(h) Reservation of seats for Scheduled Castes and Scheduled Tribes in proportion to population and not less than one-third of seats for women; reservation of posts of Chairperson in proportion to population of SC/ST in the State;
(i) Reservation of not less than one-third of the elected seats in each Panchayat (District, intermediate or Village) for women; reservation of not less than one-third the number of Chairpersons at each level; and
(j) Rotation of reservation for women.

(3) *Duration*

Five years from the date of first meeting, unless sooner dissolved as provided by the law of the State; if dissolved sooner, elections shall be held within six months.

(4) *Powers and Functions*

Legislature of a State to endow powers and authority to Panchayats to enable them to function as institutions of self-government and include powers to prepare and implement plans for economic development and social justice; undertake implementation of schemes entrusted to them by State/Central Governments; and exercise powers as delegated in subjects listed in the Eleventh Schedule.

(5) *Finances*

(a) The law by the State will provide for (i) levy of taxes, duties and fees, (ii) allocation of taxes, etc., and (iii) grants to the Panchayats.
(b) Once in five years, a State Finance Commission will be appointed by the Governor, as provided in Part IX.

(6) *Elections*

There shall be a State Election Commission which will be responsible for preparation of electoral rolls and holding of elections to Panchayats.

(7) *Continuance of Existing Laws and Panchayats*

(a) The existing laws on panchayats can be in force only for a maximum of one year, that is, up to 21 April, 1994;
(b) The Panchayats existing before 21 April, 1993 may, however, continue until the expiry of their term, unless sooner dissolved by a Resolution of the Legislature.

14

DECENTRALIZATION
African Experiences

Africa presents a picture of great complexity and confusion. The countries within it are currently in a vortex of change. The old order is changing and the governments in many countries are inventing and re-inventing institutions for organizing development efforts at various levels. The kind of experiences which many Asian countries underwent immediately after their independence are probably being repeated here. As regards multi-level planning, Kenya, Nigeria, Tanzania, Zambia, Zimbabwe, Ghana and Uganda are some countries in which decentralization as a policy objective has been tried with varying commitments and mixed results. More recently, the debt crisis and IMF prescriptions have forced the adoption of increasingly market-oriented policies. The Sub-Saharan African countries are particularly struggling with decen-tralization problems. For many of them, to decentralize or not, and if so, by how much is the question. For a non-African, it is arrogant to pretend that the problems have been understood. The problems in each country are remarkably individualistic and varied. The author has attempted to draw a picture of the decentralization trends in Ghana and Uganda in Sub-Saharan Africa, which are undergoing vital transformations. But the situation is volatile and dynamic, and even as the ink dries, changes are happening. But one thing is clear. There is an urge for decentralization. But of what kind and at what pace are the crucial questions.

1. GHANA*

Ghana (Area : 239,000 km^2 and population 14.0 million, 1989) is one of the most widely discussed African countries in the context of the imple-

* This case study of Ghana's decentralization policies was undertaken by the author during November' 91—January' 92 as FAO consultant. See 'Decentralization of Agriculture Sector Planning in Sub-Saharan Africa', by this author, (FAO, Rome.)

mentation of structural adjustment programmes. With population increasing at 3.1 per cent per annum, its population distribution is uneven with an average population density 62 km^2, but locally, the density exceeds 400 km^2. The cultivated area is about 14 per cent, but as large parts of the remaining area are either within the bush fallow cropping cycle or are unsuitable for cultivation, the area available for expansion is limited.

Ghana has a potentially rich agricultural base, which offers employment to about 55 per cent of the active national labour force. Women constitute a significant component of the labour force, accounting for about 70 per cent of the total food production. The agriculture sector is the major foreign exchange earner for the country, contributing over 72 per cent of the total foreign exchange per annum. The bulk of this is accounted for by cocoa, which is the chief export crop. Agriculture accounts for more than 45 per cent of the GDP.

At its time of independence in 1957, Ghana was one of the richer countries of Sub-Saharan Africa (SSA). Soon after independence, the Government of Ghana introduced substantial economic and institutional reforms to reshape the economy. However, these efforts were frustrated by the persistent deterioration in the International Terms of Trade and later, by the oil-induced external shocks to the economy. Since the latter half of the 1960's and 1970's, the Ghanaian economy was caught in the grip of a downward spiral, exacerbated by high and accelerating inflation and growing external structural imbalances. GNP per capita in the late 1980's was in real terms much the same as in 1950. Real per capita GDP, indexed at 100 in 1950, rose to a peak of 194 in 1962, but had fallen to a low of 86 for 1983, recovering since then. Per capita income declined by over 2 per cent per annum during the 1970's and 1980's. Recurring political problems, internal economic mismanagement and declining external conditions (particularly in the price of cocoa) all contributed to a massive economic collapse.

The government initiated in April, 1983, a series of major economic policy reforms and a package of structural adjustment measures, called "Economic Recovery Programme", that were intended to reduce inflationary pressures on the economy and reverse the declining trends in its key productive sectors. This Economic Recovery Programme (ERP)—the first phase being in 1983-86 and the second phase in 1986-1988—led to considerable macro-economic progress. The GDP has increased 6 per cent per annum; inflation fell to 25 per cent per annum; and the public sector increased its share of GDP from 1 per cent to 8.3 per cent. Notwithstanding these developments, according to World Bank assessment, with the poverty line based on per capita income of US $370 per annum, 60 per cent of the population is poor. Other indicators are just as worrisome. Life expectancy is only 54 years; infant mortality is 77 deaths per 1,000 births; the poorest are 30 per cent of the house-holds; and school enrolment for children of age 6 to 10 is only 57 per cent (World Bank, 1990). Although much has been accomplished since 1983 the considerable decline that characterized the 1970's is yet to be turned around.

Administrative Structure

Ghana has a multilevel administrative structure. Below the national level, the country is divided into 10 regions and 110 districts. Below the districts, councils/towns/unit committees are constituted. The districts are small with an average population of about 100,000 people.

At the national level, the supreme political body is the Provisional National Defence Council (PNDC). The Government of Ghana is organized into sectorial and general purpose ministries and supporting technical departments. A National Development Planning Commission (NDPC) has been constituted, but is not fully empowered. The result is that there is weak central coordination of planning activities. At the regional level, there is no political body. However, the Central Government departments are present in the regions. Although the region is supposed to be a coordinating tier, horizontal coordination is not effective for various reasons. Under the Local Government Act 1988, District Assemblies have been constituted. The District Secretary is the government appointed chief executive and political head of the district. The Central Government ministries and departments have line branches in districts to implement sectorial policies and programmes. They carry out programmes and plans determined at their headquarters. They, therefore, are not involved in the planning aspects, but are more involved in managing existing services and reporting to central headquarters. Only a few ministries and Central Government departments have a branch in every district. Some of them operate in spatial units, which are not co-terminous with statutory administrative districts (Ministry of Health, Department of Feeder Roads). There are others, which have not established district branches and, therefore, operate in the district from the level of the administrative region. Some of these ministries are now establishing district branches. Table 14.1 shows the institutional structure for decentralized planning and management.

TABLE 14.1 : Ghana : Institutional Structure for Decentralized Planning and Management

	Territorial Unit	Head of government	Planning entity	Political bodies	Administrative/ autonomous agencies	
National level	Country	Head of National Defence Council (Chairman)	National Development Planning Commission and the Ministry of Finance and Economic Planning	Provisional National Defence Council (PNDC)	Central Ministries National sectorial agencies/ Corporations	Special progra-mmes and projects
Regional level	Region	Regional Secretary	Regional Planning Coordinating units	Regional Coordinating Councils	Central government departments	
District level	District	District secretary	District Planning and Budgeting Unit	District Assembly	District administration	
Local level	Town/Area Councils/Unit Committees	Council Chairman		Local Council	Local Administration	

Planning Framework and Plans at National Level

In the mid-1980s, as Ghana began to stabilize its economy and it became necessary to think beyond "crisis management" in terms of a longer term direction for development policy, certain initiatives were made to design and establish a planning system.

National Development Planning Commission

A National Development Planning Commission was established under a law in 1989, which has been signed, but till January, 1992 (the time of this study) was not gazetted. Failure to gazette the law has naturally raised some doubts about the nature and extent of government commitment to planning. It has also slowed down the operationalization of a planning process in the country, which has also led to much confusion in establishing decentralized planning procedures. The Commission is envisaged to have a full-time chairman, who will be a member of PNDC. The Commission will also have a Secretary, five full-time Commissioners, seven part-time Commissioners and some Secretaries of State appointed by PNDC.

It is expected to have, besides the office of the chairman, five technical divisions each under a full-time commissioner. These are :

(i) An Economic Policy Division;
(ii) A Production Policy Division;
(iii) A Social Policy Division;
(iv) A Spatial Organization Policy Division; and
(v) A General Services Division.

As it existed in 1992, the commission had only a few professionals and limited activities. It was under an acting chairman and had none of its full-time commissioners in position. With only partial staffing in position, it had not fully and effectively taken on the planning functions. Part of this function still resides in the Ministry of Finance and Economic Planning. So far, the Commission has only undertaken an exercise for the "national goal-setting" and has not yet embarked on the perspective planning exercise.

At present (1992), the planning functions are divided among the Ministry of Finance and Economic Planning (MFEP) and the National Development Planning Commission. Ultimately, the latter is expected to take over all the planning functions. The planning process has not been effectively operationalized. No clear-cut division of the scope, content and responsibilities for planning at various levels has, so far, emerged. Similarly, training of staff in planning for various territorial levels has not yet been systematically established. Most of the imperfections here are a result of the delay in the establishment of a full-fledged Planning Commission and the operationalization of a time-bound two-way process of planning for the preparation of annual/five year/perspective plans.

Public Administration Restructuring and Decentralization Implementation Committee (PARDIC)

As a measure towards working out proposals for the restructuring of public administration towards decentralization and implementing such proposals with speed and vigour, a committee known as the Public Administration Restructuring and Decentralization Implementation Committee (PARDIC) was created in 1983, with the following functions :

(a) Working out the modalities for the nationwide implementation of the ministerial restructuring and decentralization programme;
(b) Assisting in the actual implementation of the programme;
(c) Arranging public education back-up for the programme; and
(d) Coordinating information on all restructuring exercises aimed at improving the performance of the public administration system.

The PARDIC has not been able to achieve all that it was charged with. However, in the several years it has been functioning, only one Ministry (Ministry of Health) is reported to have made some significant advances towards operating on the basis of the proposed new structure. As a result of PARDIC's work, ministries now have policy planning units and/or project monitoring units. But these have not transformed the role of the ministries from implementing agencies to pure policy-making and reviewing organizations, a change which PARDIC wanted to bring about. As an evaluation has put it, PARDIC's influence has so far been limited to thoughts about and not action on true restructuring exercise, although it is a fact that PARDIC has operationalized the decision of PNDC to restructure and decentralize national administration in far more concrete terms than any of its predecessors.

Planning Framework and Plans at Subnational Levels

Regional Level

At the regional level, Regional Coordinating Councils (RCC) and Regional Planning Coordinating Units have been set up under the Local Government Law 1988 (PNDC 207). The RCCs have been given the task of harmonizing District Plans at the regional level; but they have not been tasked with the responsibility for preparing coherent regional policies and strategies. There is a deliberate attempt to play down the role of the region in planning and decision-making, probably because the dominant concern is the desire to directly encourage local-level bodies and to secure genuine grassroots participation.

The Regional Coordinating Councils are expected to monitor, coordinate and evaluate the functions of the District Assemblies in the region. In their composition, they consist of a Regional Secretary (a political appointee), all District Secretaries in the Region and all Presiding Members of the District Assemblies in the Region as members. They have been entrusted with a whole range of planning and management functions—allocating resources, formulating programmes and projects, coordinating, monitoring and reviewing and harmonizing district plans, which certainly mean considerable responsibilities at this level. However, all these functions are not being performed. There is usually a Regional Economic Planning Officer under the Regional Secretary, who does not have enough supporting technical staff under him to assist him in the planning tasks. He, therefore, performs only functions, which are limited to monitoring the implementation of programmes and projects and processing tenders for the award of contracts, for which limited powers have been conferred on the Regional Secretary. The task of harmonizing district plans is accomplished in a very perfunctory manner. The plans are only examined for their consistency with Regional policies/strategies, which, in any case, are not being formulated in any systematic manner.

Thus, despite the presence of a coordinating mechanism in the form of a Regional Coordinating Council with a Regional Secretary and Regional Economic Planning Officer in position, this mechanism is not able to perform the functions expected of it. The reasons are partly structural and partly procedural, among which the absence of financial delegation must be particularly mentioned.

District Level

Under the Planning Law, the District Planning authorities have been set up which are expected to prepare District Development Plans with full participation of the local communities. The district planning authorities are to feed the Planning Commission with the required data and information under a prescribed format. However, the planning exercise at the district level has not yet started. This is largely due to the lack of skilled personnel, which such an effort demands and which is not immediately available, even if funds and salaries, enough to attract them, could be made available. The Ministry of Local Government has the responsibility for building the planning capability at the district level. In view of severe resource constraints, Mobile Planning Teams were created nominally to support the district administration in carrying out their planning functions. However, this measure does not appear to have had much impact. This is probably because the staff of the mobile teams do not have the necessary training and experience in planning. Moreover, the procedural tasks associated with planning have not yet been worked out and operationalized. It is understood that the NDPC has undertaken a programme of training for the district-level staff. However, since the structure and process for planning are not yet fully established, the training that is currently imparted to the staff of the mobile teams is rather more in the nature of a general orientation to planning techniques, rather than training in well-worked out procedural tasks.

In some districts, it is understood that District Development Planning and Budgeting Units have been created. They seem to be only engaged in collection of data and performing some monitoring functions. Under the law, they are expected to prepare a district plan and to function as the Secretariat for the District Executive Committee.

Attempts are being made to introduce what is known as "composite budgeting" in the districts, i.e. each district will be given a total sum to be allocated within certain limits to the various sectors, over which it exercises responsibility. This will replace the strictly sectorial budgeting that has hitherto been the practice for releasing funds to sub-national-level administrations.

The preparation of such a budget is still in its infancy. For the 1991 fiscal year, the Ministry of Finance and Economic Planning had issued some general guidelines for the preparation of "composite budgets" at the district and regional levels. These guidelines required that the budget items normally funded from central government sources should be distinguished from the recurrent and development budgets to be funded from District Assemblies' own general revenues. In this way, the district budget is being sought to be synchronized with the national budget.

The district revenue consists of house tax, entertainments duty, tax on certain professions, crop levy, market fees and licence fees.

In addition to the revenues, which a district may mobilize from its own resources, the Government also provides some "untied" development funds, called "ceded revenue", which can be used by the district within the framework of certain general guidelines. The Ministry of Local Government follows some scientific criteria for the allocation of the ceded revenue. In this method, equality, population and development status of the districts have been given weights. A certain proportion of the funds is divided among the districts on an equal-sharing basis, which is decided from year to year, based on the total quantum of development funds available. The remaining funds are shared by taking population and development status into account in the proportion of 3:2. The criterion of development status is related to deprivation or backwardness. For example, the presence of settlements qualifying as towns is regarded as an indicator of "developedness". Using such "rule-of-the-thumb" methods, the level of backwardness of the districts is measured. The ceded revenue allocation to individual districts (in 1990) varied from cedi 8 million to 20 million. According to the guidelines provided by the Ministry of Local Government, the ceded revenue may be utilized for undertaking the following kinds of development works :

(a) income-generating activities;
(b) rehabilitation of markets;
(c) sanitation programmes;
(d) construction of drains; and
(e) construction of schools, etc.

In order to enhance the ceded revenue, the Government has set up a committee to study and report on sharing of more revenue to local authorities.

The districts face a number of problems such as inadequate housing, transportation and office accommodation. To solve these problems, the government provides some Specific Purpose Grants under a District Resource Programme. These funds are provided against specific programmes, such as construction of offices, residences for government staff, purchase of vehicle and office equipment. It is understood that the funds provided by the Government are inadequate. But active local governments with the assistance of non-governmental organizations and benevolent societies can make up for the shortfall through their own efforts.

Overall (multi-sectorial) Decentralization Efforts

There seems to be enough political will in Ghana to decentralize the administration. This is apparent from at least two policy-level initiatives. One is in the context of preparing a draft constitution for the country, for which the Government has appointed a Committee of Experts. In its mandate to this Committee, it is stated that the proposals "should provide for a decentralized system of national administration based on a non-partisan District Assembly system, with development as its objective and including revenue-sharing clauses". In another initiative made in 1983, the Government established a committee known as the Public Administration Restructuring and Decentralization Implementation Committee (PARDIC), whose achievements were referred to earlier.

Institutional Mechanisms

Under the government's decentralization programme, District Assemblies have been constituted under Local Government Law (PNDC 207), 1988. The District Assembly (a body consisting of 40 to 70 persons or even more) functions as the highest political authority in the district.

A district Assembly consists of :

(a) The District Secretary;
(b) Two-thirds elected members; and
(c) One-third of the total membership of the Assembly appointed by the Provisional National Defence Council.

The key person is the District Secretary, who is appointed by the Provisional National Defence Council and who has been entrusted with the task of the day-to-day supervision of the departments and organizations in the districts. Thus, through the District Secretaries, the Government has got directly involved in the politics of local administration in order to give political direction at the district level.

The executive functions of the district assembly are carried out by an Executive Committee, which is presided over by the District Secretary and which has a total membership of not more than one-third of the total number of the members of the assembly, elected from among themselves. Thus, the key figure in the district administration is the District Secretary. However, the District Assembly also elects from among its own members a Presiding Member, who holds office for a term of one year. (The term of the elected assembly is three years.) The Presiding Member is not a member of the Executive Committee. He only conducts the meeting of the District Assembly and functions like a Speaker. Under the Local Development Law, the District Assemblies have been given deliberative, legislative and executive functions, which empower them with a certain autonomy in local affairs. On the development front, the District Assembly has been given the functions of coordinating, inte-grating and harmonizing the execution of programmes and projects and approve development plans for the districts and other development programmes promoted or carried out by Ministries, Departments, Public Corporations and other statutory bodies in the district.

Under the Executive Committee, five sub-committees are constituted as follows :

(a) Economic Development Sub-committee;
(b) Social Service Sub-committee;
(c) Technical Infrastructure Sub-committee;
(d) Justice and Security Sub-committee; and
(e) Finance and Administration Sub-committee.

Each member of the District Assembly has to serve on at least one of the sub-committees.

Notwithstanding the various institutional mechanisms that have been created, and the passing of a legislation with some clearly laid down procedures, the District Assemblies, as now operating, are not fully decentralized bodies. They are still evolving and passing through a transitional stage in their development.

Participation

In the way the local government and decentralization have been interpreted in Ghana, they are meant only to operate development schemes through District Assemblies supervised by the political party at the centre. Institutional arrangements, other than the elected assemblies, have not been sufficiently encouraged to become involved in the planning process and development at the local level.

In the social and cultural life of Ghana, the traditional authorities called "chieftaincy" continue to exist, albeit with different degrees of powers. The chief continues to command the traditional loyalty of most Ghanaians, particularly in the rural areas. They can no doubt play some role in the districts, by way of offering their counsel and mobilizing and inspiring the community in the execution of development programmes. They do not seem to have been given any active role at the level of the local governments established under the PNDC Law. In this respect, much can be achieved, if traditional institutions can be developed to achieve development objectives within a framework of local self-organization. In fact, people's participation has to be secured through various modes—through people's representative leaders from the village council to the Parliament, voluntary organizations, advisory bodies, consultative committees, user groups at the village level, farmers' forum, youth clubs, women's club, etc. Viewed in this light, decentralization and widespread people's participation is still an article of faith in Ghana. Nothing much tangible has, as yet, been achieved by way of mustering the people's organizations.

Overall (multi-sectoral) Decentralized Planning : Problems and Prospects

The Ministry of Local Government in Ghana has done quite a bit towards laying down the groundwork for a decentralized democratic system. Still, it has to go a long way in making decentralization functional. A partially decentralized non-integrated public administration system has emerged. However, the linkages expected between ministerial and sub-national organizations have not been established. Establishment of full-fledged planning teams at the regional and local levels has not taken place. What is in place now is partial with Mobile Planning Teams trying to bridge the gap; but it has not made much impact. The District Planning and budgeting units have been established, only in a few districts. They are yet to be linked to the national planning process. Even where they have been established, they exist only in name. Their planning functions are almost nil. They manage to put together a District Budget and forward the same to the Regional Co-ordinating Councils. The Composite Budget System of linking district budgets to the national budget is yet to be perfected. The districts do not have adequate financial resources. The Ministry of Local Government provides some specific-purpose grants under their "District Resource Programme". But it does not contain an incentive element to stimulate local contributions. On the organizational structure side, some anomalies exist. The District Secretary who is a political appointee is the Chairman of the Executive Committee, while an elected member is the President of the District Assembly. Traditional Authorities (Chieftaincy) have not been recognized and assigned any specific role in participatory development at the sub-national levels. The appointment of district planning staff has proceeded without proper training to them and provision of parallel logistic support and establishment of a bottom-up planning process. This has led to manpower wastage. In the decentralization effected under the Local Government law 1988 (First Schedule), 22 departments and organizations have been brought under the District Assemblies. As it has happened till now, not all of them are actually represented in each of the 110 districts. At the staff level, the "dual control" problem still persists. Effective and healthy procedures in this regard have not been evolved so far. Thus the desired integration of the line agencies as active inputting departments to the District Assembly and the District Plan and accountable to the district assembly for their performance has not emerged as a reality.

The region, as a coordinating tier, functions in a vacuum of authority and a clearly defined planning process. The Regional Planning Officer has no mandate to prepare a regional plan. His functions are limited to the processing of tenders for award of contracts and the monitoring and implementation of programmes and projects. The Regional Coordinating Council is unable to perform its function as an effective regional coordinating mechanism. Thus there are many mismatches, gaps and lags in the decentralization experiment that is under way. Many of the legal provisions seem to be in order. But much will depend on practice and how the decentralized programme evolves, rather than on statutory powers and responsibilities.

Status of Decentralization : A Summing-up

To sum up, Ghana is going through a period of "transition" with a new constitution in the making, with some administrative reforms in the offing and with many developments in the "melting pot" and full of uncertainties.

Decentralization became an important policy objective of the country during the 1980s, particularly after the PNDC established the Public Administration Restructuring Decentralization Implementation Committee (PARDIC) in 1983, charged among other tasks with working out the modalities for the nationwide implementation of the ministerial restructuring and decentralization programme.

Administrative Decentralization has made some headway in the important ministries. For example, the Ministry of Agriculture has all the major structural elements that are necessary for a territorial framework for operating a decentralized administrative and technical system in the agricultural sector. There are, however, notable gaps, particularly by way of participatory structures, which will become more apparent, when one puts the planning needs in a democratic decentralization context. But even in the sectoral departments, where some formal structures exist down to sub-national levels, these have not started contributing to innovate, coordinate and stimulate development activities at the various levels through an effective two-way planning process. Delegation of functions and powers to the lower levels is not adequate. Financial decentralization has not really taken off. Many issues in decentralization need to be attended to in a more systematic manner.

2. UGANDA*

Uganda (Area : 24 million ha. and population 16 million, 1989 growing at 2.5 per cent a year according to the provisional results for the 1991 Population Census) is a landlocked country in East Africa, noted for its natural beauty and promise of economic development. It used to be known as the "Pearl of Africa". The agricultural sector is critical to its economy, providing food, fibre and gainful employment for about 80 per cent of the total population. Of the country's land area of 24 million ha., 4 million ha are under arable crops, 1.5 million ha under permanent crops, 5 million ha under pasture and grazing land and 6.5 million ha under forests and the balance in lakes, swamps and rocky mountains. On the average, agriculture accounts for over 60 per cent of GDP and claims approximately 98 per cent of the export earnings and over 40 per cent of government revenue. The agricultural income is wholly generated by about 2.2 million small-scale producers, farming an average of 2 to 3 hectares. According to a survey conducted by UNICEF in 1988, 97 per cent of women in Uganda are engaged in crop production and contribute to the bulk of farm labour.

The Ugandan economy has undergone massive structural shifts in the past two decades. GDP figures supplemented by other indicators give us a preliminary picture of the major economic trends between the mid 1960's and the early 1980's. According to Gulhati,[6] the annual average percentage growth of GDP (1980 prices) was +3.9 per cent during 1967-73. It was exactly the reverse i.e. (-)3.6 per cent during 1965-73 and (-)2.3 per cent during 1973-80. For manufacturing value added the corresponding figures for the same time period are : +4.0 per cent and (-) 12.4 per cent respectively. These figures show the glaring economic setbacks experienced by the country as a result of political instabilities and civil unrest. According to Vali Jamal,[7] 'Economic Collapse' would certainly not be too strong a term for the catastrophe that hit Uganda in the 1970s.

Uganda adopted intensive reforms in the early 1980s, after almost a decade of protracted economic decline. In December 1980, Idi Amin was ousted and President Milton Obote took over as the head of the Uganda People's Congress. The new government, however, did not have a decisive civilian control over the army, and there was considerable

---

* This case study of Uganda's Decentralization policies was undertaken by the author during May-July 1991 as FAO consultant. See 'Decentralization of Agriculture Sector Planning in Sub-Saharan Africa' by this author. (FAO, Rome.)

insecurity. In this extremely fragile situation, economic reforms were launched in Uganda on the premise that economic recovery would lead to political improvements and a reduction of insecurity. Stiff stabilization and structural adjustment measures were adopted, but the policy reforms did not pay off. The reform effort was derailed toward the end of 1984. Meanwhile, the security situation worsened and elections approached. There was a military coup in July, 1985 followed by a civil war. The new Museveni Government, after considerable vascillation regarding the adoption of the prescriptions of the International Monetary Fund (IMF) and the World Bank, finally resumed relations with the IMF in 1987. The National Resistance Movement (NRM) government of President Museveni is firmly in saddle since 1986 and several progressive reforms are now under way. The country's economy is now picking up.[8]

The overall economic objective of the government is contained in the NRM Ten Points Programme, which is to build an independent, integrated and self-sustaining economy. This is to bring about structural changes involving movement away from subsistence agriculture to a more productive and diversified economic base, which would ensure food security to the population, establishment of agro-based industries to upgrade and diversify exports, and other import-substitution industries to manufacture basic consumer goods and simple capital goods. The economic objectives are operationalized in the Rehabilitation and Development Plan, initially covering the period 1987/89—1990/91, but now extended to 1994, as a three-year rolling plan, guided by a policy framework paper, which sets out the macro-economic and sector policies.

Administrative Structure

Uganda's administrative structure is organized around 38 districts. These are further divided into counties (151), sub-counties (750), parishes (3500) and villages. There are 10 regions, which are only notional and do not have any legal significance. Some sectorial ministries have their regional offices in them. But these are being phased out.

The political system is based on the National Resistance Movement (NRM), which has delegated powers to a hierarchy of Resistance Councils and Committees. The apex of the system is the National Resistance Council (NRC), which is the Parliament, being the supreme law-making body (legislature) and final arbiter of national policy. Resistance committees have been established at village, parish, sub-county and county levels.

Planning Framework and Plans at National Level

The overall responsibility for planning in the country rests with the Ministry of Planning and Economic Development (MPED).[9] It has, within its office, planning units for various sectors of activity, which perform its major functions of formulation of development plans, co-ordinating project planning activities of the entire government system, including those of parastatals, assisting ministries and parastatals in the formulation of their annual development budgets and monitoring the implementation of plans and projects. Most sector ministries have their Ministerial Planning Units (MPUs), though their sizes in terms of professional officers vary widely. A National Planning Commission (NPC) had been established in 1963, under an Act, which, however, has not met since 1970. MPED was providing the Secretariat for the NPC. Many of the former functions of the Planning Commission are now being performed by a Presidential Economic Council (PEC), which, however, is a decision-making rather than advisory body. It is the most important forum for discussion of the major economic policy proposals prepared by MPED. MPED provides the Secretariat to PEC. All functions of government planning and statistics as well as the management of the common cadre of Economists and Statisticians are vested in the MPED.

The three core planning departments in the MPED are : Macro-economic and Regional Planning Department, Sectoral Planning Department and External Aid Coordination Department. These departments along with the Ministry of Finance, Bank of Uganda, Agricultural Secretariat and National Council for Science and Technology have major roles in the planning process operating in Uganda.

The current National Plan document for Uganda is the Rehabilitation and Development Plan, 1987/88—1990/91; this appeared in March, 1987, but had been in preparation even before the NRM government came to power. It had to be finally put together in a hurried and essentially adhoc way. It is in two volumes. Volume I deals with the past and present state of the economy, goals for socio-economic reconstruction and economic and social policies. Vol. II contains profiles of the 150 or so projects featured in the plan.

Planning procedures for a two-way process of planning have not yet emerged in an acceptable form. The roles of the different actors and the coordinating bodies have to be spelt out and a participatory procedure has to evolve. A Planning Manual has been prepared for the MPED, which is intended to help improve planning in Uganda.

Planning Framework and Overall (multi-sectoral) Decentralization Efforts at Sub-national Levels

In 1972, Uganda initiated and carried out a programme of administrative reorganization, which encompassed some elements of decentralization. This was done with the aim of facilitating access to administrative services to the rural population and to establish the basis for an improved spatial distribution of social and infrastructural facilities. The political motive was for creating more jobs for the governing team and meeting the long, historical and parochial struggles of various groups for autonomy. The territorial and administrative framework consisted of nine Provinces/Regions (in place of four), each under a Provincial Governor. Similarly, 33 districts (in place of 18) were carved out, each under a District Commissioner. The Provinces and Districts were characterized by remarkable disparities in the provision of administrative infrastructure, and before these could be bridged, the economy deteriorated leading to the perpetuation of these disparities. In regard to planning and development arrangement, Uganda had established, in 1968, District Planning Teams and Committees made up of sectorial departments for purposes of encouraging grassroot planning and bottom-up planning approaches, as well as strengthening and co-ordinating sectorial planning at the district level. These had no equivalents nor interfaces at the regional and national levels. These mechanisms existed in the old districts. But the new districts which were established failed to establish similar mechanisms. In regard to devolution and delegation of powers, these were minimal. Powers were essentially concentrated in the President first and his governors at the other levels. The so-called decentralization was merely to create jobs for the compatriots.

Thus in Uganda, although some form of decentralized planning seems to have been practised even during the 60's and 70's, it is only after 1986, with the formation of the NRM Government and the enactment of the Resistance Councils and Committees Statute 1987, that a greater degree of awareness of the need for local-resource-based and area-specific district planning has emerged. At present, although there is a commitment by government towards decentralized planning, the efforts made so far are fragmentary and a systematic operationalization of the concept is yet to take off. Two important steps taken towards decentralization till 1991 are :

(a) establishment of the District Development Committee; and
(b) introduction of common cadre staffing arrangements.

It is understood that "District Planning Committees" were in existence in the 60s and even earlier for well over 30 years; but they became dormant since the early 70s.

It is understood that the District Development Committees have been constituted in 33 out of 38 districts. They are still in an embryonic stage of functioning.

Under the common cadre staffing arrangements, one Economist/Planner and one Statistician are proposed to be posted to the districts. But till mid 1991 the arrangement had not effectively taken off.[10]

Some staff, who were posted to the districts came back because there was no office space, office equipment, furniture, etc., to provide them with a working environment. At present, when the planning process at the district level has not been clarified, the functions that they will perform, etc., are quite vague. Further, most of them are new recruits from the Universities. Before they are sent as responsible planners to the districts, they must be given adequate pre-service training. All these personnel problems have not been sorted out. Besides these two officers, who will be posted to the districts, there is also one officer designated as "Population Officer" in the eight districts covered by the UNFPA project.

The responsibility for handling sub-national (Regional and District level) activities is mainly with two ministries, viz.: the Ministry of Planning and Economic Development (MPED) and the Ministry of Local Government (MLG). Within MPED, there is a separate Department for Macro-economic and Regional Planning, which deals with the policy issues relating to Decentralized Planning. The role of the Ministry of Local Government (MLG) is stated to be one of implementation of the government's district and regional planning policies and the management of the Common Cadre of Economists posted to each district. But this ministry requires considerable strengthening to enable it to play the role expected of it.

The Resistance Councils and Committees Statute of 1987[11] has laid down the essential ingredients for decentralization at the district level. Under this legal dispensation, Resistance Councils, Resistance Committees and District Development Committees provide the decentralized institutional framework, within which the people are afforded the opportunity to participate in decision-making and monitoring of governmental activities. The Resistance Council (RC) has been described as a "policy-making organ" within its area of jurisdiction. The RC system, which penetrates through the various tiers of administration, is also deemed to function as the medium for participatory development.

The District Resistance Councils are elected bodies. In each Resistance Council, a Resistance Committee (which is really executive) has been established, with nine members with defined responsibilities and functions. A District Administrator, who is an appointee of the President, is the political head. Under him is established a District Development Committee (DDC), which is the development arm of the RC. The duties of DDC include *inter alia* the preparation of the district development plans and the scrutiny of department work plans and budgets, before they are submitted to the ministries concerned. The elected representative (RC 5 Chairman) is the Vice-Chairperson of this committee. According to the Statute, this committee consists of all district chiefs of various departments, the planning officer, and the finance officer along with representatives from the RCs. The Secretary of this committee is an official designated as the District Executive Secretary (DES) entrusted with co-ordinating, integrating and accounting functions. He is an employee of the Ministry of Local Government and supervises all government programmes. Although, the Statute governing the Resistance Councils and Committees contains many of the needed provisions for the establishment and functioning of more efficient, more responsive and more democratic local authorities, these have not been fully implemented.

Presently, the local activities are governed partly by the Resistance Councils and Committees (RCC) Statute of 1987 and partly by the Local Administration Act (LAA) 1967. This is because the RCC statute of 1987 repealed only Part 1 of the Local Administration Act of 1967. The remaining part of LAA 1967s, is still governing certain arrangements in the local government, e.g. some financial arrangements between the Central Government and districts. All these provisions are highly "centralistic" in nature. Thus, at present, some "liberal" as well as "centralistic" provisions exist side by side.

The District Administrator, who is the head of the district, is also the Chairman of the District Development Committee. The elected person (RC-5 Chairperson) is its Vice-Chairman. The District Resistance Committee is also chaired by the District Administrator and the RC-5 chairperson has no place in it.

As for staffing arrangements at the district level, a dual system prevails. The district-level functionaries from the line agencies of the government are not under the strict control and discipline of the district authorities. Their loyalty is mainly to their line ministries. The District Executive Secretary (DES), who works under the District Administrator is a key functionary in the system. He has to horizontally coordinate the functions of the other district heads, who are not strictly under his administrative control. The local-level structures and functions need considerable revamping to render them more conducive to a functionally efficient pattern of decentralized development.

The districts have now been given the functions of primary education, construction and maintenance of feeder roads, primary health care and maintenance of water supply. Most of these services, perhaps with the exception of primary education, do not seem to be delivered to a satisfactory standard. The reason is stated to be want of operating funds.

The major sources of revenue for the local authority are the graduated tax collections, a range of licence and permit fees and a block grant or subvention from Central Government. Among these, the graduated tax is the most important, contributing as much as 80 per cent of the revenue in some districts. (e.g. Mbarara). The Block Grant from the Central Government is a small amount. Even this amount does not come to the local authority regularly. It is often cut arbitrarily without prior consultation. Districts cannot plan firmly on the basis of anticipated block grants. The criteria for the allocation of grants-in-aid among the districts are also not clear.

Again, both in the disbursement of grants-in-aid and the channelling of funds through departmental budgets, there are bottlenecks. Even after the allocations are decided upon and provided for in the budget, there is no guarantee that the money will be available for incurring the expenditure. A true exchequer release system does not operate automatically. Although quarterly releases are implied, in practice, the sectorial ministries make payments in driblets from month to month, as the treasury does not have sufficient resources to meet the full requirements for each quarter. Also, in many cases, the amounts released bear little resemblance to what had been budgeted.

The expenditure pattern of the districts reveals that most of the available revenues are paid out in staff salaries, with only token allocation remaining for meeting the recurrent costs of the district's services. Capital expenditure has all but ceased. It is understood that in the 60's, there used to be a "Capital Development Fund" in the Ministry of Local Government from which the local authorities could borrow towards their capital expenditure. This does not exist now. Presently, an allocation of 3 per cent from the centre's development budget is devolved to the local authorities to support the decentralized programmes in primary education, primary health care, rural roads and water supply. This is a very small amount and hardly sufficient to meet the felt needs of local communities in these areas.

At present, the district budget prepared in each district is confined to the decentralized subjects only, and is implemented by the district administration. The flow of funds through the line departments for projects operating at the district level do not find a place in it. Hence it is difficult to obtain a full developmental picture of the district.

The decentralized system of district administration in Uganda has been in operation only for a short period (just three years). The process of change has just begun. Already some weaknesses in the system have surfaced. As the decentralized system takes root, these are likely to get exacerbated. Some of the weaknesses that may need to be addressed are : the problems of vertical and horizontal interface (between and within the bureaucracy and the political executive), clarity of functions falling within the orbit of the national and sub-national levels, personnel management issues, clarity on the processual aspect of democratic decentralization, specification of new financial arrangements between the centre and the district, etc.

Looking at the present state of art of decentralized district development in Uganda, a conclusion that is irresistible is that what has been achieved so far is only partial; the government's policy commitment to decentralization of power away from the centre has to go hand in hand with several other parallel measures of decentralization : some related to structures, some related to functions and finances, some related to personnel problems and perhaps most important of all, the institution of an overall planning process and laying down of proper administrative and interactional procedures.

Administrative Decentralization

In the sectorial ministries, administrative decentralization needs much to be desired. The important ministries have regional and district offices. But the delegation of functions and powers to these offices is quite limited.

Below the district level, the reach of the administration through extension staff varies. Planning is highly centralized. In some ministries, there is no separate planning department. It is clubbed with administration. There are also serious personnel constraints. Even sanctioned posts in many ministries and departments are not filled up, as technical personnel are not available.

Apart from the vacancy rates, the government wage levels are so abysmally low that moonlighting has become a routine. This apart, even the existing staff are hampered in their effective functioning, because of some serious inadequacies in the logistic support. For instance, lack of housing and transport facilities tend to make quite a number of extension personnel posted to sub-district level, stay in the District Headquarters and to operate downwards from there. Since they do not have transport vehicles, such services are very poorly performed.

There are also serious deficiencies in regard to other facilities like office accommodation, office equipment, tables, chairs, typewriters, etc. These problems have multiplied after the number of districts were increased from 16 to 38. Thus at the district level and below, there is an unfavourable working atmosphere, which encourages absenteeism and leads to poor productivity.

Sectoral Ministries and departments need considerable strengthening. Administrative decentralization has to be vigorously pursued by strengthening regional and district offices and establishing procedures for the two-way planning process to operate.

REFERENCES

1. UNDP, New York, July 1991, 'Evaluation of UNDP support to Planning Activities in Ghana'.
2. Eghan, B.C., Draft Consolidation Report on the work done by the Public Administration Restructuring and Decentralization Implementation Committee (PARDIC), March 1990.
3. Local Government Law, 1988 (PNDC 207).
4. Chapter 11 : Decentralization and Local Government, Expert Committee Report on a Draft Constitution for Ghana, 1991.
5. National Development Planning Law, 1989.
6. Gulhati, Ravi, "The Making of Economic Policy in Africa" EDI, Seminar Series, The World Bank, Washington D.C., 1990.
7. Vali, Jamal, 'Coping Under Crisis in Uganda', International Labour Organization, 1988.

8. A Report of the Ministry of Local Government Annual Consultative Assembly for 1988-1989, MLG Annual Conference held at Kyambogo, Itek, 8-12, Aug. 1988.
9. Report of the Public Service Review and Reorganization Commission 1989-1990, Vol I—Main Report, Ministry of Planning and Economic Development, Govt. of Uganda, Dec. 1988.
10. Planning on organization and administration of thc common cadre of economists and statisticians in the Uganda Civil Service, Ministry of Planning and Economic Development, UGA/87/1008, Sep.1989.
11. The Resistance Councils and Committees Act, 1987.

15

CRITICAL LESSONS

In recent years, many countries have felt an increasing need to pursue decentralization policies and programmes more seriously than in the past. They have reached this current phase of development after passing through a wide variety of experiences. From these experiences, we derive substantial insights and understanding of the performance and prospects for decentralization. Inevitably, the decentralization performance of each country was shaped by factors peculiar to its own political, social, institutional, cultural and behavioural characteristics as well as the macro-economic imperatives. Political considerations have, particularly, exerted their influence on the pattern and pace of decentralization. In spite of the fact that the countries are heterogeneous in their various characteristics and levels of development, there are some commonalities in the challenges faced and the problems encountered. Certain problems are indeed common to all.

The purpose of this chapter is to put together the empirical evidence that is emerging from the case studies along with other sources, and to highlight from particular experiences some challenges that have to be faced, while implementing new policy approaches towards decentralization and local governance and guided by such insights point to new directions for development planning. This involves both synthesis and prognosis based on case study experiences.

Highlights of Experiences

The substantive issues discussed in the case studies may be captured in three dimensions that are relevant to decentralization. These are : Structure, Process and Stage. We may elaborate these expressions a bit to convey their real meanings. Structure implies institutional configurations; of chief interest in our context are those related to planning, coordination and participation. They constitute a "cluster" of activities and how well these are performed in their institutional contexts, individually and collectively, depends on the effective linkages that operate among them. The term "process" refers not merely to the planning process operating—whether only top-down or a two-way process—but also the functional, financial and administrative aspects of deconcentration from the centre to the periphery, that determine the degree of success of the decentralization process. It also includes the interactional and iteration procedures that make the process dynamic. "Stage" refers to the net result in the operation of the "structure-process nexus" and is the sum total of achievements in a decentralized set-up. In other words, it constitutes a measurement of decentralization, which is an intrinsically variable process within an administrative system. The variables would be many, e.g. the number of functions decentralized, the range of decision areas assigned to local authorities, the extent of devolution of authority, the ratio of local government revenues to total revenues, the degree of financial independence of local authorities, the degree of responsibilities (delegation) assigned to field personnel, the degree of inter-departmental coordination achieved, the ratio of local government employees to employees of central agencies, etc. It cannot be an absolutely precise, quantitative exercise and value judgements will have to prevail.

In a nation's context, the structure, process and stage of decentralization have to be evaluated at all the three crucial levels, viz. National, Regional and Local (District and Sub-district). In what follows, we have not gone into the details of measurement. Our limited aim here is to obtain a bird's eye view of achievements and shortfalls, as well as the problems and constraints faced by these countries, while pursuing the path of decentralized development. Such an overview throws up many important lessons.

Among the four countries, India has had a longer history of experimentation with decentralization than the others, extending over a period of nearly half a century. But India's decentralization policy has followed different impulses and taken several routes. Although decentralized planning was advocated from the 50's, it was only in the late 60's that positive steps were taken by the Central Government to decentralize planning and development activities to the state level. The states started responding from the 70's. They had to first gear up their state planning machinery so as to be able to draw up the State Plans. The centre assisted the State Governments to strengthen their planning machinery, first at the state level and then at the district levels. Thus today the capabilities for planning have been built up to some extent both at the state and district levels in the country.

However, the progress towards decentralized district planning has not been uniform in the country. In a survey of the state of art conducted in 1982-83 by the Planning Commission (Working Group Report on District Planning), it was revealed that only six out of the 22 states in the country—Maharashtra, Gujarat, Karnataka, Uttar Pradesh, Jammu and Kashmir and West Bengal—had made some innovations in the field of District Planning. Decentralization initiatives always emerged from the centre in different forms through several centrally sponsored schemes, which were really an imposition from above, a kind of "top-down planning". Referring to the failure of the Panchayati Raj Institutions and the sluggish progress towards district planning in many states, critics have not been wanting to point out that decentralization in India did not spontaneously emerge from below, except in the case of a few isolated success stories at the micro-level. It may be noted that even the 73rd and 74th amendments of the Constitution, by which devolution has been sought to be extended below the state level, is interpreted in some quarters as the "pressure tactics" of the Central Government. Of course, there are other views about it. In a federal democracy of a vast country like India, the Centre's legitimate role is to push, advise, prod and pressurize in order to improve upon the performance of planning at the sub-national levels. Looked at from this perspective, whatever has been achieved till today in the states in relation to decentralized planning is due to the effective advisory role played by the centre in this direction. The catalyst role played by the Planning Commission through its Multilevel Planning Division during 1970-80 has been particularly commendable. The various efforts made, from the detailed guidelines issued for district-level planning in 1969 and subsequently in 1982, accompanied by the continuous efforts made to strengthen planning capabilities at the sub-national levels, have stimulated the district planning activities all over the country and have gradually pushed forward the frontiers of knowledge about district planning methodologies. Currently, much attention is being paid to improve the database for district planning by developing the District Information System by the National Informatics Centre. Similarly, in order to promote improved performance in district planning, a number of centrally-sponsored training programmes are being conducted by the apex training institutions in the country. Indeed, there is much to be learnt from India, about how a Central Government can guide, stimulate and strengthen the efforts aimed at decentralized planning at the sub-national levels.

The three major lessons that we learn from the Indian experience of decentralization in the various states are :

(i) Attention to certain essential prerequisites is basic, if a decentralization strategy/programme is to succeed. The Indian guidelines have identified eight major prerequisites. These include political and bureaucratic will, functional, financial and administrative decentralization, establishing organizational mechanisms, planning machinery and provision of technical assistance and training;

(ii) Decentralization has to be pursued "in stages" as a gradual incremental process; and

(iii) Decentralization policies must be consistently and continuously pursued without major shifts and set-backs.

In the Indian experience in some states, it was revealed that decentralization, after gaining initial momentum, showed tendencies "to reverse" or back-track, a phenomenon referred to as "pendulum effect". Even when powers and functions were initially given, something was held back for parallel implementation through competing agencies, creating situations of potential conflict.

In an overall assessment, however, it may be said that decentralization has taken some root; many institutional structures and coordination mechanisms are in place. Yet, many grassroot-level participatory structures are still to evolve. On the theoretical front, quite a few methodologies have been experimented upon. The tools and techniques of micro-level planning are being refined.

While there have been some successful models of decentralization in a few states, they do not represent a model that could be replicate of the third tier of the government—the district government. Even Karnataka's Panchayati Raj System (which was hailed as a model of democratic decentralization), while no doubt breaking some new ground has still visualized the role of the elected panchayat bodies as being confined to development planning and implementation aspects only. The law and order functions were vested with the Deputy Com-missioner (District Collector), who was outside the direct Panchayati Raj institutional framework and who continued to represent the state government at the district level. Nirmal Mukherji[2] and others, who have advocated the idea of District Government, are of the view that the district governments should look after the totality of district governance, with the district bureaucracy coming squarely under them. A government publication says, 'Ultimately, what matters is, who wields the *lathi*, and if that remains with the district officer, district government will be just as unable to deliver genuine development as Panchayati Raj Institution (PRI's).[3] In sum, the local government should have total control over the large variety of functions performed by the regulatory departments and also developmental organizations, which are presently outside the purview of the Panchayati Raj Institutions but whose actions impinge upon the life of the rural people. A key issue for consideration is, therefore, whether it is possible to move to a system of panchayat/village governance, which will encompass all the Governmental functions at the local level. This is still a moot question. Undoubtedly, India's experiments towards democratic decentralization have many achievements to their credit. But there is still great scope for refinement and improvement, both in scope and content and in the methodology of planning. Efforts towards a resurgent democratic decentralization system are currently under way, following a constitutional amendment.

Although a number of initiatives were made by His Majesty's government of Nepal in the 1960's and 1970's designed to draw the district political bodies into development planning and execution, to focus and integrate line agency efforts at the district level and to encourage local resource mobilization, these did not bear fruit. This is because of a relatively muted political response and a mixture of sustained line ministry opposition, weak technical and administrative capacity of the officials at the local level and the generally disappointing local revenue mobilization efforts. It was only in the 1980's, after the promulgation of the Decentralization Act, 1982 and the rules framed under it in 1984 that some concerted efforts were made towards decentralized planning and development. The Act prescribed an important technical support role for HMG regional offices; it also provided for the establishment in each *Ilaka* (i.e. service area) of an integrated rural service centre, from which the sectorial departments will extend technical advice and material services to the Village Panchayats. It also gave an important role to Local User Groups and User Committees in the planning, execution and maintenance of local projects. The Decentralization Act and Rules were under implementation for hardly five fiscal years, when the Revolution of 1990 took place, replacing the Panchayat System by the Multi-party System. Since then, however, the dynamism and continuity of the decentralization process have been lost, because of the constant flux in the political matrix.

One major constraint in regard to decentralization is the fact that about half of Nepal's development efforts are being financed through donor aid. The donor agencies, as well as the line departments, circumvent the decentralization process, by according central status to their programmes. The "central projects" do not fall within the purview of decentralized district planning and they account for about three-quarters of public development allocations. This being the current state of affairs, decentralization involves only a limited devolution of real authority to the districts. Unless aid commitments are linked to the government's decentralization strategies, there is no hope for the total success of decentralization policies. As of now, political uncertainties, imperfect planning mechanisms and weak institutional structures hamper the decentralization process in Nepal.

In Ghana, decentralization is one of the policies being implemented, in the context of a package of structural adjustment measures, as part of the Economic Recovery Programme. With the National Development Planning Commission not fully empowered, and a systematic planning process not being operational, everything is in a transition. The Regional Coordinating Councils with their Regional Planning Coordinating units have not been tasked for the preparation of Regional Plans, but only perform monitoring, coordinating and evaluating functions. At the district level, planning has not yet started. The head of the district—District Secretary—is also the chairman of the District Executive Committee. The District Assembly elects a Presiding Member, who functions like the Speaker of the Assembly. Participation is confined to elected members only. In sectorial ministries, planning and budgeting is centralized with no involvement of the regions and districts.

In Uganda again, economic development planning and decentralization efforts are in transition. The Presidential Economic Council (PEC), the Ministry of Planning and Economic Development (MPED) and the Ministry of Finance engage in national planning activities. The National Resistance Council (Parliament) with its hierarchy of Resistance Councils and Committees play a significant role in sub-national level development matters. Decentralized planning at the district level is yet to take off. The only accomplishments are the establishment of the District Development Committees and the introduction of common cadre staffing arrangements. In the sectorial ministries, the planning process is mainly concentrated at the national level. The district level staff do not have the capacity to undertake planning functions. At the district level and below, serious inadequacies in logistic support—housing, transport facilities, office accommodation, office equipment, etc.—hamper the effective functioning of the staff in position.

Thus in the two Sub-Saharan African countries cited here, most of the prerequisites necessary for decentralization have not been met and what we find are certain "weak" forms of decentralization imposed from above. The Sub-Saharan African (SSA) situation is burdened not only by conditions reflecting their stage of underdevelopment, but also by serious policy distortions and the impact of negative exogenous shocks. An issue like decentralization is affected by political factors such as who is in the policy-making circle and how much political will is exercised for parting with powers. Most states in Sub-Saharan Africa are authoritarian, and the character of the ruler influences the process substantially. The ruler cannot afford to take any risks that may cause political instability and, therefore, may have to tread cautiously and with understanding. In the African situation, there are also other impeding factors : grossly inadequate institutional structures and their inefficient functioning, underdevelopment of human resources, weak statistical systems, highly discouraging government wage structure, poor career development opportunities to staff, poor working environment with lack of essential logistic support like housing, transport, office accommodation and office equipment, poor financial management and accountability in local administrations and so on. Many of these weaknesses can be overcome given time and will power. In such situations, devolution of authority to local bodies must be an incremental or gradual process.

An important aspect of the gradual approach is the need to push ahead first and foremost with the administrative aspects of decentralization (or "deconcentration" as it is otherwise known) in all sectors of activity to pave the way for the democratic decentralization, which may follow later. In the Sub-Saharan African context today, authoritarian regimes and the dominance of patron-client relations are likely to continue till such time as political stability is totally assured. If the past is any indication, changes which usher in a democratic political culture are likely to take a long time, perhaps some decades, if not generations. Meanwhile, it is important to assess what reforms are feasible in the context of the existing stage of political development. What we would like to emphasize is the grim reality that there is a "social and political time preference" for such reforms as decentralization. In the context of political centralism which obtains today, we argue that administrative decentralization and increased people's participation must be pursued, irrespective of other considerations. By at least decentralizing the administration in ministries, line agencies and departments, we will be capacitating the government functionaries at the lower levels and exposing them to a planning concept, which has to take a better account of local conditions and wider participation in the development process. Administrative decentralization will assist in streamlining government operations, mainly through simplification of administrative processes and procedures, to improve access of the public government services and to effect the expeditious implementation of priority programmes and projects. It will also effect better coordination of all development efforts, including the effective integration of government corporate programmes within the mainstream of national government activities. In this way, the administrative preparedness for greater decentralization or "devolution" (characteristic of democratic decentralization) can be ensured. This is a point of view counter to the extremist view that nothing short of devolution is needed to realize decentralized development.

From the country experiences reviewed here, it is apparent that several aspects of decentralization will require the attention of governments both in Asia and in Africa in order to consolidate the progress made thus far. Among these, one of the most important relates to capacitation. Ultimately, the success of decentralization will depend, to a considerable extent, on the capacities available at the local level and on an appropriate set of responsibilities being assigned to them. Also the key to generating and sustaining the momentum for decentralization will lie with the growth of properly motivated and empowered participatory groups at the grassroots level. Another consideration in this context relates to the role of voluntary agencies. In none of the countries discussed has any serious and systematic effort been made to incorporate their operations into the government's decentralized planning framework.

REFERENCES

1. The other countries, whose decentralization experiences this author, he has had opportunities to study during his career are : Bangladesh, Sri Lanka, Indonesia, The Philippines and Fiji in Asia and Pacific; and Ethiopia,

Zambia, Kenya and Tanzania in Africa. There are two publications authored by him for FAO in which their experiences have been dealt with.

(i) 'Toward Improved multilevel planning for agricultural and rural development in Asia and the Pacific,—FAO Economic and Social Development Paper 52, Rome 1985, and

(ii) 'Decentralization of Agricultural Sector Planning in Sub-Saharan Africa' FAO, Rome July 1992.

Besides the above countries, he also reviewed the Regional Decentralization experiences in agricultural development planning of the following countries of the Near East and North Africa for FAO in 1988 : Algeria, Cyprus, Egypt, Iraq, Jordan, Libyan Arab Jamahiriya, Morocco, Saudi Arabia, Sudan, Syria and Turkey. See 'Regional Decentralization for Agricultural Development Planning in the Near East and North Africa'—FAO Economic and Social Development Paper 73, FAO/UN, Rome, 1988.

2. Mukherji, Nirmal, 'Decentralization below the State Level', February 1989 (mimeographed).
3. 'Social control by Panchayats' paper in Occasional Papers, Government of India, Ministry of Rural Development, New Delhi February 1992. It is mentioned that the views contained in the paper do not reflect the views of the government or the Ministry.

PART IV

HUMAN RESOURCE DEVELOPMENT

"We should train the local officers fully and then trust them with resources and responsibility. Local institutions should move under their own steam. This perhaps is the hardest lesson for public administrators of underdeveloped countries to learn or to teach."

—*Akhter Hameed Khan*

INTRODUCTION

Decentralized planning in all developing countries faces the major challenge of "capability constraints" of the personnel for manning the planning and development tasks at the critical sub-national levels. In this context, the development of the human resources through training and retraining would constitute the "core" strategy. In systematically planning for such training, the assessment of the training needs would constitute the major first step. For any given context, such assessment has to be made with reference to the planning process in operation and identifying the key actors and key steps involved in the planning endeavour. Once these are identified, the tasks to be handled by each actor and the knowledge and attitudes to be cultivated can be derived. This helps to frame the curriculum and to outline the details of the training programme. The preparation of a basic training manual incorporating into it appropriate exercises and case studies is emphasized.

Chapter 17 is a case study and describes an international training programme conducted substantially in an inductive manner, built around a "planning exercise" in a region in a developing country. This refers to the six month training programme conducted by the United Nations Centre for Regional Development, Nagoya (Japan), revolving around a planning exercise conducted in the Bicol region in the Philippines. The planning exercise-oriented training (PEOT) approach was a highly demanding exercise, so far as the training institution was concerned, but a highly effective method of training, as far as the trainees were concerned, as it made them active participants in a live planning situation, enabling them to learn as well as to contribute to the process of planning and development. However, it was a costly and time-consuming process. The case study concludes that the PEOT approach, applied in a country-specific situation has great potential.

Chapter 18 deals with the training aspects for sub-national level planners in the context of the establishment and use of the information technology. In most developing countries, the use of Information Technology (IT) in planning is, at best, in its infancy or non-existent. While lack of physical infrastructure and financing problems may be deemed as one set of factors contributing to this situation, the other is the absence of skilled personnel. The general trend towards decentralization of planning and the large volume of data to be handled in this context make it imperative for the developing countries to adopt the Information Technology (IT) as early as possible. In this context, there is a great need to train large numbers of professionals in utilizing Information Technology in planning. The target groups for training will consist of various groups needing different skills. These are : The Designers who manage the IT systems; the information collection and processing staff; and the Users, who are divided into policy planning and decision-making level and planning and development analysis level. The interaction between the various groups is quite important and, in fact, should be a necessary element in the training strategy. A distinction is also made between "computer education" and "computer training" for the two groups which comprise the users. The former refers to educating users on what they should expect of IT and how they should make use of the information provided by the technology. The latter refers to the operation of the hardware and software. The major problem addressed in the chapter is the assessment of training needs and how to acquire a socio-economic command of the information technology, which is the crucial problem in the planning context today.

Chapter 19 squarely addresses the problem of in-service training for Decentralized planning at district level, its content, techniques, analytical tools and curriculum building. Here the author sets out his experience in Nepal in implementing an in-service training programme on decentralized planning on behalf of a multi-lateral organization—Food and Agricultural Organization of the United Nations. The training manual prepared in this context (emerging from the live situation of an action-planning-cum-training exercise) with eight modules including case studies and exercises is described. A conceptual framework for training model of an instructional cycle, in which the trainees pass through stages of "divergent thinking" and "convergent thinking", has been presented. Training for decentralized planning cannot be conceived as a one-stroke operation. The "follow-up phase" of training as well as periodical refresher training are important facts in the total training perspective.

The concluding chapter of the book observes that training for decentralized planning is a dependent activity related to the policy environment, the work or operational environment and the professional or career development environment of the personnel. In each of these environments, there are factors that are conducive or otherwise to the effective and efficient functioning of personnel. It has been postulated that the essential "prerequisites" for decentralized planning (in relation to the effective utilization of trained manpower) consist in the way the policy, work and career development environments are structured by the governments. The chapter elaborates on some aspects of these pre-requisites and their importance.

16

TRAINING NEEDS FOR DECENTRALIZED DISTRICT PLANNING

In our search for greater efficiency in setting and pursuing development goals, training becomes an important working tool. In the context of decentralized planning and implementation in particular, a well-conceived capacitation programme assumes great significance. Without this support, any government's policy on decentralization is bound to remain a mere rhetoric and a pipe dream.

It is gratifying to note that, of late, within the framework of priorities generated by our national government, the task of operationalizing training programmes to accelerate the Decentralized Planning process in the country has been given much prominence.

It cannot be overemphasized that one of the preconditions for effective training is the existence of a national training policy for the public service. When training activities are performed in an *ad hoc* manner without the guidance of a policy framework, inefficient use of scarce resources and duplication of efforts are bound to occur. The training needs of different categories of personnel and different agencies of government are numerous and varied. It is imperative, therefore, that the objectives of training, an assessment of the training needs, an overall training plan for the government, its underlying strategy and priorities in terms of the tasks to be accomplished, a systematic monitoring and evaluation of training programmes and effectively linking up training to career development are tasks that call for specific attention.

Approach to Training Needs Assessment

A systematic assessment of training needs provides an indispensable basis for the taking of informed and rational decision on the target groups to be trained and on the nature and content of the training programmes designed for their benefit. Such an exercise will make the training need-based and realistic. In the context of Decentralized Planning, where there is a big gap between the actual condition and the desired condition in the work situation, this assessment is particularly important and significant. Literature bearing on the assessment of training needs points to four different approaches for making such assessments. These are : the comprehensive analysis, the key task, the problem-centred and the core analysis.[1] These methods are, by and large, relevant to the planning of training interventions in business houses and enterprises. Decentralization of planning and implemen-tation is a *process* operating across a hierarchical government organization, characterized by many layers of decision-making and division of responsibilities. In this context, it is the planning process that is important and if this process is clearly defined, then it would be possible to distinguish the "Critical Steps" as well as the "key actors" involved, having different roles in this process. The planning process that emerges in a country will be in accordance with the current capabilities, philosophies, needs, cultural and social characteristics and administrative imperatives of the country context. Thus an understanding of the administrative structure, the rules of the planning game and the critical steps and key actors in this game are the basic determinants in any exercise on the assessment of training needs. One may, therefore, conclude that the analytical technique that is relevant to the determination of training needs is what may be called as the "Structure, Process and Key Steps Analysis" approach. This involves the identification of critical steps in the planning process and the functional roles and training specification for key actors in this activity against the background of a given organizational structure and political ethos.

A case study of the Assessment of Trained Manpower Needs for Agricultural Planning and Project Analysis for Gujarat (India)[2] was undertaken for FAO in 1984. The study was confined to a single sector, viz. agriculture, but took into account the decentralization of the planning process that was operating in Gujarat and the anticipated changes in procedures for agricultural planning that were likely to follow in the wake of decentralization. Since there was no legislative backing for the decentralized planning effort, the projection of training needs had to be based on the executive orders of the government that were in vogue and certain assumptions as to the likely changes that may occur. A similar exercise undertaken in Nepal on the other hand, is firmly rooted in a legislation—the Decentralization Act of 1982 and the rules and regulations framed under it. It, therefore, provides us with a better illustration as to how training needs may be identified in a clearly defined decentralized planning context.

Nepal's administrative structure consists of the Centre, Regions, Districts, *Ilakas*, Villages and Wards. In the decentralization process that is being sought to be operationalized, the Districts, *Ilakas*, Villages and Wards have been assigned specific roles. The declared objectives of decentralization in Nepal are to : (a) strengthen panchayat democracy, (b) mobilize maximum local resources for development, and (c) promote harmonious development.

Under the Decentralization Act and the rules framed under it, very elaborate procedures for decentralized planning and implementation have been developed. In a nutshell, it can be described as a combination of top-down and bottom-up approaches. The planning process starts with the preparation of guidelines and budget ceiling by the National Planning Commission (NPC), which communicates them to the Districts. At District level, the District Panchayat makes an estimate of its own resources, resources available to the village panchayats[3] and adds them to the ceiling coming from the Centre to project the future total resources for which it will have to plan. A major part of the resources coming from the Centre are sectorally earmarked. The District Panchayat allocates them to the various *Ilakas* (service centre areas)[4] and issues guidelines on how they should be used. This is done on the basis of Central guidelines and on an analysis of the District Profile. The remaining part of the resources from the Centre is provided as a lump sum to the District. The District Panchayat has to allocate at least 50 per cent of this lump sum to the village panchayats and provide guidelines on how to use them. The remainder may be used for district-level projects.[5] Once all this information is available, planning starts at the lowest level, the Ward,[6] where the population identifies, formulates and prioritizes projects with the help of Village/*Ilaka*/District-level officials. These projects, after selection and approval by Village bodies, are consolidated into a Village plan. The Village plans, in turn, go to the District level, where additional selection may take place. They are then, together with the district projects, included in a district plan, after approval by district bodies. Finally, the plan has to be approved by the National Planning Commission (NPC). The funds for implementation allocated by the Centre are made available by the district treasurer. Detailed normative formats have been developed for the plan, project description and district profile.

The decentralized planning process in Nepal involves some key steps and key actors as listed in Table 16.1

TABLE 16.1 : Key Steps and the Key Actors (Nepal).

Key Steps	Key Actors
1. Preparation of Guidelines and budget ceiling	National Planning Commission
2. Preparation of Village Profiles	Village Panchayat Secretary
3. Aggregating Village Profiles into District Profiles	Local Development Officer (LDO) District Planning Officer (DPO)
4. Internal Resource Estimation	Village Panchayat, District Panchayat
5. Preparation of Budget Estimate	District Panchayat
6. Resource Allocation	LDO, DPO
7. Approval and despatch of information on resource allocation	District Panchayat
8. Identification of local need-based projects	Ward Committees
9. Preparation of Village Plan	Village Panchayat Secretariat
10. Approval of Village Plan	Village Assembly
11. Technical Assistance to Village Panchayat and Wards	LDO, DPO, Sectoral line agencies, Service Centre
12. Preparation of Sectoral Plans	Sectoral Offices in the district
13. Consolidation of Sectoral Plans	Project Formulation Committee Member Secretary
14. Analyze Village Plans and despatch for approval	Project Formulation Committee
15. Prepare District Development Plan for discussion and approval	LDO and DPO
16. Amend and approve plan as required	Joint Project Formulation Committee, District Panchayat, District Assembly
17. Integration of the District Plan into the National Plan	Ministry of Panchayat and Local Development, National Planning Commission

If we consider the key actors in this process at the district level and below as the target groups for training, then we may list the following categories of people (both officials and non-officials) as those needing some training and orientation relevant to Decentralized Planning and implementation :

— District level officers, including sectoral officers (Office Chiefs).
— Office assistants in the District Offices.
— *Ilaka*-level officers (belonging to line agencies).
— Village Panchayat Secretaries.
— District Panchayat Members (Non-officials).
— Village Chairmen/Vice-Chairmen (Non-officials).
— Ward Chairmen and Ward Members (Non-officials).
— Members of Users' Groups (Non-officials).
— Whole Population of the Village.

Among the nine target groups defined above, the officer-level trainees, whether at the District or *Ilaka* level, would need training that would be more or less similar in content and approach. In regard to the training requirements, that for the "whole population of the village" will need mass communication methods through various media, audio-visuals, films and creative dramatics and hence this target group has to be treated differently. The members of the Users' Groups will need tailor-made training suited to their particular requirements. As for the other target groups (officials and non-officials), the knowledge, skills and attitudes needed for the performance of their jobs will be different and these could be derived, taking into account the tasks and functions prescribed for them under the Decentralization Act and the rules and regulations framed under it.

For a Pilot Training Programme conducted with FAO collaboration in one of the districts in Nepal (Tanahun district), the following five categories of target groups were considered and training programmes were designed for them :[7]

— District-level officers (Office Chiefs).
— Office Assistants at district level.
— Village Panchayat Secretaries.
— District Panchayat members.
— Village Chairmen/Vice-Chairmen.

The knowledge, skills and attitudes required for the above groups in the successful performance of their tasks in a decentralized planning context were recognized as different. Broadly these differences were identified as follows. Such recognition provided the essential criteria for the design of training programmes for each group, thus rendering the training for these levels both need-based and realistic (Table 16.2).

TABLE 16.2 : Essentials for the Design of Training Programmes for each Target Group.

Target Group	Knowledge	Tasks	Attitudes
(Village Panchayat Secretary) —at village level	—rules governing the planning and implementation process.	—prepare village profile	—cooperation with local population
		—identify local resources, advise on how to mobilize them	—ability to interact with technicians and take advice from them
		—formulate simple projects —fill planning formats	—ability to move closely with people and motivate them to form Users' Groups
		—priority setting and project selection —simple implementation techniques	
(Service Centre Level) —at *Ilaka* level	—rules governing the planning and implementation process	—formulate simple projects	—cooperation with and accessible to local population
		—simple implementation techniques	—willingness to go to the villages to give technical advice

(*Contd.*)

TABLE 16.2 (*Contd.*)

Target Group	Knowledge	Tasks	Attitudes
(Sectoral Officers) —at District level	—rules governing planning and implementation process	—prepare and analyse sectoral data base	—team spirit; accept coordination from LDO
		—define priorities	
		—identify and select projects	—should be open and willing to collaborate with local leaders
		—fill formats	
		—present and defend component/ sectoral plan	
		—simple implementation techniques	
		—simple M&E techniques	
Local Development Officer/ District Planning Officer	—rules governing planning and implementation process	—prepare, analyze district profile —advise on resource allocation	—dialogue with local leaders —coordination of District
	—activities, problems in each sector		
		—define priorities	—animator of meetings
		—select projects	
		—fill formats	
		—defend and present plan	
		—organize meetings	
	—simple M&E techniques		
		—integration of sectoral plans into the District Plan.	

(*Contd.*)

TABLE 16.2 (*Contd.*)

Target Groups	Knowledge	Tasks	Attitudes
(District Panchayat) —at District level	—rules governing planning implementation process —work to be done by officials at district level and problems they meet —understand official jargon and major planning techniques used at district level —simple M&E techniques	—analysis of district profile —define priorities —organize meetings —decide on resource mobilization and allocation	—development orientation —dialogue with officials and other leaders —animator of meetings
(Villagers, Ward members) —at Ward level	—rules governing planning and implementation process —work to be done by officials at Village, service centre and District level, and assistance they should provide to the Village	—identify project ideas —decide on priorities —create users' groups —manage users' group	—development orientation —dialogue with officials —Eagerness to participate in planning process and contribute to implementation of projects
(Chairmen, Vice-chairmen of Village Panchayat) —at Village level	—rules governing planning and implementation —work to be done by officials at village level and problems they meet —understand official jargon and major planning techniques used at village level	—analyze village profile —define priorities —organize meetings —Decision-making about resource mobilization	—development orientation —dialogue with officials —animator of meetings —encourage users' groups

Training Needs in Indian Context

The foregoing discussion indicates that the point of departure for assessing the training needs is the extent of decentralization proposed and the planning process envisaged and the various decentralized planning procedures associated with it, which are all defined for a given context. While in the case of Nepal, these could be spelt out through a single legislation and the rules and regulations framed under it and made uniformly applicable to all the 75 districts in the country, in a country of India's size with its federal structure, a decentralized system of planning is much more complex. The State Governments have to decide how far they can go with decentralization and then work out the planning procedures in their individual contexts. Of course, such planning procedures will be decided by the State Governments within certain nationally accepted parameters. At the present juncture, when there is so much interest, enthusiasm and some piquancy in regard to the pursuit of decentralized planning in the States, we expect vital changes in the democratic framework (i.e. Panchayati Raj Institutions) at district level and below and clear enunciation of their planning and implementation functions through legislation. The State Governments will be working out their own institutional structures and operational principles, so that these democratic institutions would become vibrant instruments for development and planning. The point that I would like to emphasize is that there would be variations among States in the procedures for planning at the district level and below and for fitting in the decentralized plans with the general planning procedure that is followed at the State and Central levels. This will also influence the estimation of training needs which, as we noted earlier, is a process-oriented assessment. One may, however, expect some commonalities to emerge in the institutionalization of the democratic framework and in the decentralization process. On that basis, we may identify the key steps and key actors and then broadly derive the training needs. A model legislation prepared by the Centre would undoubtedly assist in achieving certain basic uniformities in this regard. One expects such developments in the near future.

For the present, I would like to base my assessment of training needs for decentralized planning based on two fairly well conceived State experiments in decentralized planning in the country, viz. West Bengal and Karnataka. In this generalization, the key steps and the key actors would be as shown in Table 16.3.

TABLE 16.3 : Key Steps and Key Actors (India).

	Key Steps	Key Actors
1.	Preparation of a 'needs statement' or the most acutely felt problems of the Panchayat area.	Gram Panchayat
2.	Preparation of a series of Maps of the block, outlining the existing facilities, resources and resource use.	Panchayat Samiti
3.	Technical assistance to the Gram Panchayats to projectize their "needs" (with the help of overseers and engineers).	Block-level Overseers and District Engineers and other officials of the sectoral departments at the block/district level.
4.	Preparation of a statement of the on-going and proposed programme of plan outlay of different departments/authorities in each block.	Block Development Officer.
5.	Collating the "needs statements" of Gram Panchayats and drawing up the schemes to meet the most pressing needs of the gram panchayats.	Block Development Officer and other Block-level Officials.
6.	Approving the schemes for forwarding to the planning authorities at the district headquarters.	Panchayat Samiti
7.	Scrutiny of the block plans and schemes; Drawing up schemes aimed at (a) finding solution to major area problems in the district (b) levelling inter-block disparities in development; (c) Prioritizing development schemes in accordance with the goals and strategies of District Development.	District Planning Committee through its sub-committees.[8]
8.	Vetting of the District Plan and its final approval	District Planning and Coordination Council (Zilla Parishad)

From Table 16.3, the Target Groups needing training on different aspects could be inferred as follows :

- — The Gram Panchayat Officials.
- — The Gram Panchayat Chairmen/Vice-Chairmen.
- — The Block Development Officer and other Block level line agency officials.
- — Panchayat Samiti Chairmen and members.

— Members of the District Planning Committee and other Sub-Committees.
— Members of the District Planning and Coordination Council (Zilla Parishad).
— Heads of District Offices (line agencies).
— Assistants dealing with planning matters in the district offices.

In the case of Karnataka, the introduction of the *Mandal* Panchayat, with the retention of the *Taluka Samiti* would mean the identification of more target groups for training. Thus it should be noted that the structure of the democratic framework, the legislation defining the powers and functions of the institutions at different levels and the executive orders of the State defining the decentralized planning procedures would constitute the basic determinants of the training strategy.

When we are taking stock of the training needs for decentralized planning, it should be remembered that we are not considering in-service training alone. In this case, the pre-service training is equally important. This is because decentralization implies a big transformation in attitudes on the part of officials, who will be manning and promoting it at different spatial and institutional levels. To enable them to imbibe the right attitudes, it is necessary to introduce training for decentralized planning as an important component of pre-service training at the Central, State and local levels. What should be the content of such training should receive careful attention at this stage, when the decentralization process is being sought to be introduced in a big way in all the States in the country.

Flowing from this analysis, we may broadly group the target groups for decentralized planning in the Indian context as follows :

A. *For Pre-Service Training*

(1) Central Level	—	I.A.S. Probationers, Personnel recruited for the Indian Economic Service and the Indian Statistical Service.
(2) State Level	—	Officers recruited by the State Public Service Commissions.
(3) Local Level	—	Officers recruited by the State or Local Service Commissions.

B. *For In-Service Training*

(1) Civil servants who supervise and coordinate district planning activities at the district level (i.e. District Collectors or Deputy Commissioners).
(2) Policy-level personnel at the State level belonging to the State Planning and Statistical Departments.
(3) Personnel operating special and area-based programmes, whose plans have to be integrated into the district plans.
(4) Members of the district planning team.
(5) Sectoral functionaries working at the District level in various disciplines such as agriculture, animal husbandry, cooperation, industry, etc.
(6) Assistants dealing with planning matters in the district offices.
(7) Block Development Officer and other block-level line agency officials.
(8) Village Panchayat Officials.
(9) Non-officials of the Village Panchayats (Gram Panchayat Chairmen/Vice-Chairmen and members).
(10) Non-official members of the Panchayat Samiti (Chairmen and members).
(11) Non-official members of Zilla Parishad and District Planning Board committees (if such organizations exist) and sub-committees.
(12) Faculty in the training institutions (for Trainer's Training).

The above is a long list of target groups. If we attempt to quantify them, the numbers will be colossal and that indicates the magnitude of the task and complexity of effort involved in training for decentralized planning.

Training Needs—Wider Issues

The term "training needs assessment" does not imply only the determination of orders of magnitude of the various categories of manpower to be trained (usually termed as the "manpower requirements approach"). It is a wider term which also implies the following :

(i) The determination and quantification of the inputs in terms of training structure, equipment, manpower resources (i.e. Trainers) and finance required for undertaking training activities to satisfy the identified training needs;

(ii) The definition of the qualitative content as well as the form of organization of the training to be provided; and

(iii) Training monitoring, which involves the capturing of relevant labour market signals, especially the unit cost of producing a particular type of trained worker, the labour productivity of the trained worker and how and to what extent the knowledge and skills obtained during training by a worker is put to operational use.

In the context of the above wider connotation of the term, training needs assessment has to be seen as a process, which is to be understood as a series of connected actions and changes. It cannot be a sporadic or "on-off" activity. It needs to be visualized as something on-going, in a sense repetitive, always alert to changes and responsive to opportunities for improvement. Here information snap-shots will not do; a flow of information is required, especially for feeding the monitoring process.

Focus of Present Discussion

In this chapter only three vital aspects of training needs assessment are dealt with :

(1) A specification of the major technical tasks and steps involved in District Planning, which would determine the qualitative content of training for decentralized planning;

(2) The training objectives of different target groups and the knowledge, skills and attitudes to be developed in this context; and

(3) The basic training packages that are necessary to meet the training needs of the different target groups.

Decentralized Planning Process : Tasks and Steps

In the context of the planning process outlined earlier (with the specification of key steps and key actors), the technical tasks involved in the decentralized planning process may be visualized in terms of certain specific tasks and steps (see Table 16.4).

TABLE 16.4 : Specific Tasks and Steps.

Tasks	Steps
1. District Analysis	Preparation of Village and District Profiles, (Collection and collation of essential data to present an articulated statistical profile of the village/district.) Resource Inventory analysis : (Malady Remedy analysis). (a) Physical resources (b) Human resources (c) Infrastructural and Institutional resources. Context Analysis (a) Review of on-going development programmes to bring out development gaps and extent of resource utilization. (b) Intra-district levels of development analysis. (c) Technology appraisal. Felt needs of the rural population based on a 'Needs statement' obtained from each village;
2. Strategy Formulation	Determination of District-specific goals within the overall framework of national goals. Formulation of developing strategy for the district indicating the major thrusts and priority areas of development.
3. Sector and Project Analysis	Determination of Sectoral objectives Analysis of the development potential : (a) Productive sectors (b) Infrastructure sectors (c) Basic needs sectors. Project preparation and appraisal. Assignment of inter-sectoral and intra-sectoral priorities on the basis of resource availability, administrative feasibility and expected beneficiaries.
4. Inter-sectoral coordination	Institution of sectoral consistency checks. Analysis of primary and secondary sectors relationship.
5. Financial Resources Analysis and Allocation	Estimate investment requirements and sources of finance, e.g.

(*Contd.*)

TABLE 16.4 (*Contd.*)

Tasks	Steps
	(a) government-sectoral funds and any untied funds placed at the disposal of the local body. (b) Local resources (c) Banks (d) External aid.
	Allocation of financial resources to villages and Blocks.
6. Budgeting	Working out cost estimates of identified programmes and projects.
	Matching of identified programmes and projects with available resources.
	Determining optimal programme sequences.
7. Implementation	Phasing of development activities.
	Ensuring the orderly flow of funds
	Task adoption : Articulation of Agency responsibilities with respect to programme execution, co-ordination, monitoring and supervision of activities.
	Monitoring and evaluation.

Training Objectives

To undertake the above *tasks* and *steps* involved in District Planning with a reasonable degree of efficiency, the acquisition of certain *knowledge* (concepts), *skills* (techniques) and *attitudes* (behaviour) is imperative. It should be noted that all the three—concepts, techniques and behaviour—are intrinsically interrelated as shown below :

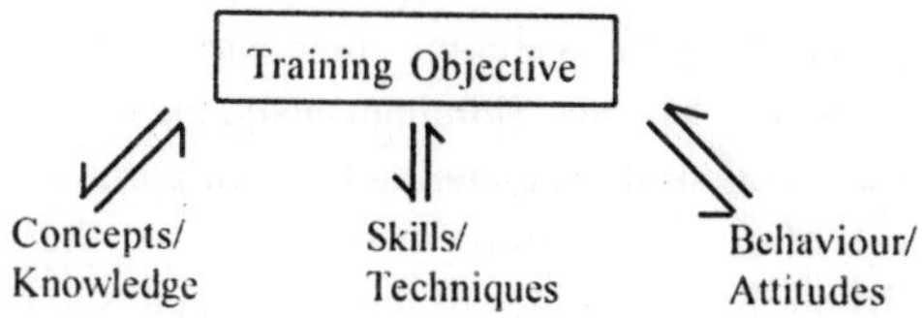

While the acquisition of all these elements—knowledge, skills and attitudes—is important to every person targeted for training, their relative emphases may vary for different training programmes, designed for different target groups, depending on the tasks and responsibilities assigned to them and the time available for training.

Knowledge

The nature of the knowledge to be imparted and the degree of its depth will vary with the requirements of each target group and the time available for training. The new entrants who will be going through a pre-service training must be enabled to acquire the following types of knowledge pertaining to :

— The district planning process;
— Tools and techniques needed for district planning;
— Participatory techniques; and
— Group dynamics.

The training programme should also equip them to acquire the required cognitive and analytical skills in dealing with both the technical system and the human system of management. It must enable them to increase their decision-making ability and stimulate critical and innovative thinking related to area-specific planning. For the district officers who are part and parcel of the district planning machinery (i.e. the personnel constituting the planning team at the district level) also the training programme must have, more or less, similar content. Perhaps, these two categories of personnel may be bracketed together for training purposes.

For the group of sectoral functionaries at the district level, who are specialists in their own right, the emphasis in training should be on the comprehensive aspects of district planning. Here the term "comprehensive" will mean that planning in one sector will have to take note of the forward and backward linkages in other sectors and that a wide range of issues involving many disciplines are to be incorporated into the planning framework. The sectoral functionaries have particularly to be enabled through training to overcome their narrow specialism and to obtain meta-disciplinary visions. Simultaneously, the training programme must also improve their skills in planning for their particular sectors with a greater degree of sophistication. In this context, they would need training specially in the techniques of resources analysis, project formulation, monitoring and evaluation.

In the case of block and village-level functionaries, the basic content of the training programme would focus on imparting knowledge and skills that may be needed : (a) to identify their area problems and prioritize them; (b) the knowledge of physical, economic and social processes that are essential to manipulate projects in such a way that the desired objectives are realized; (c) the knowledge necessary to organize groups in such a way that they are able to participate in some or all the steps of planned development at the local level (including the formation of user groups for the maintenance of projects); and (d) the knowledge necessary to mobilize local resources to effectively supplement external resources for development (self-help methods).

So far as the various categories of non-officials (at the district, block and village levels) are concerned, the training emphasis will be in the direction of increasing their understanding of the decentralization process, of enabling them to understand their particular roles and to develop the ability to communicate with the officials in a spirit of partnership and to motivate them to have a development-oriented attitude.

The above indication of the knowledge and content of the training programmes for the different target groups is admittedly general. But, for the present, we cannot go very much beyond this here. However, we may briefly touch upon two other elements that go to supplement the basic knowledge and content of a training programme. These pertain to the acquisition of some skills and attitudes relevant to decentralized planning and implementation.

Skills

The skills that are demanded for working effectively within an institutionalized planning process may be broadly considered as of two kinds :

(a) Basic	Information collection and information handling and processing. Area analysis. Resource allocation Target formulation. Project identification and appraisal. Monitoring and evaluation. Integration of programmes/projects. Participation and effective communication.
(b) Contributory skills (illustrative)	Demographic and manpower analysis. Locational analysis. Map analysis Demand analysis and forecasting techniques.

Land capability analysis.
System analysis.
Environmental impact analysis
Social accounts.

Basic Skills are those minimum skills that are required for a district planner to undertake the overall tasks of analysis and detailing of a development plan.

Contributory Skills are of a specialized nature related to the management and development of resources or related to specific sectoral aspects of planning. These are provided by varying disciplines. Since no single planner can acquire all these skills (along with the requisite degree of sophistication), selectivity is called for to determine the nature of skills to be imparted in a training programme. Obviously, this will depend on the target groups and their functions and responsibilities.

Attitudes

The third acquisition of a trainee in a training programme is the one related to attitudinal change. This is a complex process. This demands the following qualities : ability to work and interact as member of a planning team, responsiveness to divergent views and opinions, acquisition of meta-disciplinary visions including broadening of perspectives and shedding of pre-conceived notions, ability to negotiate with superiors on resource allocation and project selection, willingness to learn and innovate, sensitivity to the results of monitoring and public criticism, the ability to work with people and their representatives and the ability to manage conflicts. All these are sometimes called "social skills". Role playing protocol, (i.e. recording of a real-life situation in which interaction between human beings takes place), experiential learning, group interaction, etc., are some of the instructional techniques associated with the imparting of attitudinal change. It should be emphasized that knowledge, skills and attitudes are interrelated. It may be hypothesized that the acquisition of certain types of knowledge and skills also induce certain kinds of attitudinal change.

Training Materials

The above discussion relating to the various target groups and the broad content of the knowledge, skills and attitudes needed by them to effectively perform the various tasks and functions demanded of them in a decentralized operational context indicates that different training packages are necessary to deal with their individual requirements. While some basic knowledge pertaining to decentralization, planning process and tools and techniques of planning may be common to many of the training programmes (with, of course, different degrees of emphasis) designed for the different target groups, there will also be certain specificities and special requirements to be taken into account for these different categories. Hence different training packages tailored to the needs of the different target groups will be necessary. A systematic preparation of the training packages by the training institution is quite essential. In a number of training programmes that are conducted, *ad hoc* methods are being adopted. These consist of the training institution picking up some papers from here and there and putting them together as training materials, without looking into aspects like orderly presentation, proper sequence, balanced treatment of the subject areas, and generally the quality of the content. These lead to overlaps, and gaps in the training that is imparted. It is to redress all these short-comings in the delivery of training inputs that properly conceived, well-prepared and standardized training packages are deemed essential.

Basic Manual and Target-Group-Specific Training Packages

In the context of decentralized planning, there are certain subject areas—concepts, methods and techniques, general planning procedures, basic exercises and case studies—which may be deemed as the "essential knowledge and skills" that have to be disseminated in all training programmes catering to all identified target groups playing different roles. These essential subject areas can form the core material of a basic document or training manual. It would stress basic principles and would be fairly independent of place-specific considerations. In this way, its usefulness will be considerably enhanced, rendering it into a relevant document for adoption in diverse contexts. This basic manual should be supplemented with other target group-specific training packages which, besides indicating what portions of the "basic manual" will be applicable to each of them, would further elaborate on what other specific knowledge and skills would be relevant for each of the identified target groups. Such specific knowledge and skills may include some job-specific instruction—tasks and functions, tips for improving performance, some rule-of-the-thumb techniques, management guidance (change management skills), attitudes to be cultivated, conflict resolution techniques relevant to their jobs to be learnt, etc. In designing the course curriculum for any particular training programme, the trainer has to take into account the course duration and the nature of the target group to be trained, and then should judiciously select the appropriate course material both from the basic manual and the target group specific training packages. Thus, once the basic manual and the target group-specific training packages are ready, the training institution would have equipped itself with some standardized training materials and will be in a position to run its training programmes with some degree of confidence and competence. This is not to say that once such training materials have been prepared, the trainers can cease to apply their minds to the development of training materials. Indeed, the development of training material will be a continuous exercise. From time to time, guidelines and instructions for district and lower-level planners will be issued by the Planning Commission and the State Planning Departments. These have to be suitably incorporated into the training packages. Again, case studies must be locally produced, as these will be then more germane to the training needs of the participants. It cannot be over-emphasized that training materials must be more empirically-oriented and based on field experience, rather than merely on theory. Case studies will make this possible. In fact, participants themselves can help in the production of case studies. In this way, the training materials that have been produced will be needing constant modifications and refinements.

If the ideas on the preparation of training materials stated above are accepted, then some directions for the future are clear. The first priority in our agenda for action would be to focus our attention on the preparation of a "Basic Manual" for decentralized planning. Such a manual has to be carefully planned, as it means the production of a document that will have a lasting value and that will be guiding the training programmes organized by a large number of training institutions in the country and assisting in the acquisition of certain essential knowledge, skills and attitudes to a large number of functionaries manning different positions at the sub-national level. For lack of such a basic document, the quality of training content in local-level planning has been rather uneven in the past. While here and there, some good programmes of direct relevance to local-level planning and implementation were designed and conducted, this has not been the case with most programmes. From institution to institution, and from programme to programme within the same institution, the quality of the training content has varied a great deal. The primary reasons for the non-existence of such a basic document with any of the training institutions in the country today are, in my view, the absence of a permanent stake in many of these institutions focused on local-level planning and the absence of a permanent core faculty in them having the relevant expertise, interest and enthusiasm to engage in a year-round activity focused on local-level planning, combining training with research and consultancy assignment of direct relevance to the teaching programmes, thus helping to generate useful training materials. During my experience with training in multi-level planning when I was holding office in the Planning Commission, I found that in many of these institutions, it was not lack of resources that stifled this effort. For instance, even in those few institutions, which the Planning Commission was seeking to directly assist with liberal grants for establishing a training-cum-research-oriented faculty, nothing tangible by way of a good manual materialized. The failure may perhaps be attributed to the difficulty in assembling the right type of trainers or lack of motivated trainers or organizational constraints.

I am, therefore, convinced that if we are to focus on developing a good basic training manual for decentralized planning, which could be used directly by a wide range of target groups—both for pre-service training and for in-service training—,we must proceed on certain systematic lines, so that a productive as well as quality effort ensues from such an exercise. For this purpose, it would be necessary to pool all the expertise available in the country and to effectively bring to bear on this exercise the know-how and guidance from several sources. The training materials, already generated in a few good training institutions, must be carefully examined and used. Essential and recommended readings should be selected. Also, the tools and techniques of planning that are advocated in this manual should be simple, practical and realistic, matching the capabilities of the prevailing team of field staff, who will be really practising it every time. Further, it is important to note that the proposed manual should not be seen merely as an exercise in the pedagogic presentation of some existent and on-going knowledge and experiences. Nay, it will be going much beyond this limited task. It will be innovative and will serve to clarify many "grey areas" in the field of local-level planning methodology. Through its case studies and practical exercises, it could richly contribute towards firming up our district planning methodologies, on which there has been so much confusion.

These are the reasons why the current task of preparing the manual must be done in close association with a number of experts.

Scope and Content of Basic Manual

Now some thoughts on the scope and content of the manual will be in order. In this context the Nepal experience provides some insights. This started with a pilot District Planning exercise—the Tanahun District in the Western Development Region of Nepal. This experiment was conducted in 1984 and the basic content of the present manual owes its evolution to this pilot project exercise. The training packages prepared in this context were further refined and enlarged with the addition of new exercises and case studies. This was possible with the assistance of a number of expatriate experts and local consultants. Fresh materials, taking into account the new policy thrusts initiated by His Majesty's Government of Nepal, were added. The manual that has thus emerged consists of eight training modules, elaborated in 51 lessons under a standardized format. Twenty-seven exercises and three case studies have been built into these lessons, including one participatory planning game. These lessons have been planned ideally for a four-week Training Programme, which will have 88 training sessions of one-and-a-half-hour duration each. The readings and other teaching materials that have been developed here have been made quite flexible, so that they can be stretched to six or even eight weeks, for instance, by making the training programme into a sandwich course, divided into two phases and introducing an on-the-job planning exercise in the middle. This may also be shrunk into a two or three weeks' training course by reducing some sessions and exercises. Flexibility has also been introduced by classifying the reading materials into "Essential" and "Suggested". A modular approach has been adopted in organizing the content. The main advantages of such a modular approach are its flexibility and adaptability. It offers the users choices from which a selection of what is useful and relevant can be made and then tailored to the needs of the target groups as well as the availability of time (i.e. training duration). Each module has a score of subject areas and each subject area has its content in terms of some knowledge (concepts) and skills. The modules that were considered relevant in this exercise and within each module, the key subject areas to be dealt with are elaborated in Table 16.5. This provides us with a framework within which a fairly consistent set of themes based on some general premises could be developed.

TABLE 16.5 : Modules and the Key Subject Areas.

Modules	Subject areas
1. Understanding Development	Approaches to development-changing perceptions : (a) Growth, distribution, structural changes and self-reliance. (b) Removal of poverty and meeting the basic needs. (c) Population control, food self-sufficiency and ecological control/conservation. (d) Quality of life. (e) Reduction of spatial inequalities; development of "disadvantaged", "by-passed" and special problem areas. (f) Centralized, decentralized and participatory processes of development.
2. Decentralization and the planning process in Nepal	Decentralization : Definition; forms of decentralization; advantages; prerequisites. Review of Decentralization experiences in Nepal. The Planning process envisaged under the Act : Top-down and Bottom-up procedures. The current state of art in decentralized planning : problems and constraints.
3. District Analysis	Preparation of village and district profiles and analysis. (a) for delineating the objectives of the district plan. (b) for outlining the district development strategy. (c) for determining the priorities of development. (d) for resource inventory * physical resources * human resources * infrastructural and institutional resources. (e) for understanding the problems and potentials of the district (malady-remedy analysis). (f) for understanding the intra-district disparities in the levels of development. (g) for identifying investment opportunities (projects) Appraisal of on-going programmes. Appraisal of existing technology.

(*Contd.*)

TABLE 16.5 (*Contd.*)

Modules		Subject areas
4. Techniques and tools for district planning		Resources allocation. Target formulation. Project formulation Map Interpretation Monitoring and evaluation.
5. Plan and Programme formulation by sectors Determination of goals and objectives of respective sectors (directions of development) Analysis of development potential Establishing sectoral quantitative targets. Estimation of sectoral resource requirements e.g. capital, manpower, space etc.		*Production Sectors*
	(a)	Land resources and utilization.
	(b)	Agriculture.
	(c)	Livestock development.
	(d)	Forestry
	(e)	Fisheries
	(f)	Cottage and small-scale industries
		Infrastructure Sectors
	(a)	Irrigation.
	(b)	Energy.
	(c)	Roads.
	(d)	Marketing.
	(e)	Banking.
		Planning for Basic Needs and their location
	(a)	Health.
	(b)	Family Planning.
	(c)	Education.
	(d)	Housing.
	(e)	Drinking Water.
		Resource estimation : Government, Local, banks, external aid etc.
6. Implementation and management aspects		Implementation techniques (network, schedule, budget, task analysis). Integraton and co-ordination. Monitoring and Evaluation.
7. Popular participation		Participation in planning. Participation in implementation Participation in benefits. Participation in evaluation. Voluntary Agency participation Strengthening receiving mechanisms (user groups).
8. Documentation/ briefing room		Maps Charts Pictures/photographs Graphs District Atlas.

I have dealt with the framework used in developing a training manual for decentralized district planning in Nepal in some detail because I am of the view that this will have great relevance to a similar work that one may take up in other country contexts. I am sure that experts will agree that the scope and content of the training modules, as visualized for Nepal's context, will be more or less applicable to the Indian and other contexts too in its broad essentials. The details, of course, will vary and will have to be suitably worked out for each country's development context. The training modules realised here are :

1. Understanding Development.
2. Decentralization and the Planning Process in Nepal.
3. District Planning : An Analytical Process.
4. Techniques and Tools for District Planning.
5. District Plan Formulation.
6. Implementation and Management of District Plans.
7. Popular Participation.
8. Development Support Communication for District Development.

Role of National Academy

I feel that the Lal Bahadur Shastri National Academy of Administration in India, which is responsible for the induction training of the top-level administrators in the country, has a crucial role in the development of a basic training manual for decentralized district planning. Since the probationers, who will be later taking up positions as District Chiefs, will, after completing their first phase of training at Mussoorie, followed by a stint in the district for a fixed period of time, will be coming back to Mussoorie again for a final spell of training, they will have opportunities for field-testing the manual in their districts and thus providing a valuable feed back for making appropriate modifications and refinements in the manual. In my view, here are some great potentials which, if effectively utilized, may lead to a meaningful contribution to training the numerous actors engaged in decentralized planning endeavour, thus positively aiding the national effort in structuring the planning process at the local level along the lines of the new participatory approach, in which there is so much resurgence of interest today.

Conclusion

To conclude, the considerations and discussions in this chapter have revolved chiefly around the question of the training needs for decentralized planning, with particular emphasis on the identification of the key actors, who would be needing training, the kind of knowledge, skills and attitudes that are necessary for them and the scope and content of the training packages to be developed for this purpose. On the basis of the insights gained from my own personal experiences in an international context, I have also ventured to explore and plead for some promising directions in which the training effort could be furthered, so as to build up our personnel capabilities in an effective manner. In my view, we are discussing this subject when things are moving quite fast in India. Soon, all the States may be enacting appropriate legislations for decentralized planning and development, which would amplify signals on job requirements and procedures for decentralized planning and development, thus enabling a better assessment of training needs and a more informed approach to decision-making on various vital aspects of training for decentralized planning.

REFERENCES

1. In the comprehensive analysis approach, all facts of the job are examined with the aim of producing a detailed record of every task in the job, and the skills, knowledge and attitudes required to carry out every one of these tasks. The "key task analysis" approach confines itself to key or central tasks within a job. In a "Problem centred approach", analysis is limited to a difficulty considered to have a training solution. In the "core analysis" approach, the intention is to provide broad training which might answer to a variety of tasks, thereby presenting participants with enhanced opportunities of obtaining work within as wide a range of organizations as possible. For further elaboration on these approaches. See John Kenny and Margaret Anne Reid : *Training Interventions*, Institute of Personnel Management, London, 1986.
2. "Assessment of Trained Manpower Needs for agricultural planning and project analysis : A Case Study of Gujarat, India"–Food and Agriculture Organization of the United Nations, Rome, 1987.
3. Estimates are provided by the village panchayats.
4. There are 9 *Ilakas* in one District and 75 Districts in Nepal.
5. Which benefit more than one village.
6. There are 9 wards in a village panchayat.
7. This pilot project planning exercise in Tanahun District was undertaken by FAO in collaboration with the Agricultural Project Services Centre (APROSC) during 1984.
8. There are 3 Sub-Committees in the case of West Bengal viz. (i) A Technical Sub-Committee to look into the feasibility and estimated costs/benefits of each schemes; (ii) an Economic Sub-Committee for arranging all schemes in order of priorities, making sure of the required compatibility of and coordination between different schemes as well as consistency with the 'needs statements' prepared by the gram panchayat; (iii) A Sub-committee headed by the *sabhadhipati* for finally deciding on the contours of the district plan.

17

PLANNING EXERCISE-ORIENTED TRAINING
An International Experience*

Regional (sub-national) planning as a means to achieve a more even development within a country has been generally accepted as a tool by all developing countries. This calls for a decentralization of the planning machinery into the various regions of each country. Such a planning machinery must be composed of a multi-disciplinary team endowed with relevant knowledge and skills and capable of applying various analytical techniques for problem identification, project formulation and preparation of implementable development plans. These capabilities required of a planning team have to be systematically built up, assiduously maintained and continuously and effectively strengthened. In this context, the training of a "critical mass" of regional planners in the developing countries has assumed great importance.

The Economic and Social Council of the United Nations (ECOSOC) passed a resolution as early as 1965,[1] stressing the importance of regional development and, as one of the measures to promote it, recommended the initiation of training through the exchange of successful experiences in regional development. This was succeeded by another ECOSOC resolution[2] in 1971 which defined the major purposes of a regional (sub-national) approach to development and requested "the Secretary-General, in cooperation with the specialized agencies, the United Nations Development Programme and other multi-lateral and regional institutions, to work out arrangements by which resources can be mobilized and utilized for research and training within regional development projects supported by them".

---

* Case study prepared for the Food and Agriculture Organization of the United Nations in April 1987 and included in the FAO publication, *Training for Decentralized Planning*, Ed. by Materne Maetz and Maria G. Quieti, Vol. II, Rome 1987.

One of the specialized agencies at the international level set up in pursuance of the above resolutions is the United Nations Centre for Regional Development at Nagoya, Japan, which was established in 1971 and which has been conducting regular training courses in regional development to strengthen regional planning capabilities in the developing countries. This Chapter deals with the experience of the training approaches experimented by this institution, specially with reference to one of the well-known approaches called here the "Planning Exercise-Oriented Training Approach" (PEOT).

UNCRD—Mandate and Activities

The United Nations Centre for Regional Development (UNCRD) came into being through upgradation of an existing institution in Nagoya (Japan), called the Chubu Centre for U.N. Research and Training Programme in Regional Development, which had been started in 1968. Its major purpose is to enhance regional development planning capabilities in developing countries. In order to achieve this objective, UNCRD has organized its activities into four programme areas : research, training, advisory services and information exchange. Training is the core of its activities and the other programmes have been so devised as to be linked as much as possible by feed-in feed-back relations.

The UNCRD's training programmes broadly fall into two major activities, namely : (a) an international training programme called "General Combined Course" (GCC), intended for mid-career and advanced level officials (planners, administrators and trainers) from developing countries; and (b) a training programme focused on a particular country or region (i.e. a group of relatively homogeneous countries). The emphasis here is on the former category of international training programme.

Right from its inception in 1971 until 1987, the UNCRD has run *fifteen* international training courses. The names of these courses and their duration are indicated in Table 17.1.

As may be seen from the table, the international training programme has undergone some distinct changes in terms of duration. Three phases of change are discernible : (i) from 1972 to 1979, the courses were of a duration ranging from four to six months; (ii) from 1980 to 1982, they were reduced to a duration of three months; and (iii) from 1983 on-wards, they were further reduced to a duration of two months.

TABLE 17.1 : International Training Courses conducted in UNCRD and their duration.

	Name of Course	Duration (months)
1.	First General Combined Training Course on Regional Development (14 Feb. to 16 June 1971)	4
2.	Second General Combined Course on Comprehensive Regional Development Planning for Metropolitan Regions (14 Feb. to 16 June 1973)	4
3.	Third General Combined Course in Comprehensive Development of Region with predominantly rural characteristics (17 Feb. to 30 June 1974)	4 1/2
4.	Fourth General Combined Course on the Comprehensive Development of Rural Regions (10 Jan. to 11 July 1975)	6
5.	Fifth General Combined Course on Comprehensive Regional Development (12 Jan. to 12 July 1976)	6
6.	United Nations Asian Development Institute, Bangkok and UNCRD—Joint Training Course on Planning for Integrated Regional Development (1 Feb. to 22 July 1977)	5 3/4
7.	Training Course in Regional Development Planning (6 Feb. to 29 June 1979)	4 3/4
8.	Eighth International Training Course in Regional Development Planning (1 April to 30 June 1980)	3
9.	Ninth International Training Course in Regional Development Planning (3 March to 31 May 1981)	3
10.	Tenth International Training Course in Regional Development Planning (2 March to 31 May 1981)	3
11.	Eleventh International Training Course in Regional Development Planning (15 March to 16 May 1983)	2
12.	Twelfth International Training Course in Regional Development Planning (13 March to 14 May 1984)	2
13.	Thirteenth International Training Course in Regional Development Planning (1 April to 30 May 1985)	2
14.	Fourteenth International Training Course in Regional Development Planning (1 April to 30 May 1986)	2
15.	Fifteenth International Training Course in Regional Development Planning (1 April to 30 May 1986)	2

The change in the course duration has also meant a change in the content, scope and orientation of the programme. The year 1979 may be seen as a wastershed when a change in the approach to training was initiated and the training course was redesigned and restructured.

Until 1979, the international training course was, in a very substantial way, *inductive*, and built around a "planning exercise", usually carried out in a developing country. The course relied heavily on data collection and analysis. The duration of the courses varied between four and six months, out of which a period extending between four and six weeks was spent by trainees on in-field planning exercises.

In the latter half of 1979, the Centre took a major policy-decision to redesign and restructure the international training course. It was decided that in the restructured course :

(a) Emphasis should be placed on both the inductive and deductive approaches to training;
(b) The training methods should be strengthened by a wider use of cases, problem-solving exercises, games, etc.;
(c) Attempts should be made to standardize the course inputs without any prejudice to new ideas; and
(d) Efforts should be made to document and prepare teaching materials which can be used in the UNCRD training courses, and also made available to the training institutions in developing countries.[3]

The broad details of the course design adopted by the Centre in the 1974, 1982 and 1985 international training programmes may be seen in Annextures 1, 2 and 3. They serve to illustrate the changes in the course content introduced from time to time.

The emphasis here is on the training programme conducted by the Institution, centred around planning exercises for a specific region selected in a developing country. Four such planning exercise-oriented courses were conducted by the UNCRD focused on the following regions : Bicol Region of the Philippines (1974), Yogyakarta Province in Indonesia (1975), Sind Province in Pakistan (1976) and Nakhon Ratchasima Province (North-east Region) in Thailand (1977). In this chapter, the training programme conducted with the Bicol Region in the Philippines as the focus will be discussed in detail. The choice of this case has been determined by the author's association and familiarity with this programme, as he was Consultant to the UNCRD during this period.

Planning Exercise-Oriented Training Approach—
Rationale, Concept and Principles

The Planning Exercise-oriented Training Programme of UNCRD is based on the principle of "learning by doing". The basic idea here is that training activities cannot be confined merely to problem identification and acquainting trainees with the sophisticated techniques. More important, trainees have to learn how to work as members of a planning team and formulate implementable development plans and to increase their capacity to manage development projects and programmes. While this may sum up generally the philosophy behind the approach, the rationale for adopting this approach, as well as the concept and principles underlying it, need to be elaborated in some detail.

Originally, the programme was envisaged as a significant international *technical assistance* programme to the developing countries, intended to forge "partnership in development", i.e. partnership between those involved in development planning at the international and national levels and partnership between development planners and the people. To do so was to make a departure from the conventional type of technical assistance projects, which are aimed at formulating development plans without strengthening local planning capacities. It was argued that the conventional type of technical assistance had led the developing countries to depend perpetually on very expensive foreign technical assistance schemes. It was, therefore, proposed that a technical assistance programme with a built-in training component, which will be relevant and of direct application to the regional planning staff in each country, should be evolved. "Such a programme should be organized as a "unified input package", consisting of training, research, information systems and advisory services. . . . Furthermore, the programme should be designed to cover adequately the very diverse conditions of regions (even within each country) and bring about innovations in development planning".[4]

The basic idea was to link training with action effectively. For this purpose, the team approach to training was advocated. The approach here will be to train all the planners in the planning organization as a "team", to the extent that they acquire a critical minimum of knowledge and skills, to enable them to formulate a regional development plan for the region where they live and work. The main feature of the regional plan would be that it will be formulated by the local officials and not by a group of foreign experts. The strategy is to first build up a core group—a team of trained planners in each region concerned. This is to be followed by the provision of other opportunities (i.e. through seminars, workshops, colloquia, etc.) for decision-makers, research personnel, and specialists to upgrade their knowledge and understanding of development planning.

In this context, the proposed technical assistance model to strengthen regional planning capacities was viewed as a "Stages (or Phases) Approach". It was proposed to divide it into three main phases : Phase 1, or research and information gathering; Phase 2, or basic training course; and Phase 3, or on-the-job training. The total duration of the proposed technical assistance was envisaged at two years, more or less, depending upon the circumstances prevailing in the region concerned. It was considered that, roughly, Phase 1 will require four months, Phase 2 about six months and Phase 3 fourteen months. All these phases will be implemented in the spirit of partnership between the United Nations and the relevant institutions in the countries and regions concerned.[5]

Proposed Technical Assistance Model

The proposed technical assistance model has been diagramatically shown in Fig. 17.1.

In this model, Phase 1 is a preparatory phase which will consist of two related activities. The first activity is research on salient regional development problems. This research will be mainly of the survey type. Survey questionnaires to find out the opinion of the people on issues such as development priorities or to diagnose more sharply the causes of underdevelopment in each locality will be designed, and the surveys conducted in cooperation with local development agencies and the particular persons, who will comprise the core planning team plus research fellows.[6] Due to the limited available time, the final analysis of the survey results may be done during Phase 2, as part of the activities in the second phase.

The other activity will be information gathering from secondary sources. The information gathered will be classified and a preliminary review of the relevance and accuracy of these various pieces of information will be made. In addition, a study of the sources of information, the frequency of information generation activities of these sources, and the pattern of storage and retrieval of information in the region concerned (in relation to the national context) will be made, with the aim of improving the existing information network or proposing new information systems for regional planning in the subsequent phases. The activities in this phase will contribute to the designing of the contents of Phase 2, which will fit the needs of the country and region concerned.

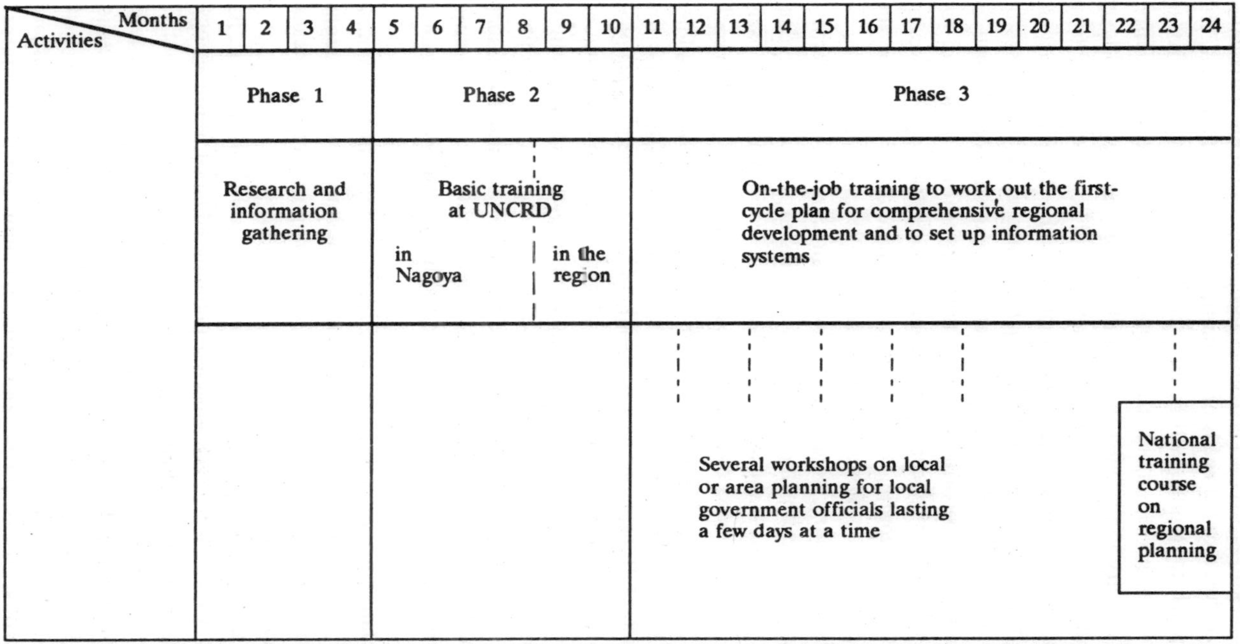

FIG. 17.1 : UNCRD's Model for Training and Technical Assistance.

Phase 2 will provide basic training for regional planning staff in the country concerned, with a curriculum designed to provide knowledge and skills tailored to the needs of the particular country and region. The team approach to training will be adopted. Each team will have five to ten members or perhaps more. The composition of each team will differ from one country to the other in terms of disciplines, sectors, and level of government representation. However, a team will be drawn mainly from a particular region with a regional development authority and will include some members coming from the national planning agency in charge of coordinating the planning being done at the regional level, as well as some members from research and training institutions located in (or nearest to) the region concerned. The composition of the team, however, could be varied according to circumstances. These teams will form the core group for the on-the-job training activities. (Fig. 17.1)

The basic training course will provide an international interdisciplinary experience. It will emphasize exchanging experiences in regional development and the team approach to learning. It will provide the basis for continuing the efforts of trainees by keeping them in touch with each other and by keeping them informed of the latest thinking on regional development. In terms of content, the training course will expose the trainees to the full range of issues in planning for comprehensive regional development. These are : (a) appropriate and applicable techniques for plan formulation, (b) issues encountered in plan implementation, (c) national-regional-local coordination as well as intersectoral coordination of development activities and of the personnel involved, (d) issues faced in mobilizing resources for regional development, and (e) issues dealing with the multilevel political and cultural context of regional planning.

The planning team will work on a specific region in the country concerned. During the basic training course, its members will be taught how to formulate a comprehensive regional development plan by means of a planning exercise.

After the basic training course is over, each team will return to its region and will form the task force for planning attached to the agency in charge of regional development. Phase 3 can now be started. Phase 3 will be an on-the-job training set of activities that will guide each task force in working out the details of the plan for its region. These details will cover projects and their interrelationships, problems of intra-regional disparities and ways to resolve them, area development plans (districts, municipalities, towns, cities, and villages), budgeting procedures, reporting procedures, and information systems required for planning in the region. The task force will work with all local government units, the political authorities, and all national government agencies concerned. Each task force, being composed mainly of members of these agencies, will operate in close collaboration with all the institutions mentioned above in order to bring about a coordinated total development effort. Each task force will learn to work within existing political and administrative realities. This will not bar it from thinking about a long-term management system for regional development.

In order to accomplish its work, each task force will have to be kept in close touch with the people and their representatives and with all government agencies through a series of workshops and through intensive and continuous consultation with groups and individuals living and working in the region. These workshops will become a systematic effort to elicit the people's ideas, analyze them meaningfully, formulate development objectives reflecting local needs, and match local resources and capabilities with these needs, in order to select feasible and acceptable priority projects for implementation. The results of these workshops and consultations will be fitted into the regional planning framework. The task force will be expected to learn how to conduct workshops effectively, in order to encourage popular participation in regional planning.

Towards the end of the third phase, after the plan for the comprehensive development of the region is completed, the task force involved will assist in conducting a national training course, of duration varying from eight to twelve weeks, for regional planners from other regions in the country. This national training course will use the planning experience in the region, where the task force worked, and will study the completed final-draft of the first-cycle plan as a case. The task force members will be the teachers for this training course, assisted by consultants and other experts, whenever necessary. In this way, the planning experience that had been gained (which otherwise will be confined to only one of many regions) will be used to spark off more regional development activities and will be diffused widely in the country.

Planning Exercise-oriented Training—Bicol Region Experience

The foregoing account briefly sets out the model, which influenced the thinking of the UNCRD in regard to the organization of its planning exercise-oriented training programme. In the actual operationalization of the idea, however, some compromises had to be made and the technical assistance model discussed above underwent some changes. The framers of the training programme, however, tried to retain its broad features. Among them, *four* features may be particularly mentioned.

First, the curriculum was built around an intensive planning exercise that occupied almost three-quarters of the course duration. The course was designed mainly for advanced level and mid-career government officials from developing countries directly concerned with comprehensive regional development planning in areas with predominantly rural characteristics.[7] The idea of plunging the trainees into the planning exercise with minimum lecture inputs was considered appropriate, as many of the trainees would be those, who already had considerable experience of actual planning and development work. The emphasis sought to be given to the training programme was working experience of inter-disciplinary planning, and not so much of abstract theoretical accounts of regional development.

The second feature was the use of an actual region, preferably backward, in a developing country. For the 1974 training programme, the Bicol region in the Philippines was chosen for the planning exercise.

Thirdly, the training programme was so planned that the trainees, after preparing the draft plan, were given the chance of visiting the case region, so that they could test the validity of their approaches and conclusions vis-a-vis real situations through interviews with local resource persons and field observations.

Fourthly, eight out of 26 trainee—nearly a third of the total number—constituting the "core group",—were selected from the country in which the case region was located (in this case, the Philippines) and were drawn from various offices related to the development of the case region, the idea being that they would be the "carry agents" of the new knowledge, working experience as well as the interpersonal rapport that would evolve during the training course to the follow-up phase envisaged in the technical assistance model.

The training course was scheduled from 17 February to 30 June, 1974. The preparations for the training programme started more than one year ahead of the event, i.e. from early 1973. Consultations were held with the Government of the Philippines concerning the selection of the case region and the conduct of the course. The Bicol region was chosen with their concurrence. Some of the senior staff members of UNCRD, assisted by some research fellows, visited the country and collected all the materials considered relevant to regional development in Bicol. These were brought to Nagoya, classified and placed in special racks in the library for the use of trainees and instructors. A research project 501, "Role of cities in attaining a desirable population distribution in the context of rapid urbanization", meant to provide inputs to the UNCRD training programmes, had been conceived earlier and the Bicol region was selected as one of the three case study areas for this project. The other two were Meerut city in India and Tsu and Hamamatsu cities in Japan. The author of this paper was the chief consultant to this project and played a crucial role in conducting these studies. In the Bicol region, the major concern of this study was to examine the role of the three cities of the region—Naga, Iriga and Legaspi—in regional economic development. The field work for the study was conducted in two and-a-half-months—September to November, 1983—and the research findings of the study were channelled into the training course in the form of training material. The UNCRD had also commissioned another study on the administrative aspects of the regional development which was conducted by Professor Raul P. Guzman of the College of Public Administration, University of the Philippines. Other relevant studies conducted in the Philippines by academics and professionals in the National Economic and Development Authority (NEDA) were also assembled. The UNCRD also prepared a bibliography of literature on Philippine development. All these documents were available to the trainees for reference. The various pre-training preparatory efforts enumerated here claimed a good deal of time of the UNCRD faculty and placed a heavy burden on them.

Apart from the indigenous training materials with specific reference to the country/case-region, a number of other training materials were also selected to cover various subject domains, considered relevant from the point of view of regional planning and development. The selection of such teaching materials followed some general guidelines. *Firstly*, teaching or training materials should be relevant to the conditions of the developing countries, in particular, Asia. *Secondly*, greater use should be made of the materials produced in the Asian countries and preferably by Asian authors. *Thirdly*, materials should take note of the vast heterogeneity of the developing countries; in other words, examples and cases should be drawn not from one or two but from a broader range of countries.[8] Selection had naturally to rely in a substantial way on the available contributions by noted development specialists. Many of them related to regional policies and theories developed in the context of Europe or USA and were not relevant to the situations prevailing in the developing countries. With the exception of a few models, the major part of regional economics was based on the institutional assumption of a market-oriented economy. Neoclassical thinking was dominant in most contributions.[9] These facts notwith-standing, the contributions of the Western authors provided the source materials for a modicum of theory, which the trainees had to be taught. At least in the first few training programmes of the UNCRD, the search for finding a suitable training literature from Asian experiences met with limited success. The situation seems to have changed appreciably since then. Judged by the volume of literature published by the UNCRD, the process of developing indigenous training materials and cases from the developing countries seems to have caught on.[10]

The training programme focused on the Bicol region was a joint effort by the UNCRD and the Government of the Philippines through the National Economic Development Authority (NEDA), Department of Public Works, Communications and Transportation and the Institute of Planning of the University of the Philippines. Details of the training course content and schedule may be seen in Fig. 17.2. The pre-training activities consisted of collection of information through surveys and their analysis and a series of UNCRD working sessions of staff members to evolve a comprehensive planning framework, apart from the research project mentioned earlier, which was going on independently. The UNCRD team was sent to the Bicol region during July-November 1973 and they conducted the analysis of surveys and the preliminary processing of data during November, 1973 to January, 1974.

The basic training course was conducted with the assistance of the UNCRD regular faculty, consultants and visiting lecturers. The UNCRD at that time had only three staff members, who had specializations respectively in : (1) economic, (2) social/administrative, and (3) physical planning aspects. They constituted the "core team of trainers".

As may be seen from Fig. 17.2, the training course started with the participation papers delivered by the trainees. This was followed by the presentation of two cases in formulating regional development plans. One case related to an experience from a developing country and the other dealt with a Japanese experience. These two cases were intended to acquaint the trainees with the whole range of issues involved in comprehensive planning which, in turn, was expected to guide the trainees in preparing the framework for the planning exercise. The planning exercise then started as a series of steps. In broad terms, the planning exercise was divided into five steps. These are :

Fig. 17.2 : UNCRD's Training Course : Content and Schedule.

	Step 1	Step 2	Step 3	Step 4	Step 5	Step 6	Step 7	Step 8	Step 9
PARTICIPANTS INPUTS	Presenta-tion	Initiate work on framework for planning exercises	Data collection and analysis	Make projections	Set objectives, quantify targets	Work out various instru-ments	Apply approaches to integrate	Consider reactions of officials, citizens	Final write-up, and reporting
TRAINING COURSE CONTENTS	Partici-pation papers reporting sessions	Two case studies in actual regional planning practice	Present state &	Projections	Objectives	Instruments to achieve	Integration of	Project	Final development
			PLANNING EXERCISE						
			potential of the region		and targets	targets	instruments	proposals	plan
TRAINING STAFF INPUTS	Comments	Presen-tation	Lectures on relevant social, economic, physical, and administrative techniques					Supervise fieldwork	Final comments
Reporting sessions and chapter write-up			1	2	3	4	5	6	7
Tentative timetable	Feb. 17 to March 15		March 18 .... May 31					3 to 28 June	
Location of training course	Nagoya .... Nagoya				.... Japan			Bicol Region, Philippines	

FIG. 17.2 : UNCRD's Training Course : Content and Schedule.

(1) analyzing the present state of the region;
(2) making future projections;
(3) setting objectives and quantifying objectives into targets;
(4) working out the instruments or the means to attain targets by sector; and
(5) applying various approaches to integrate the different elements into a comprehensive plan.

This training phase in "steps" was interspersed with lectures by training staff on relevant social, economic, physical and administrative techniques. Examples of techniques for which instructions were provided included : techniques of information gathering including the designing of survey questionnaires, classifying, storing and retrieving information quickly and accurately when needed; techniques to assess income, savings, investment levels and their distribution; techniques to analyze housing conditions, health conditions, food consumption levels, education levels; techniques to analyze the present state of industrialization, agriculture and infrastructure; techniques to analyze the people's attitudes and life goals; techniques to analyze social, economic and administrative institutions; and approaches to analyze development policies; techniques of projections by sector, such as outputs in agriculture, manufacturing, housing and transportation and by function such as employment, investment and consumption; techniques and approaches in disaggregating regional development targets as well as aggregating regional development targets into national targets; and techniques for the analysis of public investments, institutional arrangements, level measures and citizen (or popular) participation in development.

For the training course, 26 trainees were selected from 13 countries. Eight of them were from the Philippines. In order to undertake the planning exercise, the 26 trainees were divided into three working groups,[11] focusing respectively on : (1) economic, (2) social/administrative, and (3) physical aspects of planning. Each group was placed under the guidance of a UNCRD staff member, who was a specialist in the particular area. While most of the time, the working groups functioned independently to perform the relevant analysis and planning tasks concerning their subject domain, intersectoral coordination, that is most desired in the planning work, was brought about through formal/informal sessions organized at frequent intervals, during which vigorous interaction among the groups took place. In the formal sessions, intergroup reporting and discussion was arranged. It should be noted that informal interactions predominated over formal interactions. Among the four major phases of the planning tasks, viz. : diagnosis and problem identification, macro framework-building (i.e. formulation of goals, identification of strategy and setting of targets), programme/project formulation and planning for implementation, the first two phases were attempted at Nagoya and the remaining two were done during the last one and a half months' period of stay in the case region. The training course ended with a seminar to present the trainees' report to the officials and experts concerned in the country.

While the planning exercise was completed according to the time schedule, and the training programme as a whole was deemed a success in the sense that it could accomplish what was envisaged during the training period, it cannot be so said about the post-training performance envisaged in the technical assistance model. As may be noted from the model, much of the initiative for the post-training follow-up lay with the trainees selected from the country in which the case region is located. On account of the rather low-keyed follow-up performance that ensured (for several reasons, administrative and others), many of the activities that were envisaged in the original model could not materialize.[12] Later, in an informal evaluation of the programme by the UNCRD staff members, it was decided that the post-training follow up should be institutionalized and not left to the spontaneity of the trainees from the country. Accordingly, in the next training programme organized in 1975 in Indonesia, a one-and-a-half-year post-training phase was also planned. The UNCRD saw that one adviser was stationed in the case region during that period, who backstopped the activities of the trainees drawn from Indonesia by way of providing work guidelines and advisory services. Some specific work assignments were also planned during the on-the-job training phase.[13]

The outcome of the planning exercise carried out by the trainees was a document in four volumes called *Regional Development of Bicol—the Philippines*. Volume I dealt with the regional situation which contained a sector-wise analysis, bringing out the potentials, present development performance measured by critical indicators of development, and problems of and constraints to development. Volume II dealt with plan formulation, projects, objectives and targets with 11 chapters. Volume III contained programmes and strategies in 13 chapters. Volume IV set out implementation tasks, which explained the network and schedule of development activities indicating the phases, tasks and institutional framework for development. Judged by the volume of work done by the team of trainees in just three months of intensive work, as well as the wide range of problems and issues discussed in the four volumes, anyone would agree that the achievement was indeed impressive. According to an evaluation "because of this, the course seemed to have succeeded in bringing about a tremendous impact over the trainees, both intellectual and behavioural". The evaluation by the trainees themselves showed that they were highly satisfied with the experience and the exposure to techniques and methodologies of regional development. The team spirit, which was inculcated during the course, was highly commended. As a UNCRD Progress Report in 1978 states : "It can be observed that, so far, the training courses have attained the intended aim. It contributed in making the fellows broaden their horizons, so that they are better prepared for engaging in the work of coordination, the vital element of regional planning. This approach also succeeded in generating initiatives of countries in training in regional development and planning, such as on-the-job training in Indonesia following GCC 1975, and the initiation of a series of training programmes for regional planning by the Government of Thailand following the completion of GCC in 1977".[14] Nevertheless, it must be pointed out that from the planning point of view, the report contained considerable gaps, inconsistencies and inadequacies. The time constraints, and the rush with which the planning exercises had to be carried out, partly explain these shortfalls. It is needless to say that a viable comprehensive regional development plan cannot be expected to be completed in such a short period through this method of crash programme. The output that emerged from the planning exercise cannot, therefore, be called a "plan", but just a training report.[15]

Some Subsequent Development and Critical Comments on the Approach

This story of the training experience in Nagoya would be incomplete without an account of some subsequent developments and some critical comments on the approach. As the UNCRD continued this approach to training, year after year, with some refinements and changes, it was felt both necessary and feasible to consolidate these experiences into a guideline for regional development planning. This became necessary not only for streamlining the UNCRD's own training, but also for disseminating its experiences to training institutions in the countries. Hence, a series of activities were proposed as a programme of research with the following aims :

(i) To work out the methods of planning for comprehensive regional development, which can be used as operational tools for planning with specific focus on various aspects of implementation; and
(ii) To review and evaluate in a continuous manner the utility, concepts, methods and techniques that the UNCRD will employ in its training activities.

The above research project attempted by way of inductive approach—that is, through distillation of the salient ingredients from among the three planning exercises conducted until then[16]— a guideline, which set out the methods of planning for comprehensive regional development, known as "MPCRD Report (1976)".[17] It sought to elaborate methodologies addressed to the plan formulation exercise which is suitable for :

(a) A one-round regional development plan formulation exercise to be carried out in the shortest period possible;
(b) Inducing active interdepartmental coordination and collaboration;
(c) A practical planning strategy through which resilience—building of rural communities, both economically and socially—can be given first priority; and
(d) Enable all members of the team to tackle the whole gamut of developmental issues in the multilevel planning context.[18]

The thrust of the MPCRD report consists in its systematic focus on the planning process as a continuum. It does not elaborate on specific analytical techniques that are to be employed in the different contexts in the planning process,[19] but concentrates on systematization of various activities to be undertaken in the process. After reviewing the ways in which the planning exercises were undertaken, it identified seven essential steps. These are :

Step 1: Diagnosis (i.e. problem identification)
Step 2: Macro-framework building
Step 3: Sectoral Planning

Step 4: Intersectoral coordination
Step 5: Plan finalization
Step 6: Action programme formulation
Step 7: Planning for implementation.

The seven-step planning process is diagramatically illustrated in Fig. 17.3.

The planning exercise-oriented training method followed by the UNCRD went through the seven steps enumerated above, and, since the publication of the report, the training programmes conducted in the UNCRD with the above activity components have come to be known as the MPCRD approach to training.[20]

In a frank appraisal, the MPCRD approach was considered technocratic, inductive and largely a "top-down" approach. The following lacunae were pointed out :

(a) That planning for regional development is seldom a neat, logical or sequential process;
(b) That it is not merely a technical exercise; and
(c) That planning is a highly iterative effort.

After the fourth planning exercise-oriented training programme based on the MPCRD approach was concluded in 1977, an in-house investigation into the validity and utility of the UNCRD approach was initiated and a review mission assessed the activities of the UNCRD and gave recommendations for its future action. The review mission noted that the UNCRD's courses were more effective for the participants from the case region country than for those from other countries. It was observed that the success of these courses heavily depended on the commitment of the fellows. The most crucial element that may determine the extent of such commitment would be the relevance of a training course to the conditions and needs of the countries. If fellows are trained for the type of work they are bound to undertake, it is only natural that they would be highly motivated. Such a thing, however, can best be done in a country-specific training programme than in a "multi-country" training programme, as it can then be tailored commensurate to the administrative system for regional development and planning of the particular country. Based on such considerations, the mission recommended a two-pronged approach with : (a) a multi-national course for training individual regional planners, and (b) a country course for

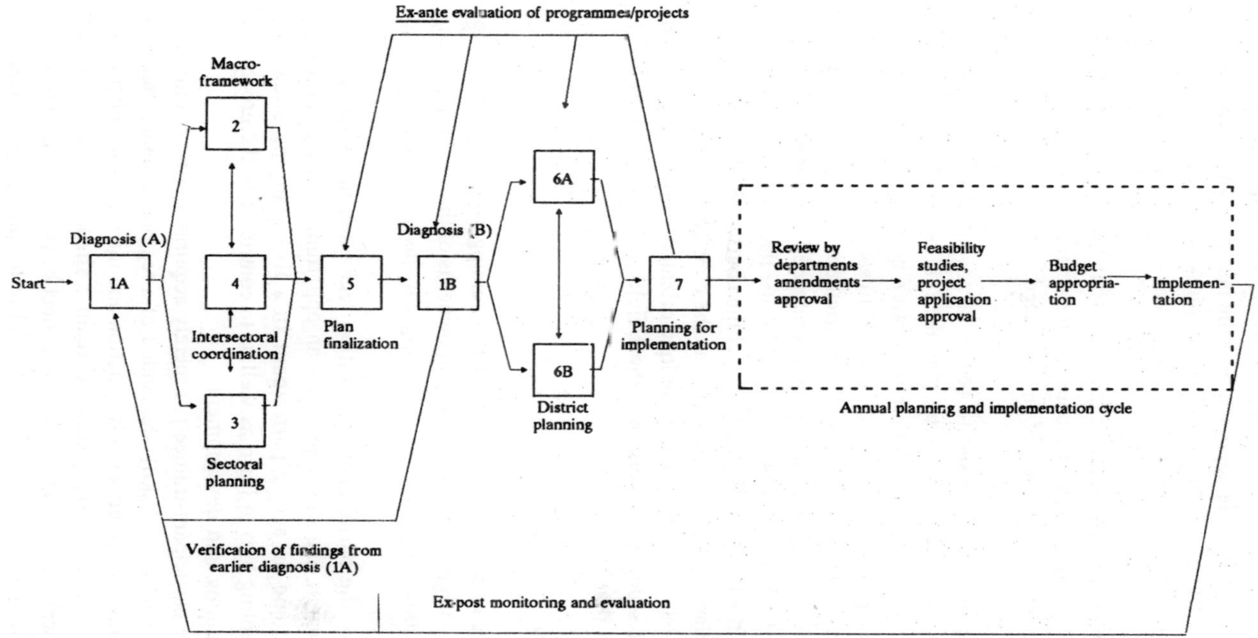

FIG. 17.3 : Planning Process : Seven Steps in a Unified System.

Source: H. Nagamine : Methods of Planning for Comprehensive Regional Development : A Paradigm. Asian Development Dialogue, Numbers 5 and 6, 1977, UNCRD 1978.

training integrated teams in two or three similar countries. The team also favoured a more deductive approach over the inductive approach followed by the UNCRD in its curriculum content for the multi-national course. Accordingly, the UNCRD now runs two kinds of courses :

(1) A general multi-national course at UNCRD, and
(2) Some country specific courses (for a single country or group of countries) conducted in a selected country.

The first one is addressed to senior or advanced-level personnel who have to, or will soon have to, play the role of promoter or trainer for regional development in their respective countries. The latter is conducted in a particular country in response to specific requests received from a government/governments. The curriculum of the multi-national course has undergone some modifications intended "to equip the fellows with knowledge and skills as a unified package that may be of common relevance to the process of planning" and the course has also been shortened. The planning exercise, which was the core of the earlier training programme, has yielded place to technique-oriented exercises, simulation games, case study presentations, short field visits, etc., apart from lectures and discussions.

Summing-up

Our objective in documenting the UNCRD training experience here is to derive some insights into the merits and demerits of the PEOT approach. In a dispassionate analysis, the following conclusions emerge :

(1) Like the participant-observation technique in social science research, the PEOT provides an opportunity for the trainee to become an active participant in a live planning situation, enabling him to learn as well as to contribute to the process of planning and development.
(2) The participant-trainee not merely acquires a critical minimum knowledge and skills demanded of a regional planner, but also learns how to effectively function and interact as member of an interdisciplinary planning team : shedding light without generating heat. The latter is a distinct behavioural and attitudinal gain that stands him in good stead in his professional career.

(3) So far as the training institution is concerned, the PEOT is a highly demanding exercise. It needs a considerable lead time to complete the pre-training activities. It demands that a good deal of data collection, analysis and research must precede the training phase. If the impact is seriously desired, then it is necessary also to plan for the post-training phase in a meticulous manner by making such institutional arrangements as necessary.

(4) So far as the time duration of training is concerned, the PEOT needs a fairly long period of time. In the UNCRD experience, about 6 months were required for the training phase alone, as it entailed field work, visits to various offices and considerable dialogue, both with officials and the people, to understand the various facets of the development problem.

(5) The pre-training and post-phase training activities are equally important and they demand at least 3 to 4 times the duration of the training phase. When the training period is of long duration, and it is meant for senior and middle-level personnel, many governments find it difficult to release such personnel for long periods. This is a practical constraint that has to be kept in view, when organizing such programmes.

(6) In terms of cost also, the PEOT is an approach which demands considerable sums of money. Firstly, there are the pre-training costs to be met. Secondly, during the training phase, money has to be provided for field work and travel.

(7) The PEOT approach, it must be understood, is not merely exercise-oriented, but also *trainee-centred.* As planning is a multi-level and multi-sectoral activity, the composition of the planning team must have a multi-disciplinary character, so that the various aspects of planning will receive proper attention. In this context, a good deal of care is necessary in regard to the *selection of trainees*, as ultimately the planning team should be representative of the numerous disciplines.

(8) In terms of its impact, however, the PEOT approach is to be highly commended. Through a judicious combination of lectures, discussions, field work and the planning exercise, it would be possible for the trainees to learn more here than through any other method.

(9) As the UNCRD experience revealed, the impact of the PEOT approach is especially great in a country-specific situation, as

it is directly relevant to the path of development pursued in the country and enables the trainees to understand the problems and prospects inherent in the development process operating in his country.

As we are aware, there is growing interest today among the developing countries towards decentralized planning and administration. New structures and procedures for planning are being introduced in many countries and some have also embarked on a process of putting power and responsibility into the hands of the "people" in the decentralized units of administration. All these have led to a growing recognition of the crucial importance of capability building among administrators and planners working at the intermediate and local levels of planning and development administration. In this context, the PEOT approach, applied in a country-specific situation, has great potential for imparting, through training, an appropriate body of skills relevant to on-going planning systems, taking various levels of government and sectoral agencies concerned, and procedures relative to coordinating conflicting interests among the levels and agencies of government.

ANNEXURE-I

THIRD GENERAL COMBINED COURSE (1974)—COURSE DESIGN

1. Participation paper delivered by the trainees.
2. Presentation of two cases in formulating regional development plans.
3. Planning exercise on a step-by-step basis.
4. Steps:

   (1) Analyzing the present state of the region.
   (2) Making future projections.
   (3) Setting objectives and converting objectives into targets.
   (4) Working out instruments or the means to attain targets by sector and integrating these means into a comprehensive plan.

5. Lectures on techniques and approaches during Phase 3, e.g. techniques of information gathering including the designing of survey questionnaires, classifying, storing and retrieving information quickly and accurately when needed; techniques to assess income, savings, investment levels and their distribution; techniques to analyze housing conditions, health conditions, food levels, education levels, techniques to analyze the present state of industrialization, agriculture and infrastructure; techniques to analyze environmental conditions focusing on the state of environmental pollution; techniques to analyze the people's attitudes and life goals; techniques to analyze social, economic and administrative institutions and approaches to analyze development policies; techniques for making projections by sectors such as outputs in agriculture, manufacturing, housing and transportation and by functions such as employment, investment and consumption; techniques and approaches in disaggregating national objectives and targets into regional development targets as well as aggregating regional development targets into national targets; the process of target-setting and working out development indicators; knowledge pertaining to the instruments to attain targets, e.g. public investments, private investments, institutional arrangements, legal measures and citizen participation in development.

ANNEXURE-II

TENTH INTERNATIONAL TRAINING COURSE IN REGIONAL DEVELOPMENT PLANNING—2 MARCH TO 31 MAY, 1982

Course Curriculum

The course deals with subjects as : meaning of development, concepts and theories, social and economic analysis, sectoral approach in planning, project planning and management, institutional dimensions and planning synthesis relative to local and regional development planning. These subject matters are scheduled roughly in accordance with the way in which the planning process usually takes place. Brief annotations are given to each of the key topics as follows :

(a) *Opening Lectures* (OL-series, 2-5 March, 1982) : A series of first-round presentations by the substantive staff of UNCRD on fundamental dimensions of local and regional development. This series will provide opportunities for the trainees to understand the overall orientation in terms of general philosophy of what development should be.

(b) *Country Presentations* (CP-Series, 8-10 March, 1982) : In order to make the best use of the heterogeneous nature of the training group, one should get to know about the situations and major problems the respective countries face. The presentations will be made for that purpose.

(c) *Development Theories* (DT-series, 15-19 March, 1982) : The essence of various development theories will be introduced in a selective manner. The trainees are encouraged to explore ways in which such theories could be made effective tools for development policy formulation.

(d) *Planning Framework* (PF-series, 18-24 March, 1982) : In addition to macro-economic planning techniques and regional income accounts, ways to organize planning processes, ways to identify crucial problems and methods of conducting an area analysis will be discussed. Utilization of electronic technologies (i.e. introduction of computers) in LDC's will also be discussed from the viewpoint of data compilation and management.

(e) *Projection and Forecasting* (FM-series, 25-26 March, 1982) : Simple quantitative skills relevant to projection and forecasting of key variables in development planning will be introduced in addition to essential theoretical issues to be kept in view in undertaking projections and forecasting.

(f) *Sectoral Planning* (SP-series, 29 March to 30 April, 1982) : Key sectors to be included into an integrated development plan, e.g. land use, environment, agriculture, small-scale industries, transport and other infrastructures, human settlement questions, public administration and development financing, education and health.

(g) *Project Analysis and Planning* (PP-series, 7-12 April, 1982) : A series of lectures and case studies relative to basic knowledge and skills of project planning (feasibility, demand analysis, consideration of alternatives, cost-benefit analysis, social profitability analysis, etc.) will be presented.

(h) *Project Management* (PM-series, 27-29 April, 1982) : Various issues relative to implementation management will be discussed through lectures and workshops.

(i) *Planning Synthesis* (PS-series, 4-8 May, 1982) : A workshop on problem identification and programme/project identification will be undertaken in order to apply some of the knowledge and planning tools dealt with during the course. In continuation, an intensive overnight workshop on a business management game will be conducted on May 7 and 8. This business game is expected to give insights into two aspects : first, it will provide an opportunity to examine the relationship between economic factors and human factors in decision-making which is basically the same between public and business administration; second, to evaluate its utility from the viewpoint of training methodology for development planners and administrators.

(j) *Case Studies* (CS-series, 14-23 April and 3-30 May, 1982) : Besides various cases taken up in relation to other lecture series, three cases will be highlighted during the course, viz. ;

(i) *Aichi Prefecture, Japan*: The whole group will be divided into three working teams and visit communities in Aichi at different stages of development and characterized by different types of developmental problems. Each team will conduct two overnight field work exercises on 14-16 April focusing on the study of strengths and weak-nesses in the planning process currently practised in each community, from the viewpoint of solving its problems and introducing a more viable development scenario into it. Briefing, interviews with various citizen groups and field observations will be arranged.

The result of field work findings will be presented on Monday, 19 April.

(ii) *South Pacific Islands*: P. Corbin, a development economist associated with the United Nations Department of Technical Cooperation for Development in New York, will introduce the case of the South Pacific Islands with the lecture sessions during the week of 19-23 April.

(iii) *Toyota Factory*: A half-day exposure to an ultra-modern production system on 22 April, 1982.

(iv) *People's Communes, China*: A ten-day study visit to China with focus on the planning process at the people's commune level will be undertaken during 18-30 May. Again, the group will be divided into three or four working teams in order to study the planning processes meaningfully. Mutual reporting sessions about the findings of the field work will take place before departure from China.

(v) *A brief study tour in Tokyo*

(k) *Japanese Experience* (JE-series) : Several introdutory lectures on Japan will be presented with focus on its socio-cultural aspects (that constitute the basis of its viable economic development) and the state-of-art of development planning. Participants are encouraged to make good use of their stay in Japan for studying various aspects of development in Japan as an insightful case for appraising the validity of development strategies of each country.

(l) *Special Lectures* (SL-series) : A few lectures will be delivered by eminent scholars. Besides, a session each on the development experience of West European countries, and the human factors on local development will be provided.

(m) *Report Writing* (RW-series) : As a requirement of the course, every participant should submit a report. For this purpose, nine sessions are earmarked for trainees to concentrate on writing.

(n) *Weekend Activities* (WA-series) : Besides regular training activities as briefly outlined above, there are several extracurricular activities arranged at weekends. Although they are basically unofficial and therefore optional, all the trainees are encouraged to participate, because these will be valuable opportunities to broaden their knowledge about Japan.

(o) *Course Evaluation* (CE-series, 12 May, 1982) : Right before the departure of trainees from Nagoya, one full day is reserved for the trainees to discuss among themselves and present the results of discussions about their evaluation on the course to the UNCRD staff.

ANNEXURE-III

THIRTEENTH INTERNATIONAL TRAINING COURSE IN REGIONAL DEVELOPMENT PLANNING : 2 APRIL TO 31 MAY 1985

The Thirteenth International Training Course in Regional Development Planning covered the following subject domains :

1. *Meaning of development : Central problems and issues*: Growth versus development; who benefits and at whose cost? income distribution and poverty; environmental conservation and resource development; socio-political and institutional issues; administration for development; sub-national planning in development.
2. *Theories, concepts and approaches* : The concept of "region"; determinants of regional growth; the "big push" and "growth poles"; "unbalanced" versus "balanced" growth approaches; the role of cities in regional development; city systems and central place theories.
3. *The regional planning process*: Theories of planning; alternative planning process; their relevance and applications; organizational and institutional requirements in relation to planning processes; synthesis of planning steps and processes; limits to planning.
4. *Economic, social and demographic analysis*: Data requirements and analytical techniques; migration; population and employment projects; construction of regional accounts; area classification; sector analysis.
5. *Infrastructure and land use planning*: Infrastructure and transport planning, spatial organization, regional land use and environmental planning.
6. *Regional social planning*: Planning for social services; planning for the poor and disadvantaged groups.
7. *Local-level planning*: Planning approaches at the sub-regional level; community participation in planning, implementation and monitoring; cross-national experiences in local-level planning.
8. *Regional plan and budget interfacing and coordination*: Inseparability of plans and budgets; budgeting as a coordination

device; intersectoral coordination; consistency with regional targets and strategies.

9. *Project planning, management and implementation*: Identification, formulation and appraisal of projects, scheduling and networking; organization and administrative feasibility; monitoring and evaluation; participation in project implementation and management.
10. *Lessons of experience*: Country experiences in formulating, implementing and evaluating regional/local development plans, programmes and projects; case studies of Japanese models in environmental, regional and urban development.

These subject domains will be examined through a variety of instructional methods including group discussions, problem-solving exercises, study tours, formal lectures and workshops. Initiative on the part of the participants in participating in the learning process will be most essential, as the course relies heavily on the principles of participatory self-learning, and experience-based learning in small groups.

Programme of Activities and Summary of Sessions

The two-month training course may be divided into two parts : the first month was devoted to the discussion of the macro and regional development problems of developing countries, regional development theory, regional development planning process, sectoral planning, projection of socio-economic variables and the Japanese experience in development; the second month was devoted to field work, project planning, project management, gaming-simulation exercise, and presentation of reports.

The distribution of number of sessions and hours by subject is presented in Table 17.III-1. Individually, the subjects with the highest time allocation are Project Planning and Gaming-Simulation with 20 hours each, followed by Project Management with 15 hours; and Regional Development Theory and Agriculture Sector Planning with 10 hours each. The rest of the subjects are either 5 hours or 2.5 hours each.

TABLE 17.III-1 : Distribution of Number of Sessions and Hours, by Subject 13th International Training Course on Regional Development Planning, 2 April to 31 May 1985

	Title of Lecture	Number of Sessions	Number of Hours
1.	Meaning of Development : Problems and Issues	1	2.5
2.	Regional Development Problems and Issues	1	2.5
3.	Politics of Development	1	2.5
4.	Regional Development Theory	4	10.0
5.	Regional Planning Process	2	5.0
6.	Organization Requirements for Regional Development	2	5.0
7.	Industrial Sector Analysis	1	2.5
8.	Social Sector Analysis	1	2.5
9.	Environmental Planning	1	2.5
10.	Projection of Economic Variables	3	7.5
11.	Transport Planning	2	5.0
12.	Japan's Aid to Developing Countries	1	2.5
13.	Community Participation	2	5.0
14.	Agriculture Sector Planning	4	10.0
15.	Industrial Development in Chubu Region	1	2.5
16.	Public Finance	1	2.5
17.	Urbanization : Problems, Policies and Management	2	5.0
18.	Interregional Resource Allocation	2	5.0
19.	Land Use Planning	2	5.0
20.	Big Cities are Good for You (Special Lecture)	1	2.5
21.	Rural Employment	2	5.0
22.	Information System	1	2.5
23.	Local Level Planning in Japan	1	2.5
24.	Community Health Services	2	5.0
25.	Small and Medium Scale Industries in Japan	2	5.0
26.	Project Planning	8	20.0
27.	Project Management	6	15.0
28.	Gaming Simulation	8	20.0
29.	Field work	8	20.0
30.	Study Tour	9	22.5
31.	Report Writing	3	7.5
32.	Presentation of Reports	6	15.0
	Total (a)	91	227.5

(a) Includes four Saturdays.

REFERENCES

1. Resolution 1086-C (XXXIX), 1965 under the title "Concerted Practical Action in the Social Field : Research—Training Programme on Regional Development", Official Records of the Economic and Social Council, Thirty-ninth Session, Supplement No. 12 (E/4061) Chapter IV.
2. Resolution 1582(L) of Fifteenth Session of ECOSOC Agenda Item No. 2, Research and Training Programme in Regional Development dated 4 June 1971.
3. Om Prakash Mathur, "What would Regional Planners know? Reflections of a Trainer"—Proceedings of the IAURREE—sonsored Conference on "Which Planning Education for which Planning Practice", held at the School of Urban and Regional Planning, University of Southern California, Los Angeles, 24-28 September, 1982.
4. United Nations Centre for Regional Development, Nagoya (Japan) : "Strengthening Regional Planning Capacities in Developing Countries", Published 1975, p. 7.
5. United Nations Centre for Regional Development, Nagoya (Japan) : "Strengthening Regional Planning Capacities in Developing Countries", 1975, p. 18.
6. The research fellows are intended as resource persons. The UNCRD proposed to recruit them from the particular country in which the planning exercise was proposed to be conducted. They constitute an important link in the chain of activities, particularly during the pre-training phase.
7. The course announcement of the 1974 programme set out that the course is designed for the following groups of trainees : (i) advanced level government officials from developing countries directly concerned with comprehensive regional development planning in areas with predominantly rural characteristics; (ii) persons engaged in training programmes related to regional development; (iii) persons engaged in research as a planning input for regional development schemes.
8. Om Prakash Mathur, What Should Regional Planners Know? Reflections of a Trainer, paper prepared for the IAURRE-sponsored Conference on "Which planning education for which planning practice", held at the School of Urban and Regional Planning, 24-28 September 1982, University of Southern California, Los Angeles.
9. Harry Richardson, "The Relevance and Applicability of Regional Economics to Developing Countries" in Om Prakash Mathur (ed) *Training for Regional Development Planning*, Regional Development Series, published for the United Nations Centre for Regional Development, Nagoya by Maruzen Asia, Singapore, 1981.
10. See the ten volumes brought out by UNCRD, Masahiko Honjo and R.P. Misra (Eds), Regional Development Series, Vols. 1 to 10, published for the United Nations Centre for Regional Development, Nagoya by Maruzen Asia, Singapore, 1981.
11. In later exercises, one more working group was added for "Macro framework building", as this was considered essential.
12. Haruo Nagamine, UNCRD's Research on Planning Methodologies : Implication to training, Paper presented at the Consultative Meeting of Experts

on Training for Regional Development, 28 January to 4 February 1980, Nagoya.

13. These included, among others, preparation of development plans for four Kabupatens (sub-provincial administrative units) in the Yogyakarta Province (the case region) as well as a planning manual for Kabupaten planning.
14. UNCRD, Progress and Prospects, Report of the Director, UNCRD AC IV/III, November 1978. GCC stands for General Combined Course, which is the name given to the International Training Programme on Regional Development.
15. Haruo Nagamine, "UNCRD's Research on Planning Methodologies : Implication to Training". Paper presented at the consultative meeting of experts on Training for Regional Development, 28 Jan. to 4 Feb. 1980, Nagoya.
16. Bicol (Philippines, 1974), Yogyakarta (Indonesia, 1975) and Sind (Pakistan, 1976).
17. MPCRD stands for "Methods of Planning for Comprehensive Regional Development".
18. H. Nagamine, "Methods of Planning for Comprehensive Regional Development : A Paradigm," *Asian Development Dialogue*, Number 5 and 6, UNCRD 1978.
19. Three reasons were attributed for *not* going into specific techniques, viz.: (1) there is already a considerable amount of literature on various analytical techniques; (2) prevailing conditions of data paucity and unreliability in developing countries often makes intellectual, well-balanced judgement and knowledge of planners about the real situations far more fundamental in the planning work; and (3) it was felt that once a viable procedural framework was established, there would be little problem in introducing various analytical techniques in appropriate contexts as integral parts of the exercise, keeping in view the data availability.
20. The MPCRD approach has been criticized for its lack of a theoretical frame-work of analysis, for not making any reference to the vast body of literature on the theory and practice of economic planning and for avoiding the use of growth models, simultaneous equations, regression analysis, linear programming and other hard techniques which are the stock in trade of conventional economic planning. The view that conventional theories and techniques are considered to be irrelevant to the needs of practical planning in the developing countries has been questioned. See George Abbott : Methods of Planning for Comprehensive Regional Development : Planning or Play-Acting? Coexistence, 21:233-245, 1984 Martinus Nighoff Publishers, Dordrecht, The Netherlands.

18

TRAINING IN INFORMATION SYSTEMS FOR SUB-NATIONAL DEVELOPMENT PLANNING

The last two decades have seen some important changes in the field of development planning. So far as the developing countries are concerned, these changes may be perceived in three major directions, viz. : (a) changes in the orientation of planning from the emphasis on public sector investments to measures contributing to a direct attack on poverty and an improvement in the quality of life; (b) changes in the structure of planning from a centralized approach to a more decentralized approach directed towards improved subnational development planning; and (c) an enormous need for disaggregated data and information for planning purposes.

With the changes that have come about, not merely the need for data and information at disaggregated levels has grown, but also the need for some extremely specialized and specific information in relation to the development strategy adopted has become imperative and urgent. While the information provision activity in the developing countries is yet to respond fully to the varying perceptions of development planning and the different strategies introduced from time to time,[1] there is no doubt that a lot of fresh data and information are now being generated in the developing countries through resource and socio-economic surveys. Further, the application of sophisticated techniques like remote sensing has also helped to update natural resource inventories. With these developments, the increases in the variety and volume of territorial data (topographic, administrative, environmental, demographic, socio-

---

* Keynote Paper prepared for the Expert Group Meeting on "Training in Information Systems for Local and Regional Planning in Developing Countries," UNCRD, Nagoya (Japan), 1986.

economic, and other data) being generated today in any country have become quite appreciable. Simultaneously, tremendous development leaps have taken place in the field of information technology based on the multiple application of micro-technology and optical electronics, which have placed at our disposal tools that can quickly collect, store, process, and transfer data and information of all kinds. Many experts in the developing world now feel that what we are dealing with here is nothing less than a powerful "technological avalanche", which is unstoppable because of its innate dynamism and also because of the economic conditions of today's international market-place. Juan Rada, a Chilean expert in communications technology, when analyzing the problems of computer technology as it affects the developing world, has concluded as follows :

Information technology is a reality, and a rapidly expanding one. The question, therefore, is how to master the changes and deal with these issues to the best advantage for development strategies. What is needed is a socio-economic command of the development of science and technology.[2]

The crucial question, therefore, seems to be : How to acquire socio-economic command of the developments in the field of information technology. The only way that this problem can be tackled in the developing countries is by mounting a large-scale training and retraining of manpower for the relevant target groups—a task that needs to proceed with the utmost speed and in greater depth than it has up to the present.

Need for Integrated Approach

The new information technology is bound to influence planning in many ways :

(a) more data and information will become available;
(b) more quantitative analytical procedures will be technically possible;
(c) most mapping and graphics will be computer produced; and
(d) greater use of cost models and other performance models will be possible.

In order to take advantage of the new possibilities and their potential, it would be necessary for any country adopting the new information technology to establish the following prerequisites :

(a) reliable collection of data at the sources and a knowledge of how to feed these into the system;
(b) a viable communications network;
(c) a sound personnel base with experts conversant not only with the technical side of their equipment but also with the methods of handling the vast volume of statistical material; and
(d) knowledgeable experts in government (i.e. in the ministries of finance and planning), who are able to evaluate the material so as to make decisions which help the development of the country.

Contemporary debates on information technology are dominated by design issues. They are led more by technology rather than by human resources or organizations. The latter emphasis is important for the effective absorption of technological progress and for building up indigenous capabilities, which can purposefully and profitably utilize the information technology and all the new possibilities that it affords. The use of information technology cannot be contented with a "stand alone" applications approach. Blind pursuit of technical objectives will fail to generate the expected high performance standards and net benefit levels.

In order to derive the best advantage, the use of information technology has to take note of the requirements of different groups in the real-world situation. These groups will include data generators, policy-makers or top-level administrators, planners, development analysts, and system designers. In the current preoccupation with system designing, the other players in the game have been neglected. Technology seems to have run ahead of the dream of decision support. The systems developed have not been able to do the jobs needed and a "mismatch" has grown.

The task today seems to be to arrest the shift of the pendulum and to restore some balance to the approach. In a multilevel planning system, the task will be to enrich the capacity of the information technology so that the multitude of transactions occurring at a number of discrete points or area levels, where policy-makers, planners, development analysts, and system designers may interface, would be rendered purposeful, meaningful, and mutually beneficial. This demands an integrated approach to training so that technical success in information technology is matched with the ability to use the system for an improved subnational planning and for providing effective feedback for innovative designing of systems. The integrated approach to training here is meant to impart relevant knowledge, skills, and attitudes to both designers and users so that they become partners in a shared exploration of a system's capabilities. It should be noted that this implies both "machine training" (i.e. teaching individuals the use of a specific piece of kit and software) as well as "machine education" (i.e. providing the necessary orientation about the capability of the information technology) so that the best use could be made of the products of the system.[3]

The State-of-the-Art and Planning Needs in the Asian and Pacific Region in Regard to Information Technologies

Before one goes into the substantive issues of training, a quick overview of the contemporary developments in subnational development planning in the countries of the Asian and Pacific region is being undertaken. This involves the data and information needs for meeting their planning requirements, and the state-of-the-art in information technology.

The review undertaken in this context revealed that most of the countries in the region have been grappling with the problem of decentralization of development administration since they came out of the colonial yoke, and they are making various efforts to link planning and management functions at the regional and local levels to self-government institutions. More recently during the 1970s and early 1980s, they have been making more serious efforts towards decentralizing development planning and management functions to the subnational areas in their countries.[4] These efforts have taken diverse forms, reflecting various political systems, administrative structures, and developmental policies.

Recent developments in these countries show that national governments are seeking to push the relevant planning and decision-making tasks to some chosen subnational levels in their hierarchical set-up and to endow these levels with corresponding authority and responsibility. One of these important responsibilities relates to the generation, processing, and flow of information back and forth along a network of communication linkages to direct the country's socio-economic development. The state-of-art of the decentralization process in this direction in many of the countries shows that the "authority structures" (i.e. decentralization of planning and decision-making functions and delegation of power and control functions) have not matched with "information structures" (i.e. the design and implementation of data and information networks).

In regard to changes in the orientation of development planning, the major thrust in all these countries has been on implementing certain decentralized development programmes aimed at the alleviation of rural poverty. These programmes have necessitated the building up of strong databases touching on poverty, unemployment, and standard of living at the disaggregated level of the rural household. The inadequacy of the databases on these aspects has been noted as a serious deficiency hampering a quantitative assessment and analysis of the dynamics of change in the situation regarding poverty.[5] Further, the magnitude of data to be handled for these programmes and for building profiles of the poor in terms of income or expenditure, measures of the quality of life (e.g. literacy and infant mortality rates), indicators of working conditions (e.g. wage rates), and the like is astounding.[6]

Manual handling of such data has given rise to a lot of problems in implementation. In some countries, like India, the sheer magnitude of the data-handling problem is compelling the government to go in for computerization.

However, the absence of certain prerequisites are hampering such developments. These include : (a) lack of an adequate number of trained personnel who can manage and operate the system; (b) lack of a reliable power supply to operate the computers; (c) absence of a properly functioning telephone network to transmit data; (d) lack of adequate capital to purchase the new technology at a time when hardware prices are falling, but software is becoming dearer and is not adapted to the needs of the developing countries; and (e) lack of qualified programmers who can redesign the software or write new programmes.[7]

As for the development of information technology, the progress in the developing countries is quite uneven. But there are also some significant breakthroughs in a few countries. China has developed a Resources and Environment Information System (REIS) with an extensive application of computer and remote sensing technology since 1980.[8] As a result of the great importance that has been attached to the research and application of REIS by different departments, institutions, and specialists in China, REIS has made substantial progress in a short time in many aspects, such as theoretical applications, formulation of standards and norms, laboratory experiment, system development, and practical applications. Its application in economic construction, regional planning, environmental protection, and the designing of engineering projects has yielded certain economic and social benefits.

India is evolving a Natural Resources Data Management System (NRDMS) in which thirteen advanced technical institutions in the country arc collaborating.[9] The goals of the NRDMS are :

(a) to make an assessment of natural resources (e.g. land, water, atmospheric environment, and human resources) of the areas under study;
(b) to utilize the information for the purpose of planning and development at various levels; and
(c) to establish a computerized monitoring system for evaluation of development projects and programmes during the execution phase.

For district planning, five pilot projects have been chosen in different parts of the country, and an integrated composite software package for district planning (called "GRIDS") has been developed by one of the participating institutions, the Institute of Coastal and Offshore Research (INCOR), and is being pilot-tested. The concurrent monitoring being attempted for the Integrated Rural Development Programme has been completely computerized. Training programmes are also being organized for different categories of target groups. The first such programme for middle-level personnel (technicians and planners) was conducted in May, 1986.

A second direction in which some developments have taken place in India is in regard to the development of information systems for urban and regional planning.[10] Currently, the task of identifying the data needs and suggesting ways and means for developing and implementing two systems are under way, viz. the Urban Information System (URBIS) and the Regional Information System (RIS). Pilot studies in two towns have been undertaken to test the relevance of URBIS.

A third major development in India is the implementation of a Computerized Rural Information System Project (CRISP) at the district level being developed by the National Informatics Centre (NIC) which is the nodal agency for implementation. Initially the project is being implemented on a pilot basis in 10 selected districts in the country. By 1989, it is proposed to cover 150 districts, i.e. one-third of the country. The software technology proposed for the programme will enable the processing and monitoring of complete information in regard to two sets of programmes operating in the rural areas, viz. area programmes and beneficiary programmes. CRISP is being developed and implemented to ensure its integration into the district-level computer network, which is to be set up by NIC in the future.

In Thailand, development plans and information systems are mostly manual.[11] The only exceptions are the existence of subnational information systems for the Eastern Sea Board (ESB) development implemented during 1982-83 and the development of the Highland implemented during 1984-85.

Nepal does not have any organized systematic information system.[12] Piecemeal approaches to information generation and dissemination are designed by some sectors independently to serve their own specific needs and purposes. It has been keenly felt that the Integrated Rural Development (IRD) Programme needs a reliable and valid database for effective planning and management of IRD. There is also a lack of interagency coordination in data collection activities.

The only computerized information system in Sri Lanka operating in the state sector at the subnational level is that developed for the Kalutara district with the collaboration of United Nations Economic and Social Commission for Asia and the Pacific (ESCAP).[13] The pilot project is designed to process such data at the district and sub-district (divisional) levels to meet the requirements of local planners and administrators. The project also attempts to design a geocoded information system to present data on a spatial basis.

In Indonesia, a regional database for physical planning is being developed in the Ministry of Public Works.[14] The National Coordinating Body for Survey and Mapping (BAKOSURTANAL) installed the COMARC computer-assisted cartographic system in 1979 to meet users' expanding demands for topographic information. The geographical information system or regional data base has been installed in the Data Processing and Mapping Centre (PUSDATA) of the Ministry of Public Works. In the near future, Indonesia will be strengthening and upgrading institutional capability for the purpose of developing a data and information system on land resources at the national and provincial levels and for the physical planning process. A project was established in October, 1984 with technical aid from the Asian Development Bank.

From this account, it may be seen that the applications of information technology in most countries in the Asian and Pacific region is in very formative stages of development. Even in some of those countries which have reported the existence of some computerized information systems (e.g. Sri Lanka, Thailand, or Indonesia), these developments have been due to external support. It is apparent that for most Third World countries, it is extremely difficult to develop and promote information technologies on their own. Some threshold countries, such as China or India, have developed a few technology enclaves, but they are yet to develop the technology on a countrywide scale. For many other countries, the start-up conditions seem to be simply too unfavourable.

It is in this context that a search for feasible solutions and compromises is necessary, and a "blending" of old and new technologies is recommended. Such a blending strategy would be advantageous, because the information technology in this case will not replace, but supplement, existing technologies. Whether a country uses high technology or appropriate technology, the training needs are bound to be the same, as even the latter approach implies preparation for a continuous and rapid transition. Indeed, it would be true to say that the training needs for these countries are infinitely greater and more urgent, as time is running out and the third world is being steam-rollered by technological progress.

Thus, a graduated approach for the dissemination of information technology is recommended for the developing countries. This approach should take note of the various constraints and provide for the following :

(a) Smooth transition from existing to new technology;
(b) optimum utilization of existing equipment and skill;
(c) possibilities of upgrading equipment in case of growing demand;
(d) wide diversity of outputs to meet all types of needs; and
(e) possibility of step-by-step progress in establishing equipment to allow for staggered investments and training.

The training programmes should also be designed by taking note of the above approach.

Target Groups and Approach to Training

We may now outline our ideas for an "integrated approach" to training for the developing countries in the field of information systems. Our discussion in the second section of this paper has revealed that any training programme intended to realize the full potentials of information technology must encompass a large category of target groups consisting of people who will be managing and controlling the information technology (the designers), those engaged in data collection, processing, and feeding into the system (survey and data collection specialists—or SDCS), and those who will be using the output of the system (the users). In the user category, we may distinguish two subgroups, viz. policy planners and decision-makers, and planners and development analysts.

Our strategy for training in information technology should be based on the principle of encouraging mutual interaction among the three target groups identified above for promoting further learning, research, and innovation. For this purpose, the nature of interaction and output achievement envisaged could be as shown in Fig. 18.1.

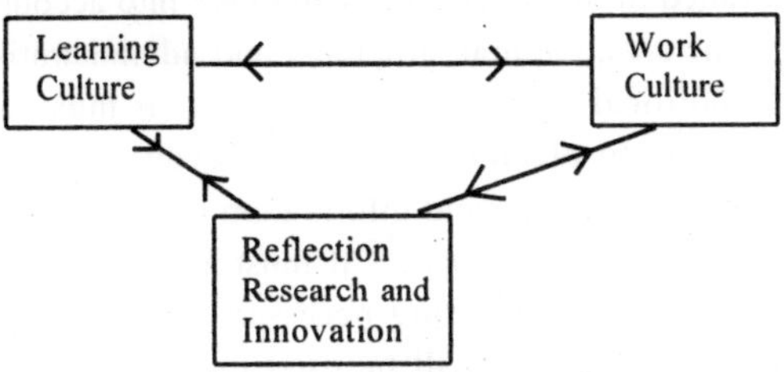

FIG. 18.1 : Mutual Interaction Strategy.

In this conception, each target group would be at once the agent of knowledge individually and also the beneficiary of learning collectively, while working together during the training period. The interaction between them would provide scope for reflection on what they are doing, so that further learning and innovation can take place. In this way, the formal training programme can become a strategy for carrying out innovative adaptations in information technology. This would mean that more dialogue should be encouraged between the development experts and the technical experts, so that the former will be able to know the potentials and capabilities of a particular information system, and the latter will be enabled to understand the intentions (i.e. the objectives) and the data and information needs, as well as the processing and analytical needs, of the planner. In this way, the development experts would be encouraged to use sophisticated analytical tools including statistical analysis of data and preparation of models using simulation and other techniques. The technical experts, on the other hand, will get feedback about users' needs and thus will be enabled to innovate and develop various software applications suited to different planning requirements. Thus, better linkages will emerge between data management endeavours and the decision-making processes that make use of the data.

It is the institution of these linkages that will make the greatest difference. It is, therefore, emphasized that unless an integrated approach to training in this manner is adopted, the overall implementation of information systems would seem destined to fumble in the dark.

Focus and Content of Training Programme for Different Target Groups

In order to attain the expected high performance standards and net benefit levels, the information technology strategy adopted for any country must be attuned to the users' needs and take into account the multilevel planning structures, cultural structures and administrative organization, as well as political and economic realities. It must capture the goal concepts related to planning at various levels in a country and must recognize the distinct data and information requirements of the different phases of the planning process.[15] It must also take note of the various steps of information processing necessary for planning and the major analytical techniques that will be used in the planning process in the country.

Accordingly, any training programme designed for the different target groups must include within its curriculum the following key knowledge dimensions :

(a) Education about the multilevel planning process in the country; goals for specific area levels of planning, and relevant national and regional policies in the country.

(b) Data and information needs for different levels and different phases of planning.

(c) Planning procedures and information processing steps relevant to the planning process operating in the country at various levels.

(d) Planning techniques relevant to the planning process, e.g. basic techniques for data collection and analysis, techniques for project and programme appraisal and feasibility analysis, econometric modelling and forecasting techniques, and techniques for monitoring and evaluation.

(e) "Computer education" to educate particularly users to think about the ways to use the information that the technology can provide and to sensitize them on the system's capabilities, hardware and software developments, and graphic information system.

(f) "Computer training" to train those who would operate and maintain the information system for particular jobs with dedicated applications, i.e. imparting to them special competence in some important skill areas including designing and development of software.

The above six dimensions of knowledge, indicated only in the very basic outline form here, may be deemed to constitute the core curriculum for a training programme on information technology. However, the training programme for the different target groups that we have identified (i.e. the designers, the SDCS and the users) cannot be patterned mechanically on the same lines. Their different requirements have to be kept in view. Accordingly, the proportions of the mix of knowledge and skills to be imparted will differ from the different target groups. Thus, the information kit of (a) to (d) above may be deemed generally common to all the target groups, though the intensity and detail of treatment may vary. The programme intended for the designers would lay emphasis on the information kit set out in (f). The programme for the SDCS would lay emphasis on the information kit outlined in (c) and (d). The programme for the users, again, will vary in detail and depth depending on the composition of the target group. The policy planners and decision-makers will mainly receive awareness education about the possibilities and potentials of information technology, and orientation related to managerial issues. The second user category of planners and development analysts, on the other hand, will receive more detailed training on the use of the system for sophisticated planning exercises.

As for the organization of the training programme, our emphasis is on an "interactive method", in which all the target groups will be brought together for the maximization of net benefits. While some aspects of the training programme will be common to all, they may branch out for particular orientations after going through a common curriculum initially. This would be an ideal method. The more the training programmes are patterned on this model to draw different target groups together and encourage active interaction among them, the better it would be for the end result of training.

We may also draw a distinction on training methods suited to different target groups. The following mix is illustrative :

(a) Designers :	Lectures; case studies; exercises and demonstrations; interaction with user groups.
(b) Survey and Data Collection Specialists :	Lectures; exposure to computers and microprocessors; demonstrations of limited applications; interaction with designers and data collection agencies.
(c) Users :	
(1) Policy Planners and Decision-Makers	Through intervention in ongoing programmes conferences, symposia, or seminars (purposeful intervention through the gate-crash method); sensitization through demonstration and display techniques (poster sessions); exchange of experiences in open seminar discussions; interaction with designers and producers of hardware components.
(2) Planners and Analysts	Workshop method; case studies; exercises and demonstrations; limited lecture sessions; interaction with designers.

Preparation of Training Packages or Modules

A major challenge for training is the preparation of training materials. This is a task in which both national and international agencies should collaborate. Taking into account the desirable orientations or thrusts to be imparted to the training of different target groups, a set of training packages or modules may be outlined. Broadly these could be as is shown in Table 18.1. Each module will consist of two major parts, viz. (a) theoretical framework, and (b) illustrations, case studies, background notes, and reading references. It will also consist of written material and teaching aids such as slides and audio-casettes.

Prospects and Priorities for Future Action

The present trends towards subnational development planning in the developing world indicate that notwithstanding the limited accomplishments in the field of information technology at present and the inadequacy of the national infrastructure systems in many countries of the region, the prospects are that the new technology will not remain alien to them for long. This optimism is induced by the fact that in the wake of the decentralized planning efforts that are under way in these

TABLE 18.1 : Training Modules for Target Groups.

Training Modules	Target Groups			
	Designers	Survey & Data Collection Specialists	User (1)	User (2)
1. Multilevel planning : goal concepts and the planning process	X	X	X	X
2. Data and information needs for subnational development planning (in a multilevel planning framework)	X	X	X	X
3. Organization and flow of data for local and regional planning and its integration with the national system of statistics	X	X	X	X
4. Processing of data (for different levels of subnational development planning and its presentation)	X	X		X
5. Information technology, hardware and software aspects : thematic mapping package for display data —elementary		X	X	X
6. —do— —advanced	X			
7. System design aspects	X			
8. Management information system for planning (a) data for plan formulation (b) implementation and monitoring (c) evaluation/performance appraisal	X	X		

User (1) : Policy Planners and Decision-makers.
User (2) : Planners and Analysts.

countries, the need for data and information and their handling and processing to meet the planning requirements have grown tremendously, and there is keen interest among the countries to switch over to the new technology as early as possible. These trends were clearly brought out in the discussions that took place in Visakhapatnam in December, 1985. How quickly the new technology will be absorbed in these countries will depend on the speed with which the prerequisites for its introduction are met. This underlines the need for massive training programmes in this direction in each country. In this context, concerted action is necessary both within particular countries and at the international level in the field of training and supportive activities.

The priority task of the countries in the region is to increase national training activities. They should make efforts to improve and expand their training activities. The setting up of specialized training centres solely for imparting training in information technology is unnecessary, as it would be a costly and lengthy affair. Perhaps the approach could be for this training activity to find its way into existing training centres in such related fields as national planning and sectoral management, public administration, urban planning, and social development. The national focal points for training must be identified, and they should be formed into a network so as to facilitate exchange among them of information on applications and dissemination of training material.

International bodies can render invaluable assistance to the developing countries in this regard. This assistance can be in a number of areas such as the design and preparation of training courses, provision and exchange of experts for teaching, exchange of training material and new software developments, training of trainers, organizing promotional courses for specific countries which need such intervention, and post-training evaluation of results. International agencies can also provide catalytic assistance to establish and promote the training network in each country. They can especially provide appropriate networking tools to foster communication between users, such as the establishment of information dissemination centres (IDCs), newsletters, and arrangement of periodical seminars and workshops.

Efforts of UNESCO and Proposals for the Future

Among the specialized agencies of the United Nations system, the United Nations Educational, Scientific and Cultural Organization (UNESCO) occupies a unique position in that it has specific and sizable programmes devoted to information per se, ranging from libraries and archives to information and data systems. In 1976, the General Information Programme (PGI) was established to provide a focus for UNESCO's activities in the area of scientific and technological information, documentation, libraries and archives management. This programme incorporated the UNISIST programme which was created in the late 1960s and produced a set of methods, norms, standards, and guidelines designed to helping the creation of compatible information systems and services and their inter-connexion in order to facilitate information exchange throughout the world. An inter-governmental council consisting of representatives of 30 member states determines the policies and programmes of PGI. The UNISIST II Inter-governmental Conference of 1979 recommended the extension of the programme to cover information and data for development so as to meet the needs of development planners, policy-makers, and administrators at one end of the user spectrum, and at the other end, those of people at the grass root level.

UNESCO's activities in the information area are essentially designed to enhance the capacity of member states to handle, transfer, and share information and information resources and the effective utilization of information and data in development activities. Such information and data may be either generated within the country or may flow in from abroad or else accessed there. UNESCO's action involving assisting member states in formulating national information policies, developing libraries, archives, or information system infrastructures, training information personnel, and making users increasingly aware of the value of information per se. Such assistance may take the form of support for consultant missions; the provision of norms, standards, and guidelines for information handling and systems inter-connexion; the organization of seminars and conferences; or support for training courses, workshops, and demonstrations of information systems and their use. The PGI/UNISIST programme has provided a framework within which member states and international organizations can collaborate by sharing resources, developing compatible international information systems designed to be linked to a flexible global network for the exchange of information, and taking part in programme activities.

During the first phase of the implementation of the programme, UNESCO's activities concentrated on the formulation of information policies, norms and standards for information handling and systems inter-connexion and on the provision of assistance for the development of infrastructures and information manpower. In its Second Medium-Term Plan, 1984-89, following up on the recommendations of expert consultations and the suggestions of member states, PGI/UNISIST has placed emphasis on : (a) users' needs, (b) operational activities, (c) regional cooperation, and (d) introduction of modern information technology in the developing countries. This shift in emphasis will also facilitate the move towards establishing a global cooperative information network.

Among UNESCO's recent activities in the field of information and data for subnational development planning, the following may be specially mentioned :

(a) UNESCO/PGI supported a programme in collaboration with the International Institute for Aerospace Survey and Earth Sciences (ITC), Enschede, The Netherlands brought together development planners and information specialists from developing and developed countries in a series of seminars enabling exchange of ideas and experiences in development planning and information support systems. The papers and proceedings of the meetings have been published.[16]

(b) As a practical follow-up of the above activities, UNESCO, organized an Asia-Pacific Regional Seminar on Information for Subnational Development Planning at Visakhapatnam, in December, 1985. The Visakhapatnam Declaration called on the governments of the region to develop a national information policy and to establish, with international assistance, an Asia-Pacific Regional Cooperation Programme on Sub-national Development Planning with one or more nodal organizations in selected countries in the region to coordinate developments and exchange experiences with national contact points. This would particularly help in manpower development for data and information support systems for subnational development planning.

Following the Visakhapatnam call, UNESCO received a proposal for the setting up of a nodal organization at the Institute for Coastal and Offshore Research (INCOR) in Visakhapatnam. Another initiative in the region which might contribute to the proposed programme includes a joint project for international cooperation in teaching and research in rural and regional development planning at the Asian Institute of Technology, Bangkok, in collaboration with the Institute of Social Studies, The Hague.

If two centres could be established with one concentrating on the South Asian region and the other on the Southeast Asian region, it would make possible the provision of useful inputs for, and coordination of, regional efforts to improve information systems for subnational planning and the training of personnel in the developing countries of the region. If the United Nations Centre for Regional Development were to complement these efforts by initiatives to establish a centre to cater to the needs of the East Asian region, it would complete a network in the Asian region.

(c) With a view to advising member states on the initial planning and further expansion of training programmes and to teach in special subject fields, UNESCO provides expert services to the countries upon request. For example, in the field of data for development, support has been provided to an ESCAP/UNESCO project aiming at the use of microcomputer technology at the district and divisional levels of administration in Sri Lanka. In such operational projects, training is invariably built in as a component. Similarly, UNESCO has supported various consultancy missions specifically in the field of train-ing in the information area.

(d) As part of its regular activities of promotion of international and regional training, UNESCO sponsors 10 to 15 international or regional courses and seminars every year on various subjects and at different levels, giving priority to courses for teachers and managers of information systems and services. It is expected that some of these will be devoted to data for development in the coming years.

(e) As a preparatory effort in this context, special reference should be made to the support given by UNESCO for the preparation by the Data for Development International Association of teaching aids on the establishment, coordination, access to, and utilization of socio-economic and administrative information systems. The training kit or package that is being developed contains eight modules covering existing types and structure of information systems and their utilization; theoretical and technical aspects of information systems, strategy, and management as well as the modalities of access to information systems; graphical, cartographic, and statistical tools; geocoding theory and application; and recent developments including cartographic information on microcomputers and remote sensing. Information for local planning needs is given particular emphasis. The training package available for wide distribution and testing in English and French. It is hoped that this package will meet many of the requirements outlined in Table 18.1 of this article, particularly modules 5 to 8.

(f) As a follow-up of the recommendations of the Visakhapatnam seminar, UNESCO hopes to promote the establishment of a software demonstration and training centre for subnational planning information system application which could serve the Asian and Pacific region. An inventory of software packages is planned and activities in other regions may be developed in the future. Cooperation may be developed in this context with the Spatially-Oriented Referencing Systems Association (SORSA).

International organizations like UNESCO, HABITAT, ESCAP, FAO, and UNCRD, are assisting the governments in the developing countries to deal with the problems and opportunities presented by information systems for subnational development planning. The need is to coordinate the various efforts and to encourage the networking of the various governmental, training, and research institutions engaged in the field of information system for development planning in the different countries of the region. Training of both information specialists and users, whether formal in nature or simply informal exchanges of experience, represents a key factor in such cooperation. The efforts of UNESCO summarized in the above paragraph are particularly signifi-cant in this context. In this way, the developing countries would be able to benefit from existing experiences in information systems for development planning and to learn more about the complex relationship between information and planning through cooperative studies, projects and seminars.

REFERENCES

1. Sundaram, K.V., "Data and Information Needs for Subnational Planning", Keynote paper presented at the UNESCO Seminar on Information Systems

for Subnational Development Planning, Visakhapatnam, India, 16-20 December, 1985.

2. Rada, Juan, "The Microelectronics Revolution : Implications for the Third World", *Development Dialogue*, 2, 1982 : 41-67.
3. From the standpoint of training, this distinction between "machine training" and "machine education" is quite significant. For a definition of these terms and their implications for an organization's successful use of information technology, see : S. Barrett and S. Baddeley, "Information Needs for Local Authorities : Small is Beautiful", Paper contributed to Joint UDM-SORSA Symposium on Information Needs for Local Authorities, The Hague, 2-6 June, 1985.
4. For a good documentation of these changes see FAO "Toward Improved Multilevel Planning for Agricultural and Rural Development in Asia and the Pacific".
5. See Rizwanul Islam, Ed., "Strategies for Alleviating Poverty in Rural Asia", Bangkok : ILO-ARTEP, 1985.
6. For one district in Karnataka State in India, beneficiary profiles had to be built-up for the following number of persons against various poverty alleviation programmes :

(a) Integrated Rural Development Programme	—	3,000 persons
(b) Negilubhagya Scheme	—	2,500 persons
(c) Gobar gas schème	—	1,200 persons
(d) Antyodaya programme	—	2,000 persons
(e) Wells scheme	—	1,656 persons

See Sanjoy Das Gupta, "District Level Computerization : The Karwar Experiment", Paper presented at the UNESCO Seminar on Information Systems for Subnational Development Planning, Visakhapatnam, India, 16-20 December, 1985.

7. Inga Krugmann-Randolf, "High Technology : What Chance for Developing Countries?" *Development and Cooperation*, 3, June/July 1985.
8. Jianbang, He and Yang Kai, "Research and Progress in the Resources and Environment Information System in Some Chinese Institutions : A General Survey", Paper presented at the UNESCO Seminar, Visakhapatnam, 16-20 December 1985.
9. Rama, Rao, R.V. and P.C. Raju, "Natural Resource Data Management System for Planning", Paper presented at the UNESCO Seminar, Visakhapatnam, 16-20 December, 1985.
10. Nair, P.K.S., "URIS in India : Information Needs", Paper presented at the UNESCO Seminar, Visakhapatnam, 16-20 December 1985.
11. Jettorntrum, Krisorn, "Subnational Information Systems : Thailand, A Brief Note", Paper presented at the UNESCO Seminar, Visakhapatnam, 16-20 December 1985.
12. Khadka, Shyam S. and Padma Shrestha, "Information System for Planning Integrated Rural Development Programme, Nepal", Paper presented at the UNESCO Seminar, Visakhapatnam, 16-20 December 1985.
13. Abhayagunawardhana, H.A., "Use of Microcomputers at the District Level : The Kalutara Pilot Project", Paper presented at the UNESCO Seminar, Visakhapatnam, 16-20 December 1985.

14. Moersidi, Suroso, "Regional Data Base for Physical Planning", Paper presented at the UNESCO Seminar, Visakhapatnam, 16-20 December, 1985.
15. The Visakhapatnam seminar contributed to a clarification of the goal concepts for a multilevel planning structure and the related information needs. See Sundaram, "Data and Information Needs for Subnational Planning".
16. DeMan, W.H. and A.D.J. Schaap, Eds., *Proceedings of the Workshop (on) Information Requirements for Development Planning in Developing Countries*, (Enschede : International Institute for Aerial Survey and Earth Sciences, 1980. This has been followed by W.H. De Man, *Conceptual Framework and Guidelines for Establishing Geographic Information System Capable of Integrating Natural Resources Data and Socio-economic Data for Development-Oriented Planning, Monitoring, and Research*, Paris : UNESCO, 1984.

19

IN-SERVICE TRAINING FOR DECENTRALIZED DISTRICT PLANNING
Experience of Nepal

The success of any training venture will ultimately depend on :

(i) Proper assessment of training needs and the identification of target groups for training;
(ii) Preparation of well-conceived training materials in the form of Training Manuals, addressed to different target groups;
(iii) Designing of a need-based instructional system, which combines academic rigour with practical orientation; and
(iv) Institutionalization of training, with a core training team engaged in year-round research-cum-training activities.

This chapter aims to set out the experiences gone through by the author in implementing an FAO assisted and Swiss funded project for an in-service training programme for decentralized planning in Nepal during 1988-1990, which touches on all the above aspects. However, the emphasis is particularly on the development of a training manual, the conceptual framework for training based on a model for an instructional cycle for action-oriented training, and the issues involved in the designing of curriculum for training in decentralized planning.

The author took up his assignment in the project (FAO/GCP/NEP/035/SWI Phase-II) in July, 1988, with counterpart assistance from the Agricultural Projects Services Centre (APROSC) in Kathmandu, which had a training section with a core team of trainers. The FAO assisted project with Swiss funding, in fact, commenced during 1983 and the author's association was only with the second phase of the project. During the first phase, the APROSC Training Section (APROSC-TS) initially concentrated on faculty capability building for running training programmes focused on Project Planning and Monitoring and Evaluation and later diversified its activities to include training programmes for District Agricultural Planning and Decentralized Planning, so as to meet the changing needs of His Majesty's Government of Nepal. During the second phase of the project, technical assistance by FAO was focused on capacitation of the faculty for running training programmes in decentralized planning.

During the first phase of the project, the training needs for decentralized planning were assessed and six categories of target groups were identified. Later, a training-cum-technical assistance cycle was initiated in one of the districts of Nepal, viz. Tanahun district in the Western Development Region. This experience, besides providing training services and helping one district to prepare a plan, also enabled the training institution (APROSC-TS) to prepare a first draft of training materials. These needed considerable refinement and systematization before they could be turned into a comprehensive Training Manual. In the meantime, a number of changes took place in Nepal during the operationalization of the Decentralization Act and its bye-laws. There were also new policy initiatives introduced by HMG/N like the emphasis on basic needs, etc. In this context, it was realized that it was necessary to have a fresh look at the training materials available, fill up their gaps, introduce new elements and turn it into a systematic manual, which can be used by all training institutions in the country.

The author took up the above challenging task in 1989. To begin with, it was necessary to obtain a consensus on the scope and content of a Training Manual for Decentralized Planning. For this purpose, a background paper[1] was prepared which was discussed in an Expert Group Meeting[2] participated by 36 experts drawn from government and non-governmental institutions (including academic institutions and research organizations) in Nepal, which agreed with the approach. It was decided to follow a modular approach for the preparation of the manual, in view of its flexibility and adaptability and a scheme of eight modules along with the subject areas falling within them was outlined. The titles of the eight modules were as follows :

1. Understanding Development
2. Decentralization and Planning Process in Nepal
3. District Planning : An Analytical Process
4. Techniques and Tools for District Planning
5. District Plan Formulation
6. Implementation and Management of District Plans

7. Popular Participation
8. Development Support Communication for District Development.

The Manual : Its Structure

The eight modules of the Manual have been structured into 67 subject areas (lessons or discussion sessions) and incorporate 16 exercises and 3 case studies, besides one participatory planning game. (See Annexure–I) Each subject area is structured under a standardized format as follows :

* Subject Brief.
* Purpose of the Session.
  — Reading.
  — Essential.
  — Recommended.
* Lesson Content.
* Suggested References.
* Discussion Questions.
* Exercises (where relevant).

The manual is essentially methodology and technique oriented. It has been designed in such a manner that the lessons can be easily amended or modified as necessary after the feedback from users. The readings in the manual have been classified into "Essential" and "Recommended." The Essential Readings form part of the text of the manual and are usually in the nature of compact and synthesized briefs, either specially written for this manual or a seminal paper contributed by a well-known expert on the subject, which sets forth all the essentials. The Recom-mended Readings appear in a separate volume and are meant as a helpful guide to the trainees as well as the trainers for broadening their background, as also for refreshing and updating their thinking on these issues.

A unique feature of the manual is the incorporation of a wealth of bibliographic material for each lesson under "Suggested References". They seek to cover all the major contributions pertaining to the subject made by Nepali intellectuals and others. These are intended as additional technical sources and reference materials to prepare a knowledge/sensitivity base and are meant to assist those who would like to study further at a later stage. They are also intended to be of assistance to the trainers in the training institutions who, at any rate, must be fully conversant with all the standard literature on the subject. Originally, it was the intention of the authors of this manual to make this section into an annotated bibliography. But owing to constraints of time, this could not be done.

The 67 subject lessons (including exercises, group discussions and other activities) have been planned ideally for a four week training programme, which will have 88 training sessions of one-and-half hour duration each. The readings and other teaching materials that have been developed here have been made quite flexible, so that they can be stretched to six or even eight weeks, for instance, by making the training programme into a sandwich course, divided into two phases and introducing an on-the-job planning exercise in the middle. This may also be shrunk into a two or three weeks' training course by reducing some sessions and exercises. The needs of the participants of the course should be taken into account, in a creative way, in selecting and scheduling subjects. Several adaptations will be required while designing the training curriculum suited for each occasion, and here the trainer's needs and perceptions will undoubtedly be quite important.

Knowledge, Skills and Attitudes Needed for Decentralized District Planning

The manual addresses itself to a systematic process of planning, which implies the following essential steps :

(a). Data and information collection and processing for macro-framework building (Goals/Objectives setting, selection of lead sector(s) and strategy formulation);

(b) Area diagnosis or district analysis involving resource inventory and malady-remedy analysis;

(c) Project/scheme identification and formulation;

(d) Plan formulation involving establishment of spatial and tem-poral linkages within an integrated framework; and

(e) Implementation planning, including monitoring and evaluation.

The successful performance of the tasks implied in the above planning steps presupposes the acquisition of some basic knowledge, skills and attitudes. The "Essential Readings" included in the manual provide the knowledge about the concepts and methods of planning. This knowledge component includes concepts like Development,

Decentralization, Area Development, Integration and Coordination, Communication and Public Participation. Since District Planning is essentially "Participatory or Negotiated Planning," a participatory planning game has also been advocated and its methodology indicated.

As for the skills, to be developed among the government functionaries to practise the simple district planning methodology advocated in the manual, the following two kinds of skills may be mentioned :

Basic Skills

* Data and information collection, handling and processing.
* Area diagnosis or district analysis.
* Resource allocation.
* Target formulation.
* Project identification, formulation and appraisal.
* Integration of programmes and projects.
* Implementation techniques—networking and scheduling.
* Monitoring and evaluation.
* Participation.

Contributory Skills (Illustrative)

* Demographic and Manpower Analysis.
* Spatial location analysis.
* Map analysis.
* Demand analysis and forecasting techniques.
* Land capability analysis.
* Systems analysis.
* Environmental impact analysis.
* Social accounts.

Basic skills are those minimum skills that are needed for a district planner to undertake the overall tasks of analysis and detailing of a development plan.

Contributory skills are of a specialized nature related to the management and development of resources or to specific sectorial aspects of planning. These are provided by varying disciplines. Since no single planner can acquire all these skills, selectivity is called for to determine the nature of skills to be imparted in a training programme. Obviously, this will depend on the target groups for training and their functions and responsibility in the work situation.

Apart from the components of knowledge and skills, another important acquisition in a training programme is the one related to attitudinal change, which is a complex process. Ability to work and interact as a member of a planning team, responsiveness to divergent views and opinions, acquisition of meta-disciplinary visions including broadening of perspectives and shedding of pre-conceived notions, ability to negotiate with superiors on issues like resource allocation and project selection and their locations, willingness to learn and innovate, sensitivity to the results of monitoring and public criticism, the ability to work and communicate with people and their representatives and the ability to resolve conflicts are some of the elements of attitudinal change that are considered desirable for a successful district planner. These are also termed "social skills." Role playing (i.e. recording of a real-life situation in which interaction between human beings takes place), experiential learning, group interaction, etc., are some of the instructional techniques associated with the efforts to bring about an attitudinal change. It should also be mentioned that knowledge, skills and attitudes are inter-related. It may be hypothesized in this context that the acquisition of certain types of knowledge and skills also induces certain kinds of attitudinal change.

Major Steps and Analyses

The major steps and analyses involved in District Planning which are discussed in the manual are :

(i) Data and information collection and processing.
(ii) Analyses needed for macro-framework building (i.e. goal/objective setting : strategy formulation, etc.).
(iii) Analyses needed for plan formulation, viz. :
   * Area (district) analysis.
   * Analyses for project identification and formulation.
   * Analyses for formulation and integration of development proposals.
   * Analysis for implementation planning.

The above steps and analyses are illustratively shown in Fig. 19.1.

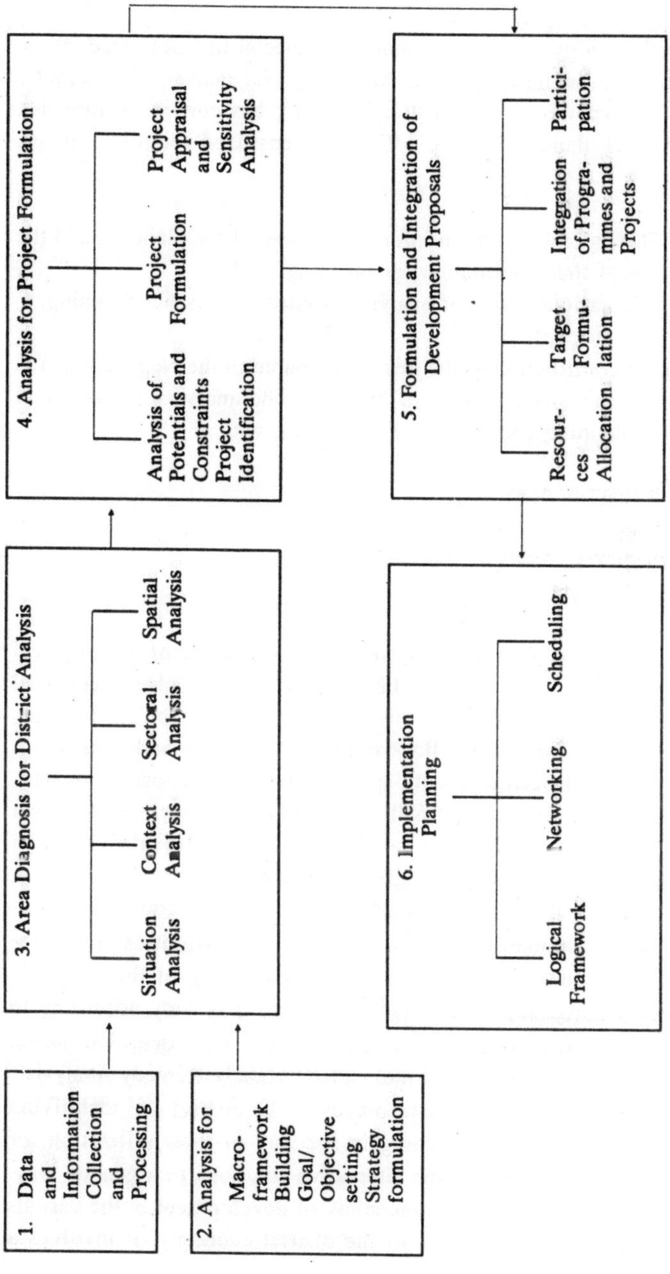

FIG. 19.1 : Major Steps and Analyses Involved in District Planning.

Area (District) Analysis

In the methodology of district planning, a special mention needs to be made about the diagnosis step, viz. Area or district analysis. The author's 30 years of experience with district planning has convinced him that grassroot-level planners are not sufficiently sensitized about two things, viz. :

(i) The critical minimum information needed for planning and the use of that information for planning; and
(ii) The various kinds of analyses needed for district planning.

A major contribution of the manual prepared in the Nepal context is in clarifying these two aspects of learning. The analyses necessary in the district planning context are of four types, viz.:

1. Situation Analysis;
2. Context Analysis;
3. Sectorial Analysis; and
4. Spatial Analysis.

The "Situation Analysis" phase involves a study of the physical environment in which the plan is to be prepared. It will involve an appraisal of the factor endowments of the district, such as geographical location, climate, biological resources (flora and fauna), geology and minerals. It will be mostly descriptive with quantitative dimensions indicated, wherever possible. This analysis will give an idea of the factor endowment potentials and constraints and can also lead to the identification of homogeneous sub-regions, e.g. agro-climatic zones.

The context analysis will include an analysis of the existing resources—water, human resources, economic opportunities and infrastructure. The analysis results in an understanding of the district's development constraints and potentials. These may vary according to agro-climatic zones. A number of "stresses" are also identified during this step. This step is also sometimes called "Malady-Remedy Analysis". It would involve reviewing the resources of the district and identifying specific problems that are coming in the way of their utilization for development and suggesting the alternative solutions in a general way.

Sectorial analysis involves the study of development in the various production and welfare sectors of the district economy. It involves a critical analysis and study of the development potentials and constraints in the individual sectors of development, the present levels of development and the strategy options for future development. It also involves an analysis of the on-going development programmes in terms of their financial outlays, inputs, outputs, targets and achievements.

Spatial analysis involves a study of the locational and development factors and an appraisal of the existing infrastructural facilities and social services available in different point locations, identifying the gaps in spatial coverage of social services and building up a hierarchical network of rural service centres and growth centres with their vertical and horizontal linkages.

Fig. 19.2 illustrates the above four major components of Area (District) Analysis.

Conceptual Framework for Training : Model of an Instructional Cycle

We may now turn our attention to the use of Training Manual for developing the professional competencies of the government functionaries. This relates to issues of learning-teaching processes and the organizational sequence of the training programme in order to facilitate easy learning and effective internalization of the knowledge and skills imparted during the training course. This is called here as the "Instructional Cycle". A model of an instructional cycle for Decentralized Planning at the district level in two phases has been worked out. Its essential ingredients are set out below. (See also Fig. 19.3).

This model presupposes two phases of training, one to promote among the trainees a process of "divergent thinking", and the other in which they develop what may be termed "convergent thinking". The first phase is a period during which the horizon of understanding of the trainees on development issues gets widened, their short-sightedness or "blinkers" are removed, and they acquire meta-disciplinary visions to enable them to become good and effective planners. This is a phase of long-duration training, during which the essential knowledge and skills are imparted and some "ancillary competencies" are developed, e.g. skills in gathering relevant information, in processing or analyzing the information and in assessing alternatives. The classroom training part consists of three inter-related activities, viz. : (i) Seminars/Workshops conducted by the core trainers to impart the essential knowledge (concepts and methods); (ii) Special lectures by academics and specialists providing some holistic perceptions on some selected issues related to development

COMPONENTS	Situation Analysis	Context Analysis	Sectoral Analysis	Spatial Analysis
BASIS OF CLASSIFI-CATION	Natural factor Endowments (Static Endogenous Factors)	Endogenous Factors (Dynamic)	Development Factors * Exogenous through National Policies * Induced through Inter-regional Interaction * Endogenous through Local Effort	Locational Factors Development Factors
TECHNIQUES	Qualitative Quantitative	Qualitative Quantitative	Qualitative Quantitative	Qualitative Quantitative
COVERAGE	Geographical Location * Physiography * Climate * Biological Resources * Geology * Minerals	Land Resources * Water Resources * Human Resources * Demography * Socio-cultural * Economic Characteristics of the Area (District) and Population	Programmes, Financial Outlays, Inputs, Outputs, Targets, Physical Achievements and Problems and Constraints for Development in Key Sectors * Agriculture * Irrigation * Animal Husbandry * Health * Industry * Education	Settlement Hierarchy * Vertical and Horizontal Linkages * Convergence of Services. * Locational Decisions
OUTPUT	A General Idea of the Factor Endowments of the District; Intra-district disparities Division into Homogeneous Sub-Regions, e.g. Agro-Climatic Zones	Understanding of * Level of Development (Intra-District Disparities) * Potential and Constraints to Development * Identification of lead sectors * Formulation of Goals	Understanding of * Levels of Development (Intra-District Disparities) Outputs * Potentials and constraints * Sectoral Objectives and Sub-objectives * Strategy Options	Existing Level of Development in Infrastructural facilities and Social Services; Gaps in Spatial Coverage identification of a network of Rural Service Centres and Growth Centres

FIG. 19.2 : Characteristics of Area (District) Analysis.

Source: K.V. Sundaram, 'What kinds of analytical skills a district planner should possess" (Mimeographed, 1987).

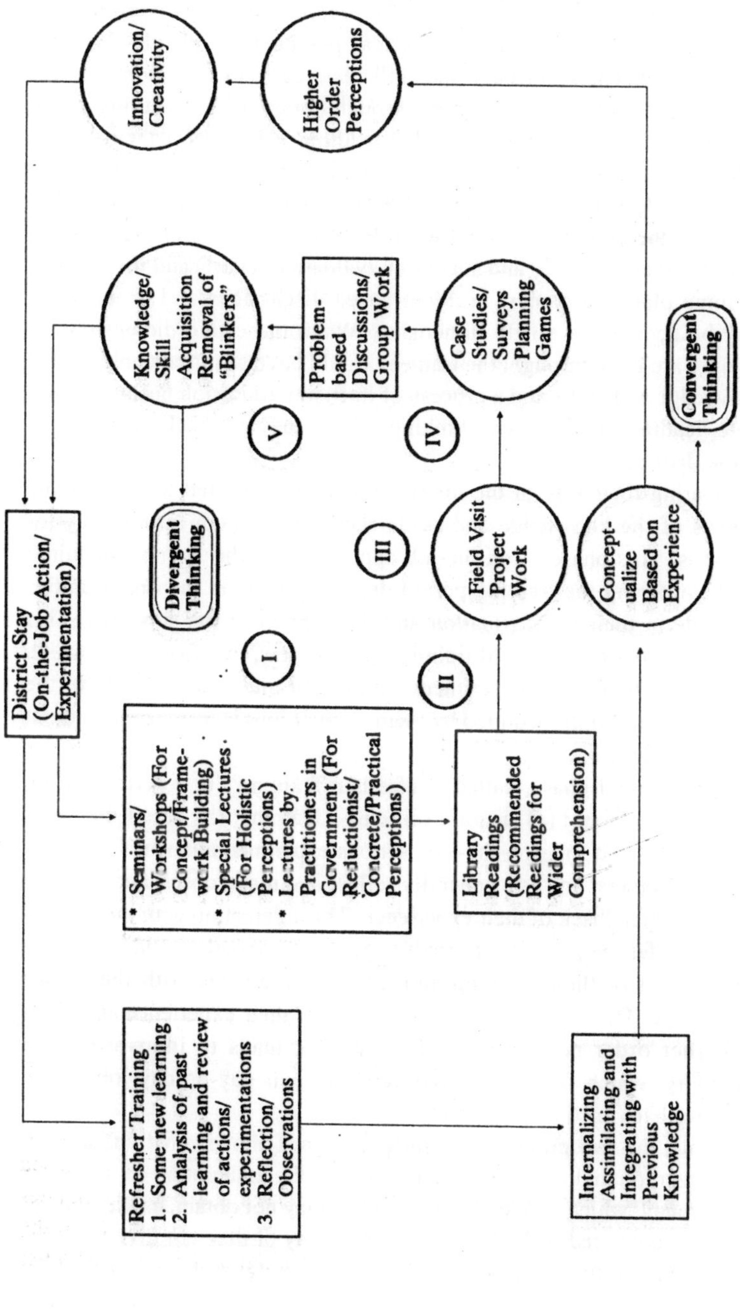

FIG. 19.3 : Model of an Instructional Cycle for Action-Oriented Decentralized District Planning.

planning; and (iii) Some lectures by practitioners in Government to provide reductionist/concrete/practical perspectives on planning for development. The knowledge and skills derived from classroom lectures and exercises is further augmented through library readings during which the participants study recommended readings selected for them by the training faculty. A third dimension of training relates to field work, during which a field exercise is conducted by the participants under the supervision of the core trainers. A fourth dimension consists of presentation of selected case studies and survey or evaluation reports and the practice of some planning games. Problem-based discussions and group work may be deemed as a fifth dimension. When these five dimensions of training are gone through, the trainees would have acquired considerable knowledge and skills and a process of intensive education becomes complete, leading to "divergent thinking". Then they get back to their jobs in the district.

During their stay in the districts, they are expected to apply some aspects of the knowledge and skills acquired by them in their day-to-day jobs. This phase of on-the-job application of the learning acquired by them during the training period depends much on the opportunities available in their work situation and the support of the superiors. This constitutes the first cycle of training. In our view, this first cycle, which enables the trainees to experiment with or put into practice some of the knowledge and skills acquired by them on their jobs is incomplete without a second cycle.

The second phase, called 'Refresher Training', is a period during which the trainees : (a) acquire some new learning; (b) recall their past learning; (c) get their on-the-job actions/experimentations reviewed by the core trainers; and (d) generally reflect and make observations in the nature of a feedback of their experience. This interaction with the trainers and other fellow participants enables them to internalize and assimilate a good part of their learning and integrate the same with their prior knowledge. This helps them to conceptualize their experience and leads to higher order perceptions. This, in turn, leads to innovation and creativity, which find expression again in their day-do-day jobs when they get back to their districts.

Thus the two phases of training described above constitute a complete instructional cycle. In actual practice, the assumption of a "closed experiment" which is implied here may or may not obtain, as the trainees may be transferred from their jobs, which may or may not give them the same opportunities for application of their learning; or there may be other hindering factors preventing them from either applying their knowledge to their work situations or come again for a refresher programme, as envisaged here.

Curriculum Planning

Having dealt with the model of an instructional cycle, we may now turn our attention to the operational issues relating to curriculum planning and implementation. The observations made here derive from a practical experience of running a four-week programme of Trainer's Training in decentralized planning at the district level in APROSC.

The basic framework for a curriculum for training in Decentralized Planning already exists in the training manual, which details out the relevant subject areas to be covered during a training course. In the four-week Trainer's Training conducted by APROSC, the objective was to render the participants capable of organizing and conducting courses on district planning as trainers (using the manual) or as resource persons for planning. Thus the emphasis was on developing their skills as potential trainers or planners. On the whole, 76 sessions (each of one and a half hours' duration) were planned as shown below :

	Major Subject Areas	No. of Sessions	Percentage
1.	Training Principles, Methods and Techniques	10	13.2
2.	Understanding Development and Planning	5	6.6
3.	District Analysis	23	30.0
4.	Project Planning	6	8.0
5.	District Plan Formulation	3	4.0
6.	Implementation, Monitoring and Popular Participation	7	9.2
7.	Field Workshop and Report Preparation	16	21.0
8.	Baseline-setting for Evaluation, Course Evaluation and Study Sessions	6	8.0
	Total	76	100.0

Course Sequence and Curriculum Implementation

The course was designed in the following sequential order :

1. After introducing the course objectives, the participants were given a questionnaire to establish the baseline of the skills and

knowledge possessed by them on the areas to be covered by the course.

2. The first four days of the course were focused on principles, methods and techniques of training in order to make participants familiar with the whole process of training, adult education, use and misuse of training methods and aids and ways of evaluating training. This is important because the participants' major responsibility after completing the course would be to organize regional and district-level courses on district planning.
3. In the sessions on planning, a few general planning conceptual sessions were followed by specific district planning sessions. Module three (District Planning—An analytical process) of the manual was extensively delt with during this period, covering district profile, situation analysis, context analysis and sectorial analysis. These sessions constituted the bulk of the total time duration (30 per cent) of the course.
4. This was followed by six sessions on project planning techniques dealing with identification, formulation and appraisal of district-level small projects.
5. Having learnt the necessary tools and techniques for district planning, various aspects of district plan formulation like objective setting, approaches and strategy formulation and plan presentation, etc., were covered. With the completion of the sessions relating to plan formulation, the planning component of training was completed.
6. Implementation, monitoring and evaluation, and popular participation were covered at the end of the course. These sessions enabled the participants to become familiar with the simple techniques and concepts related to implementation planning and monitoring and evaluation. Two sessions on popular participation were also introduced at this stage.
7. The last part of the course was devoted to the field workshop, in which participants visited a nearby district to apply some of the tools and techniques of district planning learnt during the course. This field-work exercise constituted more than one-fifth (21 per cent) of the total time duration of the course. Before the commencement of the field-work exercise, the participants were given a hand-out titled "Guide Points for a Field-Oriented Exercise on District Analysis", which set out the various steps

and procedures for conducting the field exercise and the expected outputs from it. These steps and procedures were also explained to the participants during a briefing session, before they set out on the field visit.

Pedagogic Methods

In the course methodology, the following pedagogic devices were employed, taking note of the fact that the participants were to play, in future, the dual role of a trainer and a planner :

* For the classroom teaching of techniques, concepts and principles, the lecture method was used.
* For imparting the necessary skills and techniques, the lecture method was combined with the group exercise and case study methods.
* As the participants, in their role as future trainers, were to use the teaching materials, they were fully sensitized and made familiar with the content of the manual. Therefore, extensive reading hours were allocated. For this purpose, the selected readings were indicated to them.
* The practical aspect, that of providing the participants with the opportunity to assess the quality of the information available in the district profile and of collecting any additional information, was realized through a field workshop. For this purpose, the participants were taken to a nearby district, where they were asked to assess the district profile, collect additional information, as necessary, and formulate general goals and objectives, strategy approaches and programme for district development. On this basis, they prepared their group reports, which were presented in a plenary session before all participants and trainers.

Some Concluding Observations

The experience of Nepal, while implementing a training programme for decentralized planning, discussed in this paper enables us to draw some conclusions.

Firstly, any training manual prepared for decentralized planning must emerge from the live situation of an action planning-cum-training exercise. Such an exercise would enable the training institution to render the teaching materials as close to realities as possible. This would help in the greater impact of training in the on-the-job performance of the trainees. In the case of Nepal, the existence of a well-conceived Decentralization Act along with its rules and bye-laws, which set out the planning process clearly and also provided clues to the varied job-oriented inputs required for the different target groups was a distinct advantage.

Secondly, the experience showed that despite the existence of a manual, the trainers cannot rest in their arm-chairs, but need to continually engage themselves in studies, first for updating the manual in terms of new procedures, rules and regulations introduced by the government from time to time, and secondly to undertake area-specific case studies to illustrate the use of specific methods, tools and techniques for district planning. This means that the training professionals must eschew "ivory towers" and "get their hands dirty", by frequently going to the field and conducting studies. Thus the preparation of teaching materials is a continuous activity and cannot be terminated with the preparation of a training manual. Action research is an important component here, as it is only through action-research that problems confronting decentralized planning could be experienced and innovative solutions found.

In the case of Nepal, for instance, the Training Manual was prepared at a time when the Decentralization Act was in force. Hence, it was based on the procedures laid down in the Act and the planning process envisaged therein. But during the time of its finalization, the country had gone through a revolution, which replaced the partyless system by a multi-party democracy. As such changes take place in a country, the manual will have to undergo appropriate changes in the relevant portions. Thus, the training manual in any country must constantly adapt itself to the changing socio-political circumstances.

Thirdly, training for decentralized planning cannot be conceived as a one-stroke operation. The ideal would be a sandwich type of training, in which the trainees, after an initial exposure to some knowledge and skills, go back to their jobs in the district for about six months or even a year, during which they prepare a plan for their districts. Then they come back to the training institution for a refresher phase, during which their plans are reviewed. If this is not possible, fairly long-term training (at least of four weeks' duration) should be designed, in which at least 20 to 25 per cent of the time of the trainees must be spent in field exercise focused on particular aspects of district planning. In the case of Nepal, a field exercise focused on "District Analysis" (confined to situation and context analyses) was conducted during the four week period of training.

The experience showed that such an exercise would be quite demanding for the trainers, who have to meet several pre-requisites for the exercise in order to save time for the trainees during their field-work stage.

Fourthly, the follow-up phase of training is quite important in the case of training in decentralized planning. This is accomplished in our model through "Refresher Training", during which the trainees will be able to provide valuable feed-back to the trainers, which will enable them to constantly make amendments in their training materials, to render the same more and more operational.

Fifthly, the training for decentralized planning must cover the entire spectrum of actors involved in the process, right from the centre to the lowest administrative unit (e.g. village, ward, etc.) at the local level. The training manual prepared in the case of Nepal is now addressed to the district-level government functionaries only. Other manuals with different orientations have to be prepared for the different target groups, as capacitation has to be aimed at all levels. When training programmes are designed for sub-district-level functionaries, greater focus needs to be on the motivation of people, community participation, self-reliance, diligence and cultural development, elements which will require appropriate value orientation, attitudinal change and community participation for local development. Evidently, this task should figure as an important item on the future work agenda of the apex training institution in the country, if it is to fulfil its mandate in totality for the comprehensive training focused on local-level planning.

Lastly, in a radical approach to training for decentralized planning, the participants themselves must be enabled to decide the content of the curriculum. In this case, a structured design by the training institution will yield place to a design proposed by the trainees themselves, based on an assessment of their own needs. This approach will be really the culmination of a participatory approach and particularly relevant in a Trainer's Training, where the participants happen to be senior personnel, who are already well versed in some components of the curriculum.

ANNEXURE-I

Module	Subject Areas	T1	T2	T3	T4
	A. *Development Concept*:				
1. Under-standing Develop-ment	1.1 The Meaning of Development	—	4	—	—
	B. *Development Context*:				
	1.2 Nepal's Economy	—	1	—	—
	1.3 Environmental Factors in Development	1	1	—	—
	1.4 Nepal's Population Dynamics	—	1	—	—
	1.5 Basic Needs and Quality of Life	1	1	—	—
	C. *Development Institutions*:				
	1.6 The Planning Process and Methodology in Nepal	1	1	—	—
	1.7 Development Finance and Resource Mobilization	—	2	—	—
	D. *Development Considerations*:				
	1.8 Regionalization and Planning	—	2	—	—
	1.9 Target Group Development	—	3	—	—
	1.10 Outstanding Goals which Remain to be Achieved	—	6	1	—
2. Decen-traliza-tion and the Planning Process in Nepal	2.1 Concept of Decentralization	1	—	—	—
	2.2 Planning from Below : Concept and Method	1	—	—	—
	2.3 History of Decentralization in Nepal	1	—	—	—
	2.4 The Decentralization Act, 1982	1	—	—	—
	2.5 Prerequisites for Decentralization	1	1	—	—
	2.6 Disaggregation of National Targets	1	1	—	—
	2.7 Review of the Decentralization Experience in Nepal	1	—	—	—
	2.8 Corrective Measures to Improve the Functioning of the Act	1	1	—	—

(Contd.)

(Annexure-I (*Contd.*)

Module	Subject Areas	T1	T2	T3	T4
3. District Planning: An Analytical Process	3.1 The Planning Cycle at the District Level	1	—	—	—
	3.2 The Scope and Content of District Plans	1	1	1	—
	3.3 Basic Concepts and Definitions	1	—	—	—
	3.4 Situation Analysis				
	3.4.1 Concept	1	—	1	—
	3.4.2 Natural Resource Endowment	1	—	—	—
	3.5 Context Analysis :				
	3.5.1 District Profile	2	1	—	1
	3.5.2 District Background	1	—	—	—
	3.5.3 Land Utilization Pattern	1	—	—	—
	3.5.4 Water Resources	1	—	—	—
	3.5.5 Demographic Features	1	—	—	—
	3.5.6 Economic Characteristics	1	—	—	—
	3.5.7 Social Characteristics	1	—	—	—
	3.5.8 Summary of the Context analysis	1	—	—	—
	3.6 Sectoral Analysis :				
	3.6.1 General	1	—	—	—
	3.6.2 Agriculture Sector	1	—		—
	3.6.3 Irrigation Sector	2	—	—	—
	3.6.4 Animal Husbandry Sector	1	—	—	—
	3.6.5 Industry Sector	1	—	—	—
	3.6.6 Health Sector	1	—	—	—
	3.6.7 Education Sector	1	—	—	—
	3.7 Trend Analysis	1	—	1	—
4. Techniques and Tools for District Planning	4.1 Information Needs vis-a-vis Existing Data Base	1	1	—	—
	4.2 Methods of Information Collection	1	—	1	—
	4.3 Map as a Planning Tool	1	—	—	—
	4.4 Spatial Planning	1	—	—	—
	4.5 Project Planning				
	4.5.1 Project Approach to Planning	2	1	—	—
	4.5.2 Project Planning Cycle	1	—	—	—
	4.5.3 Project Identification in the Context of District Planning	1	—	—	1

(*Contd.*)

Annexure-I (*Contd.*)

Module	Subject Areas	T1	T2	T3	T4
	4.5.4 Project Formulation and Analysis	3	—	—	—
	4.5.5 Project Appraisal and Sensitivity Analysis	2	—	3	—
	4.5.6 Selection of Project at the District Level	1	—	—	—
	4.5.7 Project Report Writing	1	—	—	—
	4.6 Manpower Planning	1	1	—	—
5. District Plan Formulation	5.1 Plan Objectives	1	1	—	—
	5.2 Plan Approach	1	—	—	—
	5.3 Stating Strategies	1	—	1	—
	5.4 Sectoral Programming and Integration	1	—	1	—
	5.5 District Plan Framework and its Presentation	1	—	—	—
6. Implementation and Management of District Plans	6.1 Co-ordination	1	1	1	—
	6.2 Personnel Management	1	—	—	—
	6.3 Budgeting	2	—	—	—
	6.4 Net-Working				
	6.5 Scheduling	1	—	1	—
	6.6 Expenditure and Financial Administration	1	—	—	—

Note: T1—No. of Essential Readings
T2—No. of Recommended Readings
T3—Exercise
T4—Case Study

REFERENCES

1. Sundaram K.V. "Decentralized District Planning : An Agenda for a training manual in Nepal", APROSC Discussion Paper, Kathmandu, March, 1989 (Mimeo).
2. Report of the Expert Group Meeting for designing a Training Mannal on Decentralized District Planning, May 1, 1989, APROSC Training Section, Kathmandu, Nepal, July 1989.
3. Manual on Decentralized District Planning in eight modules—APROSC and FAO collaboration, Kathmandu, 1990.

20

FUNCTIONING AND PERFORMANCE OF PERSONNEL FOR DECENTRALIZED PLANNING
The Prerequisites

The personnel working with local authorities need to be carefully capacitated to enable them to function effectively. Training is the answer. But training for decentralized planning is a dependent activity. It may be postulated that its efficacy by and large depends on three major factors :

(a) The extent of political and bureaucratic commitment to decentralization;
(b) The nature and degree of detail of the definition of measures adopted in the country to spell out the planning process and to define the tasks and procedures to be followed by different levels for the effective implementation of decentralization; and
(c) The extent to which personnel management procedures are conducive to the appropriate utilization of trained manpower.

It may be noted here that the three factors correspond to : (1) the policy environment; (2) the work or operational environment; and (3) the professional or career development environment. We may elaborate these briefly.

1. Policy Environment

If the political and bureaucratic commitment to decentralization is strong, the commitment to training will be equally strong and serious and there will be adequate allocation of resources to the training activity. In this case, a systematic development of institutional effort for the development of human resources will be possible. The functionaries at the various levels—both government and non-government—will take to the training activity in a serious manner. All these will ultimately lead to an effective operationalization of decentralized planning and implementation of development. The net result would be the maximum impact of the positive effects of decentralization.

2. **Work or Operational Environment**

The second factor mentioned here relates to how well the decentralized planning process is conceived and how clearly and unambiguously the various tasks and procedures for decentralized planning and implementation are elaborated by the government machinery, either through executive orders or by legal enactment and to what extent the finances, powers and responsibilities are devolved to the sub-national levels to enable them to act with a degree of freedom and independent decision-making. In other words, the degree of "localism" conferred on the lower area levels to manage the development affairs. When the tasks and procedures are clearly defined, the substance and content of decentralization acquire definite meaning and clarity and they contribute to define the curriculum for training. In this way, the work environment directly influences the substance of the training activity.

3. **Career Development**

The third factor mentioned here relates to the qualifications, recruitment, career mobility and incentives for performance of the numerous personnel at different levels, who have some role or the other to play in the planning and implementation activities related to decentralized development. These have also a bearing on the effective utilization of trained manpower.

Thus one may postulate that the essential *prerequisites* for decentralized planning (in relation to the effective utilization of trained manpower) consist in the way the policy environment, the work environment and the career development environment are structured by the governments. We may elaborate on some aspects of these pre-requisites and their importance.

4. **Abilities Needed and Constraints Operating**

It is perhaps better to start from the training end. Any effective training programme for decentralized planning should be able to build up capacities among the sub-national level personnel to perform efficiently the planning, decision-making and management functions decentralized to them. To be effective, these personnel should basically acquire the capability to :

- Identify development problems and opportunities;
- Identify and devise possible solutions to development problems;
- Make decisions and resolve conflicts;
- Mobilize resources;
- Manage development programmes and projects; and
- Coordinate the local-level activities with those of various central government ministries and agencies as well as non-governmental organizations involved in development.

The above tasks demand certain specific abilities, which are :

- Ability to analyze the developmental setting and prepare a plan;
- Ability to negotiate or transact the business of planning;
- Ability to estimate and mobilize resources;
- Ability to manage development; and
- Ability to coordinate developments in the different sectors.
- Ability to effectively interact and dialogue with development beneficiaries and non-governmental organisations.

However, the development of these abilities and the effective implementation of decentralized programmes are usually retarded by several constraints. Removal of these constraints or at least minimizing their retarding effects will go a long way towards ensuring and enhancing the effectiveness of training. The following have been identified as some major constraints :

(i) environmental constraints in the policy and operational realms;
(ii) organizational constraints; and
(iii) constraints relating to personnel structures and practices.

(i) *Environmental Constraints in the Policy and Operational Realms*

We noted earlier that these included, among other things, the degree of existing political and bureaucratic commitment to decentralization, as well as the existence of legal or executive provisions and rules and regulations for implementing the decentralization programme. Clarity about decentralization policies and strategies is quite important. Where such clarity does not exist and planning procedures are confusing and coordination is weak, the result has been the undermining of decentralization policies.

So, one of the essential prerequisites is that the procedures for decentralized planning must be clearly laid down. These procedures should pertain to the definition of the actions involved in planning, the planning responsibilities entrusted to the different levels, the outputs that are expected of them, and the planning relationships existing among them. They are important, for their subject matter contributes to the training content.

Among the operational issues which constitute some essential prerequisites, we may emphasize the extent of financial decentralization made to the regional and local levels and the degree of control exercised by them over funds flowing from the centre and other sources. The method followed by the Central Government for determining the inter-regional allocation of funds, the degree of flexibility of their use, the power given to the sub-national levels to raise resources on their own and the encouragement given to them to increase their autonomy are the important factors that determine the degree of financial decentralization. Apart from suitable financial decentralization measures, certain administrative decentralization measures are also important. These include simplified procedures for administrative and technical sanctions for projects, re-appropriation powers and powers to prepare and control budgets at the different area levels.

Decentralization laws must be written concisely and regulations and directives should describe clearly the relationship among functionaries at different levels, the obligations of officials and citizens, the allocation of functions among units and the roles and duties of leaders at each level. The procedures for local participation in development planning and administration must also be spelt out in clear terms. If the rules and procedures are so clearly defined, that they are realistic and easily applicable, then the decentralized programme is likely to progress smoothly and effectively. This will also lead to an effective training, as the trainers can be told with clarity what they are to practise in reality.

(ii) *Organizational Constraints*

If decentralized planning is to be effective, then the establishment of suitable organizational structures at the different levels, linking them appropriately and instituting regular flows of communication among them are quite necessary. These measures will enable the planning organizations established at the different levels to achieve complementarity in the decentralized functions and to coordinate common activities or those that have impacts on each other.

In a decentralized planning structure, the organizational pattern has to integrate planning, implementation (including monitoring and evaluation), data collection and information feeding processes, research, training as well as people's participation. In an ideal organizational structure for a decentralized planning set-up, the planning structures, the information structures and the institutional structures for research, training and popular participation must be conceived in an integrated manner, such that they function in a complementary and coordinated manner. What is crucial in such a set-up are the linkages and information flows. The organizational inter-relationships and the procedures evolved for effective interaction among them are important. The development of the necessary organizational structures will depend on the country situation. It is not necessary that new institutional structures should be created. Rather, it would be better to create a new set of roles and relationships among the existing institutions.

(iii) *Constraints Relating to Personnel Structures and Practices*

Experience has shown that the degree to which adequate numbers of skilled technicians and managers are available determines the success of decentralization programmes. The prevailing personnel practices in most developing countries are, in a way, acting as a serious disincentive for promoting decentralized planning. Frequent transfers of personnel, on the one hand, and a service that has not been properly structured into a cadre, providing for career advancement, on the other have been the major obstacles to decentralized planning. In any system of personnel organization, talents float to the top, i.e. the tendency is for the talented and capable persons to move towards the centre. Those who are at the centre are not inclined to return to the field after having completed the necessary stint for advancement. The result is that at the local level, one finds either unwilling workers who are seeking opportunities to leave or those who have tried unsuccessfully to leave. In such circumstances, professional training programmes only assist the staff to leave. That is, the organizations simply lose their staff once they are qualified. For dealing with administrative and technical shortcomings of this nature, some "assistance linkages" must be provided. This implies support of local sub-professionals by professionals at the central and intermediate levels. This means transfer or secondment of high calibre staff from the central or intermediate levels to improve local capabilities. Another personnel problem refers to the drain of trained manpower. This problem could be minimized by constituting a planning cadre of officials manning the various technical positions in a multi-level planning set-up. When a professional cadre is constituted, the benefits of training will permanently remain with the professionals. Since they will be moving only vertically, up and down, there is no question of the training being wasted away after the transfer of the personnel, as the inputs received and the capabilities built up will continue to remain with them as an enduring endowment. Once a cadre is constituted, training can be linked to career mobility. In this way, the personnel can also be motivated to take training seriously.

The commitment for decentralized planning demands that the training of personnel at various levels of responsibility be made part of a continuing national programme. This implies that such training must be adopted as a matter of national policy and be adequately supported at all levels of the administrative hierarchy. Some concrete steps in this direction would be : (1) the establishment of a high-level coordination committee for decentralization; (2) the setting up of a national training institute for the training of trainers; and (3) establishing a network of training institutions at the sub-national levels. The best way to overcome the problem of the dearth of training institutions is to encourage existing institutions, particularly academic and research bodies, to expand their role into training by financially assisting them to shoulder these responsibilities. Such training institutions should be identified and inter-institutional collaboration among them encouraged, so that they may interact on the use of training approaches, curriculum design, exchange of training materials and experiences, evaluation of training effectiveness and support for experimentation and adaptation.

Yet another step to improve the training performance is to institute an effective follow-up by the training institution, calculated to improve on-the-job performance of the trainees. This is not strictly a pre-requisite, but a post-requisite.

The participation of international agencies can be crucial to the successful implementation of training for decentralization. They can provide the means necessary to experiment and conduct training programmes on properly conceived lines. But they have to guard against a "dependent relationship" from developing, in which the host government, without having a substantial stake in the operation, relies totally on the donor. Therefore, in such aid programmes, the donor agencies must, from the beginning, find ways to build "sustainability" into the programme.

To sum up, the training for decentralized planning and appropriate utilization of trained manpower could be considerably enhanced by effecting improvements in policy environment, work or operational environment and the career development environment. These are in the nature of essential prerequisites for an effective decentralized planning. Achieving these in the ideal manner proposed here will often be difficult, if not impossible. Herein lies the challenge of decentralization.

BIBLIOGRAPHY

Abdul Aziz, *Decentralization—Mandal Panchayat System in Karnataka*, National Institute of Rural Development, Hyderabad, 1995.

Agricultural Project Services Centre (APROSC) and Food and Agriculture Organization of the United Nations (FAO/UN), Training Manual on Decentralized Planning (District Level)—8 Modules, November 1990, Kathmandu, Nepal.

Amatya, S.L., *Rural Development through Decentralized Planning,* East-West Centre Association, Honolulu, March 1988.

Arun Ghosh, "Decentralized Planning, West Bengal Experience", *Economic and Political Weekly,* March 26, 1988.

Avrom Bendavid Val, *Regional and Local Economic Analysis for Practitioners* (New and Expanded edition), Praeger, 1983.

Bangladesh Academy for Rural Development, "The Works of Akhtar Hameed Khan," Vols. I to III, Kotbari, Comilla, 1993.

Benninger, Christopher C., "New Institutional Systems for Enhanced Regional Planning and Management" in *Regional Planning and Development*, Sundaram, K.V. *et al*, (Ed.), Heritage Publishers, New Delhi, 1990.

———, 'Institutional Strategies for Decentralization', *The Administrator,* Vol. XXVI, No. 3, July-Sep., 1991.

Bhat, L.S., *Strategy for Integrated Rural Development : Case Study of North Kanara District*, (Karnataka), Concept Publishing Company, New Delhi, 1987.

———, *et al*, *Micro-level Planning : A Case Study of Karnal Area*, Haryana, Indian Statistical Institute, New Delhi, 1976.

Centre for Earth Science Studies *et al,* Thiruvananthapuram, "Panchayat Level Resource Mapping—An approach paper" Dec. 1991.

Centre on Integrated Rural Development for Asia and the Pacific, Report on Rural Development in CRDAP Member countries 1994-95, Dhaka, Bangladesh, 1996.

Chakravarty, S., "Aspects of India's Development Strategies for 1980's", Training Division, Department of Personnel and Administrative Reforms, Govt. of India, New Delhi, July 1984.

———, 'The Planning Process in India : An Appraisal and a Framework', Planning Commission, New Delhi (mimeographed).

Chambers, Robert, *Managing Rural Development : Ideas and Experience from East Africa*, New York, Africana Publishing Company, 1972.

———, *Rural Development : Putting the Last First*, Longman, London, 1983.

Chandrasekhara, C.S., "Environmental Planning and Management for Local and Regional Development : A Conceptual Framework" Paper to the International Workshop on Environmental Manage-ment for Local and Regional Development, 9-13, June 1985, The United Nations Centre for Regional Development, Nagoya (Japan).

Chatterjee, Lata, "Quantitative Analysis for Regional Policy in Developing Countries : A response to data scarcity" in *Regional Planning and Development, Essays in honour of Prof. R.P. Misra*, Edited by Sundaram, K.V. *et al,* Heritage Publishers, New Delhi, 1990.

Chaturvedi, T.N. (Ed), *Indian Journal of Public Administration*, Special Number on Decentralization in Administration, Vol. XXIV, July-Sept. 1978, New Delhi.

Cheema, G.S. and Rondinelli, D.A. (Eds.). *Decentralization and Development : Policy Implementation in Developing Countries*, Beverley Hill : Sage, 1983.

———, Implementing Decentralization Programmes in Asia—Local Capacity for Rural Development, United Nations Centre for Regional Development, Nagoya, Japan, 1983.

———, *Institutional Dimensions of Regional Development*, Maruzen Asia, Singapore, 1981.

CIRDAP and AIT, Impact of Decentralization on Rural Poverty : An Asian Perspective, CIRDAP Study Series, No. 136, 1992.

Commonwealth Secretariat, Decentralization for Development : A Select Annotated Bibliography, London, 1984.

Consultation on Multi-level Planning and the Two-way process in Agriculture and Rural Development Planning", FAO Regional Office Bangkok, 1983.

Conyers, D., 'Decentralization of Development—A Review of Literature, in *Public Administration and Development*, 4, 1984.

Conyers, Diana, Decentralization : A Framework for Discussion, in Hasnat Abdul Hye (ed.), *Decentralization, Local Government Institutions and Resource Mobilisation*, Bangladesh Academy for Rural Development, Conilla, Bangladesh, 1985.

Dantwala, M.L., "Two-way Planning : Logic and Limitations, A critical review of Indian experience", Paper to Expert, Asian Institute of Technology, Bangkok, 1987.

Das Gupta, Ashim : 'Panchayati Raj and Decentralized Planning in West Bengal in *Decentralized Planning and Panchayati Raj.* (Proceedings of the D.T. Lakdawala Memorial Symposium), Institute of Social Sciences, New Delhi, Concept Publishing Company, New Delhi,1994.

DeMan, W.H. and A.D.J., "Schaap, A model for incorporating the element of space and some aspects of the basic human needs approach in regional development." *ITC Journal,* Vol. I, 1979, Enschede, Netherlands.

Elinor, Ostram, Larry Schoeder and Susanne Wynne, *Institutional Incentrives and Sustainable Development—Infrastructure Policies in Perspective*, Westview Press, Oxford, 1993.

FAO, UN, Rome, 'Towards Improved Multi-level Planning for Agriculture and Rural Development in Asia and the Pacific. *Economic and Social Development*, Paper No. 52, 1984.

Felicia, R. Clark, *et al,* "Getting people involved" *International Development Review,* Vol. 20, 1978, No. 1, pp. 28-31.

Fraser Taylor, D.R. and Fiona Mackenzie (Ed.), *Development from Within—Survival in Rural Africa,* Routledge, London, 1992.

Gadgil, D.R., 'District Development Planning' Kale Memorial Lecture, Gokhale Institute of Politics and Economics, Poona, 1966.

Gandhi, M.K., *Rebuilding our Villages,* Ahmedabad, Navajivan Publishing House, 1958, p.5.

Govt. of India, Planning Commission, Report of the Team for the Study of Community Projects and National Extension Service, Committee on Plan Projects, New Delhi, Vol. I, 1957.

Govt. of India, Report of the Rural-Urban Relationship Committee, Ministry of Health and Family Planning, New Delhi, 1966.

Govt. of India, Planning Commission, Report of the Working Group on Block Level Planning, 1975.

Govt. of India, Department of Rural Development, Report of the Committee on Panchayati Raj Institutions (Ashok Mehta Committee), Ministry of Agriculture and Irrigation, New Delhi, 1978.

Govt. of India, Planning Commission, Report of the Working Group on Block-level Planning, New Delhi, 1978.

Govt. of India, Planning Commission, Guidelines for Block-level Planning, New Delhi, 1979.

Govt. of India, Planning Commission, Report of the Working Group on District Planning, New Delhi, May 1984.

Govt. of India, Planning Commission and the Department of Rural Development, Ministry of Agriculture, New Delhi. Report of the Committee to review the existing administrative arrangements for rural development and poverty alleviation programmes. (CAARD), New Delhi, December 1985.

Govt. of India, Planning Commission, New Delhi, 'Towards Improved Local Level Planning for Rural Development'—Lessons from some experiences, 1986.

Govt. of India, Planning Commission, Report of NDC Committee on 'Microlevel Planning and involvement of people at grassroot level, New Delhi, April 1993.

Griffin, K., "Economic Development in a Changing World," *World Development* 9(3) : 225, 1981.

Hasnat, Abdul Hye (Ed.) *Decentralization, Local Government Institutions and Resource Mobilization*, Bangladesh Academy for Rural Development, Comilla, Bangladesh, 1985.

Hicks, U.K., *Development from Below : Local Government and Finance in Developing Countries of the Commonwealth.* Oxford : Oxford University Press, 1961.

Inayatullah (Ed), *Rural Organization and Rural Development : Some Asian Experiences*, Asian and Pacific Development Administration Centre, Kuala Lumpur, 1978.

Institute of Social Sciences, *Decentralized Planning and Panchayati Raj* (Proceedings of the D.T. Lakdawala Memorial Symposium), Concept Publishing Company, New Delhi, 1994.

Iqbal Narain, 'The idea of democratic decentralization', *Indian Journal of Political Science*, Vol. XXI, No. 2.

Jain, L.C. *et al. Grass without Roots : Rural Development under Government Auspices*, Sage Publications, New Delhi, 1985.

Jain, S.P. and Hochgesang Thomas W., *Emerging Trends in Panchayati Raj in India*, National Institute of Rural Development, Hyderabad, 1995.

Johan Galtung *et al, Self-Reliance—A Strategy for Development*, Bogle L'overture Publications Ltd., London, 1980.

Joung Whang, *Management of Rural Change in Korea,* The Seamaul Undong, The Institute of Social Sciences, Korean Studies Series No. 5, Seoul National University Press, 1981.

Khan, Mohammad Mohabbat and Zafarullah, Habib Mohammad, "The Decentralized Planning Process in Bangladesh," H.S.D. Research Report No. 19, Asian Institute of Technology, Bangkok, 1988.

Konrad Adenaner Foundation, *Decentralization : The Example of Federalism in the Federal Republic of Germany*, Sankt Angustin, 1994.

Korten, David C. and Klauss Rudi (eds.), *People-Centred Development : Contributions Towards Theory and Planning Frameworks*, West Hartford, Connecticut, Kumarian Press, 1984.

Korten Davrd C., Community Organization and Rural Development : A Learning Process Approach, *Public Administration Review*, Vol. 40, Sept.-Oct., 1980.

Lee, Man-Gap, (Ed.), 'Toward a New Community Life'—Report of International Research Seminar on The Seamaul Movement, Institute of Seamaul Undong Studies, Seoul National University, 1981.

Leonard, David K. and Marshall, Dale R. (eds.), *Institutions of Rural Development for the Poor : Decentralization and Organisational Linkages*, Berkeley, California, Institute of International Studies, 1982.

Leonard, D. White, 'Decentralization' *Encyclopaedia of Social Sciences*, Vol. 5, New York, Macmillan 1959.

Maddick, H., *Democracy, Decentralization and Development*, Asia Publishing House, 1963.

Maetz, Materne, and Maria G. Quieti, *Training for Decentralized Planning—Lessons from Experience*, Food and Agriculture Organization of the United Nations, Rome 1987.

Meenakshi Sundaram, S.S., *Decentralization in Developing Countries*, Concept Publishing Company, New Delhi, 1994, p. 11.

Michael M. Cernea (Ed.), *Putting People First-Sociological Variables in Rural Development*, Published for the World Bank, Oxford University Press, October 1985.

Mishra, S.N., *Rural Development Planning—Design and Method, Satvahan*, New Delhi, 1984.

Misra, R.P. and Sundaram K.V., *Multi-level Planning and Integrated Rural Development in India*, Heritage Publishers, New Delhi, 1980.

———, (ed.), *District Planning—A Handbook*, Concept Publishing Company, New Delhi, 1990.

———, (ed.), *Local-level Planning and Development*, Sterling Publishers Pvt. Ltd., New Delhi, 1983.

Misra, R.P. and Achyutha, R.N., *Micro-level Rural Planning : Principles, Methods and Case Studies*, Concept Publishing Company, New Delhi, 1990.

Mosher, Arthur T., *Creating a Progressive Rural Structure to serve a Modern Agriculture*, Agricultural Development Council, New York, 1969.

Mukherjee, Amitava, *Methodology and Database for Decentralized Planning,* Vol. 3 (Parts A, B and C), Heritage Publishers, New Delhi, 1991.

———, 'Methodologies in Decentralized Planning : A Survey', *Annals of the National Association of Geographers* (India), Volume II, Nos. I and II, December 1992.

Norman, Furniss, The Political Significance of Decentralization, *Journal of Politics*, Vol. 36, No. 4, 1974.

Norman T. Uphoff and Milton J. Esman, *Local Organization for Rural Development : Analysis of Asian Experiences*, Cornell University, Ithaca, New York, 1974.

Oakley, Peter, *et al.*, *Projects with People : The Practice of Participation in Rural Development*, ILO Geneva, 1991.

Ocampo, Romeo B., "Toward more authentic Local Autonomy—Premises and Proposals for reform," in 'Papers on Decentralization and Local Autonomy'—Local Government Centre, College of Public Administration, Manila (mimeographed).

Oommen, M.A. and Datta Abhijit, *Panchayats and their Finance*, Concept Publishing Company, New Delhi, 1995.

Paul, Hirst, *Associative Democracy : New Forms of Economic and Social Governance*, Combridge Polity Press, 1994.

Ramachandran, V., "Report on the measures to be taken for democratic decentralization at the district and lower levels," Vol. I, Government of Kerala, Trivandrun, July 1988.

Ramakrishna, Hegde, 'Local self-government in Karnataka : Planning from Below' in *Decentralized Planning and Panchayati Raj* (Proceedings of the D.T. Lakdawala Memorial Symposium), Institute of Social Sciences, Concept Publishing Company, New Delhi, 1994.

Rao, V.M.; Peiris, G.H. and Tilakaratne, S., *Planning for Rural Development—The Experience of Integrated Rural Development Programme of Sri Lanka*, I.L.O./ARTEP, Bangkok, 1984.

Raul, P. deGuzman and Perfecto L. Padilla, 'Decentralization, Local Government Institutions and Resource Mobilization—The Philippines Experience' in Hasnat Abdul Hye, *Decentralization, Local Government Institutions and Resource Mobilization*, Bangladesh Academy for Rural Development, Comilla, Bangla-desh, 1985.

Ray, Jayanta Kumar, *Organising Villagers for Self-reliance : A Study of Deedar in Bangladesh,* Bangladesh Academy for Rural Development, Kotbari, Comilla, 1983.

Reddy, Y. Venugopal, *Multilevel Planning in India*, Vikas Publishing House, New Delhi, 1979.

Rondinelli, D.A.; J.R. Nellis and G.S. Cheema (1984) 'Decentralization in Developing Countries', Washington, World Bank.

Rondinelli, D.A. *et al.*, "Decentralization in Developing Countries—A Review of Recent Experiences", World Bank Staff Working Paper No. 581, World Bank, Washington, 1983.

Routray, J.K., Decentralization Process and Impact on Area Development in Selected Blocks of Orissa, India, H.S.D. Research Report No. 25, Asian Institute of Technology, Bangkok, 1992.

———, "Data Base : An aid to GIS application for decentralized micro-level planning in developing countries—Indian experience"—Paper presented to the International Conference on Geographic Information Systems organized by the United Nations Centre for Regional Development, Nagoya, at Jakarta, October 1989 (Mimeographed).

Roy, Prodipto and Patil, B.R., *Manual for Block level Planning*, MacMillan Company of India, Delhi, 1977.

Sant, B. Gurung and Prodipto Roy, *Decentralization in Nepal*, Orient Longman Ltd., Hyderabad, 1987.

Saxena, A.P. (ed.), *Administrative Reforms for Decentralized Development*, Asia Pacific Development Centre, Kuala Lumpur, 1980.

Sazanami, Hidehiko (ed.), Local Social Development Planning United Nations, Centre for Regional Development, Nagoya, Japan, 1984.

Seers, Dudley, "The Meaning of Development," *International Development Review,* No. 4, Dec., 1969.

Shah, Vimal, *Planning for Talala Block—A Study in Micro-level Planning*, Gujarat Institute of Area Planning, Ahmedabad, June, 1974.

Shaikh, Maqsood Ali *et al.*, *Decentralization and People's Participation*, National Institute of Public Administration, Dhaka, 1983.

Shiviah, M., *Panchayati Raj : A Policy Perspective*, National Institute of Rural Development, 1986.

Shrestha, Bihari K., "Decentralization, Basic Needs and the Makings of a Responsive Bureaucracy in Nepal", *Administration and Management Review,* Vol. No. 1, December 1987.

Shrestha, Raj Krishna, "Impact of Decentralization on Rural Poverty in Nepal"—Paper presented to the Expert Consultation held at AIT, Bangkok 17-20 September 1991. Jointly Sponsored by Centre on

Integrated Rural Development for Asia and the Pacific and Division of Human Settlements Development, Asian Institute of Technology.

Silverman, Jerry M., Public Sector Decentralization—Economic Policy and Sector Investment Programs—World Bank Technical Paper No. 188, The World Bank, 1992.

Simon, David, *Third World Regional Development : A Reappraisal*, Paul Chapman Publishing Ltd., London, 1990.

Sivaraman, B., *Voluntary Participation in Rural Development*, Govt. of India, Planning Commission, New Delhi, 1978.

Smith, B.C., *Decentralization, the Territorial Dimension of the State*, London, Allen and Unwin, 1985.

Sundaram, K.V., "Rural Development and Environmental Conservation", Keynote Address in *Proceedings of International Symposium* on 'The Development of Regional Agriculture and Environmental Conservation in South-East Asian countries', Kyoto, March 15-17, 1988.

———, Planning below the state level : Policies, Strategies and Methodologies, *The Indian Journal of Geography,* Vol. XIII, No. 1, 1978.

———, Poverty Alleviation in Rural Areas through Employment creation—Implication of Block Level Planning and other methodologies, *Manpower Journal,* Vol. XIV, No. 4, January-March 1979.

———, Report of a Study Tour on Local-level Planning in India (November 1979), United Nations ESCAP, Bangkok.

———, *Data and Information Needs for Sub-National Planning,* Key Note Paper to the UNESCO International Seminar on "Information Systems for Sub-national Development Planning", Visakhapatnam, India 16-20, December, 1985.

———, "An Integrated Approach to Training for the Establishment and Use of Information Systems for Sub-national Development Planning", *Regional Development Dialogue*, Vol. 8, No. 1, Spring 1987.

———, "Changing Data and Information Needs for Agricultural Planning : The Challenge for the Developing Countries", in *Information Systems for Government and Business : Trends, Issues, Challenges*, United Nations Centre for Regional Development, Nagoya, Japan, 1988.

———, "Decentralization of Agricultural Sector Planning in Sub-Saharan Africa," F.A.O./UN, Rome, 1993.

———, "District Planning—The Case of Maharashtra". *The Indian Journal of Public Administration,* January-March 1979, Vol. XXV, No. 1.

———, 'Decentralization of Agricultural Planning for Ghana', January 1992, Report prepared for the Food and Agriculture Organization of the United Nations and the Government of Ghana, Ministry of Agriculture (mimeographed).

———, 'Multilevel Planning : The Indian experience' in Lata Chatterjee and Peter Nijkamp, *Urban and Regional Policy Analysis in Developing Countries,* Gower Publishing Company, England, 1983.

———, 'Multi-level Planning, Concepts, Principles and Application to sectoral development'. In Sundaram, K.V. *et al.* (Eds.), *Regional Planning and Development* (Essays in honour of R.P. Misra), New Delhi : Heritage, 1985.

———, 'Some Recent Trends in Rural Area Development Planning, in R.P. Misra and Sundaram, K.V. (Ed.) *Rural Area Development : Perspectives and Approaches*, Sterling Publishers (Pvt) Ltd, New Delhi, 1979.

———, and Palanidurai, K.V., 'The Challenge and Response to Decentralization—The Indian Experience, an Overview', in *Decentralization: Area Development in Practice in Asia,* Harvey Demaine and R.E. Malong (Eds.), Asian Institute of Technology, Bangkok and Institute of Social Studies, The Hague, 1987.

———, 'Development from Within—A rethinking on an alternative development path in *Asia-Pacific Journal of Rural Development,* Published by CIRDAP, Dhaka, Bangladesh, Vol. IV, Nos. 1 and 2, July-Dec., 1994.

Thavaraj, M.J.K., and Handa, K.L., *Financial Control and Delegation*, New Delhi, Indian Institute of Public Administration, 1973.

Tripathy, R.N. *et al*, *Development Plan for a Block : Ibrahimpatnam, Rangareddy District*, Andhra Pradesh, National Institute of Rural Development, Hyderabad, 1979.

———, *et al.*, *Block Plan in the District frame—A Development Plan for Madakasira Block in Anantapur District*, Andhra Pradesh, National Institute for Rural Development, Hyderabad, 1980.

Uma, Lele, *The Design of Rural Development—Lessons from Africa*, Johns Hopkins University Press, Baltimore and London, 1975.

United Nations, *Decentralization for National and Local Development*, New York, 1962.

United Nations, *Local Government Reform : Analysis and Experience in Selected Countries*, New York, 1975.

United Nations, Local Participation in Development Planning, New York, 1987.

United Nations, *Popular Participation and Decision-making for Development*, New York, 1975.

United Nations Asian and Pacific Development Institute, *Local Level Planning and Rural Development—Alternative Strategies*, Concept Publishing Company, New Delhi, 1980.

United Nations Centre for Regional Development, *Training Modules : Local Social Development Planning*, Vols. I & II, Nagoya, Japan, 1988.

United Nations Research Institute for Social Development, *Measurement and Analysis of Progress at the Local Level by Wolf Scott,* Geneva, 1979.

UN\ESCAP, "Local-level Planning for Integrated Rural Development—Report of an Expert Group Meeting Bangkok 6-10", November, 1978.

Vajpeeyi, Dhirendra (ed.), *Local Government and Politics in the Third World : Issues and Trends*, Heritage Publishers, New Delhi, 1990.

Vyas, V.S. *et al., Decentralized Planning in India,* Oxford and IBH Publishing Co., New Delhi, 1985.

Weitz, Raanan, *From Peasant to Farmer—A Revolutionary Strategy for Development,* Columbia University Press, New York, 1971.

World Bank, Rural Development—Sector Policy paper, Feb., 1975.

Yadav, R.P. and Kafle, M.P. 'Development Planning in Nepal', Paper to the Expert Group Meeting on Development Planning at District Level, Kathmandu, Nepal, Oct. 24-Nov. 1, 1980. (mimeographed)

Yugandhar, B.N. and Mukherjee Amitava, *Readings in Decentralized Planning* (with Special reference to District Planning), Vols. I & II, Concept Publishing Company Ltd., New Delhi, 1991.

INDEX